D0084860

War in Kentucky

☆☆☆

War in Kentucky

From Shiloh to Perryville

☆☆☆

James Lee McDonough

The University of Tennessee Press / Knoxville

First Edition.

The paper in this book meets the minimum requirements of the American National Standard for Permanence of Paper for Printed Library Materials. ♾ The binding materials have been chosen for strength and durability.

LIBRARY OF CONGRESS CATALOGING IN PUBLICATION DATA

McDonough, James L., 1934-
War in Kentucky: from Shiloh to Perryville / James Lee McDonough. —1st ed.
p. cm.
Includes bibliographical references and index.
ISBN 0-87049-847-9 (cloth: alk. paper)
1. Kentucky—History—Civil War, 1861-1865—Campaigns.
2. United States—History—Civil War, 1861-1865—Campaigns.
I. Title.
E470.4.M33 1994
973.7'3—dc 20 94-4508
CIP

Dedicated to the memory of
Howard Ashley White

☆☆☆

Contents

☆☆☆

Figures

☆☆☆

Maps

Preface

☆☆☆

In the winter of 1862, a Union joint army-navy offensive succeeded in capturing Fort Henry and Fort Donelson, located respectively on the Tennessee and Cumberland rivers near the Tennessee-Kentucky state line. The operation was a great strategic triumph for the Federals—really the first of the Civil War—and presented many opportunities to threaten, exploit, and weaken the Confederacy. Immediately, the Rebel defensive line across southern Kentucky collapsed, and the Confederate armies retreated from northern Tennessee to Alabama and Mississippi. In the wake of the Confederate withdrawal, the Federals moved south. The Rebels mounted a major concentration of forces and attempted to throw back the Yankee advance, but the effort failed, in the bloody battle at Shiloh, one of the most notable and closely contested of all Civil War engagements.

A second Confederate attempt to counter the Union victories was then conceived. This offensive came only after still more damage—such as the Federal capture of New Orleans, the fall of Memphis, and the breaking of the Memphis and Charleston Railroad—had been inflicted on the western Confederacy. The effort took place in the late summer and fall of 1862. This campaigning is not nearly so well known as the Battle of Shiloh. In fact, both Union and Confederate operations in the western theater, in the weeks and months following Shiloh, have received relatively little attention. Instead, insofar as this period of the war is concerned, history's spotlight has been focused on Stonewall Jackson's Valley Campaign and the Peninsular Campaign, with Robert E. Lee taking control of the main Rebel army in Virginia, followed by the battles of Second Bull Run and Antietam.

This is unfortunate. I do not mean that it is unfortunate that the eastern campaigning has been heavily studied; rather, it is unfortunate that this focus has contributed to a perception that western events really did not matter much. This period, in both East and West, was very important to the Confederacy's struggle to survive.

The western Confederates, in making a second major bid to turn the war around after the disasters suffered during winter and spring of 1862, got off to a good start. The unfolding of events from Shiloh to Perryville was quite significant, with vast strategic implications. Without an understanding of these happenings—regardless of how knowledgeable one may be of events in the East that are perceived by some as both more important and more glamorous than those in the West—one's view of the Civil War in 1862 will be incomplete and, worse, markedly unbalanced. The war's western story is very significant; it is also instructive, interesting, and at times fascinating.

The following account attempts whenever possible to allow the participants, both officers and common soldiers, to tell their own stories in their own words, without any effort to correct their grammar and spelling. I have accepted at face value these accounts from letters, diaries, and memoirs, unless there seemed to be a good reason for doubting their record. Perhaps it is also appropriate to add that the reports and records in the *War of the Rebellion: A Compilation of the Official Records of the Union and Confederate Armies*, always an indispensable source in any military study of the Civil War, were unusually helpful for this project because of the extensive testimony compiled during the investigation of General Don Carlos Buell's campaigning from North Alabama through the Battle of Perryville. Finally, the author hopes that the reader will close this book with a greater appreciation of the significance of events in the Western Theater, particularly in the Upper South—in Tennessee and, even more, in Kentucky—during summer and fall of 1862, as well as of the people, Yanks and Rebs, who struggled there.

Acknowledgments

☆☆☆

To all those who have helped me in the completion of this book, I wish to convey a hearty and deeply felt "Thank you." Certain people deserve particular recognition. First, I must acknowledge the assistance of Peggy Bunnell Nims, Kentuckian, former student, and long-time friend. Her help in researching the events at Munfordville and Perryville was particularly valuable; additionally, she took pictures and located photographs at Munfordville, Perryville, and Richmond. All in all, she made a major contribution to this book.

While preparing this manuscript, I continued to benefit from research conducted years ago in the extensive personal library of the late Phil J. Hohlweck, Milwaukee, Wisconsin. Dean W. Lambert, professor at Berea College, Berea, Kentucky, spent the better part of an afternoon with me—and that when I appeared unannounced—discussing the fighting at Richmond and helping me understand that battle. Christopher Losson, author of a recent book on General Benjamin Franklin Cheatham, made available for my research several pertinent sources which he had used in his study of Cheatham. John Byrd, San Jose, California, provided a number of important books for my use in recent years. The suggestions of those who read the manuscript for the University of Tennessee Press, one of whom was B. Frank Cooling, were thoughtful and helpful in making this a better book. Also reading the manuscript and making some excellent suggestions was Thomas Belser, professor emeritus, Auburn University. My daughter, Sharon McDonough, was a major help with the maps; and my brother-in-law, John Hursh of Lewisburg, Tennessee, contributed some photographs of important railroad sites.

The staffs of many libraries, archives, and historical societies have rendered invaluable assistance. Mary Glenn Hearne, manager of the Nashville Room at the Public Library of Nashville and Davidson County; Marilyn Bell Hughes of the Tennessee State Library and Archives; and Carolyn Wilson of the Crisman Memorial Library, David Lipscomb University, Nashville, all deserve particular mention for their assistance with this manuscript and my earlier books. I also acknowledge the assistance of the staffs at the Alabama Department of Archives and History; the Robert B. Draughon Library at Auburn University, especially the Interlibrary Loan Office; the Eastern Kentucky University Library; the Filson Club; the Library of the Florida State University; the Georgia Department of Archives and History; the Georgia Historical Society; the Hart County (Kentucky) Historical Society; the Huntington Library; the Indiana Historical Society; the Military Records and Research Branch of the Kentucky Department of Military Affairs; the Kentucky Historical Society; the Mississippi Department of Archives and History; the Ohio Historical Society; the Perryville Battlefield Museum, especially Kurt Holman, manager and curator; the University of Florida Library; the University of Kentucky Library; the University of North Carolina Library; the University of Tennessee Library; the Western Kentucky University Library; and the Western Reserve Historical Society.

Since our days together as graduate students at the Florida State University and now as a colleague at Auburn, Wayne Flynt has been a good friend and a major source of encouragement. Gordon Bond, now dean of the College of Liberal Arts at Auburn, while head of the History Department was instrumental in my securing two quarters of research leave, which helped me to complete this manuscript.

Certainly I must mention the late Howard A. White, president emeritus of Pepperdine University, Malibu, California, a former teacher, long-time friend, and staunch supporter, who was very encouraging about this book. Encouraging me, too, perhaps more than he realized, was a "young fellow" whom I first met when we started the fourth grade together, Ross V. Hickey, Jr., Nashville, Tennessee.

Jennifer Pennington, secretary in the History Department at Auburn, by her knowledge of computers (this being my first book prepared on disk), saved me considerable time and frustration. For all her help I am thankful.

For well over a decade, in various capacities, Jennifer Siler, now director of the University of Tennessee Press, has been a great help with my books published by the press. Again I want to say, as I did in a previous book, that "working with the UT Press has continued to be a pleasant experience."

Finally, writing a book—which much of the time is an obsessive endeavor—inevitably affects one's spouse, who must be an understanding person. I thank Nancy for enduring yet another of these projects.

It seems that it should be unnecessary to state—but I will say it nevertheless, both because it is customary and so that no will misunderstand—that I alone am responsible for all statements of fact, interpretations, and conclusions presented herein.

James L. McDonough

Chapter 1

A Long Way from Shiloh to Perryville

☆☆☆

The telegram from Richmond came as a surprise. The day was dry and hot as Confederate General Braxton Bragg read the communiqué at his headquarters near the Mobile and Ohio Railroad in northeastern Mississippi. The date was June 20, 1862.

The telegram was from Jefferson Davis, president of the Confederacy. It removed General P. G. T. Beauregard from command of the Army of the Mississippi, the Rebel force then sprawled in and around the little town of Tupelo, and designated Bragg as his successor. "You are assigned permanently to the command . . . , as will be more formally notified to you by the Secretary of War," said Davis. "You will correspond directly and receive orders and instructions from the Government in relation to your future operations."[1]

The focus of attention now would shift away from one of the war's most volatile and most colorful generals. Popularly known as the "Napoleon in Gray," an image which his biographer indicates the general worked to cultivate,[2] Pierre Gustave Toutant Beauregard was a small but muscular and strikingly handsome man. His olive skin was accentuated by a neatly trimmed, jet-black mustache. A favorite of the ladies, he also was widely recognized as a leader of men.[3] When he came from Virginia to Tennessee in early February

1862, his reception sometimes was astounding. A Memphis editor, in a column headed "The Hero of Manassas," seemed to look upon Beauregard as a one-man gang: "There is all confidence *now* that a vandal's foot will never tread the streets of Memphis."[4]

Certainly Beauregard made an impact on people. "Something in his resounding name of Beauregard, in his Creole origin in south Louisiana, in his knightly bearing," wrote T. Harry Williams, "suggested a more exotic environment than the South of Jefferson Davis."[5]

But Jefferson Davis was president of the South—at least of the eleven southern states that made up the Confederate States of America. He did not care for Beauregard and, despite the Creole's proclamations about the absolute need for concentration of forces and taking the offensive in a campaign that would carry to the mouths of the Tennessee and Cumberland rivers ("most probably" even taking St. Louis, said Beauregard),[6] all that Davis had observed were words and retreat. Thus the "Napoleon in Gray" had been removed from command.

The army's new commander, General Braxton Bragg, was quite different from the man he replaced. At forty-five years of age, Bragg was only a year older than Beauregard.[7] But Bragg—sour, quarrelsome, frequently pessimistic—looked rather haggard and appeared to be considerably older than Beauregard. In fact, the special correspondent for the *London Times*, William Howard Russell, when he first had seen Bragg about a year earlier, had described him as "a tall, elderly man."[8] Bragg may not have deserved the term "elderly," but he definitely looked older than his age (he was in his mid-forties). And, compared to Beauregard, Bragg certainly was not good-looking.

Appearance never had been one of Bragg's strengths. Entering the United States Military Academy at West Point in 1833, the North Carolinian had been depicted as a "tall, ungainly plebe, almost uncouth in manner, but bright and engaging in conversation."[9] His intelligence, however, was paired with, and impaired by, certain qualities that were to spell trouble for Bragg and those closely associated with him. At the academy it had been noted that he had "an unusual frankness of expression, extending even to harshness, brusqueness, rudeness."[10]

In the years after West Point, Bragg had become known in the old army for integrity, efficiency, discipline, and—as a result of actions in the Mexican War—courage. He also had developed a pronounced reputation for being contentious. An oft-repeated story illustrates this characteristic. Once Bragg, while serving as both a company commander and the post quartermaster at a certain fort, in his former capacity had requested supplies, only to deny his own request in the latter capacity. He topped off the ridiculous episode by exchanging disputatious letters with himself until, finally, he turned the matter over to the fort commander for resolution. That officer, noting that Bragg had quarreled with every officer in the army, remarked that now he was even quarreling with himself.[11]

This tale conveys, if nothing else, the impression many held of Bragg. U. S. Grant said that Bragg had an "irascible temper" and was "naturally disputatious."[12] Perhaps Bragg never quarreled with himself, but he certainly quarreled with many people, including Jefferson Davis, with whom he had a somewhat bitter confrontation in the last decade before the Civil War.[13]

There was about Bragg a no-nonsense air that probably revealed much of the inner self. A tireless worker and a rigid disciplinarian, the general, according to one of his biographers, "actually enjoyed managing detailed affairs."[14] Many of the soldiers thought he was unreasonably strict. During the Mexican War—in which General Zachary Taylor's order at the Battle of Buena Vista ("Double-shot your guns and give 'em hell, Bragg") helped make Bragg famous—somebody attempted to murder Bragg by planting a bomb under his tent.[15] Thus far in the Civil War, no Confederate soldier had attempted to kill Bragg; however, in a popularity contest with Beauregard, Bragg would not have stood a chance. An Alabama doctor wrote to his wife that Bragg was an awful despot and that service under the Tsar of Russia would have been preferable to service under Bragg. (The doctor wanted a furlough to visit his wife, whom he had married the previous year, and Bragg had canceled furloughs.) One of the Rebel soldiers, Sam Watkins, wrote that Bragg's name became a "terror to deserters and evil doers," claiming that men "were shot by scores." Another said that the general had hanged sixteen men on a single tree.[16]

Such accounts obviously were exaggerated, but it was soon after Shiloh, on the retreat from Corinth, that an incident occurred which did much to brand Bragg as an unreasoning stickler for the letter of the law. Bragg gave orders that no gun be fired, lest the retreat route be revealed, and set the penalty of death for disobedience. Subsequently, a drunken soldier fired at a chicken and accidentally wounded a small black child. The soldier was tried by court martial, was sentenced to be shot, and was executed. Some of the facts of the event soon were distorted, or ignored, and the story circulated that, because a Rebel soldier had shot at a chicken, Bragg had had the soldier shot—a soldier for a chicken.[17] Although he was falsely maligned as a result of this incident, there is no denying that Bragg tended to alienate a lot of people, including both superiors and subordinates. Getting along with others did not come easy to him.

Indeed, Braxton Bragg was, as Steven Woodworth writes, "a complicated personality." Highly self-disciplined, he valued self-discipline in others, observes Woodworth, and, "when a person fell short in that trait, as was often the case, Bragg could be a very strict disciplinarian. This had made the troops he commanded some of the best drilled and trained in the Confederate army. Even so, he exercised a paternal care for his men, seeing to their welfare and even visiting hospitals and making attempts (however clumsy) at joking with them."[18] Bragg may have cared for others—he probably did—but in conveying that concern to others he often failed. Nevertheless, there were some (probably a minority) who seemed to take pride in having experienced Bragg's training. Private William E. Bevens of the First Arkansas said that "the old general trained us to walk until horses could not beat us."[19]

Confederate General Braxton Bragg. Courtesy, Library of Congress.

Here it seems worthwhile to quote Richard Taylor, son of the former president of the United States and later a lieutenant general under the Confederacy, who visited with Bragg soon after his appointment as army commander:

> Possessing experience in and talent for war, [Bragg] was the most laborious of commanders, devoting every moment to the discharge of his duties. As a disciplinarian he far surpassed any of the senior Confederate generals; but his method and manner were harsh, and he could have won the affections of his troops only by leading them to victory. . . . Many years of dyspepsia had made his temper sour and petulant; and he was intolerant to a degree of neglect of duty, or what he esteemed to be such, by his officers. A striking instance of this occurred during my visit. At dinner, surrounded by his numerous staff, I inquired for one of his division commanders, a man widely known and respected, and received this answer: "General — is an old woman, utterly worthless." Such a declaration, privately made, would have been serious; but publicly, and certain to be repeated, it was astonishing. . . . From that hour I had misgivings as to General Bragg's success.[20]

Appearance, manner, and popularity aside, General Bragg impressed many people, including President Davis, as being a man who could successfully command an army, one who possessed good organizational ability, skill in campaign planning, energy, discipline, and a strong sense of duty. Yet, as one of his biographers has pertinently observed, he was too ambitious to be satisfied with himself or others, and represented "an unusual combination of potentially dangerous eccentricities and high ability."[21] An ominous observation. For better or worse, the fate of the Confederacy's main western army, to be known for much of the war as the Army of Tennessee, now was in the hands of General Braxton Bragg.

The telegram from President Davis placing him in command not only came as a surprise to General Bragg, it also left him in a very uncomfortable position. In years to come—when Bragg and Beauregard no longer were on cordial terms and Bragg was a prime mover among those who attempted to hold Beauregard responsible for the so-called "lost opportunity" at the Battle of Shiloh[22]—Bragg probably would not even have lifted one of his heavy eyebrows at the thought of replacing Beauregard. Perhaps he would have delighted in doing just that. In summer 1862, however, Bragg was a friend of General Beauregard and on better terms with President Davis than he had been in a long while, their antebellum hostility now buried for the good of the cause. Bragg realized that he was caught in the middle between two men, Davis and Beauregard, who had come to despise each other.[23]

Three days earlier, Beauregard, having informed Richmond that his health necessitated "a short rest" but neglecting to specify where he was going, had left for a spa north of Mobile known as Bladon Springs. Promising afterward to "retake the offensive," Beauregard had placed Bragg in command until his return.[24] The promise to "retake the offensive" probably struck a dissonant chord with the government, because, since taking command at Shiloh—the defeat that he insisted upon calling a victory—Beauregard had only retreated. Beauregard had just arrived in Mobile when the news of his removal reached him. The information came not from Richmond, however, but in a telegram sent by Bragg .

The army's new commander, presumably contemplating both the awkwardness of the situation and the tremendously heavy responsibility suddenly laid upon his shoulders, said he was "almost in despair" and that he envied Beauregard. Shortly after Bragg's message arrived, Beauregard received the official word from the government in Richmond. The notification, wrote Stanley F. Horn in his landmark study, *The Army of Tennessee* (1941), "was a curt note from the Secretary of War enclosing a copy of the President's telegram to Bragg."[25] On the surface, at least, Beauregard took the news reasonably well, even telling Bragg that, while he could not congratulate him, he was "happy for the change," and he offered Bragg the service of his own staff. Not long afterward, Beauregard said that Bragg, to his knowledge, had "not a superior in the service." Apparently Beauregard genuinely held Bragg in high esteem. Immediately following the

Battle of Shiloh, Beauregard had "earnestly and urgently" recommended Bragg to Richmond as replacement for the slain Albert Sidney Johnston as commander of the army. Bragg, for his part, responded in kind, vowing never to be jealous of "so pure a man and eminent a General as Beauregard."[26]

There was a kernel of truth, however small, in Beauregard's statement that he was "happy for the change." He remained for the summer in the Mobile–Bladon Springs area, continuing to relish his acclaim as the hero of Fort Sumter and Manassas ("Bull Run," the United States called it). There he was "wined and dined by the best families" and, perhaps above all, "found much pleasure" in the company of a local novelist, Augusta Evans. To a friend, Beauregard wrote that "it would not do" for him to see the lady "too often, for I might forget 'home and country' in their hour of need." Long after the war, Augusta and he were still corresponding.[27]

Despite the special attractions of southern Alabama, there is overwhelming evidence that Beauregard was deeply bitter about the manner in which President Davis had dealt with him. In a private letter he spoke of Davis as "a man who is either demented or a traitor to his high trust. . . . , a living specimen of gall and hatred." Davis himself viewed Beauregard as having left the Army of the Mississippi without just cause—as, in essence, having deserted his post. Later, when Beauregard's health had improved and his supporters in the Confederate Congress requested that Davis restore him to command of the western army, the president became enraged. Beauregard, he said, should not have left the army, "even if he had to be carried around in a litter." Davis affirmed that, "if the whole world were to ask me to restore General Beauregard to the command which I have already given to General Bragg, I would refuse it."[28]

The enmity between Beauregard and Davis would go with them to the grave—and, in a sense, beyond it. When Davis died while in New Orleans in 1889 and was laid to rest in that city's famous Metairie Cemetery, Beauregard, long a leading citizen of New Orleans, confided to family members that he was not sorry to learn that

Confederate General P. G. T. Beauregard. Courtesy, Library of Congress.

Davis was dead, because the two had "always been enemies." Four years later, when Beauregard himself died and also was placed in Metairie, within a few weeks the body of Davis was removed and reinterred in Richmond. "The timing of the removal," wrote William I. Hair, ". . . shortly after Beauregard's body was taken there, probably was not coincidental." Mrs. Davis, who made the decision to remove her husband's body to the former Confederate capital, knew, continued Hair, "that her husband and Beauregard could not stand being near each other while alive, and it surely occurred to her that they would not want to be near in death."[29]

☆☆☆

Possibly General Bragg, for his part, might have welcomed a restoration of Beauregard. There is no question that Bragg had been given command at a time when the Confederacy's fortunes were at a low ebb. The truly critical situation of the Confederacy in June 1862 never has been generally recognized—certainly not by popular readers and not even by some historians. The losses suffered were catastrophic, and the suddenness with which the losses all happened made them seem the more appalling. The extent of loss in the first six months of 1862 would have seemed absolutely incredible to most southerners when they had celebrated Christmas in December 1861.

At that time the Confederates—vital and confident, some frankly arrogant—still had expected, as they had early on, that the war soon would be over. They reveled in the intoxication of their early triumphs. In the opening land "battle" of the war at Big Bethel, Virginia, two Yankee columns attempting to rendezvous were so badly managed that they fired at each other by mistake, inflicting several casualties, after which they were defeated by the Rebel force although they outnumbered the latter three to one. Also, at Wilson's Creek in Missouri, the Federals had been compelled to retreat after a fierce fight. At Ball's Bluff, Virginia, the Yankees had been whipped again.[30] Above all, of course, the Confederates relished the memory of Manassas, the war's first engagement that could properly be called a battle—and the only "big" battle of 1861. They fought on Virginia soil, just a few miles from Washington, D.C., where the southerners of General Joseph E. Johnston and General Beauregard had driven the Yankee army back to its capital, initially in panic and finally in rout. Compared to this victory, such minor Confederate setbacks as occurred in West Virginia soon had been forgotten.

But for those Confederates who contemplated the future in late 1861, such memories of the past were grossly misleading as to coming events. Nothing had yet occurred to compare with what now was about to happen. The casualties at Manassas, Wilson's Creek, Big Bethel, Ball's Bluff—in fact, all the carnage of 1861—soon would pale into relative insignificance when contrasted with the horror of a single engagement in early April of the new year: the Battle of Shiloh. The killed and wounded of all those 1861 clashes put together would fall far short of the number of killed and wounded at the so-called "place of peace"—the meaning of the Biblical word Shiloh, a name given to the Methodist meeting house that stood on the battleground. Shiloh was by a wide margin the biggest battle, in numbers engaged and in casualties, both of the Civil War and of American history up to that time. Yet it accounted for only a portion of the inconceivable Confederate losses suffered by early June 1862.[31]

While the damage was done in many places and in various ways, nothing equaled the disasters the Confederacy experienced on the western rivers. Indeed, the war's first really significant campaigning began on the great Mississippi's paralleling waterway to the east, the Tennessee, and, still farther to the east, the Cumberland River, the defense of which the Confederate authorities had neglected. In early February 1862, a combined land and water invasion force under U. S. Grant and Andrew H. Foote breached the Confederate defensive perimeter across southern Kentucky. Driving south up the Tennessee and Cumberland, the Federals captured the bastions protecting those vital waterways, Fort Henry and Fort Donelson.

The importance of these Union victories can hardly be overstated. Robert S. Henry, in his book *The Story of the Confederacy* (1931), writes, "Fort Donelson, in many ways, may be considered the critical event of the civil war."[32] Bruce Catton writes that "Fort Donelson was not only a beginning; it was one of the most decisive engagements of the entire war, and out of it came the slow, inexorable progression that led to Appomattox."[33] Most recently, Frank Cooling, in a study of the fall of the forts, writes of "the expedition that broke open the war in the West."[34] Presumably, in this evaluation he is referring to Fort Henry as well as Fort Donelson—which makes Cooling's analysis even more to the point than the others.

Fort Henry fell to the Federals first—and with ludicrous, almost incredible ease. Located on the east bank of the Tennessee River a short distance south of the Kentucky state line, Henry was "miserably located" on low ground, "not well planned, poorly armed,"[35] and "threatened almost as much by the rising river as by the approaching Yankees."[36] The Confederates put up a fight against Andrew Foote's gunboats for about two hours. With one-third of the Rebel fortifications under water, the single ten-inch Columbiad with sufficient range to duel the gunboats accidentally spiked, and a rifled 24-pounder burst, the handful of Rebel defenders commanded by Brigadier General Lloyd Tilghman, decided to surrender. Most of the garrison already had been sent to Fort Donelson. "The river had risen so high," writes Stanley Horn, "that when Foote's officer approached to receive the surrender his cutter could sail right through the sally port."[37] Meanwhile, U. S. Grant's troops still were sloshing through the muddy bottoms and, beyond serving as a potential threat to the rear of the fort, had played no role in taking the fortification. Thus the fall of Fort Henry, with the U.S. Navy doing the work, was indeed a decision on the river.

The fall of Fort Henry opened the Tennessee River as an avenue of penetration all the way to the Alabama and Mississippi state lines. Advancing via the Tennessee River, which parallels the Mississippi, proved just as good as moving down the Mississippi itself. Actually, it was better in some ways: it enabled the Federals to flank the Confederates at Columbus, Kentucky, on the Mississippi River, and immediately to break one east-west railroad, the Memphis, Clarksville

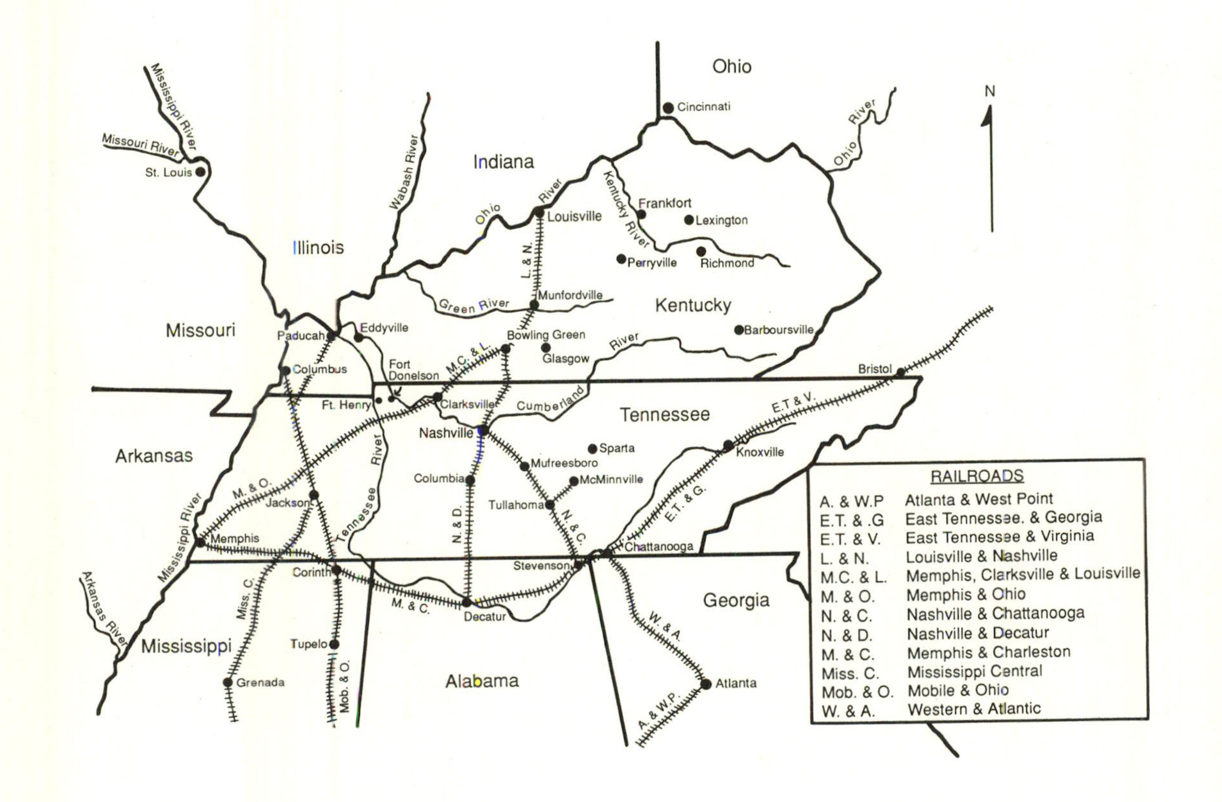

The Western Theater.
Map prepared by Sharon McDonough.

and Louisville, which crossed the Tennessee only seventeen miles south of Fort Henry. Three gunboats did the work of destroying the bridge. This meant that communication between Confederate forces on the Mississippi at Columbus, Kentucky, and those at Bowling Green, Kentucky, the center of the Rebel line, was severed—severed except for the far longer rail route from Columbus south to Corinth, Mississippi, then across part of northern Alabama (via the Memphis and Charleston Railroad) to Decatur, and finally the last leg, northward into Tennessee through Columbia and Nashville into Bowling Green. The gunboats then continued (south) up the Tennessee, knocking out other bridges and cutting telegraph lines, all the way to Muscle Shoals, Alabama, where the town of Florence was surrendered by its mayor to S. Ledyard Phelps, commander of the expedition. Within the next four months, in the wake of the fall of Fort Henry and the opening of the Tennessee River, the Yankees took control of Corinth and its all-important Memphis and Charleston Railroad line, the Confederacy's main east-west rail link. Thereby they outflanked Memphis, which fell four months to the day after Fort Henry.[38]

The fact was that, with Fort Henry in Yankee hands, the Confederates could do nothing but retreat. Even before Grant could get his troops across the twelve-mile neck of land from Fort Henry to take position at Fort Donelson, Rebel General Albert Sidney Johnston already had decided to abandon Bowling Green, Kentucky. Sending half of his troops to Donelson in hopes that the fort somehow could be held, he retreated with the remainder toward Nashville.[39] With Fort Henry in Federal hands, the center of the Kentucky-Tennessee defensive line at Bowling Green was being abandoned.

A Kentucky soldier wrote to his wife on February 15, "The time of our severest affliction has now come; our state is about to be abandoned by our armies—a disaster caused by. . . the surrender of Tillman." The fall of Fort Henry would "wake up" the South, he thought. "Before they would not believe that a southern army however weak could be driven back, and would do nothing, in spite of General Johnston's remonstrances."[40]

Suddenly it was a different war. Fort Henry was like the first domino that, in falling, set in motion the collapse of an entire row. Barring a military miracle of sorts at Fort Donelson, the Confederacy soon would be trying to recoup in northern Mississippi and Alabama.

There would be no miracle at Fort Donelson. Only ten days after the fall of Fort Henry, Fort Donelson collapsed, following some hard fighting amply mingled with Confederate bungling—all taking place in cold weather accentuated by snow and sleet.[41] The fall of Fort Donelson resulted in the Union's capturing fifteen thousand Confederate prisoners and opening a second avenue of invasion, via the Cumberland, to Tennessee's capital city, Nashville. These events insured the collapse of the entire Rebel defensive line across southern Kentucky and propelled General Ulysses S. Grant into the limelight as the North's first successful commander.

The fall of the two forts was the first turning point of the war—and not Antietam and Emancipation, as has been popularly believed. What followed in the next few weeks, as the pressure of the Federal onslaught mounted steadily and rapidly, was a series of Union triumphs, several directly or indirectly attributable to the fall of Henry and Donelson, that left the western Confederacy struggling for its life. Simply put, the foundation of the Confederacy had been split open.

Why has this generally not been recognized? Frank Cooling offers the most telling indictment. Noting that both Yanks and Rebs seemed to forget the forts as they reminisced about other engagements, he writes that "historians perpetuated the amnesia about the meaning of Henry-Donelson by portraying these battles as minor affairs."[42] The failure of historians ties in with the long-standing emphasis on the eastern theater of war, characteristic of the majority of people, whatever their credentials, who have studied the conflict. Even at the time, most people in the North probably failed to perceive the far-reaching implications of the river triumphs. (After all the majority of northerners, like many people today, probably did not know where the rivers were.) However, the man who eventually was to lead the Union armies to victory in the war saw the meaning clearly. Grant, writing to his wife soon after the momentous events, said that the advance on the Tennessee River gave the Federals "such an inside track on the enemy that by following up our success we can go anywhere."[43]

Perhaps not literally "anywhere." But Grant certainly was right about the vast potential of the advance on the Tennessee. If the Tennessee was the most important stream, the Cumberland was not inconsequential. As the dominoes continued to fall, the Cumberland River yielded a tremendous prize. When Nashville—the first Confederate state capital to fall—was abandoned a week after Fort Donelson surrendered, the western Confederacy lost a major city which, "including its suburbs, contained very nearly thirty thousand inhabitants."[44] This number was twice as large as Atlanta's population, for example. But Nashville represented more—much more—than the number of its residents. "Nashville was," wrote Stanley Horn, "the largest and most important city south of the Ohio River, with the exception of New Orleans, and occupied an important strategic position."[45] That position, in addition to being located on the Cumberland River, was defined largely by extensive railroad connections: north, via the Louisville and Nashville; south, via the Nashville and Decatur, to a junction with the Memphis and Charleston; southeast, via the Nashville and Chattanooga, with connections to the Deep South; and west, via the Nashville and Northwestern, to the Tennessee River.[46]

Following the outbreak of war, Nashville rapidly had been transformed into a major arsenal and supply depot. Nashville's warehouses, as Stanley Horn puts it, "were bursting with food and clothing accumulated by the Commissary and Quartermaster Departments." One plant was "manufacturing 100,000 percussion caps a day"; others were turning out sabers and muskets. Two foundries "were . . . casting cannon, and one of them was turning out rifled guns. The highly valued rifling machine had been made from plans obtained by a spy sent to a northern arsenal after the beginning of the war."[47]

With the abandonment of Nashville, the western Confederacy had lost its most important city for the manufacture and storage of all manner of war supplies, from heavy ordnance to shoes, flour, and bacon. The Rebel loss of Nashville obviously constituted a very serious blow. But the total loss in Middle Tennessee amounted to much more. The state of Tennessee was the greatest iron-ore producing region in the entire Confederacy. Most of the state's furnaces, forges, and bloomeries were located south of Fort Donelson and between Nashville and the Tennessee River, a distance of about sixty air miles, in the area the Union army had just penetrated. The heart of Tennessee's growing industrial complex and its great war potential were gone, virtually irreplaceable resources for the Confederate war effort.[48]

The Union army under Don Carlos Buell, which had advanced from Louisville, occupied Nashville. Meanwhile, the army that had taken Fort Donelson returned to the Tennessee, proceeding upriver (southward) all the way past Savannah to Pittsburgh Landing. Farther to the west, the grand advance continued, as Federal General John Pope applied pressure on the Mississippi River. When Columbus, Kentucky, was evacuated after the fall of the twin forts on the Tennessee and the Cumberland, the Rebels attempted to hold the Mississippi farther south, in the vicinity of the Kentucky-Tennessee-Missouri boundary.

The key points were Island Number Ten, a major fortification in the southern end of a big loop of the river, and New Madrid, a Missouri town farther downstream (although north of the island because of the river's big loop in that direction) on the west bank of the Mississippi. Three forts with seven guns each were trained on the river at New Madrid, while Island Number Ten boasted thirty-nine guns, including a sixteen-gun floating battery. General Pope, coming from the north, of course, could not approach New Madrid by river because of the island's batteries. The position was far more vulnerable to land approach, anyway. Coming in from the northwest, Pope had claimed the town for the Union by March 14.

This left Island Number Ten almost completely isolated, as the Federals then controlled the west bank of the river both above and below the island. The low land to the south was becoming impassable, as the river was rising. The island, formidable as it was, was about to be cut off.[49]

Thus it appeared that the Confederates soon would be falling back again, perhaps all the way to Fort Pillow, only fifty river miles north of Memphis. Mrs. Braxton Bragg, never one to hesitate in offering criticism or giving her husband advice, wrote to the general, who had left Pensacola and Mobile to help reinforce the retiring Confederates: "In truth we can not retreat much more without coming upon the enemy on the Gulf." If the southern soldiers "continue to behave so disgracefully we women had better take the field and send them home to raise chickens."[50]

Truly the events of February had produced a southern disaster of unparalleled magnitude. Soon the Union army was approaching dangerously close to what suddenly had become the most strategically important Confederate town west of Chattanooga: Corinth, Mississippi, a railroad junction only twenty miles from the Tennessee River, where the north-south Mobile and Ohio Railroad crossed the east-west Memphis and Charleston line. If the Union army captured Corinth, Memphis would be untenable, and thus the Mississippi River soon would be opened to Federal forces for several hundred more miles. Even more significant, the Union army would control "the vertebrae of the Confederacy"—as former Confederate Secretary of War General Leroy P. Walker appropriately termed the Memphis and Charleston Railroad.[51]

This was the railroad which Secretary of War Judah P. Benjamin said "must be defended at all hazards." So serious was the matter that the Confederate cabinet actually discussed the possibility of abandoning Richmond in order to defend it.[52] If this line were broken, southern east-west communications would be forced to go south all the way to Vicksburg and Meridian, Mississippi; move on to Mobile, Alabama (perhaps proving Mrs. Bragg a better prophet than she realized); then proceed north by a route through Montgomery, West Point, and Atlanta; and finally turn back northwestward to Chattanooga, before continuing northeastward to Virginia. A more damaging strike against the Confederacy's ability to move troops and supplies quickly in the west is difficult to conceive.

But the Rebels, smarting, angry, and embarrassed by the Federal successes, concentrated in force around Corinth. They assembled from all over the South—from Mobile, Montgomery, Pensacola, New Orleans, Jackson, Nashville, Memphis—determined to muster enough strength to roll back the onrushing Yankee army and reverse the tide of war in the Western Theater.

The Confederates needed to protect the Memphis and Charleston Railroad; they needed to recover the central and western portions of Middle Tennessee; they needed to regain control of the Cumberland and Tennessee rivers. They were gathering for a battle that appeared to be a "must" for them to win—or they would be fated, in the face of ever-mounting Federal strength, to continue the struggle from a drastically changed and weakened position. Their effort culminated in the great battle at Shiloh.

There the Confederates sacrificed thousands of their soldiers in the attempt to turn back the Federals. They almost succeeded. The Rebels were so close to victory on April 6 that one marvels that the U.S. Army was able to escape disaster. Early in the fighting on that Sunday morning, the southerners possessed a numerical advantage of perhaps five thousand men; more important, the element of surprise—not absolute, but certainly effective—was on their side. The Rebels took the initiative and held the momentum. They were also aided by the fact that the encampments of the Federal army lacked any tactical formation and had no field fortifications. Green troops manned the advance camps, and only about fifteen hundred men protected the critical left flank and the route to Pittsburgh Landing by which Union reinforcements might arrive.[53]

Although victory at Shiloh clearly was within reach of the Rebels for a few hours, history records a Union triumph. The Confederates lost an opportunity to undo a large portion of what the Federal Army had accomplished during the winter and early spring. When they failed, the pressure of the Federal onslaught mounted steadily.

On the Mississippi, the advance of the Yankees continued, as they applied pressure that gradually forced the Rebels to give up another stretch of the great river. On April 7, about seven thousand Confederate soldiers became prisoners, as Island Number Ten, the strongest fortification on the river, surrendered to the U.S. forces. As the Rebel army that had fought and lost at Shiloh, suffering more than ten thousand casualties, trudged back into Corinth that same night, this was the news that greeted its commander, General P. G. T. Beauregard, who had replaced the slain Albert Sidney Johnston. "The fall of Island Number Ten was a disaster of no mean proportions," was Stanley Horn's evaluation.[54] Besides the blow to both the Mississippi River defenses and Confederate morale, the loss of Island Number Ten struck still another blow at what some have considered the Confederacy's "most vulnerable spot—manpower."[55]

Soon the Confederates also were compelled to evacuate Fort Pillow, only fifty miles north of Memphis, and the Federals then quickly closed in on the Bluff City, which was occupied by Union forces on June 6—still more decisions on the rivers.

Meanwhile, at the mouth of "the Father of Waters," the onrushing Blue juggernaut already had taken the Crescent City. The impact of this capture was devastating to the Confederacy. The population of New Orleans was four times greater than that of any other southern city. But the importance of New Orleans, like that of Nashville, cannot be understood simply as the number of people dwelling there. New Orleans also was the wealthiest of southern cities. It boasted the largest sugar refinery in the world, was the capital of King Cotton, and was the foremost export port on the North American continent. The city was second only to New York in imports and enjoyed the distinction of being the banking capital of the South. "The fall of New Orleans not only had military and economic impact, but also diplomatic results," Frank Vandiver writes. "If the South could not protect so vital a city, it must be weak indeed."[56]

The U.S. triumph in taking New Orleans also had been a river decision, and it had been set up, in no small degree, by the recent events on the rivers to the north. Benjamin F. Butler, lawyer and politician from Massachusetts, whose occupation of New Orleans was to make him infamous to southerners, commanded eighteen thousand troops, with whom he hoped to capture the Confederacy's principal port. But the real work was done on the river, seventy-five miles below New Orleans, by a naval expedition commanded by the crusty sixty-one-year-old David G. Farragut, born in East Tennessee. Having gone to sea as a boy, he was a veteran of the War of 1812 and the Mexican War, and probably was, as he has been described, "the most remarkable naval commander of the [Civil] War."[57]

New Orleans, stripped of its seasoned defenders, who had gone to Corinth for the concentration preceding the Battle of Shiloh, hoped that the Federals could be stopped downriver at the site of two forts, one on each bank, called Jackson and Saint Phillip. Supporting the forts were a few Confederate ships and a number of fire rafts. If the Yankees got past these defenses, the defense of the city would depend on about three thousand militia, under Mansfield Lovell, in New Orleans itself—virtually a hopeless task. On the night of April 24, Farragut ran his ships past the fort. Historian James McPherson succinctly describes the fighting and the result: "The fleet weighed anchor and moved single file up the channel. . . . The forts opened fire with 100 guns; the ships replied with their broadsides; the intrepid Confederate fleet tried to ram some of the Union ships and to push fire rafts against others. . . . Despite the sound and the fury, Farragut got through with only one ship sunk and three disabled."[58] Continuing upriver to New Orleans, Farragut, at the foot of Canal Street, trained his guns on the Crescent City; but he soon discovered that the militia had fled without even firing at him.

Charles Dufour calls it "The Night the War Was Lost," the title of his book detailing the action.[59] While he claims too much for the significance of the city's fall, clearly the loss of New Orleans was another major blow to the Confederacy. This loss, and the other Union triumphs on the western rivers, made up a series of events, occurring in the brief span of four months, that together placed the western Confederacy in a very precarious situation.

Farragut was not yet through. Steaming upriver—while Butler received the surrender of southern troops who mutinied at Jackson and St. Phillip, before coming on to occupy New Orleans—Farragut received the surrender of Louisiana's capital, Baton Rouge. Pushing still farther north, Farragut also took Natchez's surrender, but at last was forced back by the powerful guns of Vicksburg, high on the bluff above the Mississippi. The result was that "from New Orleans to Vicksburg, the [lower] Mississippi was a 400-mile Union highway by the end of May."[60] And, as previously noted, Memphis fell to the Federal fleet advancing southward on the great river by June 6. Now the Crescent City would serve as a secondary base for the attempt to complete the opening of the Mississippi. Thus the Federals had a death grip on the Mississippi Valley; and, without the valley, the Confederacy would be rent asunder, vulnerable to piecemeal strangulation by its adversary.

From Fort Henry and Fort Donelson on the Confederacy's northern border to New Orleans on the southern, the decisiveness of the Union campaigning in winter and spring 1862, which had cost more than forty thousand Confederate casualties, hardly can be exaggerated. Most of the results never were to be undone even briefly, and none at all permanently. Afterward, with the fall of the much-publicized fortress at Vicksburg in summer 1863 and the surrender of Port Hudson farther south a few days later, the forces set in motion by the momentous events of 1862 ground inevitably to their conclusion.

☆☆☆

While the worst damage to the Confederacy clearly was inflicted in the Western Theater, the situation was hardly encouraging anywhere. Union General Ambrose Burnside captured strategic Roanoke Island on February 8. Other important Atlantic coastal positions, such as Albemarle Sound and Port Royal, were in Federal hands, strengthening the Union's ability to tighten the blockade of the Confederacy. In early March, the *Monitor* had come forth successfully to check the Rebel breakthrough in the development of ironclad warships, battling the southern *Virginia* (*Merrimac*, as she previously had been known to the Federals) to a standoff at Hampton Roads. And, on the Gulf front, from Florida to Louisiana, few resources of significance remained under southern control, except for Mobile.[61]

In the Trans-Mississippi theater, the Confederate forces of Major General Sterling Price joined with Brigadier General Ben McCulloch in northwestern Arkansas; and the entire command of sixteen thousand troops, led by Major General Earl Van Dorn, headed northward, planning to strike into Missouri, with St. Louis as the objective. The capture of that great city, thought Van Dorn, would enable the Rebels to control the state and so take a major step toward mastering the Missouri and Mississippi rivers. But blocking the Confederate advance were the Federal forces of Brigadier General Samuel R. Curtis, some 10,500 in number, positioned just south of Pea Ridge, not far from Elkhorn Tavern, a sometime stagecoach stop for the Butterfield Overland Mail Company, which stood beside the telegraph (wire) road. Declining to assault the Yankees, who were dug in on high ground above Little Sugar Creek, Van Dorn attempted a turning movement against the Federal right flank, climaxed by a two-pronged attack.

In a wild, confused two-day fight on March 7 and 8—in which McCulloch was killed; casualties were heavy on both sides; and two regiments of Cherokee Indians, led by Albert Pike (whom Van Dorn refused even to acknowledge in his official report), fought for the Confederates—the outnumbered Yankees held out until the Rebels, running short of ammunition, at last retreated. The Union victory at Pea Ridge (Confederates called it Elkhorn Tavern) meant that Missouri would remain in Federal possession, while the Rebel government of Missouri would spend the war in exile.[62]

Even in the Far West, Rebel efforts had been likewise unproductive. Invading up the valley of the Rio Grande, southern General

Henry H. Sibley's army of four thousand men, mostly Texans, reached Santa Fe, New Mexico, by March 1862, with dreams of claiming what is now New Mexico, Arizona, and possibly even California for the Confederacy. It was not to be. In mid-April, at the Battle of Glorieta Pass, Colonel Edward R. S. Canby's Union regiments from New Mexico and California, assisted by Colorado volunteers, turned back the Rebel bid for the Southwest. Sibley led the survivors back into Texas, while vital supplies of gold and silver from the rich western mines continued to flow eastward to finance the Union war effort. Thus the Rebel hope of a California port came to naught.[63]

The Yankees, more than a hundred thousand strong, also were knocking on the doors of Richmond. By late May, they were, in fact, less than ten miles east of the Rebel capital. Although outnumbered nearly two to one, the Confederates, commanded by General Joseph Eggleston Johnston, launched an attack at Seven Pines (Fair Oaks) on May 31. The plan, based on a classic principle of war, was to throw the mass of the Rebel force against an isolated segment of the enemy. The smaller wing of the Federals was believed to have been separated from the U.S. main force by the rampaging waters of Chickahominy Creek. But the Rebel concept was badly executed, and the Federals on the south bank of the creek were reinforced by comrades from the north bank, leading to a confused two-day melee that produced about six thousand casualties on each side, including General Johnston, who was severely wounded. Thus the leadership of the Confederates passed to General Robert E. Lee—hardly a comforting thought for many a Confederate.

Hindsight provides the historian with a seemingly infallible tool for analyzing the past. How easy it is to remember Lee's contribution at Cerro Gordo Pass in the Mexican War, to recall that President Lincoln once offered Lee command of the U.S. forces, and, of course, to recollect the Virginian's later and sometimes brilliant exploits commanding what he termed the Army of Northern Virginia. How easy it is to forget, on the other hand, his first campaigning in West Virginia in 1861, which was viewed as a failure by many a soldier. Soldiers and newspapers, some later to praise him almost as a demigod, then had dubbed him "Granny Lee." It is true, as one historian writes, that "Lee's first campaign almost ruined his reputation before it had a chance to become established."[64] There was little to generate any widespread optimism as Lee took command of the Rebel forces defending Richmond.

Clearly the situation in the Eastern Theater in June 1862, at the time when Braxton Bragg took command of the Confederate army at Tupelo, Mississippi, was very serious; like Lee, Bragg already had some critics harping at him. There was more to the criticism than Bragg's reputation as a strict disciplinarian. Some thought, with reason, that his performance at Shiloh—particularly at the "Hornets' Nest," the name given by Confederates to a strong Union position that became the scene of prolonged and bloody fighting—had been less than impressive.

By late morning of the first day at Shiloh, Bragg had been commanding the majority of Confederates who were making costly frontal assaults against the position. Bragg had thought that the Hornets' Nest could be reduced by bayonet charge. After several such attempts had failed, it became obvious to many subordinates that something other than frontal assaults—even less effective when conducted in a piecemeal fashion—was demanded. Yet Bragg refused to change the tactics which, in the eyes of others, had proved a failure.

Not only were his tactics very costly in terms of manpower, but also the Confederates paid a price in time. The Yankees, under General Grant, were given valuable time to organize a strong defensive line covering Pittsburgh Landing on the Tennessee River, to which the whole Union army could fall back. This shortened line, on higher ground, with reinforcements coming by river to the landing, placed the Federals in position not only to hold out, but in fact to take the offensive and win the battle the next day. In short, Bragg's management of his troops at Shiloh—at least against the Hornets' Nest—hardly merited praise.[65]

When the Confederate retreat from Corinth began, some of Bragg's men, together with conscripts from other units, deserted and headed for home. "No wonder," writes Stanley Horn, that "morale slumped when [Bragg] was raised to the high command."[66]

"Bragg and Beauregard are at a discount since their retreat," wrote T. J. Koger of the Forty-First Mississippi to his wife. Koger was a captain in Company A, who earlier had reported that "unless we whip the Yankees [at Corinth] and whip them thoroughly, the whole valley of the Mississippi is lost."[67] Doubtless many Confederates had felt as Koger did, and the retreat from Corinth, following the defeat at Shiloh, constituted a double blow to Rebel morale that made Bragg's task as the new army commander especially difficult.

Yet Bragg also was praised after Shiloh, at least in some quarters. The *New Orleans Daily Picayune* lauded him: "General Bragg and staff were the last to leave the ground, though he was frequently urged before to retire, saying that he would never leave the battlefield so long as one of his soldiers remained before him." The paper claimed Bragg's "heroic valour and generalship" had gained for him "imperishable fame."[68]

One of the army's surgeons, writing to his wife from Tupelo, said, "General Bragg has been put in command of the Western Department and Beauregard superseded and now we have the right man in the right place. General Bragg is the most energetic and daring General we have and you will hear before long of something being done." The doctor also wrote that "the stories you hear of the demoralization of this army and desertions are greatly exaggerated. . . . Under the excellent rule of General Bragg the drills are regular and the men satisfied . . . , ready for a move."[69]

Governors of some states praised him. Most important, Jefferson Davis made him a full general, elevating Bragg to a position as the Confederacy's fifth-ranking officer.[70] Since Davis probably knew little or nothing of Bragg's shortcomings at Shiloh, to the president Bragg seemed the reasonable choice to replace Beauregard. As noted above, Bragg did give the appearance of being a man who could successfully command an army.[71] After Bragg was made a full general, his wife wrote that his usefulness thereby was increased; she added an intriguing comment that this relieved him "from obeying the commands of our vain glorious Bishop [Polk]" and ominously observed, "What you can *now do*, or indeed any one, is the important question."[72]

In touching on the relationship between Leonidas Polk and Braxton Bragg, Mrs. Bragg focused attention on a very tender command problem that potentially posed serious difficulties for both Bragg and Polk—and, of course, the Rebel army as well. Certainly Mrs. Bragg was correct, too, in what she implied about the absolutely critical situation facing her husband and the army. The recent achievements of the U.S. forces in the Western Theater, especially the triumphs on the rivers, presented a challenge to General Bragg and the western Confederates that clearly was without precedent—a challenge that threatened soon to put an end to the young Confederate States of America.

Thus, whatever Braxton Bragg, in the words of his wife, could "*now do*" needed to be done quickly. Initially at least, the general indeed rose to the challenge. Within a short time, regardless of the problems and the critics, Bragg devised and inaugurated a plan. Shifting to a new line of operations, he successfully led a turning movement, on a magnificent scale, to the east at Chattanooga and thence northwest into Middle Tennessee. Effectively deceiving the enemy in his front, and using the railroads to best advantage, Bragg was able to place his forces in position to threaten the Federal rear, compelling the enemy to retreat or have its supply line severed.

Strategically, this Rebel movement was more promising than the earlier advance against the Federals at Shiloh. If the Confederates had won at Shiloh, the victory obviously would have been a great boost to their morale, as well as a setback to the Union; but a triumph there would not have opened up the opportunities that Bragg's turning movement presented. There was no railroad to follow north from Shiloh. The nearest line was the Mobile and Ohio, several miles to the west, that ran through West Tennessee and into western Kentucky at the Ohio River, reaching the strategic hearts of neither Tennessee nor Kentucky. A victory at Shiloh would not have provided an opportunity to move north on the Tennessee River, because the Confederates had no naval forces with which to contest Yankee control of that stream. Also, there were no good roads leading north from Shiloh to any place of major importance.

But when Bragg moved into Middle Tennessee in summer 1862, he could advance, if he chose, along the railroad from Chattanooga to Nashville, an excellent communications line. If he could compel the Union to fall back from Nashville into Kentucky, as in fact occurred, another rail line would be at his disposal for a continuing advance. Also, moving to Chattanooga would present an opportunity for Bragg to achieve a concentration of Rebel forces, joining up with the troops in East Tennessee. And it would place the enemy in northern Alabama in a situation in which they must either retreat or have their communications severed. At this point, anyway, it seemed possible that, as the surgeon told his wife, Bragg was "the right man in the right place."

If events in Middle Tennessee developed favorably, a movement into Kentucky was a real possibility. If Kentucky could be joined to the Confederacy, then, as will be seen in a later chapter, the war would take on quite a different complexion. It just might be possible for the Confederacy to gain its independence from the U.S. Braxton Bragg's campaigning was about to see—albeit not quite in the manner that he would have preferred—the scene of conflict transferred to Kentucky. That movement finally came to a climax on October 8, 1862, southeast of Louisville, at the little town of Perryville. There an intriguing, confused, and bloody encounter, in the very heartland of "the dark and bloody ground," was to unfold between Yanks and Rebels. Despite being outnumbered approximately three to one, the Confederates, strange as it seems, still had a chance to win at Perryville.

It was a long way from Shiloh to Perryville. More important, the campaigning from Shiloh to Perryville—encompassing Bragg's turning movement, the battle for the bridge at Munfordville, the fight at Richmond, and the struggle at Perryville—would do much to determine the ultimate fate of the Confederacy. The campaigning signifies the high-water mark of the Confederacy in the Western Theater. But before Bragg could begin his offensive, and while he mulled over his options, the triumphant Federals at Corinth, still buoyed by their recent successes, had been moving again, trying to take yet another major strategic point: Chattanooga, Tennessee.

Chapter 2

Working on the Railroad

☆☆☆

It was decision time for the Union army at Corinth, Mississippi. What would be the next objective? The question would be answered by Henry Wager Halleck, a forty-seven-year-old general—known to fellow West Pointers as "Old Brains" because of his scholarly background and authoritative writings on military science—who had come from his St. Louis headquarters to take field command after the Battle of Shiloh. Halleck consumed about a month marching and (mainly) entrenching, while taking the army to Corinth, a distance of about twenty miles from Shiloh. Then he discovered that the Confederates had evacuated the town, retreating to Tupelo. Not surprisingly, criticism was leveled at Halleck for being overly cautious; there is much truth to Grant's laconic, caustic summation: "Corinth was conquered at Shiloh." Grant and Sherman both thought a rapid move and attack on Corinth would have found the outnumbered Rebels unprepared effectively to resist. Perhaps Halleck's generalship in the move on Corinth paved the way for further criticism of his actions in the days to come.[1]

With the capture of Corinth, the Union had achieved a major objective: breaking the Memphis and Charleston Railroad, that "vertebrae of the Confederacy," as former Confederate Secretary of War

Leroy P. Walker had described it, and, as a bonus, had broken it at its junction with the north-south Mobile and Ohio Railroad.[2] Thus, in early June 1862, General Halleck, with more than one hundred thousand men, rested at Corinth, sitting on top of the greatest railroad prize in the Western Theater of the war.

To this point Halleck had fared rather well, especially considering his situation four months earlier, before the Federal advance against Fort Henry and Fort Donelson. Halleck's Department of the Missouri then had formed one-half of a faulty Union command structure, the other part being the Department of the Ohio, headquartered at Louisville, under Don Carlos Buell. The two departments had been separated by the boundary of the Cumberland River; the arrangement had encouraged competition rather than cooperation between the generals. Nothing of note had been accomplished by either commander. However, as Halleck and Buell stewed over the command problem, U. S. Grant, with Halleck's approval and with the cooperation of the navy, proceeded to move on Fort Henry. Successful there, Grant simply sent Halleck word that Fort Donelson was his next objective and advanced to take it, too.

Suddenly Grant was a national hero, but Halleck was not particularly impressed with his ordinary-looking subordinate who wore an old slouch hat and habitually chomped on the butt of a cigar. Grant had ventured to Nashville for a conference with Buell soon after that city fell to the Federals following the surrender of Fort Donelson. A communications breakdown had left Halleck out of touch with his general; and, probably, Grant's recent triumphs and the attendant publicity had triggered a bit of jealousy. Grant was suspended from command, only to be reinstated when an accident incapacitated his replacement, General C. F. Smith. The reinstatement came just in time for Grant to win the Battle of Shiloh, although he was surprised by the enemy attack at Pittsburgh Landing, which found him residing in a mansion nine miles down the Tennessee River. Again Halleck had benefited from the generalship of his increasingly illustrious subordinate.

By this time, Halleck had the command he wanted. The Department of the Missouri and the Department of Kansas, together with the western portion of the Department of the Ohio, had been consolidated into the Department of the Mississippi, dating from March 11. Halleck had been assigned to command Buell's army, then operating in Tennessee, as well as his own. Shortly after the Battle of Shiloh, Halleck arrived at Pittsburgh Landing and, for the first time, took command of his forces in the field. Grant was named second in command, but his army was placed under George H. Thomas, and there seemed little for him to do. Following Shiloh, criticism of Grant, in some circles, was considerable; and this criticism, coupled with Halleck's previous misgivings about the general, probably explain Halleck's decision actually to demote Grant, in the guise of a promotion. Dissatisfied by the demotion, and probably disturbed by his very near defeat at Shiloh, Grant considered leaving the army, only to be talked out of it by Sherman—fortunately for the Union.[3]

Now the question facing Halleck was what to do next. The answer was not obvious, although some of the general's critics have argued that it was.[4] Criticism of Halleck doubtless developed for more than one reason. He had become "top dog" in the Western Theater's command structure; generals in such positions often are targets of barbs from those who are ambitious to unseat them, as well as from historians who are unimpressed by a particular general's performance. In this case, it is very tempting to criticize Halleck, particularly because it can be argued that Halleck's achievements were primarily the work of subordinates: Grant, Sherman, Buell, and others. It should also be noted that, up to this point in our account, the Union had developed what was basically a two-pronged assault on the western Confederacy: one advance via the Mississippi River and the other via the Tennessee River. This two-pronged advance meant that the Mississippi Valley had been the main focus of Federal effort, and some military leaders (and later some historians) thought that it should remain so.

On the other hand, Herman Hattaway and Archer Jones, in *How the North Won*, point out that the waterways "which previously served [the Federals] so well" no longer were available. South on the Tennessee River, the Yankees had come to break the Memphis and Charleston. South on the Mississippi, they had advanced to take Memphis; north on the Mississippi, they had struck to capture New Orleans and had moved beyond Baton Rouge to threaten Vicksburg. Where, then, could they go by water?[5]

Clearly Halleck no longer could move by water. The Tennessee River lay off to the east in northern Alabama, where the rapidly receding water level soon would make navigation impossible, and the Mississippi was a hundred miles to the west. Future campaigning, whatever the objective, would be different for Halleck's command. The general simply could not keep advancing on the Tennessee, using it as a line of communication, as the Federals had done since February.

One of Halleck's options was to go for Vicksburg, and "Old Brains" has been taken to task for not mounting a major campaign against that fortress on the Mississippi. Allan Nevins, for example, bitingly comments, "Generalship indeed! Halleck had thrown away a month. . . . Once in Corinth, instead of using his irresistible concentrated force to seize a key position of the enemy, like Vicksburg, he dissipated it."[6]

But it should be remembered that the Federals on the Mississippi, the victors at New Orleans and Baton Rouge, were not yet through with the effort to take Vicksburg. In fact, it was anticipated—perhaps not very realistically—that Vicksburg would fall to the combined forces of Farragut moving upriver from New Orleans, and the Yankee river fleet under Charles Davis advancing downriver from Memphis. If this strategy did not work, then Halleck would send help. He wrote to Secretary of War Edwin Stanton on June 12: "If the combined fleets of Farragut and Davis fail to take Vicksburg, I will send an expedition for that purpose." Again, on June 25, Halleck wrote to Stanton: "It is hoped that the two flotillas united

Union General Henry W. Halleck. Courtesy, Library of Congress.

will be able to reduce [Vicksburg]."[7] These Federals did make a determined effort to reduce that fortress and did not give up the campaign until late July, when hundreds of Yankees were dying of disease. By then, Halleck long since had committed his forces elsewhere.[8]

Not only was Farragut expected to dispose of Vicksburg, but also the problem of disease loomed large in Halleck's thinking. This was the first summer for the Federals to campaign in the Deep South, experiencing the extreme heat, the sweltering humidity, insufficient clean water. "If we follow the enemy into the swamps of Mississippi there can be no doubt the army will be disabled by disease," Halleck told Stanton.[9] Farragut's expedition, plagued by illness, proved that this potential difficulty was not a minor worry.[10]

If Halleck moved overland toward Vicksburg, he would face two further difficulties. One was the danger from Confederate cavalry raiding his railroad communications, as Grant was to learn a few months later in his first effort against Vicksburg. Nathan Bedford Forrest and Earl Van Dorn then played havoc with Grant's railroad at Jackson, Tennessee, and Holly Springs, Mississippi. The other problem was that the Confederate army at Tupelo would be on Halleck's left flank, not a pleasant scenario to contemplate.

Halleck, of course, might have opted to go for the Rebel army at Tupelo first, the move which other Halleck critics contend he should have made. Bruce Catton, for instance, states that "the only really sizable Confederate Army in all the West was the one which, passing from Beauregard to Bragg, was now being permitted to reorganize and refit at Tupelo, Mississippi. . . . Everything the Confederacy held west of the Alleghenies depended on that army, because if it ceased to exist Halleck's troops could go anywhere they chose to go."[11]

Catton's position is not without merit. But, as Halleck saw it, a move on the Rebels at Tupelo presented the same difficulties as a move on Vicksburg: subjecting his army to disabling disease and stretching out his supply line as a tempting target for the southern cavalry. Another consideration adds to the complexity of the total picture. While professional military training might emphasize conquest of enemy armies, at this stage of the war, many political leaders—and, for that matter, many military leaders, including Halleck—saw the conquest of territory, with the hope of tapping the latent Unionism present in the South, as a major objective of the Federal armies.

While the arguments for keeping the Union force concentrated and moving on the enemy army at either Vicksburg or Tupelo have substance, the decision by no means was an obvious one, and General Halleck was not a fool. Given what he knew *at the time*, and taking account of political considerations—particularly the president's views—as well, his decision, whether seen as the best military option or not, certainly is understandable.

It was better, reasoned Halleck, to use a portion of his troops to guard his lengthy supply line, and address the nasty difficulties of administering conquered territory, than to remain concentrated. Consider the railroads, for example; as James McPherson notes, "Halleck's detachment of several brigades for railroad repair and guard duty was not so obtuse as it is sometimes portrayed, for as the rivers dropped below navigable stage the armies became wholly dependent on rail supply. . . . Other brigades had to be detached from combat forces for the politically necessary tasks of policing and administering occupied territory."[12]

General Halleck was convinced that he could defend the rails; administer the towns and cities, preserving order; and still move offensively with part of his command. But the advance would not be southwest. The decision, instead, was to turn east—turn east and now follow the railroad rather than a waterway. The objective, clearly defined, was one of great political import, dear to the heart of the president. The objective would be Chattanooga, Tennessee.

Chattanooga has a name as fascinating as that of any city in the country. The name obviously is of Native American origin. According to one story, *Chattanooga* was the aboriginal name for Lookout Mountain; it was thought to be a half-anglicized Cherokee term, derived from *Chatta* (crow) and *nooga* (nest) but usually rendered, in more grandiose fashion, as "eagles' nest" or "hawk's nest." The name

Chattanooga also has been explained as a phonetic descendent of *Chadonaugsa*, a Creek term meaning "rock that comes to a point."[13]

By Civil War days, Chattanooga still had less than five thousand citizens, very small by any standard, and especially small in comparison to Nashville's twenty-five thousand or thirty thousand, or Richmond's more than forty thousand. Certainly, Chattanooga was not important for its size. Neither was the city venerable for its age. Far from being an old southern community, like Charleston, New Orleans, or Richmond, the city technically had formed part of the United States for less than a quarter of a century before the Civil War began—that is, only since the Cherokee Indians had been removed by the U.S. Army, led by General Winfield Scott. In Scott's command had been a young lieutenant, Braxton Bragg, who had just graduated from West Point, in the class of 1837.[14]

Chattanooga was located in an impressive setting, known for its scenic views. Missionary Ridge, to the east of the town, affords several impressive vantage points. Lookout Mountain and Signal Mountain offer magnificent panoramas of the general area, especially of Moccasin Bend and the canyon of the Tennessee River.

But of course the Federals were not interested in Chattanooga for its scenic views. Chattanooga was significant militarily for one reason—one very important reason. It was a natural passageway north and south, east and west. This was true, first, because of the Tennessee River. Even more momentous, however, were the railroads.

In 1862, Chattanooga was a railroad town. One is tempted to designate it *the* railroad town of the Confederacy. No other southern city, not even Atlanta, equaled it in this regard at this time. To the northeast lay the East Tennessee Railroad to Knoxville, Bristol, and on into Virginia. From the west came the Memphis and Charleston from northern Alabama, and the Nashville and Chattanooga from Middle Tennessee, with connections to Louisville and the Ohio River. To the southeast ran the Western and Atlantic to Atlanta. From Atlanta ran rail connections with Virginia through the Carolinas, and with the munitions and iron works of central Georgia and Alabama.

It is an understatement to say that, if the Union could possess Chattanooga, the Confederacy's rail communications would be severely damaged. Federal control of Chattanooga would mean much more to the Union than depriving the Rebels of railroads, however—important as that unquestionably would be. The Yankee potential for making war on the Deep South from a staging base such as Chattanooga was almost unlimited, as General William Tecumseh Sherman eventually demonstrated so convincingly. The rail lines into Chattanooga made it the natural center for waging war against the southeastern Confederacy. If the Union could take it, Chattanooga was the key to splitting the South along a second corridor, Nashville-Chattanooga-Atlanta, much as the Confederacy was already split along the general line of the Mississippi, with Forts Henry and Donelson, Shiloh, Corinth, Memphis, and New Orleans. If the Federals had succeeded in taking Chattanooga in summer 1862, or if Farragut had taken Vicksburg, few ever would have questioned Halleck's decision to go immediately for Chattanooga. Clearly it was a judgment call, but one not without merit.

With the hearty approval of President Lincoln, General Henry W. Halleck inaugurated Don Carlos Buell's East Tennessee campaign. On June 9, "Old Brains" Halleck gave Buell his orders for the move across northern Alabama toward Chattanooga. In the interest of a balanced view of the larger context of the war in the Western Theater, however, it should be remembered that, while the Lincoln administration might regard East Tennessee Unionism as a major goal for military support and the East Tennessee Railroad as a strategic military prize, military leaders like Grant and Sherman, as well as the midwestern political base from which Lincoln himself hailed, regarded the reopening of the Mississippi as the primary war aim. This meant that Buell's East Tennessee operation was relegated to second place in the overall picture of campaigning in the West—a somewhat subtle point, but one necessary for a full appreciation of the realities of the Union war effort.

☆☆☆

The concept of an East Tennessee campaign certainly was not new to Buell, who had been hearing about it since the previous year when he was commanding in Kentucky, and hearing about it from the highest authority, President Lincoln. The president had wanted an early advance from north central Kentucky, preferably through the Cumberland Gap and into the Knoxville region. It would "cut a great artery of the enemies' communications," Lincoln wrote.[15] The president referred, of course, to the combined lines of the East Tennessee and Virginia Railroad and the East Tennessee and Georgia Railroad. Federal control of that artery, east of Knoxville, would be a major setback for the Rebels' east-west communications, compelling the Confederates to use a pronounced exterior line. Instead of a relatively straight route from Chattanooga northeastward to Richmond, they would be forced to follow a long, circuitous path, south to Atlanta and deep into South Carolina before finally turning north, winding through the heart of North Carolina, and coming into Richmond by a back door.

Writing to Buell that he would rather have a point on the railroad south of Cumberland Gap than to capture Nashville—which was not on a major east-west railroad—the president had also argued for the East Tennessee project because "it is in the midst of loyal people, who would rally around it, while Nashville is not. . . . My distress is that our friends in East Tennessee are being hanged and driven to despair."[16] The desire to rescue the loyal people of East Tennessee was reiterated throughout the president's correspondence.[17]

The Appalachian Valley of East Tennessee was one of the largest wheat-producing areas in the South, as well as a region blessed with abundant resources of saltpeter, lead, and copper. The Confederacy's ability to feed its soldiers and produce gunpowder, bullets, percussion caps, and bronze artillery would be damaged if East Tennessee were in Union hands. The workshops and foundries in Georgia and

South Carolina also would be cut off from their supply of coal. Undeniably, there were good arguments for the Federals' moving into East Tennessee.[18] Only the avenue of advance was new, and the Chattanooga approach had to be more pleasing to Buell, who had been deeply concerned about the supply problems associated with Lincoln's earlier ideas for a move through the Cumberland Gap. As for Lincoln, he simply wanted East Tennessee and was "greatly delighted" with the advance on Chattanooga through northern Alabama.[19]

The campaign appeared to be strategically sound. General Buell would be given sufficient strength for the undertaking. The powerful Union army at Corinth, numbering more than one hundred thousand soldiers, had been split up, with Halleck sending William Tecumseh Sherman with two divisions to Memphis and John McClernand with two divisions to Jackson, Tennessee, while Halleck himself remained with a force at Corinth. Buell would advance eastward with four divisions, commanded by Brigadier Generals Thomas L. Crittenden, Alexander McD. McCook, William Nelson, and Thomas J. Wood, totaling approximately thirty-five thousand men. Ormsby Mitchell, who had moved into Huntsville earlier and had been urging the Chattanooga campaign upon Halleck, was waiting to join Buell in northeastern Alabama with ten thousand more troops. Also, the staunch Virginian, George H. Thomas, whose loyalty to the Union had caused a break with his sisters that never would be reconciled, was at Iuka, Mississippi, ready to march with eight thousand soldiers to reinforce Buell. Two more divisions were promised by Halleck if needed, and, finally, General George Morgan's division at Cumberland Gap, about ten thousand strong, was subject to Buell's command as a part of the Army of the Ohio. The number of troops available seemed adequate.[20]

The campaign promised to keep Rebel forces separated. Certainly it would be difficult for the main Confederate Army in the West, which had fallen back from Corinth, to join with Edmund Kirby Smith's command in East Tennessee, if Buell's strong force was interposed between them.[21] To realize such a Rebel junction by railroad, the Confederates at Tupelo would be forced to drop south

Union General Don Carlos Buell. Courtesy, Library of Congress.

all the way to Mobile, Alabama, and then proceed northward by a circuitous route through Alabama and Georgia back up to Chattanooga, all the while hoping that Buell, with a direct route along the Memphis and Charleston Railroad, did not get there first.

Indeed, it was the Memphis and Charleston Railroad—expected to provide a supply line for Buell's army—that seemed to cement the strategic soundness of the advance on Chattanooga. Louisville and Nashville would constitute Buell's supply depots. Nashville was fed by both rail and water, via the Louisville and Nashville Railroad and the Cumberland River. From Nashville, Buell would have two rail lines supporting him in northern Alabama—the Nashville and Decatur line, which joined the Memphis and Charleston line at Decatur, Alabama; and the Nashville and Chattanooga line, which met the Memphis and Charleston line at Stevenson, Alabama.

The Federal movement would be across four Alabama counties lying north of the Tennessee River—Lauderdale, Limestone, Madison, and Jackson—where Union sentiment was substantial.[22] Thus, at the time of its inception, Buell's advance on Chattanooga appeared to be strategically feasible. It should be noted, however, that General Buell later testified that he had not been in favor of the route through northern Alabama and had expressed his views to Halleck, but had been overruled. "My own idea had been to strike a little farther north, through Middle Tennessee and McMinnville."[23] This would not have required attempting to protect as much railroad supply line.

Was Don Carlos Buell the man to lead the campaign? The general was a West Point graduate and a veteran of the Seminole and Mexican wars.[24] Stern in expression, formal in manner, and stocky in physique—sometimes he displayed his arm and upper-body strength by clasping his wife about the waist, holding her off the floor straight out before him, and then lifting her to sit on a mantle[25]—Buell possessed a good mind and conveyed the image of a successful, albeit somewhat withdrawn, leader of men. While his lack of enthusiasm for an East Tennessee campaign through Cumberland Gap had been disappointing to Lincoln, Buell had arrived at Shiloh in time to reinforce (some said to save from destruction) Grant's army on the second day of battle.[26]

In summer 1862, the evidence available on Buell's generalship would have had to be judged as more positive than negative. There were no compelling reasons for not entrusting the Chattanooga campaign to his direction. Even today, when all the evidence presented at the Buell Commission investigation is carefully scrutinized with 20/20 hindsight, the general's conduct of the campaign appears responsible and reasonable.

Why, then, was the campaign a failure? Buell's great problem, which became worse as the army advanced, was how to feed his army. The old cliché that an army marches on its stomach certainly did not originate with this movement across northern Alabama, but never could it have been applied more appropriately. The daily requirement of food and forage was considered to be three and one-quarter pounds for a man, twenty-six for a horse, and twenty-three for a mule.[27] Buell's railroad supply line, expected to be a major contributor to the campaign's success, proved to be a nightmare.

A rail journey from Louisville to any given point in northern Alabama involved some three hundred miles of track or more. Clearly, the railroads were vulnerable in scores of places. On the Nashville and Decatur line, there were twelve important bridges on the forty-five-mile stretch between Nashville and Columbia alone, with the bridge over the Duck River at Columbia 65 feet high and 600 feet long. At Culleoka, ten miles below Columbia, a high trestle extended 1,100 feet.[28] Midway between Pulaski and Athens, the railroad first went through a curving tunnel about a quarter of a mile long, soon crossed a 700-foot bridge over the Elk River, and then traveled a long, high trestle just south of Elkmount, Alabama.[29]

The Nashville and Chattanooga road was equally vulnerable. For example, there was an important bridge only twelve miles south of Nashville at Antioch.[30] Between Antioch and LaVergne, the road crossed several trestles. Then there were major bridges over the Stones River, the Duck River, and the Elk River. And two miles south of Cowan, Tennessee, the long tunnel, 2,228 feet, which is still used today, was an inviting target. South of the tunnel, the grade was steep, presenting still more opportunities for destructive work.[31]

Tunnel south of Cowan, Tennessee. Photograph by John Hursh.

There were dozens of creek crossings on both these roads, as there were on the Memphis and Charleston from Corinth to Stevenson.[32] Once Buell's army progressed beyond Stevenson, the Memphis and Charleston would be exceedingly vulnerable, with a bridge nearly a mile long necessary to span the Tennessee River at Bridgeport, while beyond, on the approach to Chattanooga, were high and flimsy trestles.

Bringing the army's provisions the first leg of the journey south, from the Ohio River at Louisville to Nashville, was anything but simple. Besides the usual numerous creek crossings, there were two wooden trestles which would make prime targets. Both were about eighty feet high and five hundred feet long, stretching through rugged Muldraugh's Hill, four or five miles north of Elizabethtown. Most inviting of all were the twin tunnels, still used today, about eight or nine miles north of Gallatin, Tennessee. Dug through porous slate under an outcropping of the Cumberland Plateau and supported with heavy timbers, the "Little South" tunnel was about six hundred feet long, while "Big South" was nearly one thousand feet in length.[33] Even if all these vulnerable points could be defended against guerrillas and Confederate cavalry, there were both a shortage of rolling stock and the necessity of providing ironclad boxcars to protect train crews against the sniper fire of guerrillas.

From the first, the railroad could not be defended. As was common at this stage of the war, the Union cavalry was no match for the Confederate cavalry forces. The Confederate superiority resulted from better leadership, better tactics, and more experience. These factors more than compensated for any inferiority in numbers. At this period, even the numbers sometimes favored the Rebels. About the time that Buell's forces were arriving in the Athens-Decatur-Huntsville sector of northern Alabama, the bridge over the Elk River on the Nashville and Decatur Railroad was destroyed, along with the trestle a few miles south of the bridge. The break in the railroad compelled the Federals to haul supplies about forty or forty-five miles over a rough wagon road from Reynold's Station to Athens. Even the elements seemed to be against the Federals, as high water washed away a portion of a bridge over Duck River.[34]

Buell put his men and animals on half rations and began repairing the railroad, which took many long, hard days of work. Colonel W. P. Innes, of the First Regiment Michigan Engineers and Mechanics, described the rebuilding of the span over the Elk River: "It was 700 feet long and 58 feet high, in about 20 feet of water. That was the heaviest bridge built. Four companies were employed on that work, with a large infantry detail. At that time we worked incessantly at it, rain or shine. . . . I had two companies at the same time engaged on what is called the heavy trestle . . . ; we rebuilt 1,050 feet of it; that was about 64 feet high."[35]

Even north of this destruction, where the wagons began their long trek at Reynold's Station, the railroad was not bringing sufficient supplies. Colonel Edward M. McCook, Second Indiana Cavalry, who was in charge of guarding the wagon train, testified during the investigation of the Buell campaign that "very frequently wagons had to wait [at Reynold's Station] for the want of supplies coming on the railroad. Supplies did not arrive fast enough at one time to furnish loads for the wagons; at other times two hundred and forty or two hundred and fifty wagons a day were sent off with supplies when they were there to load into the wagons."[36] Lieutenant Colonel Francis Darr, chief commissary in the field for the Army of the Ohio, supported this testimony, saying that "the supplies wagoning around the railroad break did not come fast enough either to supply the army day by day or to accommodate a quantity for any forward movement."[37]

General Buell, at the same time, was trying to get the Nashville and Chattanooga Railroad in shape to assist in supplying his army. The superintendent of railroads for the Army of the Ohio was John B. Anderson, who alternated his repairing force between the Nashville and Chattanooga road and the Nashville and Decatur line. On the Nashville and Chattanooga, three bridges were rebuilt over Mill Creek, track and trestles repaired between Antioch and LaVergne, and the bridge over Stones River rebuilt.[38] It is obvious from Anderson's testimony that Rebel guerrillas and cavalry had been quite destructive. After additional work on the Nashville and Decatur track, Anderson's crews returned to the Nashville and Chattanooga road and, as the superintendent reported, "proceeded to erect a bridge at Garrison's Fork, 57 miles southeast from Nashville; commenced a trestle work at Normandy; I do not know the amount of repairs made there without reference to the record; then to Duck River and Elk River. . . . The work at Elk River was finished on the 12th July."[39]

Perhaps, at this point, General Buell thought that the worst of his frustrations were behind and that the Chattanooga campaign at last would develop favorably. The completion of repairs at the Elk River bridge meant that the Nashville and Chattanooga was open to Stevenson, Alabama. Buell's advance now had carried beyond Stevenson, where the Nashville and Chattanooga joined the Memphis and Charleston, providing an additional supply line. Attempting to insure that the road would not be destroyed again, Buell had placed work gangs all along the line and had stationed at Murfreesboro two regiments of infantry, a detachment of cavalry, and a battery, with the idea that this force could move in either direction if the vital rails were threatened again.[40]

The general had needed some good news. Aside from all the railroad supply problems, a doubly disturbing report had come from Halleck on July 8. The Confederate army was on the move, its destination uncertain: "General Grant thinks it is Memphis, others Corinth or Tuscumbia, and others again your lines at Chattanooga." The Rebel force might be approaching Buell from the rear flank or moving to occupy Chattanooga. Halleck's message also said:

> The President telegraphs that your progress is not satisfactory and that you should move more rapidly. The long time taken by you to reach Chattanooga will enable the enemy to anticipate you by concentrating a large force to meet you. I communicate his views, hoping that your movements hereafter may be so rapid as to remove all cause of complaint, whether well founded or not.[41]

Halleck's telegram seemed to stun Buell, especially the part about Lincoln's displeasure. "I was so astonished at the message that I made no reply until three days afterward," he later reported.[42] In fact, it was only after receiving a blunt dispatch—"I want to hear from you. H. W. Halleck"—that Buell responded. Detailing the problems faced, Buell contended that to reach Chattanooga quickly would be useless if his army were not in condition to fight when it got there. "The advance on Chattanooga must be made with the means of acting in force," he said; "otherwise it will either fail or prove a profitless and transient prize." Stating that "arrangements are being pushed forward as industriously as possible," the general added: "The dissatisfaction of the President pains me exceedingly."[43]

There must have been an element of reassurance and some satisfaction for Buell in Halleck's response the following day. While saying he could see both sides—Buell's difficulties and Lincoln's impatience—"Old Brains" assured Buell of his personal good will and, implying the superiority and camaraderie of professional soldiers, urged Buell to be more tolerant of the amateurs above them who had "no conception of the length of our lines of defense and of operations." Halleck promised that he would "properly explain" Buell's movements to the president.[44] He soon would have a chance to do so in person, for Lincoln had just named Halleck general-in-chief of all U.S. land forces; within two weeks, Halleck would be in Washington assuming his new position.

Halleck's reassurance to Buell arrived on July 12, the same day that Buell received the good news that the railroad was repaired. The first trainload of supplies would be steaming out of Nashville bound for Stevenson on July 13. Finally Buell would be able to take his army off half rations,[45] and the move on Chattanooga could progress with renewed strength—or so he thought.

☆☆☆

July 13, 1862, a Sunday, was the forty-first birthday of Confederate Brigadier General Nathan Bedford Forrest.[46] It was also the date of his first independent operation as a brigade commander. He had already established an enviable reputation as a daring cavalry leader in Kentucky at Sacramento, as well as at Fort Donelson and Shiloh.[47]

In fact, Forrest rapidly was becoming both a great war leader and a legendary hero. While quite adept in the employment of profanity, he did not smoke or chew tobacco or drink alcoholic beverages. He possessed a terrible temper, an unbending will, and an amazing presence of mind on the battlefield. The troopers had great respect for him, and many of them also feared him.[48]

Forrest had told his command of his birthday. He said that he wanted to celebrate it in a memorable manner, "particularly since he would have occasion to do so near his birthplace," close to Chapel Hill, Tennessee. The aroused troopers shouted promises to contribute whatever they could to the festivity.[49]

The objective was the little town of Murfreesboro, thirty miles southeast of Nashville. Of course, it was the railroad that gave the town military importance. Forrest had been assigned the mission of disrupting Buell's line of communication, with the goal of preventing any aggressive enemy advance on Chattanooga.[50]

Moving in on Murfreesboro from the east, as rapidly as the dim predawn light permitted, Forrest's cavalry column was fourteen hundred strong.[51] The troopers, who had been riding from the village of Woodbury since one o'clock in the morning, gained the outskirts of Murfreesboro before sunrise, where they surprised and captured a group of Federal sentinels who were given no chance to sound an alarm. Forrest later reported that the pickets were captured "without firing a gun."[52] From these prisoners, Forrest learned the disposition of the Union soldiers in the town, realizing at once that the enemy was not properly concentrated.[53] Having been apprised at Woodbury of a large number of Confederate sympathizers held in the Murfreesboro jail, some of whom were condemned to death,[54] the Confederate commander determined to make the most of his opportunity.

The Union garrison, about equal in number to that which Forrest was bringing against it,[55] was under a new commander, Brigadier General Thomas Theodore Crittenden. A thirty-year-old graduate of Centre College, Danville, Kentucky, Crittenden had studied law under his uncle, Senator John J. Crittenden of Kentucky, and then had set up practice in Lexington, Missouri. From there he had entered the Union service soon after the Civil War began. Crittenden had just taken over the Murfreesboro post on the morning of July 12. He realized that the Federal camps were badly separated, reportedly due to a sparse water supply, but he was in no particular hurry to draw them closer together.[56] After all, Crittenden was advised, no Rebel force had been "nearer than Chattanooga, with the exception of small parties of guerrillas," since the Union had occupied Murfreesboro, "and there was no danger of an immediate attack."[57] The new commander did order that the cavalry patrols, which rode out each day on the turnpikes emerging from the town, should be doubled in number, but nobody informed Crittenden that the patrols came in each night, leaving all five roads open.[58]

Thus the Union force remained vulnerable. The Third Minnesota Infantry and a Kentucky battery were camped about a mile and a half northwest of the village, while on the eastern edge of the town lay the Ninth Michigan Infantry and a detachment of the Seventh Pennsylvania Cavalry. Detailed as a provost guard was one company of the Ninth Michigan. It was located in the center of Murfreesboro, guarding the courthouse and the jail.[59]

Just at dawn, with no one in the Union camps yet awake "except a few cooks chopping wood for the breakfast fires,"[60] Forrest's cavalry struck. Divided into three columns, one segment charged into the camp of the Michigan infantry and the Pennsylvania cavalry, while the other Rebel units pounded into Murfreesboro, part of the troopers surrounding and storming the jail to free the prisoners and the others sweeping through the town to attack the Minnesota regiment on the west.[61]

Instantly, Murfreesboro was in an uproar. "We sprang from our beds and rushed to the windows to see the streets full of gray-coated, dusty cavalrymen," wrote a lady of Murfreesboro, "while . . . the glad cry of 'our boys have come' rang from one end of the town to the other. . . . That day . . . was the happiest day experienced by the citizens of Murfreesboro during the war."[62] The day may have brought

Confederate General Nathan Bedford Forrest. Courtesy, Library of Congress.

happiness to some, but for others the hours of fighting meant terror and even tragedy. One such person was Mollie Nelson, a little girl struck in the face by a stray bullet. She wore the ugly scar of battle for the rest of her life.[63]

Forrest's attack, meanwhile, had not developed according to plan. The greater part of one regiment, instead of turning off to charge the enemy on the eastern side of the town as ordered, became confused and rushed on into Murfreesboro. And the Federals, despite being rudely awakened from their sleep, were fighting with courage and determination. The Union forces west of the town, forewarned by the noise of battle coming from Murfreesboro, had advanced to a little rise of ground about a mile from the square where they were drawn up with a section of artillery on each flank. Here they were making a good fight. The Confederates, both east and west of town, were stymied.[64]

Then Forrest asserted his genius for battle. The vigorous, tall (around six feet, one inch) cavalryman, who had been born in Bedford County, only twenty-five miles from Murfreesboro, was a tough, aggressive fighter.[65] And Forrest seemed to be getting even tougher as the war progressed.

Riding west of the town with a band of men, Forrest swept around the Union flank and charged into the enemy camp, driving off and capturing the guards, destroying tents and baggage, and spreading panic.[66] A few Confederate officers tried to persuade Forrest to be satisfied and ride away before Federal reinforcements from Nashville might arrive. Furious and determined, the general replied abruptly: "I didn't come here to make half a job of it. I'm going to have them all."[67] Leaving only seven companies to hold the Federals in check on the west, he next thundered back through the town and, with additional troops shifted from the other fights, brought the weight of his command against the beleaguered enemy east of Murfreesboro. With his troopers ready to attack, Forrest then demanded that the Yankees surrender.

The message was the first of a type he would resort to several times in the future.[68] It was simple and direct: "Colonel: I must demand an unconditional surrender of your force as prisoners of war or I will have every man put to the sword. You are aware of the overpowering force I have at my command, and this demand is made to prevent the effusion of blood. I am, Colonel, very respectfully, your obedient servant, N. B. Forrest, Brigadier General of Cavalry, C.S.A."[69]

At noon the Federals east of Murfreesboro surrendered. The Rebel "Wizard of the Saddle" then could marshal his forces against the enemy west of the town. Forrest's cavalry pounded in that direction again, and once more he sent in a note demanding immediate surrender in order to spare "the effusion of blood." The Minnesota colonel, Henry C. Lester, requested a conference with the Ninth Michigan's Colonel William Duffield, who, by then, was a prisoner of Forrest's command. So that Lester could be assured that the rest of the Union garrison had surrendered, the interview was arranged. Forrest also arranged for Lester to see something else as he walked through the town to the house where Duffield was held: glimpses of Rebel soldiers marching through the streets. Actually, although Colonel Lester did not know it, he was seeing the same Confederate column being maneuvered back and forth, again and again. Lester too surrendered.[70]

The total number of Federal prisoners was between eleven hundred and twelve hundred officers and men, and the value of captured property was probably $250,000. By six o'clock the raid was finished, and the last of Forrest's command, which was relatively unscathed, had departed from Murfreesboro by the same road on which it had come.[71]

Before leaving town—and most significant from General Buell's perspective—Forrest had destroyed the depots containing all government supplies that could not be transported and wrecked the Nashville and Chattanooga railroad bridges in the immediate vicinity. The supply train from Nashville would not get past Murfreesboro, and Buell's soldiers in northern Alabama would remain on half rations.[72]

☆☆☆

For General Buell, July 13 had been a disastrous day, but certainly it was not the only one. The repair crews had barely completed their work near Murfreesboro when Forrest struck again. Bolder than ever, he appeared near Nashville on July 21 and wrecked all three bridges over Mill Creek. General William Nelson's division, which Buell had sent to Murfreesboro immediately after Forrest's first foray, marched to intercept "that devil," as William Tecumseh Sherman later called the cavalryman. Forrest, however, took a side road, passing within a few hundred yards of the Yankees, and once more made his escape into the mountains east of Woodbury.[73]

Again the Union repair gangs went to work, and within a week they had the railroad ready to operate. The first train pulled into Stevenson from Nashville with 210,000 rations on July 29. Another train followed on July 30, and the troops went back on full rations of food.[74]

Although this progress was encouraging, the advance was now seriously stalled by the need for a bridge—1,400 yards long[75]—over the Tennessee River at Bridgeport. Lumber for the pontoons was difficult to acquire. Colonel W. P. Innes of the engineers later testified: "The [pontoon] boats were finished about the 20th of August, except putting the bottoms together. They would have been finished long before if we could have got the timber." Innes said there was only one mill on the railroad "that could saw the long timber required for the bridges, and I ran that mill day and night, not only with the force belonging to the mill, but with the detail from my own regiment."[76]

The bridge problem involved not only getting the timber cut, but also securing nails, oakum, and pitch. Buell's chief of staff, James B. Fry, in an August 10 message from Huntsville to Captain Judson D. Bingham, quartermaster at Nashville, conveyed the frustration his commander must have felt: "The nails for [pontoon] boats were purchased three weeks ago and sent to the Nashville depot. . . . They have never come. Find them and send them at once. . . . The oakum and pitch had to be sent for to Louisville and Cincinnati. Look this matter up without a moment's delay. The articles should all go to Stevenson, to Colonel Innes, Engineers."[77]

Buell not only was worried about the bridge; he also now had the ominous report that Braxton Bragg had arrived in Chattanooga and that his whole army was following.[78] Perhaps Buell's concluding remark to Halleck, as he informed "Old Brains" of this development, contained a touch of criticism: "You can judge yourself of the probability of the concentrating of a heavy force against Middle Tennessee, now that they have nothing to apprehend in Mississippi."[79]

The next few days again brought Buell news from Halleck of continued dissatisfaction in Washington "at the slow movement of your army toward Chattanooga." The Nashville and Decatur Railroad was not yet in good order. Colonel Darr testified: "On August 6 a trial train was run over the Decatur and Nashville road for the first time from Nashville to Athens; the bridges were pronounced unsafe and the trains suspended. It was not until August 11 that loaded trains could pass safely over the road."[80]

By August 11 there was another piece of good news: Lieutenant Colonel Judson D. Bingham, depot quartermaster in Nashville, at last had located nails and oakum for the railroad span at Bridgeport. "I found the nails and oakum for boats in the railroad shop this morning," he said. "I did not know they were here. They will go forward to Stevenson on the next train." Not all was good news though, because "the pitch has not yet been found," continued Bingham. He had heard that eight barrels were "at some station" between Nashville and Huntsville. Consequently, he was conducting an examination "to ascertain if the pitch ever passed through here."[81] At this moment, General Buell probably would have been perfectly content to accept the elusive pitch as his chief problem. Overall, prospects for the bridge were looking much brighter.

Unfortunately for Buell, when good news did come, it often seemed to be eclipsed by bad. This time the bad news was catastrophic. John Hunt Morgan, one of the most dashing figures of Confederate legend, had struck the Louisville and Nashville Railroad—and in the worst possible way.

Morgan, a Kentuckian, was thirty-seven years old and six feet tall. Well proportioned and handsome, with a fair complexion and

Confederate General John Hunt Morgan.
From *Battles and Leaders of the Civil War,* ed. Buell and Johnson.

grayish-blue eyes, already he had become a folk hero unusually attractive to many women, who, as his victories—although never major ones—made him famous, thronged in large crowds to adore him.[82] But as his biographer, James A. Ramage, persuasively argues, Morgan was more than an ideal romantic cavalier. Ironic as it may seem, Morgan actually contributed to making the Civil War more hellish. Using the tactics of guerrilla warfare, which "he intuitively adopted," Morgan made his own rules, "killed pickets, masqueraded as a Union officer, and employed civilians in the fighting, setting off a cycle of escalating violence" that was changing the nature of the war.[83]

In the early morning hours of August 12, Morgan captured the railroad guard at Gallatin, twenty-five miles north of Nashville, surprising Colonel William P. Boone, who was sleeping with his wife in the local hotel. Boone's pickets all were slumbering; they reportedly surrendered without firing a shot, and 125 Federals were captured in the town.[84]

Morgan himself boldly confronted the railroad station agent, declaring himself to be a Union officer searching for Morgan. The agent wished him luck, saying something to the effect of "I wish I could meet the damned guerrilla." Morgan then introduced himself and proceeded to disarm the shocked agent.[85]

With the enthusiastic help of many of Gallatin's citizens, Morgan's men piled wood on several flatcars, coupled them to a captured locomotive, and steamed northward toward the strategic objective, "Big South Tunnel." Surprising and capturing the Union guards at the tunnel, the Rebel raiders then torched the wood on the flatcars, sending them and the locomotive, with a full head of steam, racing into the tunnel and crashing against a barrier of cribbed crossties. The locomotive's boiler exploded and a great fire swept the tunnel. The roof supports burned, causing the slate rock to give way and blocking the tunnel with debris and fallen rock. The fire spread to a vein of coal, which burned and smoldered for days.[86]

General Buell's supply line had been dealt a disastrous blow. More than three months were to pass before the tunnel could be used

Between the twin tunnels north of Gallatin, Tennessee. Photograph by John Hursh.

again. Morgan had not finished his work of destruction, however. At Gallatin he burned forty railroad cars, as well as large caches of government stores. A bridge was burned one mile south of the blocked tunnel; another burned at Pilot Knob, south of Gallatin; a trestle destroyed; and six hundred feet of track wrecked.[87]

John Anderson, the superintendent of railroads, later testified that the railroad damage between Bowling Green and Nashville, *leaving out the tunnel*, "could not have been repaired by 90 men in twenty days."[88] As for the tunnel, to go around it by wagon was a worse problem than had been encountered in connection with the earlier break in the Nashville and Decatur Railroad at the Tennessee-Alabama line. As Colonel Innes testified, the road around the tunnel was "very bad indeed; impracticable for teams."[89] Asked how long it would have taken to make it practicable, Innes said, "You could not do it, on account of the elevation to be overcome."[90] And the tunnel did not cool sufficiently for work crews to begin repairing it for a long time, according to Anderson's testimony,[91] not to mention that many workers, scared of the possible reappearance of Morgan and his dreaded raiders, refused to start repairs without adequate protection.[92]

Indeed, Morgan did reappear. Some of his men had remained in town for the very purpose of stopping any Federal work crews that might be sent to clear the tunnel. On August 16, this news was reported to Federal headquarters in Nashville. A flustered orderly was heard to exclaim: "Hell is to pay and the Devil's on top. Morgan is at Gallatin again!" Actually Morgan himself was not there yet, but he soon would be, called forth by an event on August 19.

A Union infantry command from Nashville, about three hundred strong, appeared in Gallatin, proceeding from house to house and taking all males of twelve years and older. More than sixty, among them several older men, were arrested and forced to start walking the railroad track toward Nashville where, they were told, they all would be hanged as spies for helping Morgan. This news was brought to Morgan's camp at Hartsville near midnight by a breathless young boy on a horse, crying out what had happened to the men of Gallatin. Within a few minutes, Morgan and his troopers were riding to the rescue.[93]

About halfway to Nashville, they caught up with the Yankees and their prisoners. Morgan was leading the advance, having pledged, "No quarter today boys." According to Morgan's account to Virginia French of McMinnville, "The first Yankee I came up to had an old man, nearly exhausted, driving him forward at the point of the bayonet—he was perhaps 80 years of age—I think that was the only time in my life that I felt all humanity leave my heart." Morgan forced the Union soldier down the railroad embankment. Although the man threw down his weapon and begged Morgan to spare him, Morgan himself was setting the example of "no quarter" and shot the Federal at close range.[94]

As Morgan's biographer Ramage writes, "There is no telling how many prisoners were killed after they surrendered that day." Morgan said of the Federals, "There were so many of them that when they threw down their arms we couldn't shoot them all."[95] Evidently "all humanity" had left the heart of a number of people—Federal and Confederate—during spring and summer of 1862. The struggle for the railroads had become a mean war.

Chapter 3

God and Kentucky

☆☆☆

Abraham Lincoln, soon after the Civil War began, wrote: "I think to lose Kentucky is nearly the same as to lose the whole game." No American of his time has been more widely quoted than Lincoln, and the president's statement about Kentucky is among the quotations that appear most often. Lincoln also is said to have remarked, "I hope to have God on my side, but I must have Kentucky."[1]

This emphasis on the importance of Kentucky certainly was not misplaced. Elaborating on the issue, Lincoln said, "Kentucky gone, we can not hold Missouri, nor, as I think, Maryland. These all against us, and the job on our hands is too large for us. We would as well consent to separation at once, including the surrender of [Washington, D.C.]."[2]

Lincoln probably was right about the decisive impact if those three slave states had joined the Confederacy. Missouri had the largest white population of any slave state, while Kentucky ranked third, just behind Virginia. Historian James McPherson has calculated that Kentucky, Missouri, and Maryland "would have added 45 percent to the white population and military manpower of the Confederacy, 80 percent to its manufacturing capacity, and nearly 40 percent to its supply of horses and mules."[3]

The president undoubtedly was correct in his judgment that Kentucky was the most crucial of the border slave states. This was not because of Kentucky's sizable population, its numerous resources, or its many ancestral ties with Virginia which molded "southern" attachments and sympathies, however. While all of these clearly contributed to Kentucky's significance, the crux of the matter was the state's strategic location. One need only look at a map and examine the course of the rivers in order to understand the importance of Kentucky in the Civil War. "A Confederate Kentucky," wrote historian James Rawley, "would have thrown the southern frontier to the Ohio [River], fronting on the southern portions of Ohio, Indiana, and Illinois—where 2,600,000 persons had a sentimental attachment to the South. . . . [Kentucky's] northern river boundary could afford a natural military frontier for the southern armies."[4]

For nearly five hundred miles, the Ohio River winds westward, meandering along the northern border of Kentucky toward its confluence with the Mississippi. Shortly before meeting the Mississippi, the Ohio is joined by two of its major tributaries from the South, the Cumberland and the Tennessee. If the Confederates could control Kentucky, they would have a natural defensive barrier at the Ohio River. Even more important, they would deny to the Federals—who must overrun and conquer the Confederacy if they hoped to save the Union—the best avenues of invasion, the waterways into the South.

The Cumberland River, in the hands of the Yankees, was a route into the heart of Middle Tennessee at Nashville; the Tennessee River penetrated to northern Alabama; and the Mississippi, of course, pierced the Confederacy all the way to the Gulf. The importance of these waterways for moving men and materials can scarcely be overemphasized.

Nor was it a matter of small import that Confederate control of Kentucky would take away from the Federals yet another avenue of invasion—the iron horse. From the great river port of Louisville on the Ohio, the Louisville and Nashville Railroad provided an obvious line of advance straight into the Confederacy at Nashville. As previously noted, rail connections ran from Nashville to Alabama at both

Decatur and Stevenson on the Memphis and Charleston line—in other words, directly into the central theater of the war. Also, from Columbus, Kentucky, the Mobile and Ohio Railroad extended directly south through Jackson, Tennessee, to a junction with the Memphis and Charleston at Corinth, Mississippi, and thence through most of the length of Mississippi to Mobile. From Bowling Green, Kentucky, the Memphis, Clarksville and Louisville Railroad ran through West Tennessee to the Mississippi River at Memphis.

The United States badly needed to possess Kentucky. There is no question about that. If the Federals controlled Kentucky, they controlled the principal avenues, both waterways and railways, for invading and waging war against the heart of the western Confederacy. To lose Kentucky might not have been "to lose the whole game," but it would have made winning "the game" much more difficult. And win, of course, was what the North had to do. The Confederacy, in order to succeed, only needed to maintain itself. The Federals had to take the offensive, had to invade and conquer. With Kentucky in Rebel hands, that task would have been much tougher.

Lincoln must have breathed a lot easier after September 1861, when Confederate Bishop-General Leonidas Polk took it upon himself to seize Columbus, Kentucky, violating Kentucky's declared neutrality. Up to that time, the U.S. and the Confederacy alike carefully had respected the state's position. Both Jefferson Davis, who possessed more political understanding and concern than Polk, and Lincoln had perceived that whichever side defied Kentucky's neutrality likely would drive the state into the camp of the other. But Polk, fearing that the Yankees were about to seize the bluffs on the Mississippi River at Columbus, determined to strike first. His high-handed action, taken under what he later alleged to be "the plenary powers" delegated to him by Jefferson Davis, was, in the judgment of historian Steven E. Woodworth, "one of the most decisive catastrophes the Confederacy ever suffered."[5]

Ignoring Davis's instructions to withdraw the Confederate troops from Columbus, and passing up an opportunity to save face by plac-

Confederate General Leonidas Polk. Courtesy, Library of Congress.

ing the responsibility on Gideon Pillow, Polk boldly declared that the troops had acted upon his orders and that they would not be removed.[6] The predictable result was that Kentucky's aroused legislature, predominantly Unionist, denounced the Rebels and invited the Federal government to drive them out. Union forces quickly moved into Louisville and other places, particularly the key town of Paducah, Kentucky, a few miles north of Columbus, where the Tennessee River flows into the Ohio. Federal control of the mouth of the Tennessee negated the value of Columbus to the Rebels, for, as soon as the Yankees advanced on the Tennessee, Columbus would be outflanked.[7]

Bishop-General Polk had intended to take Paducah as well as Columbus, but he had been too slow, allowing the Federals under Grant to steal a march on him. Thus Polk's violation of Kentucky's neutrality in taking Columbus was a political blunder that drove Kentucky into the arms of the Federals, while his failure simultaneously to seize Paducah was a military blunder that might render his hold on Columbus useless. Polk seemed always to act with great confidence (perhaps the result of his having served for many years as a man of the cloth); even so, he began the war badly and never showed any notable improvement.

By late fall 1861, in the eyes of the Federals, then, Kentucky seemed reasonably, if not irrevocably, secure in the camp of the Union. But there were numerous Confederates who never had given up on Kentucky's joining their cause. Many a Kentuckian who had gone south to join the Rebels—and some 35,000 did so in the course of the war[8]—believed that Kentucky could yet be added to the list of Confederate states. Certainly Jefferson Davis, like Lincoln a Kentuckian by birth, never had forsaken the dream that Kentucky still might enlist under the southern banner. Kentucky, like Tennessee, really was a Confederate state held in bondage—or so many believed by summer 1862. Given a fair chance, they thought, Kentuckians would rise to throw off the Yankee oppressor and cast their lot with the South.

Like the Federals, the Confederates could read maps, and now,

Confederate General Edmund Kirby Smith.
Courtesy, Military Records and Research Branch,
Kentucky Department of Military Affairs, Frankfort, Kentucky.

following the Yankee triumphs on the western waters in winter and spring 1862, they were keenly aware of the strategic value of possessing Kentucky. The war, they thought, could be turned around if Kentucky could be occupied and held, thus depriving the Federals of the rivers and the railroads. Perhaps "God and Kentucky" might be found, after all, taking their stand on the side of the Confederacy.

In late summer 1862, the Confederacy would make its bid for the Bluegrass State. The endeavor would become known to some people as "Bragg's Kentucky Campaign." Actually, the man who had more to do with it than any other was a native of Florida, sent from Virginia to command the Department of East Tennessee.[9]

Major General Edmund Kirby Smith, thirty-eight years old in May 1862, had spent his first twelve years in St. Augustine and, according to his biographer Joseph Parks, never forgot "the hot sands, fresh mullet, . . . orange groves . . . [and] the carefree and exciting life" of his native state.[10] Smith's family, however, decided that the bright young boy should pursue a military career, and sent him off to an appropriate preparatory school at Alexandria, Virginia, just outside Washington, D.C. In 1841, he received an appointment to the U.S. Military Academy at West Point, graduating in 1845. Ranked twenty-fifth in a class of forty-one[11] and known by the nickname "Seminole," Smith finished just in time to gain some combat experience in the Mexican War, where he served with distinction. He also had a tour of duty at West Point as a mathematics professor, followed by frontier service with the Second Cavalry Regiment, and held the rank of major when the Civil War began.[12]

Casting his lot with the Confederacy, Smith was appointed a brigadier general shortly before the Battle of Bull Run. There his brigade chanced to arrive precisely at the right time and place to play—in concert with Jubal Early's brigade—a decisive role in enveloping the Yankee right flank and so beginning the repulse (eventually a rout) of the Federal forces. Unfortunately, Smith was severely wounded as his command was deploying for the attack, and Colonel Arnold Elzey took over, leading the brigade to its triumph.

Following the battle, Smith was taken to Richmond where, as he recovered from his wound, he became something of a social celebrity and hero. He came to be hailed as "the Blucher of Manassas"—a reference to the Prussian general whose reinforcement of Wellington at Waterloo turned the day against Napoleon—despite the fact that, in actuality, it was Smith's second-in-command, Arnold Elzey, who had assumed command when Smith was wounded, whom President Davis had praised with this tribute.[13] Part of Smith's recuperation period was spent at Lynchburg, where the general found a wife, Cassie Selden, the girl who, in Mark Boatner's words, made the general a shirt "on the joking promise that whoever made the garment would get the handsome [man] who went with it."[14] Smith and his new bride managed to get away to Florida—President Davis extending his sick leave—for a honeymoon at Smith's beloved St. Augustine, after which he was promoted to major general and sent to head the Department of East Tennessee.[15]

There the general faced a tough task in late spring 1862. Defending a front from Cumberland Gap on the north, through Knoxville, and down to Chattanooga on the south—180 miles, he calculated[16]—Smith knew that enemy forces were moving against both of his flanks. While neither Federal force was more than ten thousand strong, Smith's whole command, known as the Army of East Tennessee, numbered only about ten thousand, and they were poorly armed.[17] Clearly the Florida native faced a dilemma: concentrate his forces against the Federals on one flank, leaving the enemy unopposed on the other; or divide his forces to defend both flanks, leaving Smith badly outnumbered in each place.

The obvious solution, reasoned Smith, was reinforcements. He diligently sought them from various places: the governor of Georgia; General John C. Pemberton at Charleston, South Carolina; General A. R. Lawton at Savannah, Georgia; and, of course, the War Department in Richmond.[18] For example, he wrote to Governor Joseph E. Brown of Georgia on May 27:

> The movement of the division of the enemy in North Alabama point unmistakably to an attack on Chattanooga. The force threatening this department by way of Cumberland Gap prevents my meeting such an attack with anything like adequate numbers. . . . Can you not send me two or more armed regiments, or arms to put in the hands of those who are without them? . . . Any assistance which you may render me at this critical juncture will greatly redound to the cause of our country, and be thankfully received.[19]

While Governor Brown certainly was distressed by the impending threat to Chattanooga, he continued to react basically as he had earlier, calling upon Richmond and Jefferson Davis for help and suggesting strategy to the president.[20] The upshot was that Edmund Kirby Smith received considerable sympathy but very little assistance.

And then the situation got worse—much worse, in fact. By mid-June, Smith had learned that a Union army under General Buell was moving across northern Alabama, apparently with the objective of taking Chattanooga. The Federals, with a division already strung out east and west of Huntsville, which now could be added to Buell's army, were about to concentrate an overwhelming force on Smith's Chattanooga flank. If the Yankees kept coming, Smith faced a crisis.

At that point the War Department finally began, in the last days of June, to get Smith some help as the general seemed about to be forced to abandon Cumberland Gap and concentrate his troops to defend Chattanooga—a movement in accord with the president's wishes.[21] By this time, however, the mass of Yankees approaching Chattanooga was so numerous that piecemeal reinforcements would not suffice. Something drastic would have to be done or Chattanooga would be lost. The only Rebel force strong enough and close enough to be of any real assistance to Smith was General Bragg's army at Tupelo, Mississippi. Already, on June 26, Bragg had sent one division of some three thousand men under John McCown by rail to Chattanooga, where the unit arrived on July 3.[22] Bragg also had told

Smith that he would move with his main force to put pressure on the Federals from the rear—a declaration that must have lifted Smith's spirit. Due to lack of wagon transportation, however, Bragg was still in Tupelo when McCown arrived in Chattanooga. Thus Smith continued to call for help from Bragg.

On July 14, Smith told President Davis that the Yankees had "an overwhelming force that cannot be resisted except by Bragg's cooperation."[23] Nathan Bedford Forrest, Smith said, had been sent into Middle Tennessee to "delay Buell's movement till Bragg's columns make their appearance." Shortly after writing this, Smith would learn how very successful Forrest had been in contributing to this objective, through the surprise attack at Murfreesboro. Five days later, Smith again was telling Richmond how much he needed Bragg: "The safety of Chattanooga depends upon his co-operation."[24] The next day Smith said that Bragg's "co-operation with the force in East Tennessee is all-important."[25] And the same day, July 20, Smith wrote to Bragg: "Buell has completed his preparations, is prepared to cross near Bridgeport, and his passage there may be hourly expected. General [George] Morgan's command moving on Knoxville from Cumberland Gap. Your co-operation is much needed. It is your time to strike at Middle Tennessee."[26]

While Smith stewed, fearing that Chattanooga would soon be lost, Bragg seemed a Confederate Hamlet, unable to make up his mind. To stay put and wait for the next move of the Federals at Corinth was not a viable option, even if Bragg had wished to do so, which probably he did not. The southern people expected action from their new commander. Already there had been far too much retreating—and waiting—by the Confederates. The Rebel army also expected an offensive, and when Bragg took command he promised the army exactly that. On June 27, addressing his new command, Bragg told the troops: "Soldiers, great events are impending. . . . A few more days of needful preparation and organization and I shall give your banners to the breeze. . . . But be prepared to undergo privation and labor with cheerfulness and alacrity."[27]

No doubt many a Rebel, if given the choice, would have preferred Bragg's promise of "privation and labor" while advancing, as opposed to similar sufferings while retreating. The Forty-First Mississippi's Captain Koger, in another of his many letters to his wife, had described the hardships of the retreat from Corinth to Tupelo. Complaining, among other things, of all the "baggage," he especially deplored the pistol and sword he carried. "My hip is skinned where [the pistol] rubbed," he wrote, and the sword was "a great nuisance," a "useless appendage," and if it were not required by army regulations, Koger said, he "would thro it away." The troops were suffering "from measles, diarrhea, mumps and home-fever," Koger wrote, and he, particularly, was "greatly annoyed" by the men in a nearby tent who "are 9 or 10 of the most vile, obscene, blackguards that could be raked up this side of the bad place, outside of a jail or penitentiary. From early morn to dewy eve there is an uninterrupted flow of the dirtiest talk I ever heard in my life." In various ways, Koger articulated a pronounced dissatisfaction with army life in camp at Tupelo.

But Koger also asserted, "Let the word come 'forward' and set our faces to the enemy and we will tell you a different tale. I am no [professional] soldier but it does seem to me that a little less ditch digging and a little more daring, go-ahead fighting would do better, even tho it cost . . . more lives. I hate running away as bad as any . . . man." No doubt Koger also hated being separated from his wife, whom he admonished time and again: "Write—Write." (Later he would be frustrated—"deeply seized," as he expressed it—to learn that many of the letters they both wrote never reached the other.) Koger's extensive letters indicate clearly that he wanted to get on with the war. If Braxton Bragg would please the captain, and others like him, an advance was imperative.[28]

Bragg intended to take the offensive. There is no doubt of that fact. One option, which the general first seemed to favor, was to advance directly north and confront the enemy forces under Halleck that still remained in the vicinity of Corinth and West Tennessee. Actually, this move had little to commend it. While it was true that the Federals had divided their troops (a move generally considered unwise unless there are extenuating circumstances), sending Buell across northern Alabama toward Chattanooga, Halleck, using the railroads, could quickly concentrate a much larger force at Corinth than Bragg had in his whole army. Furthermore, upon taking command, Bragg did not have enough wagon transportation to haul the supplies that were imperative for his army to take the offensive. Whatever course he picked, the Confederate commander first had to acquire more wagons.

Another option for Bragg was to advance against the rear of Buell's column, in the hope of relieving the pressure on Smith at Chattanooga. This would place Buell between two Rebel forces. At the same time, of course, the movement would place Bragg's army between Buell and Halleck's forces. Possibly, the hunter might become the hunted, caught in the pincers of one force as large as his own and another even larger.

Bragg had yet another option, one surely attractive to the military mind, because it would quickly concentrate major Confederate forces for an offensive campaign. Bragg might shift his army to Chattanooga by rail, unite with Edmund Kirby Smith, and move into Middle Tennessee against Buell's communications through Nashville. Buell would be compelled to withdraw to protect his communications and perhaps could be maneuvered into fighting against superior numbers in a disadvantageous position. But would the railroads hold up for the transfer of the Rebel army? The journey would cover nearly eight hundred miles, using half a dozen railroads of varying gauge, with the troops having to be ferried across Mobile Bay. And what of Mississippi? Would the Yankees overrun the state and take Vicksburg if Bragg moved to Chattanooga? If such a transfer of base succeeded, it would have to be done fast, before the Yankees knew what was happening. Every option appeared fraught with risk and uncertainty.

Bragg seemed to take a good while mulling over his options. This is not so difficult to understand when one remembers that only recently—on June 20—Bragg, suddenly and unexpectedly, had been thrust into the position of army commander. A host of responsibilities and problems confronted him. Matters of organization, command, supply, and discipline, as well as strategy, demanded his time, thought, and energy. It was not possible for the general immediately to assume the offensive, even if he had already known the direction in which he wanted to move—which, of course, he did not. A certain amount of caution was appropriate; no laurel wreath would be awarded to the new commander for leaping into a major mistake.

While Bragg contemplated his options, gathered his wagons, and attended to various responsibilities that no army commander can escape, the Rebel soldiers at Tupelo continued their long, tiring bout with boredom and all the dissatisfactions of everyday life in an army. "I am tired of camp life," said a member of the Thirty-Third Alabama. Reporting that there was widespread sickness in his company, the soldier noted that "it makes the duty very hard on the rest." When not on guard duty or work detail, it seemed that always there was drill. "We have just now come off a battalion drill and I am very tired," he wrote, as he specified the burdensome equipment—cartridge box, ammunition, and heavy gun—that he was required to carry.[29]

One of the usual results of dissatisfaction and inactivity is the proliferation of rumors, and the Confederate camps were inundated with these. Captain Koger reported hearing that "the Yankees [were] falling back from Corinth, scared by old Stonewall's advance and alarmed for Washington City. Also that France and England have intervened in our quarrel at last." Koger "hardly knew" whether he was "pleased or not." Explaining such a surprising comment, he continued, "After our retreat I don't feel like quitting, even if we could do so, without a chance of thrashing the rascals first. But I expect it is all a lie, so I will not count on what I fear to be false." Indeed it was "all a lie," but Koger's comments are a testimony of how strongly held was the opinion of some Rebels that they were yet going to "thrash the [Yankee] rascals."[30] Meanwhile, General Braxton Bragg had determined his course of action.

As numerous historians have argued, Bragg's ultimate decision to move the army to Chattanooga was influenced by a number of factors, possibly even including, as Bragg's modern-day biographer has proposed, a suggestion from his wife Elsie.[31] Whatever Bragg may have considered, the move on Chattanooga, if accomplished rapidly, seemed to have a better chance of succeeding than the other options; moreover, if successful, it clearly promised the greatest potential gain.

On July 21, from Tupelo, General Bragg informed President Davis of his plan in a communiqué that is remarkable both for its brevity and its decisiveness: "Will move immediately to Chattanooga in force and advance from there. Forward movement from here in force not practicable. Will leave this line well defended."[32]

Obviously Bragg was not asking permission, but simply announcing his decision. One wonders if the general felt that he had been a bit abrupt, because the following day he again addressed the president, adding a little more information: "Obstacles in front connected with danger to Chattanooga induce a change of base. Fully impressed with great importance of that line, am moving to East Tennessee. Produce rapid offensive from there following the consternation now being produced by our cavalry. Leave this State amply protected by Van Dorn at Vicksburg and Price here."[33]

At the same time, Bragg wrote a much more complete summary—of both his reasons and his plans—to Beauregard, interestingly, to "beg" the Creole's "candid criticism," in view of "the cordial and sincere relations we have ever maintained." To lose Smith's line would be "a great disaster," and "to aid him at all" from Tupelo would render Bragg "too weak for the offensive against Halleck, with at least 60,000 . . . in my front. . . . It seemed to me then that I was reduced to the defensive altogether or to the move I am making." Bragg would "throw" his cavalry forward "toward Grand Junction and Tuscumbia," creating the impression "that I am advancing. . . . Before they can know my movement I shall be in front of Buell at Chattanooga, and by cutting off his transportation may have him in a tight place." Thus Bragg's plan was set forth for Beauregard, with Bragg tossing a final accolade to the horse soldiers: "Our cavalry is paving the way for me in Middle Tennessee and Kentucky."[34]

No doubt Bragg was well pleased when he learned that Beauregard was in hearty agreement—hardly a surprise, considering the Creole's penchant for grandiose offensive movements. On July 23, Bragg was on his way, rolling south on the rails toward Mobile. The transfer was to be quickly and smoothly accomplished, probably the premier effort in the history of Confederate rail operations, as approximately thirty thousand infantry were moved from Tupelo to Chattanooga within a few days. Only the artillery, wagon trains, and cavalry did not ride the rails, following instead the dirt roads from Tupelo across northern Alabama to Rome, Georgia, and thence northward to Chattanooga.

The first trains carrying the Rebel infantry were steaming into the little town on the banks of the Tennessee on July 29, and Buell's army was still miles away to the west. Bragg had left sixteen thousand men under Earl Van Dorn to defend Vicksburg, and another sixteen thousand under Sterling Price to confront the Union forces in northern Mississippi. Meanwhile, he united the balance of his troops with Kirby Smith before the Federals knew what was happening, placing them in position, as Bragg told Adjutant General Samuel Cooper, "to strike an effective blow through Middle Tennessee, gaining the enemy's rear, cutting off his supplies, and dividing his forces, so as to encounter him in detail."[35]

It was a brilliant move. There was no doubt, as subsequent events clearly demonstrated, that Bragg had chosen the best option available and the best plan for dealing with Buell's army in northern Alabama; in doing so, he just might be giving the Confederates an opportunity to turn the war around in the Western Theater. According to biographer Grady McWhiney, the Confederates, "thanks to Bragg, now had a chance to regain all they had lost. Up to this point in his offensive he had done everything right."[36]

As the troops moved north, realizing that the army was taking the offensive, spirits were high and confidence was at a peak. Events seemed to be developing as the surgeon Carlisle had prophesied earlier in a letter to his wife, "Our army is now in fine fighting trim and General Bragg is anxious to strike a blow and will surely do it. I have strong hopes of watering my horse in the *Ohio* before long. Would like to send you a little good wine from . . . Cincinnati."[37] The Third Florida's Thomas B. Ellis and his brother James L. Ellis were members of Company C, an outfit known as "The Wild Cats." They had "a wild cat skin stuffed and [mounted] at the head of the engine that bore [the unit] to Montgomery and on to Chattanooga."[38] Another Florida native, Augustus McDonnell, wrote that "before arriving at Chattanooga we were greeted by smiles and cheers . . . from the ladies" at every station along the road. "At some places refreshments were prepared for us by the fair hands of the women. I think the ladies in Georgia, as a general thing, are more enthusiastic and evince more genuine concern for the soldier than anywhere else I have passed through."[39]

From Chattanooga, a soldier in B. Franklin Cheatham's division, M. Jinkins, soon wrote to his father that he believed "Tennessee and Kentucky will be under the shield of the Confederate flag before Christmas. The spirit is in the South," he continued, "to avenge the foul wrongs that has been heaped upon her and she will have vengeance, cost what it may. There is no use talking about submission or the South being whipped. . . . It is impossible. The South," Jinkins affirmed, "will fight for half a century before she will give up."[40]

Unfortunately for the Rebels, the chances for lasting, significant achievement were not to be realized. When Bragg arrived at Chattanooga on July 30, major seeds of failure already had been sown. The ensuing campaign was to become one of the war's best examples of what happens when command is not unified and there is no clearly defined military objective. The latter, to a marked degree, may be traced to the former. Perhaps the Confederates would have failed under any conceivable circumstances, but their chances certainly would have been greater if they had not violated these basic principles of generalship.

The problem of a divided command rests primarily upon the shoulders of Jefferson Davis. After removing Beauregard, Davis reconstituted the command structure in the West, making East Tennessee a separate department. Thus Kirby Smith was an independent commander, reporting directly to Richmond, something Braxton Bragg did not realize until he actually reached Chattanooga.[41] Bragg found the situation disconcerting. He was somewhat relieved by a letter from Smith, received en route to Chattanooga, in which the East Tennessee commander proposed the very move upon which Bragg had embarked.[42] "There is yet time for a brilliant summer campaign," said Smith. Promising that he would "not only co-operate with you, but will cheerfully place my command under you subject to your orders," Smith thought there was "every prospect of regaining possession of Middle Tennessee and possibly Kentucky."[43]

When Bragg and Kirby Smith met in Chattanooga on the afternoon of July 31, their relationship was certainly cordial.[44] Kirby Smith had to be pleased that Bragg was bringing the troops necessary to ensure the defense of Chattanooga, something for which the Florida native had been pleading far and wide. Also, if Buell's army could be neutralized, the way might be opened to move into Kentucky, a campaign already pressing on Smith's mind.[45] As Kirby Smith sat down with Braxton Bragg to discuss strategy, he probably was in a most cooperative frame of mind.[46]

Bragg had a large map of Kentucky and Tennessee on the wall, and the two generals conferred until the early morning hours of August 1.[47] Surely the possibility of moving into Kentucky was discussed, but how much and under what circumstances are matters of conjecture. One thing is sure: a basic plan of campaign was agreed upon. Since Bragg's army could not take offensive action for some ten days to two weeks—until its transportation came up—General Smith would unite his troops, reinforced by some of Bragg's infantry, and move against the Federals under George Morgan at Cumberland Gap. With Morgan out of the way, Smith then would rejoin Bragg and, as Bragg said in his letter to Richmond, "Our entire force will then be thrown into Middle Tennessee with the fairest prospect of cutting off General Buell, should that commander continue in his present position."[48] At the same time, Price and Van Dorn were to combine their forces to "strike and clear West Tennessee of any force that can be left to hold it."[49]

The plan was good, calling for a united force to move into Middle Tennessee and deal with the Yankees under Buell. Once Middle Tennessee was recovered, with Buell either trapped or forced to withdraw into Kentucky, then Bragg and Smith might push on into Kentucky, using the railroad through Nashville for supplies and reinforcements. Farther to the west, theoretically at least, Van Dorn and Price also would be pushing into Kentucky—or anyway into Tennessee. The crux of the campaign was Bragg's and Smith's combined forces either eliminating Buell's army or compelling its withdrawal into Kentucky.

Bragg said that he and Smith had "arranged measures for mutual support and effective co-operation."[50] A few days later, Bragg told Smith: "Neither of us have any other object than the success of our cause. I am satisfied no misunderstanding can occur from the necessary union of our forces."[51] For his part, Smith responded: "I deem it almost superfluous to say that I will make no movement that your judgment does not sanction. . . . Where the first thought of each of us is the success of our cause no misunderstanding can arise."[52] Thus, "mutual support and effective co-operation" would carry the Rebels to victory, Bragg's superior rank giving him overall command when the armies were joined.

If it all sounded too good to be true, it was. Kirby Smith, for some time, had been developing a case of "Kentucky fever." The incubation period was nearly over, and Smith was about to be manifestly smitten. His obsession with Kentucky would bring about the death of any "mutual support and effective co-operation" with Braxton Bragg.

When Smith went to Chattanooga in late July to confer with Bragg, he already had Kentucky on his mind. Early in July, as Smith had considered how best to deal with the Federals at Cumberland

Gap under George Morgan, he had thought about a cavalry strike against the Yankee communications that would carry deep into Kentucky, "destroying the bridge over the Kentucky River, a blow" that would "so cripple the enemy's resources as to compel the evacuation of [Cumberland Gap]."[53]

Before long, Smith was thinking of more than a cavalry strike into Kentucky. On July 16, the colorful Colonel John H. Morgan, leading about a thousand men on a raid through central Kentucky, sent Smith a dispatch that made a tremendous impression on the East Tennessee commander. The message was from Georgetown and said: "I am here with a force sufficient to hold all the country outside of Lexington and Frankfort. These places are garrisoned chiefly with Home Guards. The bridges between Cincinnati and Lexington have been destroyed. The whole country can be secured, and 25,000 or 30,000 men will join you at once."[54]

The flamboyant Morgan did not know what he was talking about. Morgan's personal charisma, plus mounting discontent with Union government in Kentucky, had misled the raider into thinking that the Confederacy enjoyed widespread support.[55] While many people had greeted Morgan with cheers and some had produced food and drink, only a few had joined up with his dashing troopers. Morgan then retired from the state.

Reality mattered not. Morgan's telegram had an electrifying effect, and Kirby Smith began to dream of leading an invasion of the Bluegrass, where, he supposed, thousands would flock to the grayish hue of the Confederacy. Soon after, on the same day that Smith wrote Bragg promising not only to "co-operate" but also to "cheerfully" place his command under Bragg if Bragg would move his main force to East Tennessee, Smith also wrote to General Carter L. Stevenson, who was commanding a division near Cumberland Gap, sending him a copy of Morgan's July 16 dispatch and speculating that "the most favorable opportunity" might be at hand which would "probably enable you to enter Kentucky."[56]

J. Stoddard Johnston, recently arrived from Kentucky, also contributed to the Bluegrass fever. Conferring with Bragg, he argued that it was "a good time to go to Kentucky," and, meeting with Kirby Smith in Knoxville on August 16, Johnston no doubt made the same argument. He said that Smith was glad to see him.[57]

Humphrey Marshall, another Kentuckian who desperately wanted to lead troops into the Bluegrass, was also at hand. A native of Frankfort, Kentucky, Marshall was a West Point graduate who had pursued a career in law and politics. Standing five feet, eleven inches tall and weighing in at over three hundred pounds, the colorful brigadier general was in his fifty-first year. Earlier Marshall had penned an amazing letter to Vice President Alexander H. Stephens, speaking of "my [daring or darling] purpose of penetrating Kentucky . . . where my name is known and where *the people* will flock around *my* banner as the Italians did to that of Garibaldi. I am not mistaken . . . and they have been looking for *me* as for their deliverer from accursed bondage."[58]

By August 9, Kentucky was weighing very heavily on the mind of Kirby Smith. He wrote to Bragg, contending that he could not reduce Cumberland Gap without a long siege—"more time than I presume you are willing I should take"—and proposing another plan: "As my move direct to Lexington, Kentucky, would effectively invest Morgan, and would be attended with other most brilliant results in my judgment, I suggest my being allowed to take that course."[59]

Kirby Smith's proposal would drastically alter the plan of campaign agreed upon with Bragg at Chattanooga. Surprisingly, Bragg apparently acquiesced at once, responding the next day: "It would be inadvisable, I think, for you to move far into Kentucky, leaving Morgan in your rear, until I am able to fully engage Buell and his forces on your left." In conclusion, Bragg sounded an optimistic note: "Van Dorn and Price will advance simultaneously with us . . . and I hope we may all unite in Ohio."[60] It was about this time that Bragg remarked, in a jocular vein not often manifested, given his stern personality, that his troops had "promised to make [him] military governor of Ohio in ninety days."[61]

Bragg's August 10 dispatch to Kirby Smith was all the Florida native needed to justify his move into Kentucky. The only question for Kirby Smith was the schedule of departure. If Morgan should evacuate Cumberland Gap, Kirby Smith said he would, "of course, follow him and fight him wherever I can find him. Otherwise I will remain in position in his rear until you think I can move rapidly upon Lexington." Smith could not resist, however, adding his opinion that "every moment we delay will lessen the great advantages to be gained by an immediate move upon Lexington."[62] As far as Kirby Smith was concerned, the Chattanooga plan to join Bragg for a movement into Middle Tennessee first might as well never have been formulated. Neither did it matter that Bragg's wagon transportation was not yet available, so Bragg could make no immediate advance to support Smith's movement, wherever it might take him. Not only was Smith ready to go, but he wanted to leave for Kentucky at once.

Kirby Smith also was making his case for the Kentucky venture to Jefferson Davis. Rather than investing Morgan at Cumberland Gap, "the true policy," he told the president, was "to move into Kentucky," which plan he had "urged upon General Bragg." If Kentucky "be as ripe for the move as all representations indicate, it must involve the abandonment of Middle Tennessee by the Federals." Politically, Smith continued, "now is the time to strike at Kentucky." In the latter part of the letter to Davis, Smith said he had just received a letter from Bragg which "sanctions my move on Kentucky; but the delay which it necessitates is to be regretted." Finally, Smith wrote, "My advance is made in the hope of permanently occupying Kentucky. It is a bold move, offering brilliant results."[63] The East Tennessee commander now was totally in the grip of Kentucky fever.

Kirby Smith is relatively easy to understand. He certainly had been thinking about Kentucky for a long time, conceivably even working to get Bragg's forces to Chattanooga as a prerequisite for launching, as he phrased it, "my move on Kentucky."[64] More puzzling is why Bragg so quickly accepted a change from the solid plan projected at Chattanooga for a united drive into Middle Tennessee.

Was it the awkwardness of the command situation? There is no doubt that Bragg was embarrassed when he got to Chattanooga. In attempting to pursue a policy of cordial cooperation with a fellow department commander, perhaps Bragg could not bring himself to insist forcefully upon the original strategy. Maybe Bragg found the thought of curbing the ambitious Smith—a man who insisted to his wife that, regardless of what others might say, he was not ambitious[65]—too unpleasant to make the effort. Too, Smith was not close at hand, and he had some of Bragg's best troops with him.

It is also conceivable that Bragg, like Kirby Smith, fell victim to Kentucky fever—even if his case was less virulent than Kirby Smith's. Surely Kirby Smith had talked to Bragg about Kentucky when they met in Chattanooga. As Bragg reflected on the discussion, Kirby Smith's points may have seemed more potent. When J. Stoddard Johnston conferred with Bragg in Chattanooga, advocating a move into Kentucky, he recorded in his diary that the general "told me it was with that purpose for which he was then massing his troops from Alabama to Chattanooga, and he was very glad to see me as he knew nothing of the state, its routes, and topography."[66] Thoughts and talk of Kentucky were "in the air" during summer 1862 and may have affected Bragg.

In fact, it was on August 10 that another Kentuckian and friend of J. Stoddard Johnston, the former vice-president of the United States, John C. Breckinridge, was writing to Bragg: "We must fight them next autumn in Kentucky and make them begin at the line of the Ohio with their newly raised forces, or Kentucky and Tennessee will be lost to us. A strong movement will give us large accessions in both these states."[67]

Whatever the reasons, General Bragg, having made a brilliant transfer of base to Chattanooga, and having projected a sound plan for unified action that promised to recover Middle Tennessee, suddenly succumbed to Kirby Smith's destruction of that same plan. The result would be no unified movement and no clearly defined objective.

As if all this were not bad enough, Van Dorn and Price had difficulty achieving the hoped-for cooperation, further illustrating the problems that arise when command is not unified. General Bragg, of course, had authority over both Van Dorn and Price, but, because of the distance from Mississippi to East Tennessee, where Bragg's campaign would be initiated, he felt he must rely upon the good judgment and cooperation of the two generals in Mississippi. The matter sounded simple enough in Bragg's instructions to Van Dorn, written from Chattanooga on August 11:

"In view of the operations from here," said Bragg, "it is very desirable to press the enemy closely in West Tennessee. . . . If you hold them in check we are sure of success here." While Bragg felt that he could not give positive instructions "when so little is known and when circumstances may change daily," the general did expect his subordinates "to strike at the most assailable point." Also, whenever Van Dorn and Price joined forces, Van Dorn's rank would give him the command of the whole force.[68]

But Price and Van Dorn would not join forces for several weeks, and they could not agree about where to join up or where to strike. On August 27, Price wrote Van Dorn, urging the latter to join him in the vicinity of Tupelo and move on the enemy at Corinth. This would "regain control of the railroad." After having driven the enemy from Corinth, "we may then decide upon the future conduct of the campaign."[69] Two days later, Bragg sent Price a dispatch indicating that Buell's whole force was retreating toward Nashville and, thinking William S. Rosecrans, then in the Corinth region, would follow, ordered Price to try and prevent a junction of the two Federals. From this point on, Price wanted to move northeastward as soon as possible.[70]

Van Dorn, however, did not seem impressed with the urgency of moving toward Nashville. Anyway, he could not have his troops in motion as soon as Price. Furthermore, he wanted Price to move west and join up in the vicinity of Grand Junction and advance from there into West Tennessee. Then he wanted to move into Kentucky and to the Ohio River.[71]

As Van Dorn expressed it in a message to Price on September 8:

> If Rosecrans has crossed the Tennessee . . . do you not think it would be better for us to join forces at Jackson, Tennessee, clear western Tennessee . . . and then push on together into Kentucky, along the Ohio River? . . . We, joined on the Ohio, would be between Buell's army and the [Federal] forces from the west and prevent junction, or by crossing eastward from the Ohio behind Buell could join Bragg and aid him in case of need.

Van Dorn was also writing the secretary of war, requesting that he be given command of the movements of Price, "that there may be concert of action."[72]

The next day, Price responded to Van Dorn: "I am sorry to say that I feel General Bragg's repeated instructions compel me to move without any further delay toward Nashville."[73] There would be further delay, however, and by the first of October, Price and Van Dorn still would be in Mississippi. The correspondence of these two generals, along with their correspondence with Bragg, provides further evidence of the overall vagueness of the Confederacy's Kentucky campaign, as well as the freelance nature of that campaign.

Thus, in late summer 1862, the Confederates were moving into Kentucky. Edmund Kirby Smith was heading toward the Bluegrass. Braxton Bragg, farther to the west and after changing plans, would advance into central Kentucky from Middle Tennessee. Still farther west, Earl Van Dorn, hoping for the assistance of Sterling Price, wanted to march into western Kentucky after driving the Federals from West Tennessee—assuming, of course, that Van Dorn and Price first could agree on how to get out of northern Mississippi.

The southern objective, loosely conceived, was to bring Kentucky into the Confederate camp. Whether this meant taking Louisville, or Lexington, or some point or points on the Ohio River, or the railroads, or all these—or some other strategic places—never was defined. Coordination of the effort depended solely upon the commanders' cooperation with one another. But how could they cooperate—assuming they were of a mind to do so—when the goal of the campaign was, at best, vaguely defined?

The only way that, under the circumstances, the Rebel invasion of Kentucky could succeed (other than a total Federal collapse) was if the Kentuckians, by tens of thousands, were to rise and take up arms for the South. Lacking unity of command, lacking specific military objectives, and lacking superior numbers of troops, the Confederacy, in order to triumph in Kentucky, would have to have massive help from Kentucky—and perhaps from God as well.

☆☆☆

Yet another general had been giving a lot of thought to Kentucky. That general—because of his strong will that could be both a blessing and a curse—just possibly might have contributed toward a unified command and specific objectives, if the reins of authority had been placed in his hands. General G. T. Beauregard had been enjoying the hot springs, and the welcome company of Augusta Evans, at Bladen, Alabama; clearly, however, he longed to be back in the war. Ever since Jefferson Davis had removed him from command following the retreat from Corinth, he had chafed under his enforced absence from the conflict. For a person of Beauregard's ego and ambition, it must have been terribly distressing to know that *the* great event of his lifetime now was proceeding without his participation.

Beauregard decided, near the end of August, to send his ideas on what the western Confederates should be doing both to Braxton Bragg and to the War Department at Richmond. Having heard that his "just expectation" of being returned to command "upon the restoration of [his] health" was "to be disappointed," the general wrote that he still hoped his ideas could be "of service to our arms and to our cause."

Beauregard's letter of September 5 to Richmond certainly demonstrates that the hard lessons of the previous winter's campaigning had been impressed upon the mind of the colorful Creole. The essence of the matter was that the Rebels badly needed to take control of Kentucky. Beauregard first pointed to Louisville and Cincinnati as primary objectives for controlling the line of the Ohio River, and he elaborated on the best procedure, as a prerequisite, for Bragg to get Buell's army out of northern Alabama. The "Napoleon in Gray" then focused upon those water routes by which the Union had opened up the Confederate heartland six months earlier.

"We must, . . . as soon as practicable, construct strong works to command the Tennessee and Cumberland Rivers," he said. Beauregard knew that the old sites in Tennessee would not do. This time, the forts must be in Kentucky. "The best position for said works," he elaborated, "is about 40 miles below [north of] Forts Donelson and Henry, not far from Eddyville, where those two rivers come within one and a half miles of each other." At that point, there existed "a commanding elevation where a strong field work could be constructed" to defend the rivers. That was not all. This time, if the Rebels were going to do it correctly, there must be "a series of batteries, armed with the heaviest guns," along the bank of each river and "bearing directly on obstructions placed in each of said rivers."

The Creole also wanted a rapid advance of the troops in northern Mississippi, from Grand Junction to Fort Pillow, where, on the Mississippi, north of Memphis, they could interdict the Federal line of communications to Memphis and below. Too, continued Beauregard, "from Fort Pillow I would compel the forces at Corinth and Jackson, Tennessee, to fall back precipitately to Humboldt and Columbus, or their lines of communication would be cut off also." "We would thus compel the enemy to evacuate at once the state of Mississippi and Western Tennessee."[74]

What Beauregard wanted was concentration, followed by rapid advances and maneuver. His ultimate objective was the strategic points, mainly in Kentucky, needed to control the rivers and railroads, without which the western Confederacy was lost. It is true that the general had a flair for extravagant plans and maneuvers. Perhaps his plans were too ambitious for the Confederacy's resources to support. Quite possibly the controversial Beauregard, long a favorite whipping boy of some historians, might have proved no better than anyone else the Confederacy had to lead operations in the Western Theater. But he was a strong-willed character who insisted upon running the show and who had some definite ideas about objectives—factors that the western Rebels really needed in the summer and fall of 1862. For better or worse, however, Jefferson Davis would see to it that Beauregard never again exercised command over a major Confederate army.

Chapter 4

Retreat to Nashville

☆☆☆

The last pontoons burned fiercely. The floats for the railroad span—fourteen hundred yards long—of the Tennessee River at Bridgeport, Alabama, were going up in smoke, destroyed by the same engineers who had just finished constructing them. The United States Army was retreating.[1]

The fiery destruction of the new bridge symbolized both the war's hellish violation of the serene and resplendent river valley, and the sudden and unexpected reversal of the war's course in the Western Theater. Major General Don Carlos Buell's promising advance on Chattanooga and East Tennessee, which had carried virtually all the way across northern Alabama to within thirty miles of Chattanooga, was finished.

The strategic railroad junction at Cleveland, Tennessee, was not to be taken and held. There, about thirty miles east of Chattanooga, iron rails led south to Atlanta or north to Knoxville and Virginia. President Abraham Lincoln had said that he prized this objective as "fully as important as the taking and holding of Richmond."[2] But the campaign was over; during the last days of August 1862, the Federals were falling back rapidly into Middle Tennessee.

☆☆☆

It was quite a reversal from the events of springtime. Then the triumphant Federals, in the wake of the Confederate collapse initiated at Fort Henry and Fort Donelson, had moved into northern Alabama soon after General Albert Sidney Johnston's forces had evacuated the region. Johnston, of course, had gone west for the concentration of Rebel troops at Corinth, Mississippi, which had preceded the Battle of Shiloh. The Union occupation of Huntsville, Alabama, like a great tidal wave sweeping in from the sea, had gone virtually unopposed, as a Yankee division under command of Ormsby Mitchell moved south from Nashville. The U.S. troops then had spread out east and west to occupy points on the railroad. Some weeks later, General Buell had moved into northern Alabama with his army. Federal strength throughout the area had been formidable.

From the first, however, the Federals had experienced, in one form or another, the wrath of many people who either sympathized with the Confederacy or resented the intrusion of the Union forces. Several of the soldiers in blue, both men in the ranks and officers, left letters, diaries, and memoirs that yield valuable insights into their experiences. Writing of the events in northern Alabama, and sometimes along the Mississippi-Tennessee periphery as well, during those spring and summer days of 1862, these men generally showed an initial optimism upon entering the region but eventually succumbed to some degree of discontent with their situation.

A number of soldiers commented on the beauty of the area, their first impressions of the towns and countryside often being favorable. Tuscumbia, Florence, and Athens all were "neat, tidy places," according to Theodore R. McBeath, an attorney from Leitchfield, Kentucky, who served as quartermaster for a Union regiment. He also added, as he wrote to "Nannie," a young woman he hoped to marry, that the towns "have been roughly treated by our army."[3] The Forty-Second Indiana's George Morgan Kirkpatrick thought that Hunts-

Tennessee River at the railroad crossing, Bridgeport, Alabama.
Photograph by John Hursh.

ville was "a beautiful place" and was pleased to find "a large spring of cool water" where he was able to camp for "a long time."[4]

George W. Landrum of the Second Ohio regiment also was impressed by Huntsville, praising the town and region profusely: "I have never been in so pretty a little place before, nor have I ever seen a more beautiful valley than this. The views from any of the hills or mountains are magnificent and grand." On the negative side, Landrum said Huntsville was "the worst Sesesh town we have had the fortune to get into; no attempt to disguise their sentiments, they boldly proclaim that they are Secessionists." He was particularly irritated by "the 'five to one' business"—the notion that one southerner supposedly could "lick" five Yankees. "They say that was meant for the eastern men," Landrum recorded, and "not the men of the west; that they always looked upon the western men as their equals in a fight." The Ohio native thought it was "a pity" that a division of "real live

Yankees" was not with "our army of the west, so that we could take this last little morsel of conceit out of them."[5]

Expectably, not everyone thought that all of northern Alabama was pleasing to look upon, although most praised Huntsville and some used it as a standard of comparison. The Third Ohio's John Beatty, for example, remarked that the town of Decatur, Alabama, "is a dilapidated old concern, as ugly as Huntsville is handsome." Beatty was pleased to be along the banks of the Tennessee River, where "fine, large fish" might be caught. One night he remarked, "We have a buffalo for supper—a good sort of fish—weighing six pounds."[6]

A number of Union soldiers, not surprisingly, recorded their impressions of the women they encountered, evidently being disturbed by the females' open hostility. Some of the Federals were convinced that the women were playing a major role in persuading the young men of the South to join the Rebel forces. The Twenty-Ninth Indiana's Bergum H. Brown wrote his mother that "the women of the country would sour milk, half sugar at that. The city girls are better—all very pert but so delicate—why one told me yesterday, when I went to buy milk of her—cows milk—that she did not know how to unlock the cellar door—had to go and call a servant. . . . What splendid wives," he sarcastically concluded, "not to know more about supporting themselves than infants."[7]

John Beatty thought that the men of Huntsville had "settled down to a patient endurance of military rule." But the women were another story. Beatty said they were "outspoken in their hostility, and marvelously bitter." He thought "the foolish, yet absolute, devotion of the women to the Southern cause does much to keep it alive. It encourages, nay forces, the young to enter the army, and compels them to continue what the more sensible know to be a hopeless struggle."[8]

To George Landrum the southern females were "fiends in woman's form." They are "heartless, soulless, and barbarous," he told his sister, as he wrote from Huntsville. Some of the Federal soldiers had died of disease, and, as the funeral procession, on the way to the cemetery, passed by "a female college," Landrum wrote, "the girls would come out to the gate, giggle, clap their hands, and give every evidence . . . of their joy at seeing a Union soldier carried to his grave. [The school] became such a nuisance that the general ordered it to be taken possession of for a hospital." Landrum thought the general "ought to have burned it to the ground."[9]

Most of the Union soldiers were getting their first look at slavery, and their writings often reflect their impressions of "the Peculiar Institution." The Twenty-Ninth Indiana's Jack F. Pase obviously did not disapprove. Remarking in a letter that his company had "some of the rankest kind of Abolitionists . . . but I don't think the number increases," Pase found the southern weather "very pleasant . . . , just warm enough to suit me," concluding that "I think I shall settle down here . . . if Congress confiscates all Rebel property, kidnap 200 or 300 Negroes, etc., etc."[10]

William R. Stuckey, Forty-Second Indiana Infantry, after observing slavery for the first time in Alabama, also approved. Stuckey had enthusiastically joined the army months before, saying at first that he was "well contented" with soldiering and was a member of "the best drilled regiment in the brigade"; but, after experiencing danger from guerrillas and bouts with sickness and loneliness—he had married a short time before enlisting—and having had his money stolen, he concluded that he had been "a fool to volunteer." But slavery seemed to commend itself to him, and on August 15, 1862, he wrote his wife from Alabama: "We have two Negros a cooking for our company and if we can get home this fall I intend to fetch two for to wait on you and two for to help me to work."[11]

Whatever they thought of slavery, positive, negative, or indifferent, some of the Federal soldiers readily took advantage of the blacks whenever an opportunity presented itself. Jesse B. Connelly of the Thirty-First Indiana recorded in his diary on July 27, 1862, while in camp near Athens, Alabama, having just come from Mississippi, that "the roads were almost lined with darkies of both sexes out to see the Yankees pass. Also to sell milk, cornbread, pies, and onions, for all of which they asked an exorbitant price." Connelly said that "in a great many cases, soldiers without money and void of principle stole the entire stock in trade of some poor darkies, knowing the poor negroes dare not resist."[12]

George Kirkpatrick was straightforward in recalling the role of at least some members of the Forty-Second Indiana in such matters. Speaking of the period when the regiment was stationed at Huntsville, Kirkpatrick wrote: "We often met the colored people coming down from . . . the mountain with eggs, chickens, corn, etc., to sell. We were like Ben Butler," he said, "and we called everything contraband, and said we had orders to confiscate it; so we lived high, for as they came out they would have other things that looked good to us, and so it went."[13]

Undoubtedly the situation was very difficult for the slaves, and many suffered, sometimes from both Federals and Confederates. James S. Thomas of the Tenth Indiana wrote to his sister on August 6, 1862, that "the Secesh hang negros like sixty down here; our brigade found one hanging on a lim over the road yesterday."[14] John Beatty revealed the difficult position that some blacks found themselves in: "Billy, my servant, tells me that a colored man was whipped to death by a planter who lives near here [Decatur], for giving information to our men." Beatty said he did not doubt it. "We worm out of these poor creatures a knowledge of the places where stores are secreted, or compel them to serve as guides, and then turn them out to be scourged or murdered." Beatty concluded that "there must be a change in this regard before we shall be worthy of success." He also thought there were "not fifty negroes in the South who would not risk their lives for freedom. The man who affirms that they are contented and happy . . . is either a falsifier or a fool!"[15]

Regardless of what the Federals in northern Alabama thought about slavery or anything else—whether the appearance of the region, the southern women, the problems of loneliness and sickness, the white people in the depths of poverty, the length of the war—

increasingly their attention was focused upon two things: acquiring enough food to eat and evading the guerrillas or bushwhackers who constantly harassed and disrupted Union activities. "All the crops are a failure here except potatos and apples, peaches," wrote James F. Mohr to his brother from a camp near Stevenson, Alabama, on July 25, 1862. Earlier, he had written from Florence that "for the last three days we had moldy crackers that a dog would not eat." Now he vowed to do whatever was necessary to find food: "I can get along if any can for where there is anything to get I will have it. I do not care what it cost if it is even life itself."[16]

Many Federals must have experienced feelings similar to Mohr's. A man from Illinois, W. E. Patterson, recorded that "our near neighbor and friend" was "a secesh gentleman with two sons in the rebel army. We guarded his property, devoured his fruit and confiscated two or three of his juvenile negroes."[17] Bergum H. Brown, who said that the inhabitants of Huntsville were "sesech to the handle and not ashamed to own it," also thought they had "paid dear" for their sentiments because "the whole country has been ravaged by both armies." Everything of value that could be used "has been used." Brown recorded that Federal forces at Battle Creek, on "half rations for some time," scoured the country "for miles in search of provisions. They drive in cattle, sheep, and gather anything in."[18] And John Beatty wrote: "The bread and meat we fail to get from the loyal states are made good . . . from the smokehouses and granaries of the disloyal. Our boys find Alabama hams better than Uncle Sam's sidemeat." He claimed that "every time [John Morgan] destroys a provision train," the hearts of his troops were "gladdened and they shout 'Bully for Morgan!'"[19]

But the fact was that, as summer came on and an unusually long, dry spell succeeded the wet spring, the possibilities of successfully foraging in northern Alabama diminished—especially considering how many soldiers, Confederate and Union, already had picked over the region. Added to the lack of food was the constant threat of guerrillas. The result was that violence, brutality, and reprisal became more and more common. John Beatty, in fact, played an important role in the escalating harshness of the war.

While riding a train from Bellefonte to Huntsville, the train was fired upon at the little village of Paint Rock, resulting in several men being wounded. Beatty stopped the train a short distance from the town, took a file of soldiers, and proceeded to burn the town, while taking three citizens—one he said was "a notorious guerrilla"—with him to Huntsville, where they were held in prison. Paint Rock, according to Beatty, was "a rendezvous for bushwhackers and bridgeburners." He promised that, henceforth, "every time the telegraph wire was cut we would burn a house; every time a train was fired upon we should hang a man." The burning of the town created a sensation and was a harbinger of more violence to come.[20]

The war in northern Alabama, and in southern Middle Tennessee as well, did become quite brutal during late spring and summer 1862. At Athens, Alabama, allegedly in reprisal for guerrilla activities, Federal Colonel John Basil Turchin, formerly of the Imperial Russian Army and a veteran of the Crimean War, turned the town over to his three regiments, who (making no distinction between citizens who were loyal and those who were disloyal to the Union) raped servant girls and plundered the people of thousands of dollars in property.[21] Theodore McBeath strongly disapproved of Turchin. He wrote to Nannie that Turchin's men "have been committing some of the most outrageous and unprovoked depredations . . . that you could possibly imagine. The thieving rascals have stolen everything they could get their fingers on, and those articles that were useless to them were destroyed. John Morgan and his band are gentlemen in comparison with these scamps."[22]

The death of Yankee Brigadier General Robert McCook, like the sack of Athens, also received widespread attention. McCook was sick and riding in an ambulance on his way from Athens, Alabama, toward Dechard, Tennessee, on August 6, when he and his escort were ambushed by guerrillas and the general mortally wounded.[23] The *Nashville Daily Union* reported that McCook's infuriated soldiers proceeded to the plantation of a man they believed had led McCook into a trap "and demolished everything on his premises. We learn they also wreaked their fury on the heads of the rebels in the vicinity."[24]

The newspaper report was basically accurate. General George H. Thomas, in reporting McCook's death, said that McCook's regiment was "very much enraged, and before they could be stopped, burned and destroyed some four or five farm-houses; but Colonel [Ferdinand] Van Derveer, by great exertions, succeeded in subjugating them to discipline before night and they are quiet now."[25] It was reported in the *Ohio State Journal* that, when Dan McCook heard of his brother's death, he said, "I'll never take another rebel prisoner as long as God gives me breath."[26] No doubt some Federal soldiers felt the same as Dan McCook. The Twenty-Ninth Indiana's Bergum Brown wrote to his mother about the death of Robert McCook, saying, "It must be a very forgiving spirit that will see such work and not swear to take no more prisoners. . . . The time for milk and water manner of doing business is past. This war has gone far enough and if it requires half a million more men let them be had, for they are in the North and if they are not willing to volunteer, let them be drafted."[27]

Only a few days before General McCook's death, a young woman was murdered in the woods near Battle Creek, Tennessee, about two miles from her home, where all her family were found murdered also. The soldier, whose report was carried in the *Nashville Daily Union*, said he recently had eaten dinner with the family. "We buried her there," he continued, "among the rocks and pines of the mountain, and seven of Ohio's sons vowed by her grave that her death should be avenged."[28]

About the same time, four Union soldiers were found hanged nearby. Colonel Marcellus Mundy of the Twenty-Third Kentucky Infantry (Union) reported that he knew of two cases near Pulaski where citizens who had declared themselves for the Union were hung by guerrillas and left hanging in the woods. "Their wives came to me to Pulaski and reported the facts," testified Colonel Mundy. "I afterward sent an officer with a party of men to have them decently taken care of and to search for the guerrillas till they could find them. I did not find them; if I had I should have retaliated by hanging them."[29]

The Third Ohio Cavalry's John W. Large, writing from his camp near Decatur, claimed that the "Rebels won't stand and fight"; instead, he said, they "lie behind bushes and murder." Consequently, Large reported, "our boys [have resolved] to take no more prisoners but shoot every man they see in the woods."[30]

It seemed that a soldier was not safe from guerrillas even when answering the call of nature in an apparently peaceful countryside. Colonel Edward M. McCook, Second Indiana Cavalry, told of a Federal shot and killed by gunfire from a house while he sat down to relieve himself in a field.[31] And at Huntsville, on August 8, after a series of firings into trains by guerrillas, Federal authorities ordered that ministers and leading churchmen who had been active secessionists were to be arrested and placed on board the trains. Evidence of cruelty and brutality was all about, as both the Buell investigation and the newspapers established. General Buell took a lot of criticism because he tried to stop Federal soldiers from plundering. He had Colonel Turchin court-martialed and dismissed for the Athens debauchery, but by the end of the summer Turchin had been reinstated and promoted to brigadier general.[32]

Buell generally pursued a benevolent policy which strictly forbade arrest, pillaging, or other harassment of peaceable citizens by the army. "We are in arms," Buell told his soldiers, "not for the purpose of invading the rights of our fellow-countrymen anywhere, but to maintain the integrity of the Union and protect the Constitution."[33]

Union newspapers, many of them circulated among the soldiers in northern Alabama, were highly critical of Buell's "Rosewater Policy" of conducting the war. The term "Rosewater" denoted a policy of leniency toward the enemy; of conducting a "soft war," as opposed to a harsh and unrelenting fight against the South. At this stage of the conflict, the "Rosewater" policy still reflected Washington's official thinking about the Confederacy, its hope of bringing out a strong showing of latent Unionism. In this respect, Buell was of the same mind as many Union generals, such as George B. McClellan. But the situation was changing in summer 1862. More and more people in the free states, as well as men in the Federal army, were demanding a "hard war," with confiscation, destruction, and other harsh treatment of southerners. Perhaps the common man, as sometimes is the case, was ahead of the political leaders in recognizing the direction in which the war would go.

The troops saw Chicago, Louisville, Cincinnati, and Nashville papers frequently and Indiana and Pennsylvania papers occasionally.[34] According to Colonel Mundy's testimony, only the *Louisville Journal* refrained from condemning Buell.[35] One July issue of the *Cincinnati Gazette*, for example, lashed out at Buell for "guarding the property of secessionists, while his own soldiers are suffering." The paper quoted a letter from a soldier saying Buell had "endeavored to make his army a mere police force for the better protection of rebels." This soldier claimed Buell "personally" ordered the arrest of a lieutenant in the Sixth Indiana who was "going into a house to buy a few vegetables!" The paper editorialized: "Confiscation is an indispensable adjunct to our arms. . . . If we would conquer in this war we must value the Union as everything and slavery as nothing."[36]

The *Nashville Daily Union* almost daily criticized the general, charging on August 3 that guerrillas were "swarming all over the country, plundering Union men," and referring to "Generals Buell and Rousseau, sitting snugly in their tents like squires in the office, listening to the complaints of rebels about chickens stolen, negroes sloped, peach orchards plundered, when all around the guerrillas are growing bolder and making both [rail] lines to Huntsville more unsafe than before."[37] Another day the paper editorialized that "the Union man who tries to shape his course so as to please rebels, will succeed only to the extent that he turns rebel himself."[38] There were those who claimed that Buell was disloyal, and some of his soldiers bitterly resented his efforts to stop the plundering.[39]

General Buell believed that, if the discipline and fighting tone of soldiers was to be preserved, they must be restrained from pillage and plunder. The Gallatin, Tennessee, tunnel disaster had resulted, at least in part, he believed, from lack of discipline. The general determined to make an example of the Federal command that allegedly had been captured without firing a shot.

He ordered the arrest of Colonel Boone and his men upon their return to Union lines after parole. He also commanded that railroad guard posts must hold out "to the last extremity" and pled with Halleck for more cavalry: "We are occupying lines of great depth, . . . swarming with the enemy's cavalry and can only be protected with cavalry. It is impossible to overrate the importance of this matter."[40]

Buell further detailed two regiments of infantry for railroad guard duty, put his men once more on half rations, and placed all his cavalry under Brigadier General Richard W. Johnson of Kentucky, who was given the mission to seek and destroy John Hunt Morgan. With seven hundred troopers, Johnson, an 1849 West Pointer, set forth vowing to end Morgan's depredations. (He boasted that he would bring Morgan back in a band box.)[41]

Johnson caught up with Morgan near Gallatin on August 21 and quickly proved that he was not the man—or at least that those in his command were not the men—to deal with Morgan's cavalry. Johnson was compelled to retreat, and finally he and a part of his force were captured while attempting to cross to the south bank of the Cumberland River.

The next day General Buell received not only the news of Johnson's defeat and capture[42] but also, and worse, a report from Alexander McCook saying that three of his spies had come in that morning with important news. Indeed, the news was significant—and alarming.

Braxton Bragg was across the Tennessee River west of Chattanooga. Fifty regiments were said already to have crossed. "The troops that are crossing are well armed and have good artillery," reported McCook. "The advance of the enemy has reached the top of Walden's Ridge," he continued. "This news is reliable. The enemy intend marching upon McMinnville."[43]

To the beleaguered Buell, this message threatened the *coup de grace* to his collapsing East Tennessee campaign. No longer could Buell speak confidently, as he had to Halleck two weeks earlier when he indicated that he was prepared to find the reports of Confederate strength (which ran as high as ninety thousand) in East Tennessee exaggerated. Buell had told Halleck that he planned to march upon Chattanooga "at the earliest possible day, unless I ascertain certainly that the enemy's strength renders it imprudent. If, on the other hand, he should cross the river I shall attack him, and I do not doubt that we shall defeat him."[44]

Now Buell shifted his headquarters to Dechard, Tennessee, on the Nashville and Chattanooga Railroad and directed that all trains be employed to transfer into Tennessee the supplies accumulated at Bridgeport, Stevenson, and Huntsville.[45] Nothing had gone well for Buell all summer. Since Morgan had wrecked the tunnel north of Gallatin, the situation had seemed impossible. The Cumberland River had been too low for shipping into Nashville since about mid-July.[46] A trickle of supplies had been brought by light draught boats from Clarksville to Nashville, but even this trickle had been cut off when the Rebels took Clarksville about August 20. Thus Buell had been effectively denied all supplies out of Louisville, and already his army was eating up what rations had been collected at Stevenson for the planned march on Chattanooga.

Morgan's claim that the "Big South" tunnel never could be repaired[47] was, an exaggeration, of course, but the task did take weeks of hard work. The new military railhead—to be established by building a long siding and an unloading ramp ten miles north of the tunnel at Mitchellville, from whence supplies might be carried by wagon to Nashville—was not yet ready. The journey would be a long, time-consuming trek, anyway, through Tyree Springs and Goodlettsville to Nashville.[48] And it could not equal the railroad in volume carried.

To receive supplies from the Tennessee River or by rail from Memphis also had proved impossible. Lieutenant Colonel Francis Darr, chief commissary in the field for Buell's Army of the Ohio, testified that by the middle of July, the Tennessee River was so low that navigation above Pittsburgh Landing was possible only for the "very lightest draught boats."[49] From Eastport, Mississippi, to Tuscumbia, Alabama, the situation became worse. The low water at Colbert's Shoals, a few miles above Eastport, made any navigation dangerous, time-consuming, and, worst of all, inadequate.[50] The railroad from Memphis was of no help, because it could hardly carry enough supplies for the troops stationed at Corinth; moreover, the only locomotives available were too heavy for the bridge over Bear River, east of Iuka. Anyway, the Rebels struck the railroad between Tuscumbia and Decatur, near Courtland, destroying bridges and putting the line out of order about July 25.[51]

There had been no hope that the Federals might live off the country for any extended period. Not much subsistence could be found in northern Alabama, and what existed, as Colonel J. B. Fry, assistant adjutant-general and chief of staff of the Army of the Ohio, said, "was so scattered as to render it impracticable for a concentrated army to gather enough for its daily use. There was no salt meat, but few cattle, and the corn was standing in fields often at a considerable distance from each other."[52]

A bad crop year, with grain in very short supply in northern Alabama, had first seen the Confederate army of twenty-five or thirty thousand, falling back from Kentucky, take provisions for some two weeks. That army was followed by General Ormsby Mitchell's Yankee force of eight or ten thousand, which drew upon the countryside for several more weeks before Buell's army arrived. A judge who had lived in the Huntsville area for forty-five years testified that he had never known such scarcity.[53]

Soon after Buell arrived in Huntsville, reported Lieutenant Colonel Darr:

> all the trains were immediately organized for the purpose of foraging, and the country in northern Alabama as far south as the Tennessee River was scoured for forage and subsistence, and everything that could be gathered without absolutely starving the women and children was taken. . . . The

> county north of the Memphis and Charleston Railroad was also visited thoroughly by our forage trains. The result . . . was . . . a small quantity of old corn, left by the rebels, and only gathered in a few bushels at a time from different plantations. Subsistence of no account was brought or could be found, except a few almost worthless cattle and sheep, and these not enough to justify hunting for them.[54]

The testimony of the Buell investigation, highlighted by the report of Lieutenant Colonel Darr, which is detailed and comprehensive, demonstrates that Middle Tennessee was in no condition to provide much, if any, more support for the Federal Army than northern Alabama.[55] The overall evidence is convincing that Buell's army could not have lived off the country, nor been supplied by river. For his campaign to succeed, the railroad supply line was absolutely essential. As Buell himself well summarized the matter: "My wagon transportation was not sufficient to cover breaks in the railroads north of Huntsville and to advance beyond Bridgeport at the same time."[56]

By mid-August, after the Louisville and Nashville tunnel was blocked, the number of wagons available no longer mattered. The Rebel cavalry had destroyed Buell's rail supply line for the foreseeable future. Colonel J. B. Fry testified that "the [rail] road was destroyed almost as fast as it was repaired."[57] There was no way to build up stores for supporting an advance.

Critics of the campaign's failure have blamed General Buell—an easy, inviting target—particularly since he proved, more than once in his career, that he was not an aggressive general. The Chattanooga campaign, so goes the argument, could have succeeded *if* it had been assigned to a determined commander; to a general willing to take all the supplies that the country afforded for his army, regardless of how many innocent people suffered; to a leader who would have moved rapidly to establish a bridgehead on the Tennessee River near Chattanooga before he attempted to build up a large accumulation of supplies; to a man whose quick movement eastward would have been complemented by a simultaneous Union advance from Corinth against the Rebels at Tupelo, holding them in place and preventing any reinforcements being sent to Chattanooga.[58]

Lightning movements and smashing blows against the enemy sound good, but they contradict the reality of the situation. General Halleck, like Buell never known for being aggressive, was not going to press the Rebels at Tupelo. Clearly this should have been initiated, if the Chattanooga move was to have any chance of success. Even if Halleck or someone else had done so, however, this would not have helped to sustain the Federal army in the field when northern Alabama was depleted of supplies. The latter is an all-important point, strongly established by the Buell Commission, which makes inconsequential the issue, relative to supplies afforded by the countryside, of Buell's waging a "soft" or "hard" war.

The country between Bridgeport and Chattanooga could not have fed his army, either, so a move on Chattanooga by Buell was stymied, even if Bragg had not been marching into Middle Tennessee. General Alexander McD. McCook put the matter bluntly during the Buell investigation: "One thing I will say: it was absolutely necessary to abandon that country [northern Alabama], whether the enemy came into Middle Tennessee or Kentucky."[59]

If Buell had been willing initially to set aside caution—especially concern for a supply line—he probably could have occupied Chattanooga within a few days, soon after he started his eastward trek. To have stayed in the little railroad town at the northern base of Lookout Mountain would have been a different game altogether. He could not have fed and supplied his men by rail or river, for the same reasons that his attempt to advance across northern Alabama was rendered impossible. The situation in Chattanooga would have been even worse, since still longer rail lines would have been involved. There was no other possibility of a supply line.

If Buell had engaged in a brutal occupation policy to wrest food from the citizens, there would have been enough for a limited stay only. Ultimately his army would have been dependent upon the ability of a rescuing force to open up a defensible railroad line before his army starved—not a very likely event. To express the matter in terms taken from World War Two, such a move by Buell really would have been going "a bridge too far"—in this instance, a number of bridges too far.

Besides, the Confederates might have come up and besieged him, as they did William S. Rosecrans's army in fall 1863. At this earlier stage of the war, however, they likely would have had more strength to make a siege work, while the Federals did not control the railroads to the degree they did in 1863, to help break a siege. Furthermore, at this stage of the war, no top Union commander, not even a Sherman or a Sheridan, could have been expected to enact such harsh occupation measures. The totality of the conflict had not "progressed" to such a degree of intensity.

☆☆☆

The obvious question confronting Buell was where in Tennessee to concentrate his force, in the face of the enemy advance from Chattanooga. His answer to this question would lead to a lot of second-guessing when the campaign was over. Already Buell had started William Nelson's division toward Kentucky. "Your mission is to meet and repel the threatened invasion of Kentucky," he said.[60] Two reinforcing divisions were coming from Grant, who had replaced Halleck when that officer went to Washington as general-in-chief. Now Buell ordered these two divisions to change direction and "move by forced marches" to Nashville.[61] Possibly these orders said something not only about Buell's acute supply problem, which he hoped could be better handled in Nashville, but also about what, ultimately, he feared and foresaw for his entire army.

General George H. Thomas advocated McMinnville as the best point of concentration. He had been in the area from Dechard to McMinnville for a few days and was then at McMinnville. "By all means concentrate here," advised Thomas.[62] Buell did not agree, saying the Federals must either concentrate farther to the east and take

Union General George H. Thomas.
Courtesy, Tennessee State Library and Archives.

the offensive, or fall back to Murfreesboro. Deciding on a forward move, he ordered Thomas to make a forced march to Altamont, about twenty-five miles south and east of McMinnville, high in the Cumberland Mountains.[63]

From the perspective of the Union high command, the proper disposition of forces would be determined by three things: Confederate intentions, location and quality of roads (including railroads), and supplies for the army. Many Federal officers, when they heard that Bragg had crossed the Tennessee at Chattanooga, thought the Rebel objective was Nashville, but obviously another course was possible for the Confederates. If Buell had not pulled back from northern Alabama at once, Bragg might have attacked him there, via the Sequatchie Valley. Once Buell retreated into Middle Tennessee, Bragg might try to move around one of his flanks with Nashville as the ultimate goal; or possibly he might strike out for Kentucky.

The Bluegrass State had to be considered seriously. Since spring, Confederate newspapers had been talking of taking Kentucky. Typical was the *Southern Confederacy*, a paper widely quoted in Union print, of which many Federal officers would have been aware. Claiming that Kentucky was rising, the *Southern Confederacy* in late May had stated: "It needs only for our army to march into that country [the Lexington environs] to have three fourths of the men at once flock to the standard of Southern Rights and Independence. . . . We hope our government will soon find some means of marching an army into that State. . . . A more serious blow could not be struck at Lincolndom."[64] Already Edmund Kirby Smith's force was well into Kentucky. Very possibly Bragg might be moving to join him, thus outflanking the Federals in Middle Tennessee and hoping to establish the Confederacy's northern boundary at the Ohio River.

To understand the Federals' problem in deciding where to concentrate to counter the Confederate options, a grasp of the nature of the terrain and the roads is imperative. Between the two forces were the Cumberland Mountains, a barrier running generally northeast to southwest, and rising about two thousand feet. There were sev-

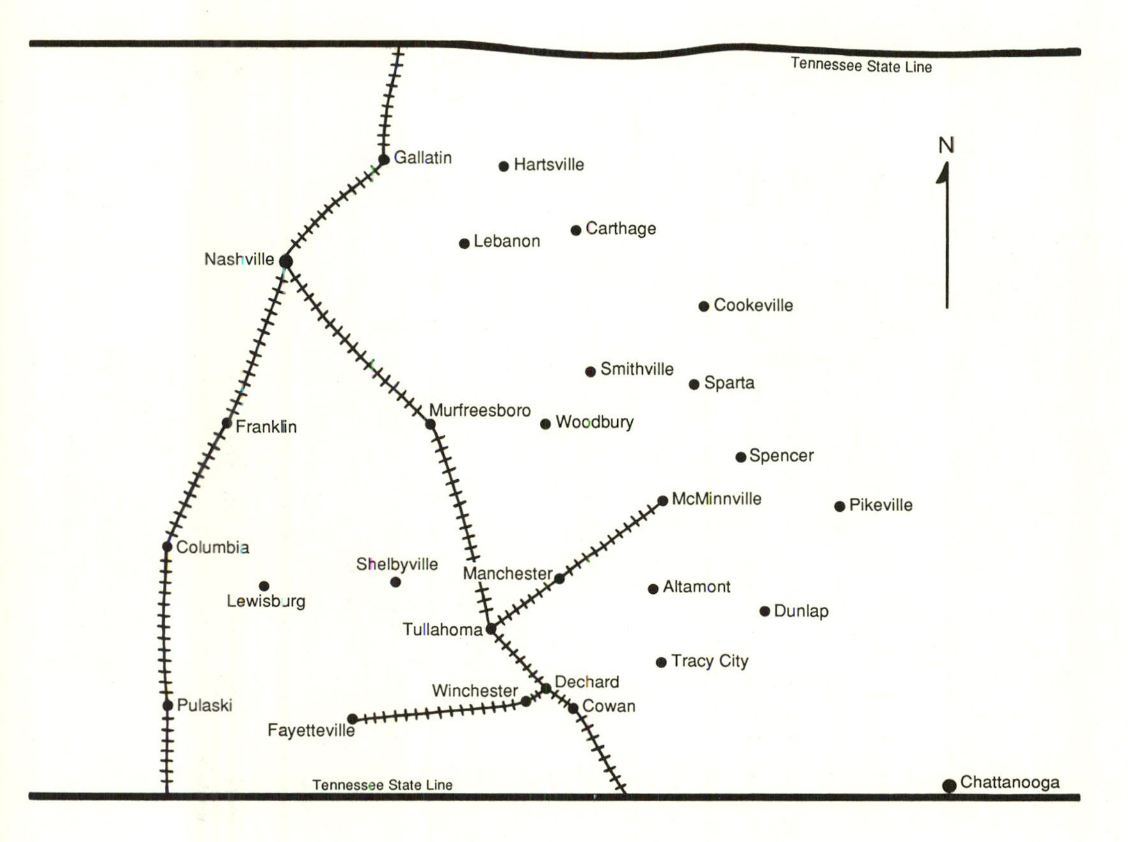

Tennessee east and south of Nashville.
Map prepared by Sharon McDonough.

eral routes by which Bragg's Confederates could leave the Sequatchie Valley and cross the mountains. To the south, the Rebels might march to Stevenson, Alabama, and across the mountains to Dechard, Tennessee. They also could cross the mountains through Pelham and move down toward Manchester. Another possibility was a road, south of Dunlap in the Sequatchie Valley, that crossed the mountains to Altamont, from which point *four roads* led down into the Middle Tennessee plains (hence Buell's desire to hold Altamont). There also was a road directly from Dunlap to McMinnville. Still another option would be to march northeast from Dunlap to Pikeville, turn west across the mountains to Spencer, where a choice could be made either to move on McMinnville or to turn north to Sparta. Once at Sparta, the Rebels might round the spur of a mountain and advance on Murfreesboro and Nashville, or head north toward Kentucky.[65]

General Thomas's advice to concentrate at McMinnville—if the issue were simply McMinnville or Altamont—was the better option. Altamont, even though it controlled several roads down the western side of the mountains, was a dangerous position. Buell would have difficulty gaining intelligence concerning Bragg's movements, both because of the rugged mountain barrier and because the people favored his enemy, especially when he had virtually no cavalry force available. Bragg might be able to slip around him and cut off his line of retreat to Nashville. An even more immediate and serious problem, as Thomas had warned Buell (and as Generals McCook, Wood, and Thomas all testified later at the Buell Commission) was that neither forage nor water was sufficient at Altamont.[66] General Wood, for instance, said, "It would have been exceedingly difficult, if not impossible, to maintain a considerable force at Altamont for any length of time or even a few days." Water, he stated, was "exceedingly scarce."[67] McCook asserted that it "was absolutely impossible" to maintain part of the army at Altamont. "I know of no place on the top of the Cumberland Mountains where a division of 10,000 men could have lived a week," he claimed.[68]

While the Federals searched for water and other necessities at Altamont, the *Nashville Daily Union* was carrying news of reported fighting in the vicinity. "This city was full of rumors yesterday," read the paper on August 28, "about a battle . . . between Bragg's forces and General McCook's division, near Altamont. It is said that Bragg was repulsed with great slaughter. If the report is not correct now, it will be, for Buell's forces will thrash the rebels whenever they get a chance at them."[69] There was, of course, no fighting at Altamont.

The most damning evidence against the position at Altamont is that General Thomas pulled out and went back to McMinnville without orders.[70] Besides his own supply problems, the danger of being flanked, and the difficulties in getting guns onto the mountains, Thomas believed that the scarcity of water and forage "and the extreme difficulty of passing over the road," which was in awful condition, would force Bragg to move his army by some other route.[71]

If Buell had concentrated at McMinnville, as Thomas wanted, he would have possessed a railroad southwest to Tullahoma, where there was a junction with the Nashville and Chattanooga line. But he would not have had to depend only on the vulnerable railroad for moving troops and supplies. A reasonably good and direct road ran from McMinnville back to Woodbury, Murfreesboro, and Nashville. For lateral movements, there was a good road from McMinnville to Manchester, as well as an adequate road in the other direction to Sparta. These roads would enable the Federals to move quickly on interior lines.

Because McMinnville offered a central location and adequate roads, General Thomas believed that a concentration there, regardless of which flank the Rebels moved on, would enable the Federals to bushwhack them. From this contention Thomas never wavered. At the time, in a letter to Buell's chief-of-staff, Colonel James B. Fry, Thomas said: "I would suggest to General Buell that a trip to this place [McMinnville] might assist him very much in maturing his plans of operations."[72] Later, at the Buell Commission, Thomas contended, unequivocally, that Bragg should have been fought north of McMinnville at Sparta. Buell's decision, however, was to fall back closer to Nashville at Murfreesboro.

Thomas argued that, when Buell took the army back to Murfreesboro, a better move would have been to go to Sparta. From there the Federals probably could have blocked the advance into Kentucky or at least forced Bragg to select a longer, less desirable route farther to the east. If, on the other hand, Bragg had changed direction toward McMinnville, Thomas thought, he could have been cut off "because the road is better" from Sparta to McMinnville than the one the Rebels would have been using from Spencer to McMinnville. Thomas contended, too, that the army could have supplied itself long enough in Sparta to fight Bragg's army.[73]

Thomas appeared to be on solid ground in arguing for the McMinnville concentration when Buell fell back from northern Alabama. Certainly the Buell Commission thought so, concluding that Buell could have stopped Bragg "by an early concentration of his army at Sparta, McMinnville, or Murfreesboro, with a view to active operations against Bragg the moment he debouched from the Sequatchie Valley."[74] Buell, for his part, finally decided that not even Murfreesboro was satisfactory. By the end of August, he had determined to retreat to Nashville. Writing to Governor Andrew Johnson on August 30, Buell described the critical situation as he saw it, said he was preparing to fall back to Nashville, and that to delay any longer "would be criminal."[75] Ironically, only the day before, the *Nashville Daily Union* had reported that the Rebels had crossed the Tennessee River and that battle was imminent. Assuming a different stance than that taken when Buell was in northern Alabama, the paper expressed great faith in the general: "It is certain they have no force comparable to Buell's in discipline and efficiency, and we feel confident he will scatter them to the winds."[76]

A very different opinion of Buell was held by a Union soldier at Nashville named James King, as he wrote to a woman called Jenny. Amusingly registering a passing distaste for what he termed the

"Southern ladies' habit of using tobacco and snuff to excess," this impassioned Federal then turned to the main subject, saying the "rebellion must be put down if every northern man is called into the field." Stating that Lincoln should have called for a million soldiers rather than seventy-five thousand, King accused General Buell of "lying before Chattanooga in a state of inactivity" while a large enemy force was allowed to invade. "I believe Jenny if the truth was only known General Buell is a rebel at heart and has done all in his power to aid the rebel cause. His very acts show him to be one."[77] Certainly other Union soldiers were thinking much the same way as King. The fact was that General Buell never had been a favorite of the men in the ranks. The half rations, hard marching, and tough work had been bad enough. But now the retreat to Nashville, they thought, was humiliating.

The retreat to Nashville meant that the Union was allowing the enemy to exercise the initiative and assume the offensive. This is *not* to say that Buell should not have protected Nashville. Quite the contrary. Nashville was being developed as the primary supply, command, communication, and political center, for Federal operations in Tennessee, Alabama, and ultimately Georgia. Fortifications were being developed all about the city. But, as Bragg's Confederates approached Middle Tennessee from Chattanooga, it was not necessary to be in Nashville in order to defend the city.

If Buell had taken up a position at McMinnville or Sparta—preferably McMinnville—he could have engaged Bragg, regardless of whether the Rebel objective was Nashville or Kentucky. Obviously Buell could not read the mind of the enemy commander. Thus he should have placed his army in a position to stop Bragg in Middle Tennessee, whatever Bragg's objective might be. By retreating to Nashville, Buell virtually invited Bragg to move into Kentucky and to dominate the Federal supply line from Louisville. In failing to contest the route into Kentucky, Buell also placed Nashville in a precarious position, dependent as the Federals were on the railroad from Louisville. Even if Buell thought that Kentucky could defend itself, that did not justify surrendering the initiative to the enemy. Furthermore, nobody at that time knew what might result once the Confederates were in Kentucky, relative to the issue of Kentucky's rising to join the Rebels. The place to defend both central Kentucky and Nashville was somewhere to the east of Tennessee's capital city.

Apparently Buell's greatest single concern had been whether he could supply his army east of Nashville. Thomas testified that, when he urged Buell to concentrate and fight at Sparta, the commander's reply was that "we had not subsistence enough at Murfreesboro to enable us to do so."[78] Thomas admitted that he "did not know the state of supplies," but he was of the opinion that they were sufficient and, when pressed to succinctly give his view, stated: "According to my judgment there was not a sufficient reason for falling back from Murfreesboro to Nashville."[79]

What, then, were the facts about the supply situation? The Buell Commission's investigation indicated that the army had twenty days' rations, which, on half rations, meant enough for forty days.[80] A wild card in all this—which almost certainly weighed heavily on Buell's mind—was how well his supplies and transportation routes could be protected from Confederate cavalry, both regular and irregular. Given his recent experience while in Alabama, this was an obvious concern. Writing from Dechard, Tennessee, to Governor Andrew Johnson at Nashville on August 30, Buell said: "So constant has been the interruption of our communications that it has been with the greatest difficulty the troops could be sustained at all." Now, he added, he was operating "virtually in an enemy's country surrounded with an immense force of irregular cavalry." Furthermore, Buell was estimating Rebel forces under Bragg at "not . . . less than 50,000" and probably "much greater," thus crediting Bragg with far more troops than he actually had.[81] Clearly Buell, fifty or sixty miles east of Nashville, felt he was out on the proverbial limb which easily might be whacked off the tree. Even thirty miles out, at Murfreesboro, the risk was too great, he concluded, and determined to fall back to Nashville.

Admittedly, it was a tough decision. Whatever Buell might have done was fraught with risk—as subsequent events clearly proved about what he did do. One may sympathize with his problems in northern Alabama and the failure to take Chattanooga. Understandable, to say the least, was his belief in "soft" campaigning relative to civilians—dubbed the "Rosewater policy" by critics but more accurately described as a conciliatory policy—across northern Alabama. (After all, the Buell Commission concluded that Buell deserved "neither blame nor applause" for the policy, because it was "at that time understood to be the policy of the Government."[82])

Buell's failure to fight in Middle Tennessee is the most troubling and questionable of his decisions. Worrying about the army's supplies, the rails, and the roads, and believing that the enemy had superior forces, Buell was convinced that he had good reasons for retiring to Nashville. The nagging problem is that Buell never, before or after this decision, showed aggressiveness as a commander. Clearly there was risk in confronting Bragg east of Nashville, but perhaps there was even more risk in not doing so. Bragg should never have been permitted to move into Kentucky without being contested.[83]

The Confederates, then, would advance into the Bluegrass State on two fronts: Braxton Bragg moved into the eastern edge of Middle Tennessee, then north across the Cumberland River, and toward Glasgow, Kentucky; while Kirby Smith, having marched into Kentucky about one hundred miles east of Glasgow, already was well into the state. The trek across barren, mountainous, hostile country had not been easy for Kirby Smith's army.

When Kirby Smith reached Barboursville, Kentucky, he reported to Bragg, on August 20, that "the roads between here and East Tennessee [were] much worse than I had supposed." He also said that the country had been "almost completely drained of all kinds of supplies."[84] Writing to his wife, Kirby Smith gave further evidence of the trials of the march. "The country is desperately union and bushwhackers have commenced operations against our detachments." He found "the people bitterly and violently opposed to us" and said that "almost a herculean effort" had been required "in crossing the mountains." Barboursville he did find to be, "or was before the war," a pretty village of about three hundred people at the foot of the mountains in a beautiful valley.[85]

The soldiers who left records were certainly in agreement with Kirby Smith about the difficulties of the country and the hostile environment—although, unlike Kirby Smith, not all found Barboursville to have any redeeming qualities. Major Paul F. Hammond, sarcastically calling it "the metropolis of this mountain region," characterized it as "a dilapidated village." Reflecting on the problems of moving wagons and artillery over the mountains, Hammond wrote that "the men fastened long ropes to the guns and caissons, and twenty or thirty pulling together, dragged them slowly but steadily over the worst places."[86] Alfred Fielder recorded in his diary that, before reaching Barboursville, which he described as "a strong Union hole," the army had climbed "the steepest mountain I ever traveled over."[87] William Lowrey of the Twentieth Alabama, recording that the march was "the first time my foot ever trod on Kentucky soil," wrote that the route to Barboursville was over a road that was "very rough." As to Barboursville, Lowrey said: "I find this village and vicinity to be greatly Union or Lincoln."[88]

Captain Hugh Black, Sixth Regiment of Florida Volunteers, in a letter to his wife Mary Ann, in Leon County, Florida, conveyed a strong optimism as he wrote that "the Federal soldiers are retreating out of [Kentucky] and we will soon have full possession of it," but he too reflected the hardships of the march. The route from Knoxville to Clinton was "the dirtiest road I ever saw, it was just like marching through a solid bed of ashes and the heat was very great and the road was crowded with a solid mass of soldiers for miles." As to Barboursville, Captain Black recorded in his diary that, after "pretty scarce" rations during the trek over the mountains, "upon our arrival at Barboursville we were informed that we could get nothing to eat [there] but green corn and beef and not much of that, but our forces had succeeded in capturing a large amount of coffee and sugar which added a great deal to our comfort." (Black also wrote that, at Williamsburg, "we got whiskey and everything that we could wish to make us comfortable and consequently we had a considerable jolification.")[89]

Leaving Barboursville, the Confederates found the advance, in some ways, even harder. Major Hammond said, "Hitherto the country was well watered. But from Barboursville to Rockcastle River there is no stream but the muddy creek just mentioned." From Rockcastle River to the foot of Big Hill, he wrote, "lies a barren, desolate region, destitute of water for men or animals. The troops suffered much from this privation" and were "exhausted by their long and rapid march."[90] William Lowrey, commenting on events after Barboursville, recorded in his diary: "The bushwhackers fire into our line. We halt, throw out the right and left companies and after skirmishing a while, take 3 of the scoundrels and march them on toward London."[91]

Undoubtedly the scarcity of water made the advance very difficult for Kirby Smith's army. Captain Frank T. Ryan later recalled an incident revealing both the hardships and the hostility of citizens along the route: "On the second day's tramp after leaving Barboursville, . . . it must have been 9 P.M., and we were still trudging along, footsore, weary and hungry, when I espied a strong, masculine-looking woman standing in the doorway of a little one-room cabin that stood several yards from the road." Ryan recorded that he bowed to the woman and, "raising my greasy wool hat, said: 'Madam, will you be so kind as to inform me how far ahead will it be before we find a stream of water?' Seeing my garb and judging . . . that we were the Southern army, she, doubtless the wife of one of those bushwhackers who had given us no little trouble ever since we reached the mountainous region," replied, according to Ryan, "with a scornful, contemptuous look," answering in "a snappish, petulant manner, 'I guess you will find it in the Ohio River.'"[92]

As Kirby Smith said, the country was "aroused," the people "all against us." His expedition, he told his wife, was "something like Cortez. I have burnt my ships . . . and have thrown myself boldly into the enemies country." The enemy was "like the Egyptians of old," he thought, and God "has hardened their hearts and blinded their eyes only to make their destruction the more complete."[93] He was proud of the march—"one of the most remarkable of the age"—that his troops had accomplished "through a mountain country destitute of supplies, with almost impassable roads and mountain passes," where "creeks, springs, and wells were dry," and the men "ragged, famished, barefooted."[94] Kirby Smith was also convinced that support would come, once his army was in the Bluegrass.[95]

On the morning of August 29, lead elements of the Confederate army cleared Big Hill and began moving northward into the Bluegrass region. But a few miles ahead, near the small town of Richmond, a Union force lay across Kirby Smith's line of march.

Chapter 5

A General Stampede to the Rear

☆☆☆

The Kentucky River would have been the best place for the Federals to stop Kirby Smith. Its banks were high, steep, and rugged. At the point where the Lexington-Richmond road crossed the river, the formidable granite bluffs, rising from the water literally at a ninety-degree angle, stretched both east and west for a great distance. Major General Horatio G. Wright, commanding the Union forces from his Department of the Ohio headquarters in Cincinnati, clearly recognized the inherent strength of such a position—especially when defending with troops most of whom were raw recruits. He instructed Major General William "Bull" Nelson, whose headquarters were in Lexington and who exercised field command in that general region, not to engage the Rebels south of the Kentucky River "unless you are sure of success." Rather, Nelson was advised to make the river the line of defense.[1]

Wright was not the only general who understood the potential Federal advantage at the Kentucky River. The Rebel commander appreciated the situation, too. Probably Kirby Smith recognized it as much or more than the Union general, and he feared that the Yankees would retreat to the river.[2] If they did, his invasion, to state it bluntly, would likely come to naught, for Kirby Smith would have no desirable options. His path into the heart of the rich Bluegrass, where he could find supplies and hoped to find recruits for his army, would effectively be blocked. To force a crossing of such a formidable barrier would cost Kirby Smith's small Confederate army too many casualties—assuming the effort could succeed at all, which would be highly doubtful. Probably even inexperienced Federal defenders could bring his advance to a halt at the Kentucky River.

To turn back meant both the failure of the invasion and an arduous trek retreating through the barren and hostile country—"a mountainous wilderness, destitute alike of food and water," Kirby Smith said[3]—still fresh in his memory. Major Paul Hammond, commenting on that region, said, "We . . . met not one man who sympathized with the Confederate cause."[4] To join Braxton Bragg, far to the southwest, would mean, at the least, allowing that general to assume overall direction of the campaign, not to mention the problems of supplying his army as he moved to join Bragg. If the Union defended at the Kentucky River, Kirby Smith would face a most unpleasant situation.

Unfortunately for the Federals, General Wright's orders to make a stand at the river were not carried out. Apparently neither of the Union generals who were in a position to determine the matter, "Bull" Nelson and his subordinate, Brigadier General Mahlon D. Manson, was as impressed with the defensive advantages of the Kentucky River as General Wright. There is no evidence in the official records, or anywhere that the author has found, that Wright's instructions to Nelson, dated August 24, about falling back to the Kentucky River were passed on to Manson, who commanded the Federal troops south of the river at the little town of Richmond. Both the context and the tone of Nelson's report and correspondence, as well as Manson's report, strongly suggest that Nelson never told Manson to fall back to the river.[5]

A native Kentuckian, Nelson was a loud, brassy, highly profane man who was six feet, five inches tall and weighed three hundred

Kentucky River between Lexington and Richmond. Photograph by Peggy Nims.

pounds. He had been a naval officer and now served as a major general of volunteers.[6] Disdainful of the feelings, opinions, and wisdom of others, he made enemies easily, almost as if he relished having them. What Nelson did immediately after the ensuing debacle at Richmond was to charge Manson with having "attacked the enemy contrary to my instructions" and "marching 5 miles to do so." The motive of Manson's actions, Nelson caustically concluded, he would "leave [Manson] to explain" to General Wright.[7] His attitude toward Manson was totally unforgiving—probably all the more so because he himself wished to escape blame for his own poor performance, both in communicating with Manson and in managing his inexperienced forces. The Rebel advance seems really to have taken Nelson by surprise.

The "instructions" that Nelson charged Manson with violating were, in Nelson's own words, "not to fight . . . , but to retreat by way of the Lancaster road." Clearly Nelson had not been planning to make a stand at the bluffs of the Kentucky River, as Wright had advised. Lancaster was a number of miles to the south of the river and southwest of Manson's forces at Richmond. Nelson's intention was to concentrate all available forces in the Danville-Lancaster region, south of the Kentucky River. "I had ordered General [Ebenezer] Dumont to proceed from Lebanon to Danville," wrote Nelson. "Also, Colonel Charles Anderson, with a brigade of three infantry regiments," continued Nelson, was "to proceed in the same direction." Nelson said his plan was "to mass the troops, knowing that the enemy would not cross the Kentucky River while 16,000 men were on their flank."[8]

Possibly this would have been an effective strategy if effected in time, but not at the late hour when Nelson acted. In fact, Nelson, by his own admission in his report, took action only when, at 2:30 on the morning of August 30, the day of the battle, he received, "much to my surprise," a dispatch from General Manson "stating that the enemy was in force in his front and that he anticipated an engagement."[9] (General Manson, not knowing where to locate Nelson, who had left on an inspection tour without informing his subordinate of his intentions or whereabouts, had sent messages both to Lancaster and Lexington.) Nelson reported that he, upon receipt of the dispatch, "immediately sent couriers" with orders for Manson "not to fight" but to "retreat by way of the Lancaster road."[10]

The result, predictably, was that Manson did not receive the order from Nelson until he had been battling the Rebels for several hours, and he could not then disengage. The time when he received Nelson's order, said Manson, was about 12:30.[11]

Nearly sixteen years later, in an article in the *Louisville Courier-Journal*, Manson stated unequivocally that he never received an order before the battle at Richmond, either to fall back or to avoid an engagement. Manson also said he confronted Nelson after the battle, upon learning of the general's charge that Manson had violated his orders, and that Nelson then admitted "he was mistaken about my having received the order in time to retreat."[12]

Of course Nelson at that time was no longer alive to dispute Manson's account, if it were not true, but Manson's story makes sense, and it is consistent with the extant sources. Nelson appears to have been rather cavalier in his management of the troops under his command, probably not expecting the Confederate challenge to materialize as quickly as it did, and thus he likely attempted to place the blame for the ensuing defeat solely upon the shoulders of his subordinate. Clearly, Brigadier Mahlon Manson did not disregard the order of his superior officer and does not deserve all the blame for the Federal defeat, as significant responsibility must rest with Nelson. Nevertheless, Manson also made a considerable contribution toward the Rebel victory at Richmond.

Manson himself had no thought—or if he did, it soon passed—of making a stand at the Kentucky River; and this in spite of his inexperienced soldiers. When Manson assumed command on August 27, he observed at once how green his troops were, saying that the soldiers "which I found at Richmond . . . had been in the service from ten to twenty-five days. Some of the regiments never had a battalion drill and knew not what a line of battle was."[13] Manson's evaluation was echoed by the leader of the Yankee Second Brigade, Charles Cruft, who wrote, "It was a sad spectacle to a soldier to look at these raw levies and contemplate their fate in a trial at arms with experienced troops."[14] Manson himself added that the soldiers "were undisciplined, inexperienced, and had never been taught in the manual of arms."[15]

Having observed this situation, Manson at once proceeded to launch into the Rebels. Kirby Smith was greatly relieved when he learned that the Yankees evidently were preparing to stand and fight;[16] in fact, he rushed to close with the Federals, perhaps fearful that they would have a change of mind and retreat. But with General Mahlon Manson commanding the Union forces, he need not have worried, for Manson was, if anything, more anxious to engage than was Kirby Smith. As soon as he learned that the Rebels were approaching, he hurried to meet them, explaining that "all the hills one and one-half miles south of me completely commanded my camp" and that "I did not think it my duty to allow the enemy to obtain possession of them without a struggle."[17] Years later, Manson said that if he had retreated and if the enemy force had proved inconsequential, he would have been considered a coward, "dismissed in disgrace."[18]

The problem was that Manson had no idea what he faced. He simply did not know the strength of the Confederate force moving toward him, probably thinking it smaller, perhaps much smaller, than it actually was. Probably, too, Manson was powerless to resist the chance for military glory that now, like some gorgeous temptress, seemed to be wantonly beckoning him. Throwing caution aside, he rushed to the fray.

Even though all of Kirby Smith's troops could not be united, the southern force was strong enough for the encounter. While an infantry division under the command of Brigadier General Henry Heth was cooling its heels far to the rear at Barboursville, near the Tennessee line, awaiting reinforcements and the army's supply train, Kirby Smith still had two infantry divisions at hand, a total number of about six thousand men.[19] The lead division, commanded by Brigadier General Patrick Cleburne, had already crossed the mountain range then known as Big Hill, while the trailing division, under Brigadier General Thomas Churchill, was coming over the range and within supporting distance.[20] In front of the infantry divisions was a cavalry brigade, about 850 strong,[21] commanded by Colonel John S. Scott, which, a few days earlier, had driven off a small detachment of Federals atop Big Hill.

Major Paul Hammond, passing over Big Hill, pertinently observed, "Here was first fully appreciated the importance of Scott's victory. . . . Numerous positions offered, in which a regiment of soldiers, with a few pieces of artillery, could have [posed] a very serious obstacle to our advance. . . . That the enemy had not seized and fortified these positions afforded General Smith great satisfaction, . . . as it furnished conclusive evidence that our movements were unknown or misinterpreted."[22] In a letter to his wife written on the night of August 29, Kirby Smith said, "We have completely taken the enemy by surprise. . . . If resistance had been made we never

Confederate General Patrick R. Cleburne.
Courtesy, Carter House Museum, Franklin, Tennessee.

could have forced the passes of the Kentucky Mountains."[23] Many soldiers remarked about the magnificent view from Big Hill as they looked northward from some vantage point to see the beautiful Bluegrass region stretching for miles before them, as far as the eye could see. There was not much time for sightseeing, however, as Kirby Smith now was hurrying to close with the enemy, despite the fact that his troops were worn by their long, rapid, and arduous march on insufficient food.[24]

Of this Kirby Smith was well aware. His men, he said on August 29, were "ragged, barefooted, almost starved, marching day and night, exhausted from want of water. I have never seen such suffering."[25] But these were veteran troops, accustomed to hardship. A total force of nearly seven thousand, many were veterans of Shiloh, while intelligence indicated that the Federal troops were mostly raw levies, against whom the Confederates could expect to have a decided advantage. Here, above all, was an opportunity to fight them south of the Kentucky River. Kirby Smith's troops could eat and rest later; now was the time to march and fight!

Even for hardened veterans, the rapid march, especially the struggle over Big Hill, was terribly demanding. One soldier, Frank T. Ryan, later said that the crossing of Big Hill "was eighteen well-measured miles," that "some of the men did not have water to last them longer than midway," and that the day's march was the most fatiguing he remembered in all his three years as a soldier. And then, when the exhausted Ryan was at last asleep on the north side of the mountain, he suddenly was aroused in the middle of the night by the terrifying cry that the horses were stampeding. Ryan said he climbed a tree, as confusion and disorder reigned for some time until the horses were secured.[26]

The Confederates undoubtedly were exhausted and in need of rest, but Kirby Smith, considering the situation as he understood it, was making the right move—a hard decision—in marching to engage the Federals south of Richmond. And in Pat Cleburne, who was commanding his lead division, Kirby Smith had an Irishman who frequently has been praised by historians and buffs alike as the best division commander produced by the Confederates in the Western Theater of the war.

Patrick Ronayne Cleburne was thirty-four years old, six feet tall, slim but broad-shouldered, with gray-blue eyes and a heavy shock of dark brown hair. He had been born on St. Patrick's Day in Ovens Township, County Cork, Ireland. The family's fortunes had deteriorated after the death of his father, Dr. Joseph Cleburne. Young Patrick, while still in his mid-teens, had been selected by his family to become a doctor like his father. However, he failed the entrance examination at the Dublin Medical School. Pat Cleburne, a sensitive young person, felt he had embarrassed the family and ran away to join the British army. By 1849, he had advanced to the rank of corporal and was assured that he had a promising future in the military. But Cleburne's family, seeking a better life, that same year decided to move to the United States of America. Patrick purchased his army discharge and joined in their "great adventure."[27]

Settling at Helena, Arkansas, Cleburne rose rapidly in the esteem of his new countrymen, working first as a druggist and then becoming an attorney active in politics. Energetic, tough, and intelligent, he made his presence felt. When the war came, his military experience served him well. Cleburne exhibited a steady, determined drive for excellence, first as a brigade commander and later as a division commander. The distinctive blue flags that came to mark Cleburne's command were to be respected and feared by the enemy. His splendid record was to become an integral part of the history of most of the major western battles until he fell, late in the war, in John B. Hood's ill-advised assault against John M. Schofield's forces at the Battle of Franklin.[28]

But Federal General Mahlon Manson, in late August 1862, probably knew nothing of either Pat Cleburne or the strength of the Rebels who were approaching him. Maybe his actions would not have been changed, had he known. He sought a fight, and that is what he soon found.

Mahlon Dickerson Manson was from Ohio, who at forty-two

years old had taught school, studied medicine, and served as an officer in the Mexican War, afterward becoming involved in state politics while working as a druggist in Crawfordsville, Indiana. Having fought in the Civil War as a colonel at Rich Mountain and Mill Springs, he was promoted to brigadier general of volunteers in March 1862.[29] Thus far in the war, he had known only victory. Now, for the first time, he was in command as the enemy came on.

☆☆☆

Some of Manson's Federal troops had found the advance to Richmond about as tough as the Confederates had. Writing to his sister Mary, on August 27, Samuel Reid of the Sixty-Sixth Indiana said, "We marched from Lexington here in one day, 26 miles. Very many of our boys gave out. . . . As we marched along, our boys pressed every darkey they could find and made them carry their knapsacks." Reid also found that food was scarce. "We have been almost starved for five or six days, the boys stealing almost everything they ate," he said. "I was so weak that I could scarcely walk, and . . . I took my revolver and one of the boys, and went to a house out in the country, determined to have my dinner if I had to kill the man of the house. Luckily for him, he was not at home. . . ." Reid found the yard "full of young darkeys, mostly naked," and asked "an old negro woman, dressed in a night gown—that is, part of her was—if I could have some dinner." Her reply, wrote Reid, was "Yes, Honey, you can have something to eat as long as their is any food on this plantation." The young soldier thought "it was a dinner sure," that seemed to be "the best of any I ever ate." Then he added, "We have plenty to eat now and will hereafter, I hope." For Reid that dinner, prepared by the black woman, truly might have been the best he ever ate. Two days before his sister Mary received his letter, she had been notified of her brother's death at the Battle of Richmond.[30]

Some of the Federals were under age to be soldiering. Henry H. Aye was a sixteen-year-old who went into camp at Terre Haute with

Company G, Seventy-First Indiana, on July 19, and, after less than a month of drill, "took a birth in a cattle car for Indianapolis." By the end of August, he was with the regiment at Richmond, Kentucky, where he said that, on August 29, "we were paid a $25.00 bonus while in line."[31] The regiment was about to more than earn that bonus the next day.

Despite their lack of experience, many of the Federals were quite confident, even cocky. Frank Ryan later recorded that some of the citizens of Richmond said that, on August 29, "the Federals had passed through the town with colors flying, bands playing, and spirits high and gay, saying that they were going only a short distance . . . merely to drive the Rebels out, when they were coming back and going to their homes to attend to their crops until needed for a similar errand."[32] Certainly this was the time-honored manner in which Americans had conceived of fighting a war, and Mahlon Manson may well have been right in saying later that, if he had retreated, he would have been considered a coward.

On the evening of August 29, however, Manson was giving no thought to retreating. He wanted to secure the high ground about a mile and a half south of his camp and close with the enemy. Manson was right in thinking that, if he were going to fight, he must not allow the Rebels to take the high ground from which they could open an artillery fire upon his camp. Receiving a mid-afternoon report that his cavalry and infantry pickets to the south were retreating, with the Confederates pressing them hard, Manson ordered his entire brigade forward.[33]

Occupying the high ground south of Richmond, Manson's force quickly stopped the outnumbered advance elements of Scott's Rebel cavalry, "capturing some prisoners, horses, and one cannon."[34] As the enemy fell back, Manson advanced farther, to the hamlet of Rogersville.[35] There he had the men bivouac, with orders to sleep on their arms. He also sent Colonel Leonidas Metcalfe's cavalry forward to pursue the enemy.[36]

When the Rebel cavalry under Scott got back to Cleburne's division, Scott informed Cleburne, according to Cleburne's report, that his cavalry "was encamped in the road in my front; that our whole front was well picketed; that the enemy were not advancing."[37] But Cleburne said he was uneasy, thinking about the "unknown force of the enemy in our front," and decided to take precautions. He formed a line of battle facing northward, told the officers of regiments that at the first alarm they should immediately bring their regiments to their prescribed position, and then dismissed them. Also, he stationed and retained a company of sharpshooters and a battery on the line, to hold position on each side of the road.[38]

These precautions proved to be wise. Soon, "firing and yelling was heard to our front," reported Cleburne, "and almost simultaneously a multitude of stragglers, consisting of part of Colonel Scott's cavalry brigade, sick men, baggage wagons, servants leading horses, came flying in . . . , closely pursued by . . . Metcalfe's command of . . . cavalry, who were firing . . . and yelling as though they were all excited with liquor."[39]

From the perspective of Colonel Benjamin J. Hill, the officer of the Thirty-Fifth Tennessee, who commanded Cleburne's Second Brigade, "the notorious Metcalfe came thundering down the road, crying 'Charge, and shoot down the rebels.'"[40] Metcalfe's Federals, on a very dark night,[41] had no idea that they were riding into a prepared line of battle. When the Confederates opened fire, the Union cavalry charge was instantly brought to a halt. Amazingly, only a handful of Federals were killed. Many more were wounded, some of them severely; thirty men were captured, as well as a number of horses. Also, one hundred stand of arms, the prized breech-loading Sharps carbines, were taken, while the Federal survivors, with "curses and threats," according to Cleburne, soon beat what Hill called "a pell-mell retreat."[42]

Thus ended the fighting on August 29, a mere prelude to what would come on the morrow. Kirby Smith ordered Cleburne to advance to the attack at daylight. In his report, Kirby Smith observed, "Although Churchill's division did not get up until late in the afternoon, and then in apparently an exhausted state, I determined to march to Richmond the next day, even at the cost of a battle with the whole force of the enemy." Cleburne said, "My men slept in line of battle without any supper, and at daylight again advanced in search of the enemy."[43]

☆☆☆

The Federals too were moving early on the morning of August 30, a day that would become, in the words of Major Hammond, "warm, clear and beautiful," a day on which "no brighter sun ever scattered the mists of early day."[44] At 4 A.M., Manson had his troops up, making coffee, filling canteens, and preparing for action. Convinced that the Confederates were advancing, at 6 o'clock Manson sent word to Richmond for Brigadier General Charles Cruft to come up with his brigade "as quickly as possible,"[45] then ordered his troops forward, taking the advance himself with the Fifty-Fifth Indiana regiment, moving south seeking the enemy.

Altogether, including Cruft's brigade and Metcalfe's cavalry, Manson had a total force of about 6,500.[46] Driving back the Rebel advance patrols that were met half a mile south of Rogersville, Manson pushed on a little farther and then formed a line of battle across the turnpike near the ten-year-old Mount Zion Church,[47] located on the west side of the road, which yet stands as the most impressive landmark from the battle's onset, and today serves as a Christian (Disciples of Christ) church. The Federal position was about five and a half miles south of the cemetery located on the southern outskirts of Richmond.

Manson placed the bulk of his forces on the east (left) side of the pike, where the ground seemed to be a little higher than on the west, and where part of the area was wooded. The Fifty-Fifth Indiana was immediately east of the pike, behind a fence. Artillery was stationed on high ground east of the Fifty-Fifth, with the Sixteenth Indiana coming up to extend the ragged line to the east in the woods. Three hundred yards to the rear was the Seventy-First Indiana, positioned to support the battery and act as a reserve. Only the Sixty-Ninth Indiana was sent to the west side of the road.[48]

Mt. Zion Christan Church. Photograph by Peggy Nims.

Apparently Manson placed the weight of his troops east of the pike because he considered that area the more defensible terrain. But in so doing, he began, probably unintentionally, a general movement of both Yanks and Rebs to the east, as each sought to protect his eastern flank, thinking the other was moving to turn it. Thus, for each side, the first movements eastward were essentially defensive, not offensive.

Across the way, in the Rebel lines, General Cleburne had decided to go forward for a better view of the Federal position. Seeing immediately that the Yankee strength was east of the pike, he made his dispositions accordingly, stationing the weight of his troops in that direction. Benjamin Hill's brigade went into position first, "in line behind the crest of a low hill which ran parallel to and about 500 yards from the enemy's line,"[49] with Preston Smith's brigade coming up in reserve and forming behind the crest of a hill to the rear. Noting a barn located on a hill to the west side of the pike, Cleburne ordered Hill to detail sharpshooters to that point "for the purpose of picking off the horses and gunners from the enemy's battery."[50] A company from the Second Tennessee, under command of Captain J. J. Newsom, got the call. Also at Cleburne's direction, Hill sent "a similar detail" from the Fifteenth Arkansas to "a skirt of woods" on the Confederate right flank in order to determine "the extreme left of the enemy's line."[51]

Soon Cleburne had a hot skirmish fire going with the Federals, as well as two batteries of artillery blasting the enemy lines. "At this juncture," Cleburne reported that he received an order from Kirby Smith, "directing me to avoid a general battle until General Churchill's division could get up. I now directed the artillery to fire very slowly and not waste a round."[52] Cleburne said the battle continued in this manner, "a mere fight of artillery and skirmishers," for over two hours. Evidently the Yankees either were firing more rapidly than the Rebels, or they did not have as much ammunition, because, as Cruft's Federal brigade advanced to reinforce Manson, Cruft reported that "we met the artillery wagons driving back to Richmond for ammunition, the supply in the boxes having been already exhausted."[53] Perhaps Cleburne's ability and experience already were having an impact.

On the Confederate side of the line, as the artillery fight progressed, the Forty-Eighth Tennessee regiment of Hill's brigade was in the immediate rear of Captain James Douglas's battery, that was firing at the Yankees near the turnpike. A member of the Forty-Eighth, Robert M. Frierson, later wrote that "one after another" of the Confederate gunners "was being carried to the rear disabled and torn by shot and shell until their captain called for volunteers from our regiment to supply their places. Just then a young man from a farm near by came upon the field and asked to be assigned to duty. Colonel Ben Hill . . . sent him forward to the battery." In only a short time, Frierson said, the volunteer was wounded, a ball imbedded in his shoulder, "but the gallant boy would not leave the field until ordered to the rear by Colonel [G. H.] Nixon," commander of the Forty-Eighth.[54] Unfortunately for the Confederates, they were not to see many volunteers like that young man during the Kentucky campaign.

Meanwhile, as Cleburne formed his line to the east, the Federal Manson was convinced the Confederates were trying to outflank him.

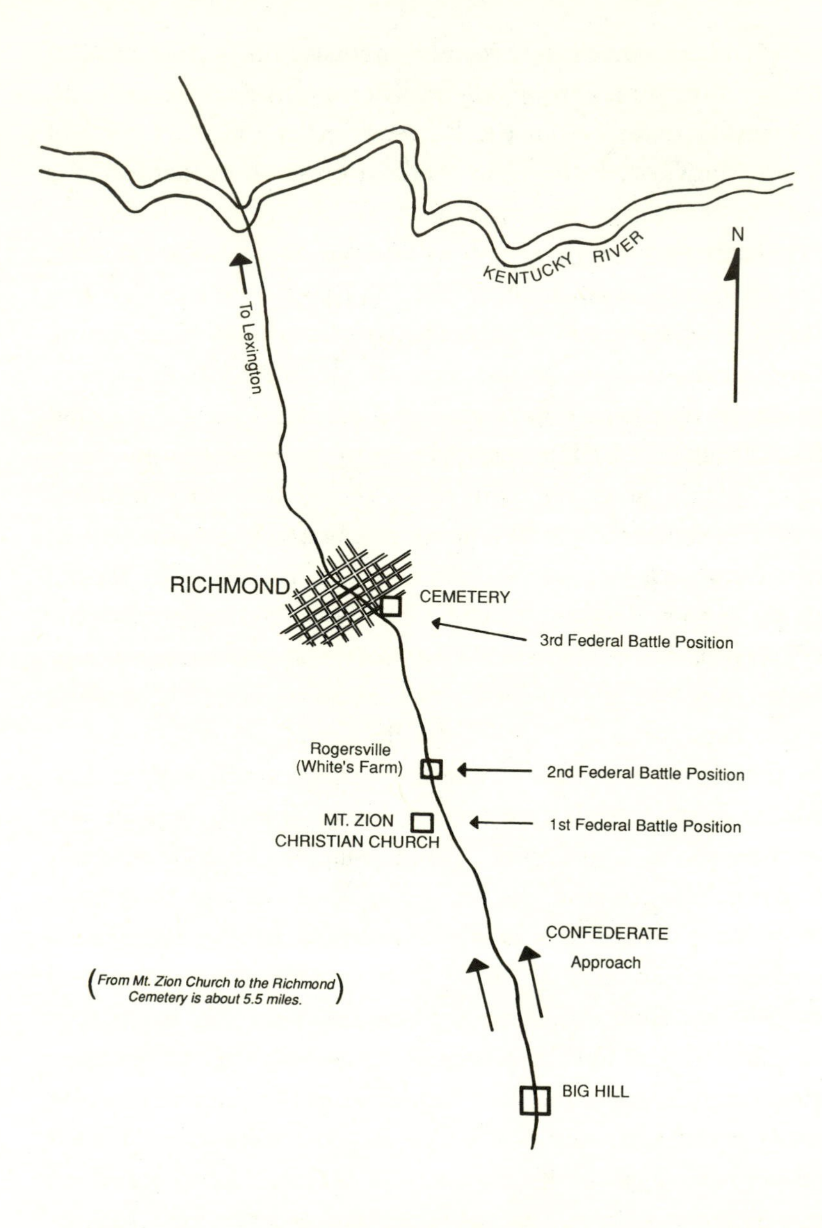

Richmond battle area.
Map prepared by Sharon McDonough.

"The rebels," he reported, "seemed determined to turn my left flank." The Union commander responded by ordering his reserve regiment, the Seventy-First Indiana, to move forward and support the left flank; then, apparently concluding that even more manpower was required, he directed seven companies of the Sixty-Ninth Indiana to move from the right to the left, thus leaving, for the moment, only three companies west of the turnpike.[55]

Cleburne's response to the Union's extension and strengthening of its line to the east was immediate. He too would marshal more manpower on that flank. Cleburne reported that "when the enemy commenced moving toward my right flank, driving back my skirmishers . . . , I ordered a regiment of Smith's brigade (the One hundred and fifty-fourth Tennessee) to be sent forward, and placed it in line on the right. . . . A close fire soon commenced on the right, and became so heavy I found it necessary to sustain the right with further re-enforcement." This time Cleburne shifted two regiments, the Thirteenth Arkansas and the Fifteenth Arkansas of Hill's brigade, under Colonel Lucius E. Polk, to support the Tennesseans on the eastern flank. Cleburne was rapidly becoming convinced that the Federals, in Cleburne's words, "had staked everything on driving back or turning our right flank and that they had weakened their center to effect this object."[56]

The fighting on the eastern flank was costly for the Rebels and soon took the life, among others, of Colonel Edward Fitzgerald, commanding the One Hundred and Fifty-Fourth Tennessee. Nevertheless, a general of Cleburne's caliber had to be pleased with the way the tactical situation was developing. He knew that, by then, Churchill's brigade must be within supporting distance, coming up in an ideal position to crush the weak Federal right and perhaps cut the enemy's line of retreat to Richmond. Thus Cleburne concluded that the time was ripe to make his own move. Sending the three remaining regiments of Preston Smith's brigade to his right flank, he thought the Rebels could overlap the Yankee left. At the same moment when Smith would open fire, Cleburne would send Hill's brigade against the Federal center.[57]

Galloping to the right, the Irishman watched for a few moments, satisfying himself that Smith's brigade was rapidly taking up the proper position. Then he started back to give his attention to Hill's brigade, poised to make its advance at the sound of Smith's guns.[58]

Everything seemed in order, but Cleburne was not to see it through. Hailed by Colonel Lucius Polk, who had been wounded, and was, according to a Rebel soldier, "as wild as a march hare from a wound in the top of his head,"[59] Cleburne paused to speak. Suddenly a bullet struck Cleburne, and in the words of his aide Captain Irving Buck, entered his "left cheek, carrying away [several] teeth on that side, and emerging through his mouth, which, fortunately, happened to be open in speaking to Polk." The bloody, painful wound temporarily deprived the general of speech, and he was forced to relinquish his command, directing Preston Smith to assume command of the division.[60]

The Rebel attack hardly could have been set up better. Kirby Smith, who arrived on the battlefield about 8 A.M., had instructed Churchill to hold one of his brigades in reserve while, with the other, he was to advance by a circuitous route to the left, hoping to take the Federal right flank by surprise.[61]

This was a good move. From behind the Federal lines east of the pike, where General Manson was located, he could not possibly have seen the Rebel column approaching his right flank. Very likely, from where he stood, Manson would not have been aware that the landscape was cut by a ravine beyond his right flank. There is no evidence that he took any reconnaissance measures in that direction. The few Federal troops on the right of the pike could not see the Rebels coming through the ravine either.[62]

Churchill picked Colonel T. H. McCray's brigade of Arkansas and Texas troops for the flanking march ordered by Kirby Smith and, "by proceeding cautiously through a corn field and a ravine," was coming up on the Federal right, west of the pike, when the attack formulated by Cleburne was launched by Smith.[63] From that point, for the Federals, everything rapidly went to pieces.

The evidence available about the Federal conduct of the battle, admittedly meager when compared to that concerning some Civil War engagements, nevertheless strongly suggests that the green Federal troops and officers were experiencing problems for some time before the coordinated Confederate attack was launched.[64]

There is, for example, no report in the official records from the Seventy-First Indiana regiment, which, stationed in reserve east of the pike was ordered forward by Manson to support the Federal left flank. General Manson simply reported that "Major [William] Conklin, of the Seventy-first Indiana, was killed while thus moving to the support of [the left flank] and bravely cheering on his men, and . . . very shortly afterward, Lieutenant Colonel [Melville] Topping fell from his horse, mortally wounded, while encouraging the men of his command."[65]

There was a soldier in the Seventy-First, however, by the name of Oliver Haskell, who kept a diary giving more details about the actions of the regiment, as well as presenting a very different perspective and tone from that of Manson. Haskell noted that the enemy's "shells were bursting among us killing and wounding several. Occasionally a cannon ball would strike the ground just in front of us and bound over us. Here M. B. Shurly was killed by a piece of shell striking him in the forehead while raising his head looking over the hill. He was," observed Haskell, "a very wicked young man."

Certainly the most interesting part of Haskell's account of the morning fighting concerns the regiment's movement to support the Federal left flank. "After lying [in rear of the artillery] 2 hours," he wrote,

> we were ordered to rise and march to the support of those engaged on the left, but our colonel, mistaking the order, commanded us to march to the right on double quick, which we did, over the road and through an old corn field; then the order was countermanded and we marched back through the field where we had been lying and . . . we met the enemies fire and here we met the 55th, 16th, and 69th [regiments] retreating in double quick. Here we was ordered to retreat which we did, not in very good order, companies separating and getting along as fast as possible. We retreated under the gall-

ing fire of the enemy for 2 miles, our men being wounded and giving out continually. I fired my piece once during this retreat.[66]

As the Seventy-First Indiana began to fall back, sixteen-year-old Henry H. Aye was wounded and taken prisoner. He said "the rebels drawed their guns to shoot me dead when a rebel major stopped them and helped me to a shade tree and left me. In about one hour I was hauled to Mt. Zion Church. . . . The church was full of the wounded and quite a number out of doors."[67]

More evidence of the blundering and disorder among the Federals comes from reports about the actions of the Ninety-Fifth Ohio, the lead regiment in General Cruft's brigade marching from Richmond to the support of Manson. The Ninety-Fifth had marched rapidly, part of the way on double-quick time, for about seven miles from its camp site at Richmond, arriving shortly after Manson had transferred all but three companies of the Sixty-Ninth Indiana from his right flank to his left. Thus Manson directed Cruft immediately to position the Ninety-Fifth Ohio on the right flank, reinforcing the three Indiana companies still there. Colonel William L. McMillen, commanding the Ninety-Fifth, reported that the regiment was then ordered to charge a Rebel battery some four hundred yards to the front.[68]

With that part of the regiment at hand, no time having been allowed for the regiment to close up ranks, the Ninety-Fifth charged the battery with bayonets. "Whilst we were thus engaged," said McMillen,

the enemy advanced his right and left wings, outflanking and driving our forces before him. Seeing that it would be reckless and useless to continue our assault upon the battery, I ordered the regiment to halt and fall back, which they did, for a time, in good order, losing, however, in addition to our killed and wounded, one hundred and sixty men and a large number of officers captured at this point.[69]

McMillen's report makes this action seem more orderly than it was. The regiment's Lieutenant Colonel J. B. Armstrong obviously was rankled by McMillen's account, later offering a "supplement" to McMillen's report. The supplement, twice as long as McMillen's report, did not appear in the official records but was published in Frank Moore's *Rebellion Records*. Among a number of caustic, biting comments, Armstrong, who states that he took command after McMillen had left the field, reported that he heard no order "to halt and fall back"; he charged that, according to those who were near McMillen, what the colonel really ordered was for "every man to save himself." Armstrong also puts the number of men in the Ninety-Fifth who were captured at this time at two hundred, considerably higher than McMillen's number.[70]

There is no doubt that the Yankee situation was desperate. The remainder of Cruft's brigade arrived just as the troops of Manson were in full retreat and, in Manson's own words, "the rout had become general."[71] The Union Eighteenth Kentucky, next up after the Ninety-Fifth Ohio, deployed and tried, alone, to check the advance of the Rebels but, after a few minutes, had to give way with severe losses. This regiment was credited by General Cruft with having "prevented the retreat at this time from becoming a rout."[72] The men and officers of most of the regiments, Cruft acknowledged, "fled in confusion to the rear through the fields." The panic, he added, "was well nigh universal. This was 10:30 A.M. At this juncture the whole thing was fast becoming shameful."[73]

Two of Cruft's regiments did not arrive in time to get involved in the battle at the Mount Zion Church and were able to fall back in good order. These were the Twelfth Indiana and the Sixty-Sixth Indiana, which General Manson then used in an attempt to rally the rest of his command about a mile in the rear of his first position. Almost at once, however, Manson changed his mind, retreating still farther—perhaps three-quarters of a mile more—until at last rallying on approximately the same ground where he had first engaged the Confederates during the skirmish of the previous evening.

Manson deployed Cruft to the right, ordering him to take the elevated ground in that direction, with two of his regiments positioned in a woods to the extreme right, while the two others formed on their left, behind a fence that fronted a field of corn. Skirmishers were deployed into the woods and the corn field. His own brigade Manson positioned to the left of the pike, behind fences, with artillery stationed both right and left.[74]

On came the Confederates, as the distraught Federals rushed to complete their deployment. The Rebels, now brimming with confidence, steadily advanced, hoping to finish the battle. Kirby Smith stayed with the plan that already had worked so well. Again he ordered Churchill to move against the Federals' right flank. At the same time, Preston Smith worked against the enemy's left. The result seemed to confirm the old adage that one should not change a winning strategy.

This time, the fiercest fighting developed on the west side of the pike, the Union right under Cruft. McCray's Confederate brigade of Churchill's division was still in the lead. When the Rebels were within about four hundred yards of the Yankee position, McCray reported, the Federals opened fire with a full battery of six pieces, rapidly followed with volleys of musketry, a fire which Churchill said was "most terrific."[75] Nevertheless, the Grayclads pressed on until they reached a fence and a ditch, about two hundred yards from the Union line, where, "finding the air literally filled with bomb-shells and Minie balls," said McCray, "I ordered the troops to lie down under cover."[76]

The Rebels remained in this position for some time—McCray said twenty minutes—while the Yankees kept firing, "the most incessant firing of cannon and musketry I have ever heard," reported McCray. The Confederates did not fire back, except for an Arkansas battery to the rear under command of Captain John T. Humphreys.[77]

Perhaps the Federals concluded that the momentum of the battle was turning. They were emboldened to charge, and the outcome was a gory disaster. As the Yankees advanced, the veteran southerners were instructed to lie still and not fire a gun until so ordered. The Federals had closed to within fifty yards when the Rebels were ordered to "rise and fire!" The cracking report of the Confederate rifled-muskets sounded up and down the line; the charging Bluecoats saw the countless little clouds of smoke appearing from scores of weapons, and a storm of bullets tore through their ranks. "The effect was terrific," reported Colonel McCray. "The advancing columns of the enemy faltered and staggered from one end of his lines to the other." Rapidly reloading and mounting the fence, the Grayclads charged, and the Federals, shocked and reeling from the effect of the terrible volley, immediately began to fall back.[78]

Some northerners fought valiantly, contesting the enemy's onrush as best they could, firing from behind trees, haystacks, corn pens, fences, depressions in the ground—whatever offered a little protection—but at last giving way and making for the rear as rapidly as possible. Both Federal generals claimed that the other's brigade had broken first. General Cruft reported that, when his brigade "broke and fled down the road," the whole of the "First Brigade had gone previously, without having opened fire during the engagement." Manson's account was quite different, asserting that, when Cruft's Second Brigade had "retreated in confusion," he was "then forced to order the left wing to fall back, . . . the enemy crowding close upon them."[79]

Regardless of which brigade retreated first, the second Federal position had been broken. The moment had to be charged with emotion for the Confederates. The Rebel commander was overcome with excitement. Rushing to the front, Edmund Kirby Smith wanted to lead the pursuit personally. His chief of staff, Colonel John Pegram, had to stop him and convince him not to risk his life needlessly.[80]

☆ ☆ ☆

The Union troops now fell back to the southern outskirts of Richmond, where they were rallied once more, this time at the city cemetery. "Bull" Nelson was on hand, having ridden some fifty miles from Lexington by way of Lancaster, using a relay of horses. Some of the soldiers cheered him, and the shouts were heard across the way in the Rebel lines.[81]

Union General William "Bull" Nelson.
Courtesy, Kentucky Historical Society.

Not all Federals were impressed, however. Oliver Haskell wrote that "General Nelson . . . lied to us . . . telling that we had 12,000 reinforcements just behind us which would be up to our assistance, when the truth was there was no reinforcements within our reach."[82] And no doubt some who had cheered Nelson soon regretted that action. At Shiloh, the blustery, swaggering general had drawn his sword, ridden straight into a crowd of stragglers, and, according to a witness, shouted, "Damn your souls, if you won't fight, get out of the way, and let men come here who will!"[83] Now, at Richmond, the general, cursing, shouting and berating the men as cowards, rode among the troops trying to rally the panic-stricken, knocking some down with his fist, using the flat of his sword to strike others, reportedly striking some of them over the head.[84] "General Nelson, in a raging temper," according to one historian, " . . . attempted to restore order by beating his soldiers over the head with the flat sides of his sword."[85]

With the help of Generals Manson and Cruft, Nelson succeeded in rallying about twenty-five hundred Federals on the crest of a low-lying ridge, the line passing through the cemetery. There the Yankees sheltered themselves behind a stone fence and the tombstones, preparing to make one last stand.[86] The position of the Union line in the cemetery seems appropriately ironical and gruesome—symbolic of the Yankees' fate on that hot summer day.

Again, for the third time, the Grayclads would strike the Federal flanks. Kirby Smith advanced Churchill on the left and Preston Smith on the right. There was one difference this time. Anticipating a wholesale Union retreat, the Rebel commander first sent Scott's cavalry galloping for the Yankee rear, in order to cut off their route of escape. After a short interval, allowing his infantry to catch their breaths while the cavalry rode around the Federals, Kirby Smith ordered the infantry forward once more.[87]

The time was about five o'clock in the afternoon, as the Confederates, many nearly exhausted, stalked toward the enemy line. The sun was lower in the west, and eerie shadows, cast by trees, head-

Cemetery at Richmond, Kentucky. Photograph by Peggy Nims.

stones of the cemetery, and gaunt men, were lengthening across the landscape, while gunsmoke once more polluted the air. The Confederates took a number of casualties. In fact, Major Hammond said, "the loss on both sides was greater than at any former period of the day."[88]

Years later one southerner remembered the struggle in these words: "We quickly formed our lines and moved on the cemetery, and in twenty minutes one hundred and forty men of the Second [Tennessee] and one hundred and twenty-eight of the Forty-eighth [Tennessee] were killed and wounded. They bore the brunt of the battle."[89]

Particularly this soldier, Robert Frierson, recalled the colonel of his regiment, the Forty-Eighth Tennessee: "In ascending the hill to the cemetery a [bullet] struck Colonel [G. H.] Nixon in the left breast, smashing his watch and striking a copy of the Testament in his breast pocket, which saved his life; our old commander, a veteran from Mexico, staggered a few paces backward, plunged forward on his hands, but struggling to his knees, loud above the din of battle, shouted: 'Forward, Forty-eighth!' Over into the cemetery we went."[90]

The disciplined, relentless Confederate troops, though worn they certainly were, could not be stopped. General Nelson, desperately attempting to inspire the Yankees to fight, lumbered about, displaying his huge bulk, and shouting to his men: "Boys, if they can't hit something as big as I am, they can't hit anything!" Within seconds, Nelson was struck in the thigh and forced from the field of battle. Some accounts say he was struck twice. The pressure of the Gray line was too much for the Federals. Nelson said they "stood about three rounds, when struck by a panic, they fled in disorder." Perhaps Nelson does not give the Union troops enough credit, but the fight clearly was not a long one. This time, when the Blue line broke, there was no hope of rallying the troops again.[91]

General Cruft penned a vivid report of the melee:

> The attack . . . was stoutly resisted for a few moments, when the whole line broke in wild confusion and a general stampede ensued. Both officers and men became reckless of all restraint or command, and rushed pell-mell to the rear, amidst a mingled mass of horses, wagons, artillery, etc., in an utter rout. . . . Officers, or men wearing shoulder straps, deliberately refused to render any assistance or respond to any order.[92]

The Union army was now more like a panic-stricken mob, streaming back through Richmond and then rushing north on the road for Lexington. The Confederate cavalry, of course, was in position to trap them. Colonel Scott had the majority of his forces posted on the Lexington road, while one company was stationed on the Lancaster road and the remainder between the two roads. On the Lexington road, where the great mass of Yankees rushed northward, Scott placed a battery to sweep the pike, and concealed his troopers on both sides of it. It was about six o'clock when the fugitives came hurrying along the road, trying to make their escape, only to become easy prey for the Rebel cavalry.[93]

Byron Smith, a member of the First Georgia Cavalry, Company J, gave the following account of what he witnessed:

> The road was full of fleeing Yankee cavalry and one piece of artillery. . . . One of the boys on the extreme left of the company shot the lead horse through the neck, and that blockaded the road so there was no more passing there. The driver of the lead horse was killed, mashed to death by the other horses. A brigade of infantry tried to escape, but when they reached the ambush they threw down their arms and surrendered.

Although Smith's story was penned half a century after the battle, it seems quite consistent with accounts written much earlier.[94] Major Hammond said the "havoc was frightful, and the Federals . . . threw down their arms and surrendered in crowds, and of the few who escaped not one in ten carried his musket with him."[95]

One of the strangest claims associated with the battle—and under the circumstances perhaps it is believable—was that of a Confederate Captain in the First Georgia Cavalry, who said that he "captured" an entire Union regiment single-handedly. When John Scott was sent to cut off the Federal retreat, the captain, whose company was acting as an advance guard, became separated from his comrades and was captured by a regiment of retreating Federals. Knowing that the Yankees were proceeding into an ambush, and fearing that he himself would be shot, the Rebel captain earnestly sought to persuade the Federal colonel commanding the regiment that he was rushing straight into a trap. Apparently convinced by the captain's pleading, the colonel asked him what to do, and the reply was: "Surrender." "Surrender to whom?" the colonel wanted to know. "To me," was the captain's answer. "I will carry you out safe." The Union colonel handed over his sword, a white handkerchief was tied to the point of it, and the Confederate captain led the Federals over to Colonel Scott, reportedly remarking: "Colonel Scott, if I haven't captured a whole regiment of Yankees, there is no devil!"[96]

Among the Federals trying to escape was General Manson, who reported:

> the enemy killed and crippled a large number of horses . . . , which entirely blocked . . . the road. It being now about 7 o'clock in the evening, . . . I at-

> tempted to make my escape, accompanied by . . . several other officers. We rode through the enemy's lines and proceeded in a westerly direction for half a mile, when we came upon a squadron of the enemy's cavalry, who commanded us to halt, and at the same time fired upon us. My horse was killed and fell upon me, injuring me severely . . . , and a short time afterward I was . . . made a prisoner.

General Nelson also was captured, but with the onset of darkness, the number of Confederates being inadequate for guarding so many prisoners, Nelson, despite his wound, managed to sneak away, conceal himself in a cornfield, and make his escape.[97]

Nelson's escape illustrates the problem, expressed by Colonel Scott, which the victorious cavalry faced: "Owing to the smallness of my force (about 850), I was unable to still guard the roads and remove all the prisoners to the rear, and consequently a large number escaped, wandering through the corn fields and woodlands, it being now too dark to distinguish them when a few paces distant."[98]

The Battle of Richmond was over—over except for the suffering of the wounded, the burying of the dead, and the sorrow of relatives and friends back home who in the days ahead would learn of the loss of loved ones. The Battle of Richmond would never be well known. Even today, when the word "Richmond" is used, most people immediately think of Virginia. Yet no less an authority than Shelby Foote has described the battle at Richmond, Kentucky, as the episode nearest to a Cannae—the great Carthaginian victory of the Punic Wars, at which Hannibal enveloped both Roman flanks, interdicted the line of retreat, and virtually destroyed the Roman army—"ever scored by any general, North or South, in the course of the whole war."[99] While the Richmond battle never could compare in numbers engaged with Cannae, the tactics and the one-sidedness of the clash indeed are reminiscent of that event.

Confederate casualties were relatively light. Of the 6,850 troops engaged, only 451 became casualties, with 78 of those killed. Of the

6,500 Federal troops engaged, 206 were killed, 844 wounded, and 4,303 were captured or missing—most of them captured—for a total casualty figure of 5,353. In other words, only slightly more than a thousand of the Federal troops escaped unscathed.[100]

The Union wagon trains and artillery also were lost, and many of the Confederates welcomed the food and supplies which fell into their hands. Captain Ryan later wrote that the Yankees "had a great quantity of stores and munitions of war . . . , and here I first saw how they were being fed—canned fruits of all kinds, condensed milk (the first I ever saw), cheese, and other edibles. They also had large quantities of clothing, shoes, hats, etc., all of which we put to good use." Ryan said the supper that he sat down to eat on the night after the battle "would grace any gentleman's table."[101]

Undoubtedly most of the Rebels felt a sense of relief on the night of August 30, when the fighting at last had ended and they could rest, eat, and feel secure as they reflected on the day's triumph. But the fact that, even when all seems to be well, life is uncertain, was demonstrated again that very evening. Captain Sterling Faulks of the One Hundred and Fifty-Fourth Tennessee, who had come through the battle without a scratch, was ordered to take his company out on picket duty. A. J. Vaughan, commander of the Thirteenth Tennessee, in an 1892 letter to Mr. French Tipton of Richmond, recorded the tragedy that followed. He said that Captain Faulks, "having assembled his men . . . started off at their head, but finding a gate through which he wished to pass hard to open, he ordered one of his men to prise it open with his musket; in doing so the gun was discharged and he was instantly killed. It made an impression never to be forgotten." Vaughan also said that "it was one of the saddest events that came under my observation during the war."[102]

The night of August 30 undoubtedly was a somber experience for many a person, soldier or civilian, Federal or Confederate, who witnessed the scenes at Richmond. All the churches were being used as hospitals, as were school buildings, the Court House, and some private homes. In some ways, the most horrible events were the amputations of arms and legs of the wounded, a very common occurrence, of course, in the Civil War, when medical practice still was primitive in its ability to assist with many wounds.

The day after the battle was a Sunday, which the Confederates spent in burying the dead, treating the wounded, gathering up the captured supplies, and preparing to move farther north. About forty Union soldiers, for example, were buried in a mass grave near the Mount Zion Church. (In 1868, they were reinterred in Camp Nelson National Cemetery.)[103] The Sixth Florida's Captain Black said that "the ground was strewn with the dead and dying soldiers—some were being buried, others were dieing, others with their legs and arms being cut off. Their sufferings were great . . . , in every hospital that could be established, there was piles of arms and legs as high as the tables."[104]

Within a few days, most of the Confederate army would be gone; but the legacy of the battle, for the citizens of the town and the surrounding countryside, was far from over. Farmers would load their wagons with food and bring in huge supplies of eggs, flour, meat, meal, cream and butter, which were distributed among the various hospitals. Some brought supplies for both sides; a few only for the Federals or the Confederates. A girl, about eight years old, later recalled that her grandfather would not give anything to the Rebels, but they did not suffer, she said, "for there were many sympathizers with the South."[105]

This little girl, Lucia Burnam, also wrote that she was sometimes allowed to go with her mother to see the sick and wounded soldiers. "I saw a man, his face . . . almost covered with whiskers, yellow as gold," she said. "I was told he had the jaundice and would not get well. The next time I was there, I saw a big bundle of what seemed to be quilts, lying on the porch floor and was told that it was a dead man. . . . It seems to me now, that it was an amazing thing that a little child should have been taken to such a place and witness such scenes, but my mother, who was going to show her sympathy, probably felt that I was safer with her than at home." Lucia added that "at all events, I was inured to scenes of danger and death, and soldiers meant no more to me than my playmates."[106]

The ordeal of sixteen-year-old Henry Aye of the Seventy-First Indiana, who had been wounded, taken prisoner, and nearly killed by his captors before being hauled to the Mount Zion Church, continued to unfold. An elderly man by the name of James Shearer, who lived nearby, taking pity upon the helpless youth, offered to take Aye home with him. "I was only too glad to accept his hospitality," said Aye, and rode in the cart that Shearer had been using to haul dead men to the church for burial. However, the lad did not meet with a kind reception from Shearer's wife, who "was almost helpless and did not think they were able to care for a wounded boy." Nevertheless, Henry Aye stayed with the Shearers, finally gaining enough strength to walk on crutches and, weeks later, was taken back home to Indiana. He had been reported missing, and his father was so overcome with grief that he had collapsed and been sick for several days. But in October, there was great rejoicing when the young man at last got home. His leg required two operations and continued to give him trouble intermittently through the years. But Aye had survived the Battle of Richmond, was discharged from the service in early 1863, and lived until 1919.[107]

The Rebels under Kirby Smith, meanwhile, were pressing on to Lexington, elated by their triumph. A makeshift force of inexperienced Federals gathered on the bluffs of the Kentucky River, then reconsidered when the Confederates approached and rapidly scattered. "When we left Richmond," said one Confederate, "we believed fully that we were invincible."[108] Entering Lexington, the southerners were received by many as if they were royalty. "When we got to Lexington the people seemed mad with joy," said Jemison Mims of the Forty-Third Alabama. The ladies, he remembered, "would almost take us in their arms, . . . the ladies not only cheered us from windows, doors and side walks, but they would run into the streets up the ranks as we marched along and seize us by the hand and welcome us. Oh, it was a glorious time, and," concluded Mims, "we forgot our blistered feet, our diet, and mean clothing, for I assure you the ladies at Lexington did not regard them."[109]

Hugh Black judged the Lexington reception as in the same vein as the one in Richmond. Ladies "old and young, rich and poor," had visited the army camps at Richmond, bringing with them "everything they could spare, and inviting the soldiers to visit them at home," while at Lexington "we were received amidst loud and continued applause, waiving of handkerchiefs, throwing up of hats, hurrahs for rebel soldiers and the Confederacy." He also noted that the people of Lexington brought food for the soldiers and in large quantities.[110] According to Captain Frank Ryan, "The day our army entered Lexington, with General Kirby Smith riding at the head of the column, was truly a glorious [one] . . . , as the ladies actually sprinkled flowers for General Smith to ride over." The ladies also gave the general a flag that he flew at his headquarters for the rest of the conflict.[111]

Kentucky fever seemed to be running unchecked in many Rebel circles. Writing to his parents in Natchez, Mississippi, from a camp near Knoxville on September 26, Otis Baker said that a young man from Paducah, Kentucky, earlier had predicted that when the Confederate "armies entered his state they would be met by forty thousand men desirous of taking up arms for the furtherance of our great cause." Admitting that he then thought such a forecast "very extravagant language," Baker affirmed that now he had changed his mind, and upon "hearing that General Smith was in need of thirty thousand stand of arms for his recruits alone," Baker said he was "inclined to think there will be even more who will welcome us with open arms and . . . enlist in our armies."[112]

Certainly Kirby Smith seemed to be caught up in the enthusiasm of the hour. To Army headquarters in Richmond, Virginia, Kirby Smith wrote from Lexington on September 6: "It would be impossible for me to exaggerate the enthusiasm of the people here on the entry of our troops. They evidently regard us as their deliverers from oppression and have continued in every way to prove to us that the heart of Kentucky is with the South in this struggle. They are rapidly rallying to our flag."[113] About the same time, Colonel John Pegram, Kirby Smith's chief of staff, was writing General John McCown in East Tennessee that "Kentucky is rising *en masse*. . . . If the arms were here we could arm 20,000 men in a few days."[114]

The day after the Battle of Richmond, Kirby Smith had written to his wife, "The destruction of the enemy of 10,000 is complete." From Lexington on September 4, he said, "I am well and have the most enthusiastic reception in Kentucky—the whole population is turning out in mass. . . . Recruits are flocking to me by thousands." Two days later, again from Lexington, he told his wife: "The Kentuckians are rising and will make one bold effort for independence and freedom. Our advance is threatening Cincinnati and Louisville." He claimed that "all of Kentucky to the Ohio is at our feet."[115]

Indeed, there was near-panic in Cincinnati and Louisville, as well as in smaller communities near the Ohio, as strenuous measures were taken to prepare for the expected Confederate onslaught. Rumors of Union disaster swept through Cincinnati. The truth was bad enough: Nelson's force defeated at Richmond with casualties exceeding five thousand; Federal troops retreating from Lexington toward Louisville rather than Cincinnati; and Cincinnati left virtually without defenders. But rumors magnified the Rebel forces under Kirby Smith until their number was alleged to be four, five or six times the actual figure. Rumor held that Confederates would attack Cincinnati in less than a week. Word was spreading that the city would be burned to the ground.[116]

To deal with the perceived crisis, Major General Horatio G. Wright, department commander, called upon Major General Lew Wallace, a thirty-five-year-old native of Indiana. Wallace had served in the Mexican War and was practicing law in Crawfordsville, Indiana, when the Civil War began. He had a background in politics, his father having served as governor of Indiana, while he himself had been elected to the state senate. Wallace appeared slight in figure, with black hair and a full beard and mustache. He had fought at Fort Donelson, but the Battle of Shiloh loomed larger than anything else in his military career. The mystery of why Lew Wallace and his division of seven thousand men never saw battle on the fateful Sunday of April 6, would be probed for the rest of his life—and long after. But before Wallace's life ended, he would be remembered, above all, as a writer, especially as author of the internationally-known *Ben Hur*.[117]

Wallace set about his task of defending Cincinnati with vigor. Fearing an uprising of Rebel sympathizers, he declared martial law. This meant a ban on the sale of alcoholic drinks; all business establishments were closed, except for services deemed essential, like food supply; and Wallace demanded that every able-bodied male be either conscripted for labor on defensive works or enrolled in the militia. His plan called for joining the defense of Cincinnati with that of the two small towns, Covington and Newport, on the Kentucky side of the Ohio River.[118]

The people responded to Wallace's leadership, and Cincinnati became a dynamo of preparations for defense. Soon "15,000 men were drilling in the streets," wrote James Ramage; "yesterday a butcher or day-laborer, today a soldier."[119] Recruits also came from the Cincinnati Police Department and the Fire Department. Soldiers who would be known as the Squirrel Hunters were gathering, too.[120] And more men were coming; coming from all over Ohio, intending to fight the Rebels at the Ohio River. Hosts of others were preparing fortifications, forts on high ground south of Newport and Covington, and long stretches of rifle pits to connect them. It was a magnificent show.

Maybe the Rebel sympathizers were awed by the spectacle. While Unionism was pronounced among the city's quarter of a million people, many citizens had Confederate leanings. Wallace's strong leadership, and the impressive response of the loyal people, assured that Cincinnati would not fall to southern insurgents—if there ever had been such a possibility. As for Rebel soldiers, hundreds, perhaps a few thousand, appeared briefly, gazing upon the city from afar. That appearance ultimately proved to be the extent of the threat to the "Queen City," for Kirby Smith seemed content to take up residence in the Bluegrass to the south. But Smith's intentions were not known in Cincinnati.[121]

Meanwhile, martial law was declared throughout Kentucky, and in Louisville all men eighteen to forty-five were forced to enroll for military drill, or stay at home. Businesses were compelled to close early, and saloons were simply closed.[122]

In command of the District of Kentucky, with headquarters at Louisville, was Brigadier General Jeremiah T. Boyle. A native of Boyle County, Kentucky (where the Perryville battle was to be fought), Jeremiah Boyle, after an education at Princeton and Transylvania, had practiced law at Danville for twenty years before the Civil War. Credited with raising four Kentucky regiments, he led a brigade at Shiloh, in Nelson's division.[123] Boyle had a tendency to become overly excited and now was formulating some intriguing messages which he dispatched from Louisville. The day after the Battle of Richmond, he appealed to President Lincoln: "News grows worse from . . . Lexington. Many of our troops captured. Rebels on the Lexington side of Kentucky River. Lexington will be in their possession tomorrow. We must have help of drilled troops unless you intend to turn us over to the devil and his imps." To Halleck he said, "We were badly defeated at Richmond. . . . The whole state will be in possession of Rebels if some efficient aid is not rendered immediately." Boyle also was writing to General Lovell Rousseau in Nashville: "The battle near Richmond was more disastrous than first reported here. Enemy at least 20,000, probably 30,000. They will have Lexington and Frankfort and the central towns and [Louisville] and other cities on the river if aid is not sent."[124]

General Boyle was not the only Federal excited. From Louisville, Governor Oliver P. Morton of Indiana dispatched a message to the secretary of war, dated September 2, at 9:45 P.M. He said, "The operator at Lexington has just bid good-by. He says the enemy were within 3 miles at 7 this evening. The loss of Lexington is the loss of the heart of Kentucky and leaves the road open to the Ohio River."[125] The governor of Ohio, from Cincinnati, telegraphed the secretary of war on the same day: "Fearing invasion at all points on the Ohio, I have called on the loyal men in the surrounding counties to organize themselves into companies and regiments for their defense."[126] On September 3, a group of prominent men wrote to the president from Louisville, saying that "the panic still prevails. Lexington and Frankfort in the hands of the rebels. Unless the State is re-enforced with veteran troops Kentucky will be overrun."[127] And down in Tennessee, General Buell, with very good reason, as he thought of his supplies from Louisville, was saying, "We must get the enemy out of Kentucky."[128]

It was not as if the only bad news for the Federals came from Kentucky, however. Four hundred miles away as the crow flies, east across the rugged mountains of Kentucky and Virginia, the day of the Battle of Richmond, August 30, had also seen the climax of the Second Battle of Bull Run, a struggle that made the first clash at Bull Run seem like a skirmish, both in numbers engaged and in casualties. Federal General John Pope, unaware that James Longstreet's Confederate corps had come up, attacked Stonewall Jackson's corps, positioned on the Rebel left, thus permitting Lee to envelop the Union left flank with Longstreet's men. The Yankees had been badly whipped, retreating to Washington with casualties numbering over sixteen thousand, compared to some nine thousand for the Rebels.[129] Both east and west, the war news was turning sour for the Federals. As Stanley Horn writes, "Dismay and despair spread through the North. Grave fears were entertained for the preservation of the Union."[130]

Meanwhile, Kirby Smith savored his triumph in the heart of the Bluegrass at Lexington. The Florida native faced virtually no organized opposition, and the road was open to both Louisville and Cincinnati. But Kirby Smith had gained his objective—Lexington—the place he had designated as his goal in letters written from Barboursville to both General Bragg and President Davis. This was the place where a Confederate presence, he said, would "give the true men of Kentucky the opportunity for rallying to our standard."[131] Thus, except for small forces sent to Frankfort and Cynthiana, as well as cavalry raiding to the outskirts of Louisville and Shelbyville and to Covington, across the Ohio from Cincinnati, Kirby Smith did not advance beyond Lexington. Content to remain more or less in control of central Kentucky, Kirby Smith settled down, apparently to await the coming of Bragg and the union of their forces.[132]

During those early September days at Lexington, in the wake of the euphoria that followed the Richmond victory, speculation about the future of the campaign became a popular pastime among the Confederates.[133] The tone clearly was one of optimism. Kirby Smith had played his part—at least in his conception of the campaign—and now, if General Bragg could defeat Buell, Kentucky would be claimed for the Confederacy. Grant would be compelled to pull back from West Tennessee and Mississippi, falling back to the Ohio River. Kirby Smith's invasion, quite possibly, was the initiative that would reverse the course of the war—if General Bragg could defeat Buell.

On August 28, two days before the Rebel triumph at Richmond, Bragg's army, thirty thousand strong, had moved out of Chattanooga, crossed the Tennessee River, and begun marching for Middle Tennessee. For a while, Bragg's location and destination became worrisome puzzles to the harried Lincoln administration in Washington. On September 7, the president asked General Boyle at Louisville, "Where is General Bragg? What do you know on the subject?" The same day, Lincoln addressed a similar inquiry to General Wright at Cincinnati: "Do you know to any certainty where General Bragg is? May he not be in Virginia?" And on September 8, the president wrote to General Buell, again revealing his fear that Bragg might have headed east: "What degree of certainty have you that Bragg with his command is not now in the valley of the Shenandoah, Virginia?" On September 10, Buell assured the president that "Bragg is certainly this side of the Cumberland Mountains with his whole force, except what is in Kentucky under Smith."[134]

Buell, of course, was right. Bragg had moved up rapidly through Tennessee's Sequatchie Valley, trekking through Pikeville to Sparta, and then on to Carthage, crossing the Cumberland River and heading for Kentucky. Actually, he had the jump on Buell, who did not realize that the Rebels were advancing into Kentucky so fast. On September 13, Bragg arrived at Glasgow, some thirty miles east of Bowling Green, and issued a resounding proclamation.

"Kentuckians," he said, "I have entered your state with the Confederate Army of the West, and offer you a chance to free yourselves from the tyranny of a despotic ruler. . . . We come to guarantee to all the sanctity of their homes and altars, to punish with a rod of iron the despoilers of your peace, and to avenge the cowardly insults to your women. . . . Kentuckians," Bragg concluded, " . . . if you prefer Federal rule, show it by your frowns and we shall return whence we came. If you choose rather to come within the folds of our brotherhood, then cheer us with the smiles of your women and lend your willing hands to secure you in your heritage of liberty."[135]

Many of Bragg's soldiers were from Tennessee and Kentucky, and the advance thus far had lifted their spirits. In Glasgow the reception was strongly encouraging. Many of the women were waving and cheering the Rebels. Some were bringing them good things to eat. One Confederate private later remembered "how gladly the citizens of Kentucky received us." He said that he "thought they had the prettiest girls that God ever made. They could not do too much for us. They had heaps and stacks of cooked rations along our route, with wine and cider everywhere, and the glad shouts of 'Hurrah for our Southern boys!' greeted and welcomed us at every house."[136]

Of course it was not only Tennesseans and Kentuckians who appreciated a warm reception and an attractive woman. Florida native Augustus O. McDonnell was another who remarked, in his diary, on September 14, about events at Glasgow, writing that the troops

Louisville & Nashville train crossing bridge over Green River.
Courtesy, Hart County Historical Society.

"were enthusiastically cheered by the beautiful women of that place. Flags and snow white kerchiefs waved, as shout after shout went up from the stalwart soldier, as he witnessed this demonstration of fidelity to our cause."[137] And a Georgia soldier, writing to his sister, gave the names of various Kentucky towns through which he had passed, noting that "the ladies cheered us on," and that there were "some of the best looking gurls I ever saw."[138] When reading such glowing accounts from various soldiers, one might be tempted to conclude that Kentucky women really were better looking than the females in other southern states. However that may be, altogether it was a pleasant time, as army life goes, for the Confederate soldiers advancing into Kentucky.

This certainly is not to say that everything always went smoothly. Some men were victims of carelessness, stubbornness, or bad luck. John J. Hogg, from Troup County, Georgia, recorded in his diary on September 8, that on the march through Tennessee "we were ordered to load our guns but not to put caps on. Some did put caps on and by so doing we got several of our men killed or wounded." In a letter to his wife Susan, written from Kentucky on September 16, Hogg told of two men in his company who "went out beyond the pickets and when they returned our picket shot them and killed one . . . and wounded [the other] severely."[139]

The problem of loneliness for loved ones seemed constantly at hand, at least for some men. While T. J. Koger continually encouraged his wife to "write, write," Surgeon Terry Carlisle's approach was quite different. Once he said, "My dear wife . . . Do write more frequently. You might write every four days and not hurt yourself *mentally or physically*, I think."[140] Of course many pieces of correspondence were either lost or arrived weeks or even months behind schedule. Meantime, the campaign proceeded.

Strategically speaking, General Bragg was in a good situation at Glasgow, having placed his force between Kirby Smith and Buell, and also in position to cut off Buell's line of retreat, both by pike and railroad, to Louisville. But, unfortunately for Bragg, twenty miles directly to the north, at the Green River, a big problem was developing at a little town called Munfordville.

Chapter 6

An Unauthorized and Injudicious Attack

☆☆☆

Black smoke billowed from the stack as the engine pounded southward from Louisville in the dark early morning hours of September 14, 1862. Its burden of rocking cars sounded a steady, monotonous clickety-clack against the iron rails of the Louisville and Nashville's line. The train was south of Elizabethtown, carrying about 450 Union troops, mostly from the Fiftieth Indiana Infantry, supported by one company of the Seventy-Eighth Indiana, when Colonel Cyrus L. Dunham, commanding, urged the engineer to greater speed, assuring him that it was "all-important for us to reach the Green River before daylight."[1]

The vital Louisville and Nashville Railroad crossed the Green River at the sleepy hamlet of Munfordville, where towered one of the most important bridges on the entire line. Munfordville got its start right after the turn of the century, as a relay station on the Louisville and Nashville turnpike, where horses for the stagecoaches were changed. Thomas Munford owned the Munford Inn, where the charge for overnight accommodations, including supper and breakfast, was fifty cents. The inn had some notable guests through the years, including Andrew Jackson, who spent the night there when on his way to Washington to be inaugurated as president of the

United States. A little boy, Thomas J. Wood, later to be a Union general in the Civil War, reportedly sat on the knee of the president-elect when he stayed overnight at Munfordville. By the time of the Civil War, Munfordville was a town numbering about two hundred people, many of Union sentiment.[2]

Set in a pleasant, agrarian community on the northern bank of the Green River, Munfordville lay about forty-five miles north of Bowling Green. The Green River's banks are precipitous in numerous places, necessitating the railroad's long, high span across the stream. *Harper's Weekly Magazine* of January 4, 1862, which carried a picture of the bridge, described it as an "elegant structure built in the fall of 1857. It is nearly 1,000 feet in length; the center pier is 115 feet high."[3]

Colonel Dunham and his Hoosier soldiers were steaming to reinforce the hard-pressed Federal garrison which was trying to defend the bridge against Confederate attack. Commanded by thirty-two-year-old Colonel John T. Wilder of Greensburg, Indiana, the Union troops were positioned on the southern bank of the stream. In fact, Dunham and his men were coming in direct response to Wilder's telegram of September 13, addressed to J. Edward Stacy, adjutant general and chief of staff, Louisville, Kentucky, which said: "Scouts and numbers of citizens coming in state that the enemy are advancing 7,000 strong, and that a force has come in between here and Bowling Green to prevent reinforcements from joining me." Maintaining that, if he had "one more good regiment and a few pieces of artillery, that force could not take me," Wilder affirmed that even "as it is, I shall do my best to prevent" being overwhelmed. But, he pleaded, "Can you send me reinforcements tonight?"[4]

As the Federal reinforcements were nearing Munfordville, Colonel Dunham was perched on the train's engine, anxiously scanning the tracks ahead for signs of sabotage, as the engineer slowed the train and moved cautiously forward.[5] "Suddenly the train gave a sickening lurch," wrote historian Hal Engerud, "swayed and rolled off the track," and came to rest in the ditch along the right-of-way.[6]

In the poor visibility before dawn, neither Dunham nor the engineer had seen where the Confederates had undermined the track and slightly spread the rails. Fortunately, because the train then was traveling very slowly, not a man or a horse was seriously injured. "The men seemed inspired with even greater confidence, as if feeling themselves under the especial protection of an overruling Providence," thought Colonel Dunham. "They were immediately formed in line of battle, an instantaneous attack being expected." No enemy appeared, however, and when a reconnaissance revealed no Rebels in the woods that skirted the railroad tracks, "the regiment was put in rapid march for Munfordville," continued Dunham. "We soon met crowds of frightened and fleeing citizens," one of whom was an acquaintance of Dunham. He informed the colonel that a Confederate command of about two thousand cavalry and one battery of artillery was posted on the northern side of the river and across the road upon which the Yankees were traveling.[7]

"But nothing daunted," Colonel Dunham reported that "our little force made a detour to the right, and, by keeping under the cover of the woods and corn fields and down ravines, eluded the enemy, and reached the river just below the bridges and opposite our works." Tired from the rough forced march, Dunham's troops halted momentarily to catch their breaths, close up the column, and allow a reconnaissance in search of a place to ford the river. Soon they splashed into the stream at a double-quick pace; and none too soon, as a rear-guard detachment had to fight off charging Rebel cavalry that had discovered their position. Onto the southern bank the Federals scrambled, then into the works of their beleaguered Union comrades, who greeted them, said Dunham, "with hearty cheers."[8]

But the Confederates too had received reinforcements—and in greater numbers than the Federals. Brigadier General James R. Chalmers's brigade had tramped northward from Cave City through the night, at the same time that Dunham's Yankees had been steaming southward from Louisville. Just before dawn, Chalmers's troops arrived in front of the Union works at the Green River. Chalmers had come at the summons of cavalry Colonel John Scott, who had been sent south by Kirby Smith to find Bragg and urge upon that general the necessity of joining forces in the Bluegrass. Scott led a Louisiana brigade and said that an easy victory could be won over an allegedly outnumbered and inexperienced Federal garrison.[9] Scott had heard that Wilder's Yankees were new recruits—less than eighteen hundred strong—and proceeded on September 13, to demand their surrender.[10] When Wilder refused, Scott decided not to make an attack until morning. Scott had learned that Chalmers's brigade of infantry had taken Cave City, less than fifteen miles to the south. If Chalmers would join him, then Scott would feel more comfortable about attacking the Federals in their Green River camp. "Scott was an impulsive man," observed Hal Engerud, "and he could not resist the temptation to 'knock off' the Munfordville garrison."[11]

Chalmers, who had surprised and captured the telegraph operator at Cave City, along with the depot supplies at that place, and torn up railroad track to stop any trains heading toward Louisville, reported that he received Scott's communiqué about 9 P.M.: "I received a message from Colonel Scott, commanding a brigade of cavalry, through one of his officers, to the effect that the force of the enemy at Munfordville was not more than 1,800 men, entirely raw troops, and that they were fortifying their position, but that the railroad and telegraph had been destroyed in their rear, cutting them off completely from all communication and re-inforcements." Also, Chalmers said that Scott told him he intended to attack "at daylight on the following morning, and desired that I would co-operate with him with a part of my force."[12]

Perhaps the prospect of an easy victory was too strong a lure for Chalmers to resist, especially if, as one of his officers thought, he was hungry for glory. Captain E. T. Sykes, Company K, Tenth Mississippi Infantry, later wrote that Chalmers was "induced" by Scott's message "to move forward on the night of the 13th—and this without orders from, or information first furnished his commanding officer—presumably, and as believed by all concerned, in the hope and

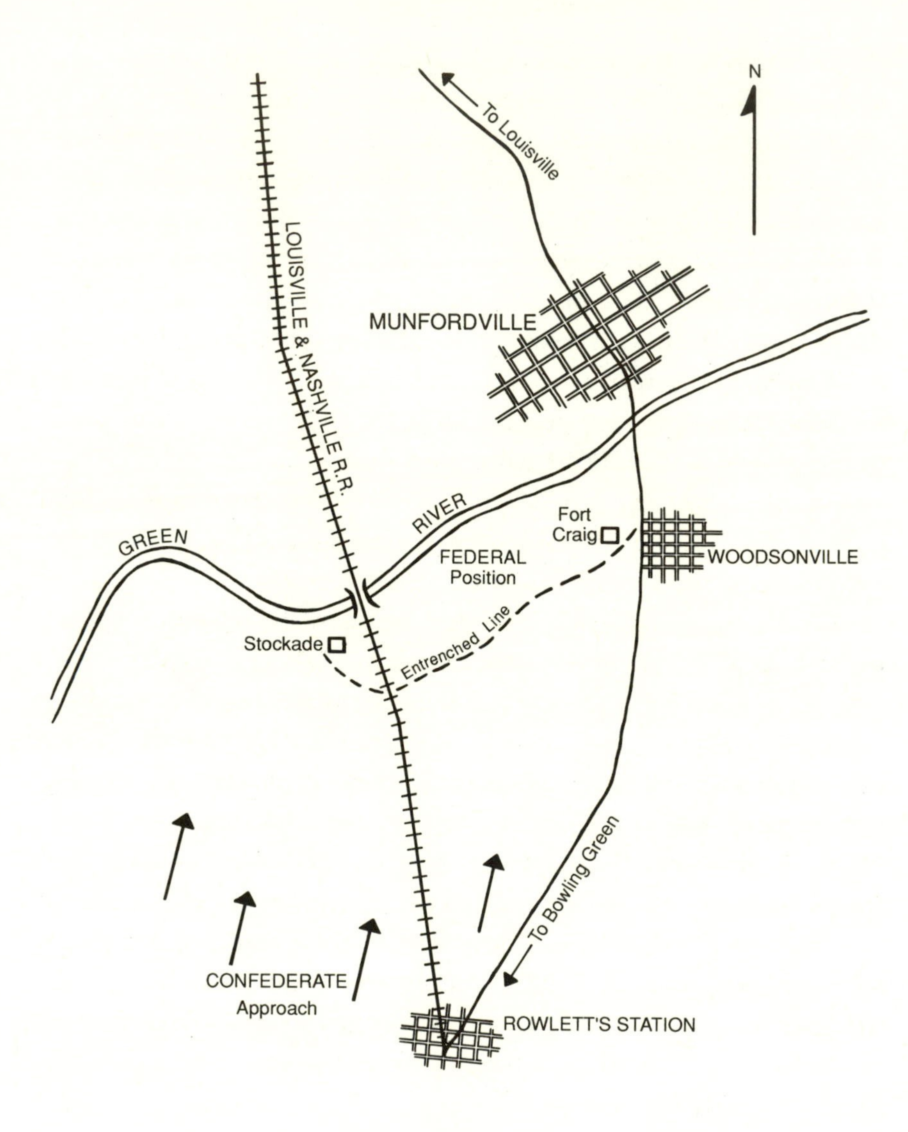

Munfordville battle area.
Map prepared by Sharon McDonough.

expectancy, by *coup de maitre* of winning promotion, cost what it may in the loss of men."[13]

Chalmers also was encouraged to join up with Scott by Federal dispatches intercepted after taking Cave City, which indicated that the Rebel army's advance to Glasgow (through which town Chalmers's own brigade recently had marched as citizens shouted greetings, waved Confederate flags, and the band played "Dixie"[14]) had "thrown the enemy into consternation along the whole line from Louisville to Bowling Green, and that they were under the impression that the force occupying Cave City was 7,000 strong and was advancing on Munfordville."[15] Glory hungry or not, from Scott's message and the intercepted dispatches, Chalmers easily could have concluded that a green, inexperienced garrison at Munfordville would be panicked into surrendering.

Thus, without consulting Braxton Bragg, the army commander who was some miles to the south at Glasgow, agonizing over the problems of conducting an improvised, two-pronged invasion, Chalmers decided to make a night march and join up with Scott at the Green River for an attack on the Federals at the railroad bridge.[16] Chalmers's venture soon would present Bragg with yet another problem.

Difficulties began at once for Chalmers when he arrived about dawn in front of Colonel Wilder's position on the south side of the Green River. A heavy fog was rising from the river, making reconnaissance very difficult.[17] Chalmers could not determine, beyond vague impressions, the extent and nature of the enemy's position. He was further deceived about the strength of the Federals when the advance of a battalion of Confederate sharpshooters witnessed a large number of Yankees fall back before them. This force of the enemy, as Chalmers reported, was estimated "at from two to three regiments," drawn up in line of battle, but "retreated with but little resistance before the advance of my battalion of sharpshooters, who drove them into their rifle pits." Chalmers said that, at the same time the Yankees fell back they also "set fire to what I supposed was the railroad bridge, but what, as I afterwards found, was a church near their principal work."[18] Chalmers was further misled, according to his report, about Federal strength and determination, when their cannon fired no more than "an occasional shot" in response to the challenge of southern artillery fire.[19]

Actually, the Federal position was well devised for repelling an attack from the south, and Chalmers, ambitious or not, likely would have pulled up and mulled over the situation carefully—and at least revised his plan of assault—if he had realized the strength of the enemy's fortifications. But the Union was supposed to be weak and inexperienced; easy victory was anticipated; and General Chalmers was not about to call off the attack merely because part of the area was shrouded in early morning fog and he did not have a clear concept of either the extent or nature of the Yankee defenses. Thus it was that the general from Mississippi launched his ill-fated assault.

The Federal defenses were formidable, thanks in no small degree to Colonel Wilder's diligence during the last few days in improving upon General Alexander McCook's earlier efforts. Back in February, McCook's men had constructed a stockade of heavy logs, banked with earth, at the south end of the bridge. This structure was on a rise of high ground a hundred yards or so west of the railroad track. Perched on the brink of the high bluff overlooking the Green River, the stockade was partially protected by a rifle trench dug around it.[20] When Wilder arrived to defend the bridge, he worked hard to strengthen the stockade, which became the right flank of his position, and also erected a large earthwork, known as Fort Craig, some distance east of the railroad, which anchored his left flank. The fort and the stockade were connected by a line of trenches and rifle pits, with the fields to the front cleared for more accurate firing, while ugly, jutting abatis (hidden in the early morning fog) threatened to impale attackers along portions of the Union position. Further, as Chalmers later noted, once he had examined the Federal position after the fight, "the passages between these works were almost entirely protected from our fire by the nature of the ground."[21] To defend the Union position, Wilder had, once Dunham's reinforcements arrived, about four thousand troops. The Eighty-Ninth Indiana held the stockade on the right, the Sixty-Seventh Indiana occupied Fort Craig on the left, and the rest of Wilder's command was stationed in the connecting trenches.[22]

Chalmers launched his attack shortly after daylight, between 5:00 and 5:30 A.M. The Rebel strength was divided (and would be dissipated) between attacking the stockade and the fort. The Tenth and Forty-Fourth Mississippi regiments were positioned to assault the former, while the latter would be attacked by the Seventh, Ninth, and Twenty-Ninth Mississippi, with Captain William H. Ketchum's four-gun Alabama Battery to render artillery support. Chalmers's attack was both poorly coordinated and plagued by blunders.[23]

Deciding that the Federal stockade could be successfully bombarded from an eminence known as "Mrs. Lewis's Hill," Chalmers sent Lieutenant James Garrity, commanding Ketchum's Battery, to open fire on the Federal right from this hill. The range, which was about one thousand yards, proved too great, and Garrity split the battery, sending one section to his right, where it could fire on the fort, while the other section moved farther down the slope of Lewis's Hill, closing the range on the stockade. Colonel Robert A. Smith, commanding the Tenth Mississippi, then was ordered by Chalmers to move his regiment to the bank of the river, to advance as close to the stockade as possible, and, "if he saw a favorable opportunity, to storm [the entrenchments]."[24]

According to the Tenth Mississippi's Captain Sykes, Colonel Smith called his captains to the center and front before the advance began: "After pointing through the haze of the early morning to the enemy's fortifications, on the top of which bayonets bristled in the rays of the morning sun, and also pointing to a fence skirting an abatis of fallen timber, he said that the order to advance would be 'By the right of companies to the front, quick time.'" With that the men moved forward.[25]

The Rebel advance seemed to be going well enough until they got close to the Union line. As they charged with cheers and yells—Smith reportedly shouting above the roar, "Follow me in," as he

Monument to Colonel Robert A. Smith south of Green River Railroad bridge.
Courtesy, Hart County Historical Society.

waved his sword and spurred his horse—the Confederates were suddenly met and staggered by a massive Yankee volley. The Confederate lines broke, and Colonel Smith was mortally wounded, as were several of his officers, while casualties among the rank and file were devastating. The Federals, continuing to load and fire from behind their defenses, showed no evidence of panic.[26]

General Chalmers, who had gained a better vantage point from which to evaluate the Federal position, had just decided that an attack by the Tenth Mississippi was unwise. He had sent an order to Colonel Smith to pull his command back. Unfortunately for the Rebels, before the order could reach him, Smith had already launched his fatal assault.[27] Seeing that Smith was already making his attack, Chalmers then hurried the Forty-Fourth Mississippi (Blythe's Mississippi Infantry, named for Colonel A. K. Blythe, former U.S. consul in Havana, who had been killed at the Battle of Shiloh when "pierced through the heart by an iron ball more than an inch in diameter") to lend support in the attack on the stockade.[28] The Forty-Fourth's commander, Lieutenant Colonel James Moore, also was shot down, mortally wounded while leading his men in this ill-timed assault upon a strong position.[29] The Rebels protected themselves as best they could behind felled trees, in ravines, and in slight depressions in the ground. They held on, and both sides engaged in a sporadic fire at each other for the better part of two hours.

Meanwhile, the Confederate attack against the Federal left flank at the fort came no nearer to success, the only consoling factor being that this assault did not cost as many casualties as that against the stockade. Sadly, some of the Rebel casualties were administered by—to use the present-day term—"friendly fire." Quite possibly, this unfortunate development may have destroyed whatever chance the Confederates had to take the fort.[30] The three attacking regiments were deployed, with Colonel Edward C. Walthall's Twenty-Ninth Mississippi first advancing to the fight, while the Seventh Mississippi was coming up on Walthall's right and the Ninth Mississippi on his left. Taking advantage of shelter provided by some houses on the hill in front of the fort, as well as the burned-out church (which Chalmers earlier had thought was the bridge burning) and a depression in the ground, the Twenty-Ninth advanced, in some cases to within twenty or twenty-five yards of the fort. "Here they halted and poured in so deadly a fire," reported Chalmers, "that the enemy were compelled to seek shelter behind their walls, and only ventured to return the fire from their artillery or by holding their guns at arm's length over the walls without exposing their persons."[31]

General Chalmers decided to try a bayonet charge. According to Colonel Walthall's report, "After firing and receiving a heavy fire for a few moments a bayonet charge was ordered by General Chalmers. I gave the command and the charge was attempted but without success, the earthworks being about 10 feet high and surrounded by a deep ditch about 8 feet wide."[32] Perhaps Walthall's account indicates that the effort to take the fort was doomed to failure, even under the best of circumstances for the Rebels. Regardless of what might or might not have been, the Confederates at this point dealt themselves a fatal blow.

The blunder is clearly detailed in Chalmers's report, which states that "a fire from artillery was unexpectedly opened from a hill in our rear, the shells falling among our ranks. Supposing that the enemy must have established a battery in our rear I ordered the Seventh and Ninth Regiments to about face and charge it." The order was quickly obeyed and Chalmers said that these regiments were within a short distance of the battery, which was falling back before them, "when I was informed that it was attached to Colonel Scott's cavalry brigade and had come up to our relief." Some relief! Immediately Chalmers halted the two regiments, with the intention of sending them against the fort once more, "but unfortunately the other regiment, not understanding in the confusion the object of the movement which had been made and supposing that a retreat had been ordered, had fallen back." Chalmers concluded that it was impossible immediately to renew the attack under such circumstances, so he withdrew all three regiments to a position in the woods.[33] Colonel Walthall, for whatever reason, does not mention the "friendly fire" in his report. He merely states that, shortly after the bayonet charge, "it being manifest that my command could effect nothing in the position it then occupied, I retired to the woods in rear of the houses above named and halted under cover of a hill."[34]

About this time Colonel Scott arrived from the north side of the river and consulted with Chalmers, saying that he had made several attempts to inform the general of his plan to use his battery in support of Chalmers's attack. None of the messages had been received by Chalmers.[35]

At this juncture, Chalmers (not knowing anything else to try and thinking there was nothing to lose, perhaps?) decided to demand that the Yankees surrender! His message was sent to Colonel Wilder about 9:30 A.M., complimenting the Federal commander on "a gallant defense of your position," and saying that "in order to prevent further bloodshed, I demand an unconditional surrender." Chalmers stated that he had five regiments of infantry and one battalion of infantry sharpshooters, reinforced by a brigade of cavalry and an artillery battery. "A short distance in my rear is General Bragg's army, and you cannot escape; the track has been torn up behind you on the other side of the river."[36]

Wilder was not to be so easily bluffed, particularly considering what he had seen to this point of the Confederate effort to overrun his position. "Allow me to thank you for your compliments," he replied, noting that he too had received reinforcements and would "defend myself until overpowered." (Wilder reported that he told Chalmers: "If you wish to avoid further bloodshed, keep out of the way of my guns.") Complementing the Rebels' determination—"Your men fight gallantly"—Wilder then made an unmistakable point about the course of the fighting thus far with this offer: "If you wish you can remove your wounded and dead. Notify me if you wish to do so." With a simple, strong statement of confidence, the Federal concluded: "I think I can hold my position against any force that you can bring; at least, I will try to do so."[37]

Chalmers decided that Wilder's offer to allow the removal of dead and wounded men should be accepted. As a result, a truce was declared. Over on the Rebel left flank, facing the stockade, Captain Sykes of the Tenth Mississippi soon found that the responsibility of implementing the truce in that sector devolved upon him as the senior officer present. Colonel Smith, of course, had been mortally wounded; Lieutenant Colonel James G. Bullard was dead; and Major James Barr, Jr., was temporarily acting on General Chalmers's staff. Sykes later penned a vivid and fascinating human-interest account of his part in these proceedings. He said that the enemy "exhibited from an embrasure of his fortifications in my immediate front, a flag of truce, when it was—due to ignorance of its sacredness—willfully fired on by one Jim Franks, a private in the company on my left." Acting quickly, Sykes first placed "the defiant Franks in charge of two men with orders to shoot him if he again attempted to fire," and then assured the bearer of the flag that it would be respected.[38]

The Federal officer, reassured, advanced; as did Sykes, the two meeting about midway between the opposing lines. The bearer of the flag of truce was First Lieutenant W. A. Bullitt, adjutant of the Third Kentucky Cavalry, "a well dressed, handsome and intelligent gentleman," thought Sykes, who observed that he himself must have "presented quite an unfavorable contrast" in appearance, having "not changed clothes since crossing the Tennessee River." From this man Sykes learned of the armistice for the purpose of removing the dead and wounded from the field.

Sykes conveyed the news to his regiment and arranged for a detail of troops to remove them beyond the crest of the ridge from which the morning's advance had begun. Then Sykes returned to the company of the Union lieutenant and the flag of truce between the lines. It turned out that Lieutenant Bullitt was supplied with a canteen of, as Sykes said, "the liquid fluid that cheers and sometimes inebriates" but that in this instance "only mellowed the soul and sublimated the lips with words of 'social commune,'" as the two shared the welcome drink. For more than an hour, Bullitt and Sykes drank and conversed, "mutually exchanging deep felt and sincere expressions and regards, and promising needed protection, should the fortune of war make either a captive of the other's army."

As they parted, the Yank presented the Reb with a flask of brandy, offering, said Sykes, "the jocular, but considerate remark, indicative of the courtly gentleman that he was, 'That you may know it is all right, I take a bumper of it to your health;' after which we separated with mutual best wishes for each other." (Several decades after the war, Sykes tried to locate Bullitt, who practiced law in Louisville for years, only to learn in 1913 that he had died some time earlier.) As events developed, Sykes did not get to enjoy the brandy that Bullitt gave him. Seeing the mortally wounded Colonel Smith lying nearby and "suffering excruciating pain," he insisted that the colonel take a drink of the brandy, even though "I knew him to be absolutely temperate." First refusing but then consenting and drinking, the colonel seemed much more in need of the alcohol than Sykes—at least Sykes thought so—and left the flask with Smith, who was carried from the field by the sergeant major and a surgeon of the Tenth Mississippi.[39]

An eight-year-old girl, Mary Brent, remembered that Colonel Smith was brought to the home of her aunt, who was not home at the time, and placed on the porch with a blanket under him. When the aunt returned, she inquired of those attending why they had not taken him in the house and put him on a bed. The reply, as the girl recalled, was: "We would not do that; anywhere is good enough for a soldier." The aunt insisted that he be placed inside on a bed, which was done. Mary Brent said that Colonel Smith lived through the night, with her mother and her aunt ministering to him, but he died the next day and was buried in a crude coffin in a corner of the garden. Eventually—according to some it was while the war was still going on, while others said it was after the war—the colonel's sister, Mrs. Charlotte Dudley, accompanied by her son, returned the colonel's body to Mississippi. There the remains were reinterred at Jackson, in Evergreen Cemetery.[40]

Many of the Rebel wounded were hauled to the railroad depot and other nearby buildings at Rowlett's Station. There they received medical attention. Those considered able to endure the rigors of travel were taken south to Cave City. Due to the lack of tools for burying the dead, the Confederates borrowed the necessary implements from the Federals. The task of caring for the dead and wounded continued, after an hour's extension of the truce, until about 6:00 P.M. General Chalmers had decided, long before this, not to renew his attack. If the assault were to be renewed, Chalmers needed help from the main body of Bragg's army.[41]

General Bragg was not at all encouraged when he learned what had happened at Munfordville. Bragg often has been described as a general whose features suggested a stern, somewhat unfriendly character. Almost certainly, this is the Bragg that Chalmers anticipated confronting after the Munfordville affair. Confederate losses had been much heavier than Federal ones, and Chalmers's report, made soon after his withdrawal from Munfordville, said that he feared his assault might have incurred the censure of army headquarters.[42] When, four days later, Chalmers made a longer report attempting to explain his actions, General Bragg wrote an endorsement thereon condemning the attack as "unauthorized and injudicious."[43]

Nevertheless, after Chalmers's debacle, Bragg felt compelled to deal with the Union force at the railroad bridge. Initially, he would have preferred simply to bypass it. There is no solid evidence that Bragg intended anything other than proceeding northward, by the route east of Munfordville, to join Kirby Smith's army. Any other thesis must rest upon speculation. But Chalmers's action had destroyed Bragg's option to bypass Munfordville, or at least Bragg thought it had. Psychologically, Bragg felt that his men did not need the impression of a defeat (or a reversal, by any definition) in their minds as the campaign progressed. Thus, on the evening of September 15, he marched to bring all of his army's strength to reduce the Federals at the bridge.[44]

The best way to take a bridge, according to the old maxim, is both ends at the same time. This assumes, of course, that the bridge is defended at both ends. In the instance of the Green River bridge, such was not the case. Only later, after the lessons of this campaign,

Confederate General Simon Bolivar Buckner.
Courtesy, Hart County Historical Society.

An older General Buckner on the porch of his home.
Courtesy, Hart County Historical Society.

did the Federals construct forts, two of them, on the northern bank of the river. In September 1862, it was particularly unfortunate for the Federals that defenses of the bridge were confined to the southern bank, because that bank was lower than the northern side. Still worse for the Federals, one of the officers who had just come up in Bragg's army knew that the northern bank was higher, knew also where safely to cross the river, and knew the best route then to follow to occupy that higher ground. From the latter, the Yankee defenders on the south side could be threatened with a devastating fire.[45]

This man was Simon Bolivar Buckner, a native Kentuckian whose home was—of all unlikely places—Munfordville. In months to come, the relationship between Bragg and Buckner would go sour, reaching a low point after the Chickamauga battle, when General Buckner and several other high-ranking Confederates tried to have Bragg removed from command of the army. President Davis retained Bragg, after which Buckner was reduced from a department and corps commander to a division commander, a perceived injustice which the

Kentuckian protested in a series of harsh and bitter letters. One of these so angered Bragg that he sent it back with an inscription reading, "Returned to writer as a paper improper and unfit to go in the records of this office."[46] But, fortunately, for the moment all this was in the future. In fact, Bragg had been very pleased when he first learned that Buckner would be joining him for the invasion. He believed Buckner's influence in Kentucky would cause a lot of men to enlist for the Confederacy.[47]

Buckner was an impressive man. He was one of two Civil War generals from the little town of Munfordville, the other being Thomas J. Wood, with whom Buckner had played along the banks of the river when they were boys, and who remained loyal to the Union.[48] Buckner was a strikingly handsome, thirty-nine-year-old West Point graduate. He had seen service in the Mexican War, then resigned his commission in 1855 and became a successful businessman. A supporter of neutrality for the Bluegrass State, Buckner finally turned down  the offer of another commission in the U.S. Army and cast his lot with the Confederacy. After the war, Buckner resumed his business career, also working as an editor and becoming involved in politics. He served four years as Democratic governor of Kentucky after his election in 1887. When possible, he always lived in the family home, "Glen Lily," about eight miles east of Munfordville, which he had known as a child and in which, in 1914, he would die, the last surviving Confederate major general.[49]

Some critics blamed Buckner for the Fort Donelson fiasco back in February—he had surrendered that Cumberland River bastion to his old friend U. S. Grant—but most people who understood the situation rightly placed the fault upon John B. Floyd, Gideon Pillow, and even Albert Sidney Johnston for allowing the Confederate force to be trapped there. After exchange in August, Buckner had been welcomed back, promoted to major general, and given a division to command in William J. Hardee's corps. Now he had the chance not only to keep further Confederate casualties at a bare minimum, but also perhaps to prevent much destruction and loss of life

* Father of Army General Killed on Okinawa?

Union General Thomas J. Wood.
Courtesy, Hart County Historical Society.

Union Colonel John T. Wilder.
Courtesy, Hart County Historical Society.

in his home town. Since he knew the territory so well, Buckner probably exercised the greatest influence of any Rebel officer in convincing General Bragg to occupy the high ground on the river's northern bank. The Federal forces thus would be surrounded and placed in an untenable situation.[50]

Soon Hardee took a position confronting the Union defenses on the south bank of the river, while Leonidas Polk's corps crossed upstream from Munfordville and made its way to the rear of the Yankee defenses, deploying and trapping the Federals. Confederate artillery positioned on the high ground north of the river then could demolish the defensive works of the enemy, probably without need for an assault. Most of September 16 was expended in getting the troops placed, while skirmish firing continued on the southern bank. Late in the afternoon, General Bragg sent a message to the Union commander demanding that he surrender. Bragg said that the Federals were "surrounded by an overwhelming force" and that "successful resistance or escape is impossible. You are therefore offered an opportunity . . . of avoiding the terrible consequences of an assault."[51]

Colonel Dunham, who ranked Wilder, was then in command but, now that the Rebels occupied the river's north bank, realized that he had succeeded only in making his way into a trap. He requested a truce until 9 P.M., which Bragg accepted, not planning any more action until morning anyway. The Federals held a council of war. They could not believe that Bragg had brought his whole force to reduce a railroad bridge garrison. Still, whether Bragg had his entire army or not, the Yankees were in a difficult position. Since the telegraph line to Louisville was yet intact, Dunham decided to wire headquarters, expressing doubt that he could maintain his position unless reinforced. The reply from Louisville was an order to turn over command to Wilder. Dunham was appalled and countered that he would not serve under a man who was his junior in rank. The next order he received was to report to Wilder under arrest.[52]

Wilder was not any more sure of what to do than Dunham had been, but he certainly knew better than to telegraph Louisville for instructions. At last he sent a message to Bragg, stating that, at a consultation of officers of his command "held since dark this evening, it is agreed that if satisfactory evidence is given them of . . . your assertions of largely superior numbers, so as to make the defense of this position a useless waste of human life, we will treat as to . . . honorable surrender."[53]

Bragg was not in a pleasant mood—certainly he was not inclined to offer something called "satisfactory evidence" of his superior force. The impatient general responded that "the only evidence" he would give beyond affirming that his force exceeded twenty thousand, would be "the use of it." Then he concluded: "An unconditional surrender of your whole force, etc., is demanded and will be enforced. You are allowed one hour in which to make known your decision."[54]

Then occurred one of the very unusual events of the war. Wilder felt that he had to know if Bragg was bluffing. If indeed there were as many Rebels as Bragg claimed, the Yankees had no chance, especially considering that the enemy held the river's northern as well as its southern bank. But maybe the weight of Bragg's army actually was deployed to the south to intercept Buell's force, thought to be marching north from Bowling Green. After all, two days before, Chalmers had said much the same thing about an overwhelming force that Bragg now said, and Chalmers had been driven back with heavy losses. Wilder was not a professional military man; thus he resorted to an unorthodox solution. Crossing the lines under a flag of truce, he called upon General Buckner sometime before 10 P.M., September 17, and amazed the Kentuckian by requesting his advice. Wilder said he had heard that Buckner was a gentleman who would not deceive him and stated forthrightly, "I came to you to find out what I ought to do."[55]

Buckner protested this unorthodox approach, yet the more he contemplated it, the more he found it irresistible, later remarking, "I wouldn't have deceived that man under those conditions for anything."[56] There was, of course, no need to deceive him, since Bragg had not been bluffing. Thus Buckner reiterated the points that Bragg had made, reminding Wilder that the Yankees were surrounded by a much larger Confederate army that was in position to bombard them relentlessly at dawn. He said that Wilder had no chance either to escape or resist with any hope of success. Wilder said he answered that, if this were the case, "there was no reason why I should not see [the overwhelming force], and that I would undoubtedly surrender if I saw it."[57]

Buckner consented, personally conducting Wilder on a tour of the Confederate lines. Colonel Wilder's adjutant was taken on a simultaneous tour on the north side of the river. Wilder counted forty-six pieces of artillery in place on the south bank of the river, while his adjutant counted twenty-six on the north side. It was obvious that Bragg and Buckner had told the truth. The Yankees were surrounded by an army several times their size, supported by strong, strategically placed artillery. As Wilder later testified before the Buell Commission, "The rebels had positions within 600 yards around us; that on the north side especially commanded us. The ground in the main work sloped toward the north, exposing the men in the works to a fire from the north side." Buckner told him at the time, "It is for you to judge how long your command would live under that fire."[58]

As Colonel Hal Engerud observed in his account of the Munfordville siege, "In the mind of Colonel Wilder the word 'surrender' carried a meaning verging on 'cowardice'."[59] But now Wilder was convinced that his position was hopeless; neither from Louisville nor Bowling Green could he expect help in time to prevent defeat and slaughter. He had only four guns, and his supply of rifle ammunition was low. The morale of his men was deteriorating. "It seems to me, General Buckner, that I ought to surrender."[60]

At this point Buckner, according to Buckner, was so caught up in the intriguing circumstances that, instead of immediately accepting Wilder's reluctant decision, he felt obligated to suggest one other factor: "If you have information that would induce you to think that the sacrificing of every man at this place would give your army an advantage elsewhere," lectured Buckner, "it is your duty to do it." Wilder had no such information. "I believe I will surrender," he replied.[61]

Nevertheless, Wilder was not through consuming time. Sometime before midnight, he was at Bragg's headquarters, accompanied by Buckner, where, with all seated at a table, the final articles of surrender were drawn up. It took awhile. For some two hours, Wilder and the Confederate commander discussed the meaning of the phrase "unconditional surrender." After a heated exchange over whether Bragg would march in or Wilder would march out, the defeated was triumphant.[62] At 6 A.M., Wilder's force marched out "with all the honors of war, drums beating and colors flying."[63]

Once the articles of surrender were signed and all procedural matters had been agreed upon, General Bragg could not resist spending some time relishing his triumph, small though it was, in grand style. After all, it was the first victory since he became commander of the army. But it was General Buckner who played the most conspicuous role. Standing in the road at Rowlett's Station, Buckner received Wilder's sword and then returned it to him, an act of graciousness that pleased the crowd.[64] Certainly Buckner's role was fitting, for, as Hal Engerud remarked, "To General Buckner must go a great deal of the credit for the skillful manner in which the Confederates organized and occupied their positions."[65] Then the Union soldiers stacked their arms, were paroled and issued rations, and started marching toward Bowling Green and Buell's army. The Rebels, of course, hoped that the paroled troops would impose a strain upon Buell's supplies.

Among the Confederates observing the proceedings at Munfordville was the Forty-First Mississippi's T. J. Koger. "I have seen a number of letters picked up by our boys in the fort," he wrote to his wife. "And I had no idea of the coarseness and vulgarity that women wrote to their husbands and brothers," he said. "There is a want of refinement and womanly delicacy in sentiment and expression which I hope can not be found any where South." Afterward, turning his remarks to the men, Koger wrote that he "heard more cursing and profanity in twenty minutes in Yankee company than I ever heard in our regiment for a week." He did add that these men were prisoners and, no doubt, "felt chafed and provoked."[66]

The scenes following the battle at Munfordville were varied. Obviously there was suffering, both physical and mental. Perhaps the latter sometimes could be worse than the former. A Union soldier from Kentucky later told of a man he saw who, while not personally injured, was in deep distress. The memory stayed with George Stewart through the years, and in 1915 he wrote of seeing "one poor soldier sitting on Mr. [Anthony L.] Woodson's fence sobbing with grief and when inquiry [was] made, pointed in the yard to three dead soldiers, whom he said was his brothers."[67] And Anthony Woodson, while not fighting in either army and not suffering any physical harm, nevertheless was one of the biggest losers in the struggle for the bridge at Munfordville. His losses were financial. It was upon Woodson's land that the fortifications were built and the fighting occurred. His barns and outhouses were burned, his timber cut, and his rail fences used for fuel. For long periods, both before and after the fighting in September 1862, troops were encamped upon his land, depriving Woodson of most of the normal income from his farm. Under an act of Congress, Woodson later claimed some twelve thousand dollars in damages to his property. After years of haggling, in about 1890, when he was an old man, Woodson finally accepted a settlement of less than five thousand dollars.[68]

Meanwhile, Bragg and his generals, continuing to savor the victory, took time to inspect the fortifications at Munfordville.[69] Bragg may have considered Chalmers's foray, which had brought the entire army to Munfordville, "an unauthorized and injudicious attack"; nevertheless, he felt compelled to congratulate his army on "the crowning success of their extraordinary campaign which this day has witnessed." The soldiers had "overcome all obstacles without a murmur, even when in the prosecution of a seemingly unnecessary labor." Thus, he continued, "nearly all things become possible." Tennessee and Kentucky he pronounced "redeemed," but he quickly cautioned that "our labors are not over. A powerful foe is assembling in our front and we must prepare to strike him a sudden and decisive blow. A short time only can therefore be given for repose, when we must resume our march to still more victories."[70]

Despite such rhetoric, the Munfordville detour really was a costly one for the Rebels. It might have been better to "write off," as an unfortunate venture of war, the 285 casualties suffered by Chalmers's command, rather than to expend still more time and resources in capturing a position that really was of no consequence when the Confederate campaigning was viewed in total—unless Bragg planned to fight Buell south of the Green River. Bragg, as one historian expressed it, had allowed "the chagrin of defeat" to outweigh "the geographical and logistical problems involved in moving the army over to the Louisville pike." That he rightly considered the march to Munfordville "a mere detour" is evident from the fact that "his request for Kirby Smith to prepare for a meeting was written *after* Bragg issued orders to march to Munfordville."[71] The "mere detour" cost Bragg much: "Time, supplies, and the advantage of moving on the Bardstown pike" all were sacrificed, "and the all-important junction with Kirby Smith would be delayed."[72] Still worse, Bragg decided to follow the president's lead and set aside September 18 as a day of thanksgiving and prayer for his army.[73] The president was not in the field. If he had been, one wonders if he would have approved Bragg's decision.

The Munfordville affair has stimulated controversy from still another point of view. Stanley Horn summarizes this interpretation of Bragg's conduct: "After an admirably devised and executed movement of more than 600 miles, he had placed his army exactly where he wanted it—squarely across the enemy's line of communication. His soldiers were inspired by the capture of Wilder's garrison and might well expect to find Buell's men correspondingly depressed."[74] Horn then contends, "There was every sound reason why Bragg should fight Buell at once, and there is some evidence that he thought of it. But he did not fight." Horn goes on to state that, "In a negative way, General Bragg's failure to fight at Munfordville was one of the great crises of the war—probably its greatest moral crisis." One would not overstate Bragg's failure here, says Horn, "by calling it a major disaster of the conflict."[75] Essentially Horn is following the arguments of Joseph Wheeler, then a colonel commanding Hardee's cavalry brigade, and of Basil Duke, who rode with the famous Rebel raider John Hunt Morgan.[76]

Robert S. Henry, a southern historian whose work preceded Horn's by a decade, took a similar view, although noting the additional option of moving on Louisville: "The Confederates . . . were between Buell and his base squarely on his line of march, and in position to fight or to march into Louisville ahead of the Union army."[77] Recently, Charles Roland has made the same argument about the vulnerability of Louisville, writing that "the Confederates probably could have taken Louisville if they had marched directly upon it from Munfordville." While Buell was marching north to challenge the Rebels, Roland observes significantly that "Bragg was between Buell and Louisville and Kirby Smith was closer to Louisville than Buell was."[78]

On the night of September 17, Bragg called a council of his generals as he mulled over his options. One possibility, since Buell had marched into Kentucky, north of Bowling Green, was to double back rapidly to Nashville, where the relatively small number of Union defenders could be easily overcome. This was what Andrew Johnson, provisional governor of Tennessee, feared most, telegraphing Lincoln that Bragg's real objective was Tennessee's capital city and that the move into Kentucky was merely a feint to draw Buell's force out of Tennessee.[79] There is some evidence that Bragg favored such a strategy. After all, his original intent, when moving to Chattanooga, had been to recover Middle Tennessee. If Bragg returned to Tennessee from Munfordville, however, Kirby Smith's army would be isolated in the Bluegrass, as Buell's force would then be between the two Rebel commands, and Bragg, understandably, wanted their forces united. In fact, as recently as September 12, Bragg had said that placing his army "between Buell and Kirby Smith" was the objective "for which I have been struggling."[80] And on September 17, he claimed: "My junction with Kirby Smith is complete. Buell still at Bowling Green."[81] This is a significant statement. Obviously the junction with Kirby Smith was not literally complete, but Bragg knew that Buell no longer was in a position to prevent the junction from taking place. Bragg's statement further confirms how important he considered the junction.

Another possibility for Bragg, equally obvious, was to hold his ground and fight Buell south of the Green River. Bragg probably thought seriously about this option.[82] He said, "My position must be exceedingly embarrassing to Buell and his army. They dare not attack me, and yet no other escape seems to be open to them."[83] If Bragg could be reinforced with Kirby Smith's army, the Confederates would have a decided numerical advantage in such a battle. Bragg thought Buell's force was considerably larger than it was.[84]

Another problem was that Kirby Smith was deployed to wait for Bragg in the Bluegrass. He probably could not come to Bragg's aid quickly enough, even if he were of a mind to do so, which apparently he was not. In fact, if Kirby Smith came to Bragg, according to his message sent from Lexington two days earlier, Kirby Smith would be seeking Bragg's help, not marching to assist Bragg. Kirby Smith had said, "Unless . . . you can either speedily move your column in this direction or make with me a combined attack upon Louisville before all of [the enemy] army arrives there, I shall be compelled to fall back upon you for support."[85] Certainly Bragg did not relish fighting Buell with what he thought would be inferior numbers, and probably not even with more or less equal numbers. Thus, joining up with Kirby Smith—which only could be accomplished by moving his army to the northeast—seemed to take priority over anything else.

That is, almost certainly, why Bragg did not move on Louisville either. Perhaps Bragg did not realize how weakly defended Louisville was. That being the case, then first to unite with Kirby Smith would have appeared all the more important—imperative, even. Too, it should be remembered that both Bragg and Kirby Smith were counting heavily on recruits in Kentucky. This was why Bragg became enthralled with establishing a Rebel government at Frankfort, which would enable the Confederacy's conscription (draft) act to go into effect. Bragg probably reasoned that it was far better to unite the Confederate armies—which would place Bragg in command, of course—and gain recruits, before risking a major engagement, especially if, as Bragg thought, he was outnumbered by the enemy. Also, in mid-September, Bragg still hoped for the success of "the two-headed command system" (as Steven Woodworth expressed it) of Price and Van Dorn, whom he had left in Mississippi.[86] Maybe those generals yet would contribute to the success of Bragg's plans in Kentucky by defeating the Federals in northern Mississippi and West Tennessee, and so opening the road for a Rebel advance into western Kentucky that would promise considerable support.

All things considered, Bragg's options at Munfordville left much to be desired. Basically, his problem stemmed from allowing Kirby Smith to change the original plan for a united move into Middle Tennessee under his command, formulated at Chattanooga. At Munfordville, Bragg was reaping the consequences of allowing the direction of the campaign to slip from his control. To regain control—uniting the Rebel forces in Kentucky and achieving unity of command—probably weighed more heavily upon Bragg's mind at Munfordville than any other factors. When viewed from such a perspective, the decision he made is understandable. If Bragg did mutter something to the effect that "This campaign must be won by marching, not fighting,"[87] this was the context that gave rise to those words.

Bragg's lack of a clearly defined objective when he moved into Kentucky was haunting him at Munfordville. While some writers have presented the campaign as if Louisville had been the goal: "Had he [Bragg] kept his eye upon the prize, the chances are that he would have beaten . . . Buell to Louisville and the . . . City would have fallen into Confederate hands."[88] Actually, there is no convincing evidence that Bragg ever had defined Louisville as "the prize" which the Rebel army sought. Bragg said that his army had promised to make him military governor of Ohio in ninety days; but the general had not specifically established Louisville, or Lexington, or any other place or places, or the enemy army, as his objective. Basically, Bragg now was conducting a kind of loose, freelance campaign, in part forced upon him by Kirby Smith's independent operation, that violated two of the most important principles of successful generalship. Perhaps the nearest he came to a clearly defined objective is revealed in the wagonloads of weapons he carried for the thousands of recruits he sought and hoped to find in Kentucky, as well as his expressions of disappointment when such recruits were not forthcoming.

Finally, it might be noted that, contrary to long-cherished popular legend, there was never any race for Louisville between Buell and Bragg, at least not so far as Bragg was concerned.

☆☆☆

September 17 is a date that stands out dramatically and tragically in the history of the Confederacy. It was the bloodiest single day of the Civil War, as Yanks and Rebs battled in western Maryland, along the banks of Antietam Creek, near the little town of Sharpsburg. When it was over, Robert E. Lee's invasion of the North had failed, and Maryland, an important border slave state, would remain loyal to the Union. Even more significantly, the Federal strategic triumph, as the Confederates were compelled to retreat into Virginia, led to the Emancipation Proclamation, which changed the complexion of the war, virtually ending the Confederacy's hope of foreign recognition and major assistance from abroad—a factor which well might have meant success for the Confederacy.

It seemed almost as if fate were aligned against the Rebels. A copy of Lee's orders, lost by some Confederate officer, had fallen into the hands of General McClellan, who thus discovered that the Confederate army was split into several fragments. Even with all Lee's forces united, McClellan outmanned the Grayclads by nearly a two-to-one margin. If the Union commander had moved quickly and decisively, he possibly could have destroyed the Army of Northern Virginia. But George McClellan was a careful man—too careful to be a successful commander.

Even after wasting time and allowing Lee to pull his army back together in front of the village of Sharpsburg, McClellan still had the opportunity to administer a smashing defeat if he used his superior manpower efficiently. Lee's decision not to retreat—once he knew that McClellan knew that the Rebel forces were widely and dangerously divided—is highly questionable.

On September 17, McClellan sent his men against Lee's positions in piecemeal fashion, the action gradually moving along the lines from north to south. There was so little coordination of effort that the engagement was much like fighting three separate battles, one on the north flank, one in the center, and one on the south flank. Even so, near the center, the Yankees almost (but not quite) broke the Rebel army in half at the "Bloody Lane." Little more than "a frazzled thread" of a line maintained the Confederate center—and McClellan had two corps that were hardly engaged at all.[89]

When the day was over, the Rebels had maintained their lines, but over twenty-three thousand Confederates and Yankees had been killed or wounded, and Lee's hopes of winning a major victory on northern soil had come to a bloody end, as more than eleven thousand of his soldiers lay dead and wounded along the banks of Antietam Creek. Another two thousand southerners were missing.[90]

That night, while Bragg, far to the west, pondered what to do next, after the surrender of the Union forces at Munfordville, Lee, at his headquarters in Sharpsburg, considered his options. Amazingly, Lee decided to hold his ground for another day, but George McClellan did not attack again.[91] In two days, the Grayclads were recrossing the Potomac, and, although Lincoln was bitterly disappointed that his general had allowed the chance to smash the Rebels to slip away, the Union had won a great strategic victory.

Meanwhile, in Kentucky, Bragg had made his decision. He would not return to Tennessee, nor fight south of the Green River. Neither would he go for Louisville. This latter decision left later armchair generals and historians an intriguing series of questions to ponder. If Bragg had moved rapidly on Louisville, when apparently he could have taken the city with ease, would such a triumph at the Ohio River have brought out the Confederate sympathizers in great numbers? At a time when the British were seriously considering recognizing the Confederacy, would this show of southern support have influenced the British decision? Would it have caused President Lincoln to rethink the timing of the issuance of the Emancipation Proclamation?

However all this might have turned out, Bragg had decided that Louisville was not his objective. "The army was not a little disappointed," wrote Major George Winchester, "when instead of 'On to Louisville' the head of the column was faced Eastward."[92]

Bragg's Confederates actually tramped northeastward from Munfordville, through Lincoln's birthplace at Hodgenville, on past Gethsemane Abbey, and into Bardstown, famous for its Old Kentucky Home. There Bragg left his army and rode with his staff to Lexington, there counseling with Kirby Smith and passing several days arranging for the inauguration of Richard Hawes as Confederate governor of Kentucky.

As usual, Captain T. J. Koger was writing to his wife in Mississippi, while he waited at Bardstown for the army's next move. "A thousand rumors are afloat, all favorable, but what to believe is difficult," he said. "We are here, wagons all packed, ready to move at a moment's notice. All our cooked food is gone. And none to cook. Waiting, Waiting." Bragg's warning to the army, back in Mississippi, of "privation and labor" when he advanced, now was manifest. "We are very uncomfortable here in an open field," wrote Koger. "The fences are all burned, water is distant and dust is plenty." Koger was on the mark with another observation, too, as he wrote on September 27: "There seems to be indecision in the plans of our generals. We are not moving, as all expected to be, on Louisville. Buell is reported to have passed us by the southern route and thus got to Louisville before us."[93]

Bragg's move to form a junction with Kirby Smith had left the road to Louisville open to the Federals, and Buell—who should have felt fortunate not to have to fight his way through—marched to the city on the Ohio as fast as he could. As Buell's troops, coming up from Nashville and Bowling Green, reached the Green River at Munfordville, they were intrigued by the recent fighting for control of the railroad bridge. Men react in various ways to scenes associated with a battle. The objects of their attention may indicate concerns that are sad, morbid, frivolous, humorous in a sick manner, or some combination of these and more. Writing an unpunctuated letter to his father and mother, describing what he saw around Munfordville, the Fifty-Seventh Indiana's James H. Jones said, "I will send a button in this that I cut of a Seceshes shirt he was laying in the side of the road with the top of his head shot of." Jones thought he knew who the dead man was, at least his rank and outfit, identifying him as "a lieutenant kearnel of the third georgia We then came on to the bridge it was a burned down the pieces was still smoking."[94]

The Federals, most of them, got only a quick look at the evidence of fighting around Munfordville, because General Buell was moving his command rapidly toward Louisville and the Ohio River. It was a very demanding forced march. W. E. Patterson of the Thirty-Eighth Illinois recorded in his diary that "the hardest march we ever undertook . . . during three years of service" was from North Alabama to Louisville. Early on the morning after crossing the Green River, Patterson said he "obtained a barrel of flour and worms in pretty equal proportions." Having "no means of separating the flour from the worms," Patterson recorded that "we made them up into flap-jacks and devoured them with much relish. After devoting about an hour to the flap-jacks we marched on with renewed vigor." After telling of the flour and worms, Patterson noted that water was "very scarce, the roads extremely dusty, weather hot and rations short." He also said that some men were "almost naked and barefoot," and that "often at the dead of night, the solitude of the forest would ring with sonorous imprecations on 'old Buell' by the exhausted soldiers whose resentment found vent in curses upon a leader in whom they had no confidence and to whose neglect of duty they ascribed the sufferings of this march." Finally, upon arriving at the city on the Ohio, Patterson said, "We were met with a cordial welcome at Louisville by the citizens who but the day before were trembling with apprehension at the near approach of the rebel army."[95]

There is no question that the criticisms of General Buell were now widespread throughout the army. If not already a "lame duck" commander, he was fast becoming such in the minds of the officers and men under him. Captain John Tuttle, who recorded in his diary that he and his men arrived at Louisville about 2 A.M. on Friday, September 26, after a very hard march, said that "during the latter part of this march free use was made of epithets 'traitor, tyrant, fool and coward' with reference to General Buell."[96]

Louisville had been in panic. William Spencer, Ninety-Eighth Ohio Infantry, who upon entering Covington, Kentucky, had written his sister that "it seems [the Union people] can't do enough for the soldiers," told his father a few days later, when he arrived at Louisville, "The citizens are fast leaving Louisville today." Spencer added that he and the other troops arriving were "throwing up entrenchments and expecting a battle."[97]

Fearing that the Rebels would be upon the city at any moment, Louisville bankers closed their doors, and merchants removed their goods from the shelves, trying to transport them across the river to safety on Indiana's shore. Louisville's commander, General Jeremiah Boyle, a man prone to excitability, told Lincoln, "No one has such troubles as I."[98] Indeed, Louisville's defenses were considered so weak that Buell instructed "Bull" Nelson, who, recovering rapidly from his Richmond wounds, relieved General Boyle and took command of the city's defenses, not to attempt a fight if Bragg attacked.[99]

Although Nelson had only raw and untrained troops, he worked with determination to restore order, to throw up entrenchments—men even working by candlelight—and to organize and drill the green soldiers. Laborers were impressed to work on the entrenchments, and blacks were taken from the county jail for the purpose.[100] "Untiring in his energy," Hal Engerud wrote of Nelson, "he drove his men night and day to complete the fortifications and to construct a second pontoon bridge across the river at the west end of town." Issuing orders for "all women and children to leave the city," Nelson announced that he intended "to fight as long as possible, then he would set fire to the city and withdraw . . . to the Indiana shore from whence he would turn his guns on Louisville and reduce it to rubble."[101]

Some residents probably thought the Federal soldiers already were reducing their property to rubble. Many soldiers were out of control, their foraging and exploring activities amounting to pillaging. A member of the Ninety-Fourth Ohio penned the following account: "At last weary and worn we reached Louisville . . . and encamped in some beautiful fields. Here, after resting," related James Mitchell, "many of us wandered away from camp. Some elegant mansions, which had been deserted by their occupants through fear . . . , were broken into by soldiers. The residence which I especially noticed was filled with men. . . . I am glad to say I had no part in the ransacking of the building, but I did open the piano and sang some of the songs I had learned at home. This was refreshing to me and I enjoyed the exercise."

Mitchell's account conjures up an amazing scene, conveying at once a disturbing collage of horror laced with a kind of sick humor: a house filled with men pillaging and plundering, while one of the number plays and sings at the piano. Mitchell said that finally, after satisfying his musical instincts, he "dug up some fine sweet potatoes and took them to my mess."[102]

This kind of thing was bad enough. Fortunately for Louisville, the situation never became so dire that Nelson had to bombard the city with artillery from the Indiana shore. By September 24, General Buell's lead division was marching into the city. Within a few days, his whole army was present. "Bull" Nelson was elated: "Major General Thomas L. Crittenden has crossed the Salt River with the advance of Buell's army," he telegraphed General Wright at Cincinnati, "consisting of 12,000 men and six batteries of artillery. Louisville is now safe," he announced. "We can destroy Bragg with whatever force he may bring against us. God and Liberty."[103] Nelson was correct about the safety of Louisville. On September 29, Buell's last division marched into the city; with all the recruits who had been pouring into town, Louisville suddenly had become one of the most strongly defended cities in the nation. It was a great day for the Union.

September 29 was also General Nelson's last day to live. While Nelson undoubtedly was a person of considerable ability, he was additionally a profane bully of a man who, as previously noted, made enemies wherever he went. "General Nelson was half liked and half disliked," wrote an Illinois soldier. Charles Francis of the Eighty-Eighth Illinois said that, "after General [John?] Pope, it was boasted of him by his admirers, that General Nelson was the 'best, finest, and most elegant and original curser and swearer in the whole United States army.'" The Thirty-First Indiana's Jesse B. Connelly thought that Nelson took "delight in hectoring the officers and men of his command," and told of an incident that took place back in June: "One of the boys in Company B drew his gun on General Nelson one day—when the General threatened to strike him with his sword and have him tied to the horse of his order—and would have shot him, but Nelson saw business in the man's eye, laughed and walked on."[104]

Major General Jefferson C. Davis of Indiana did not give Nelson an opportunity to "laugh and walk on." Nelson, thinking that Davis, who had recently arrived from Mississippi, had not been showing sufficient zeal in preparations for the defense of Louisville, had scathingly reprimanded that general.[105] Davis left in a rage and evidently became obsessed with getting back at Nelson for what he perceived to be an unforgivable insult. He went to Indianapolis, where much sympathy was to be found among the Hoosiers. Among these was Governor Oliver P. Morton, a powerful political figure who, convinced that Kentucky was not doing enough for the Federal cause, had been directing new Indiana regiments into the Bluegrass and acting, some thought, as if he were governor of both Indiana and Kentucky. After the Battle of Richmond, as we have seen, Nelson had blamed the Federal defeat on General Mahlon Manson, a military appointee of Morton's. Nelson also had blamed the Indiana regiments for fighting poorly. Indiana casualties had been heavy, and many Hoosiers felt the real blame should be placed on the Kentuckian

Union General Jefferson C. Davis.
Courtesy, Tennessee State Library and Archives.

Nelson, who, though responsible for the troops, had not even been on the scene until the battle was all but lost. As if Nelson had not already angered Indiana enough, he described the Hoosiers as "uncouth descendants of 'poor trash' from the mountains of Kentucky, Tennessee and North Carolina."[106]

Jefferson C. Davis, along with Governor Morton, returned to Louisville and approached Nelson in the lobby of the Galt House Hotel on the morning of September 29. There was a confrontation in which the five-foot, eight-inch Davis accused the gigantic Nelson of having insulted him and said he was demanding satisfaction. Annoyed, Nelson said something like "Go away, you damned puppy," only to have Davis crumple a hotel desk card which he held in his hand and throw it in his face. Nelson responded by slapping Davis with the back of his hand. Nelson then proceeded up the stairs toward his room, evidently intending to meet with General Buell a little later, but Davis immediately procured a pistol from someone nearby, followed Nelson, and in the hall shot and killed the general.[107]

Lieutenant Colonel Thomas C. James, in a letter beginning "Dear John," penned an interesting account of the episode on the same day when it occurred. "We are all in commotion here," he wrote on stationery carrying the Galt House letterhead. "Major General Nelson was shot and killed at my room door this morning about 8 o'clock by Brigadier General Jeff C. Davis of Indiana, whose face he had slapped a moment before." James thought that Nelson was a "very rough" man who used the "most frightful language; he cursed me terribly on Wednesday for nothing, telling me that he would put me in close confinement for asking him which order I was to obey when he had given me conflicting orders." James, however, gave Nelson a qualified credit for later making "the best apology that such a brute could make when I returned from a scout two days after." James said that Nelson had lived only a few minutes after being shot—long enough, however, that a Reverend Mr. Talbot "baptized him five minutes before he died." "There is scarcely an officer that is a gentleman that has not been cursed by Nelson if he has met him in business," continued the lieutenant colonel. And while "no one seemed to regret his death," yet "all deplored the shooting of one general by another."[108] That, at least, was James's opinion.

Probably many, particularly Indiana soldiers, felt much as did James A. C. Dobson. A member of Company K, Seventy-Ninth Indiana Volunteers, Dobson wrote of Nelson's "blind and merciless tyranny upon the large army of recruits" gathered at Louisville. "The expressions of approval and satisfaction with which both officers and men received the news . . . that General . . . Davis had shot and killed . . . Nelson at his hotel, for a gross and insolent insult . . . ," said Dobson, "will be pardoned by those who can appreciate the extreme feelings of resentment which we all held toward him."[109]

Jefferson C. Davis—whose presence in Louisville initially had sparked a rumor that the president of the Confederacy was in town and that reportedly caused some Unionists to flee across the Ohio[110]—was arrested. He was never tried, however; and soon afterward, having been freed, he resumed his command. However much some people may have disliked Nelson, and with good cause, it was alarming that the general could be murdered and his murderer never even be brought to trial.

Buell was distraught at the murder of Nelson, but the military situation demanded his attention. Reinforced by two divisions from Grant, while another was on the way,[111]—the very thing that Braxton Bragg had hoped Van Dorn and Price could prevent from occurring—Buell was reorganizing his army and preparing to move out of Louisville in search of the Rebels.

President Lincoln, however, was understandably upset, even dismayed, by Buell's retreat from northern Alabama to the Ohio River without ever engaging the enemy. He ordered General George H. Thomas to take command of the army. Buell would have been removed, had not Thomas refused to accept the command, arguing that Buell's preparations were complete, the army was about to advance, and the commander should not be replaced on the verge of the campaign, especially when Thomas was not sufficiently familiar with the plans to proceed immediately.[112] Thus General Buell retained command. On October 1 he moved out of Louisville, heading generally southeastward, seeking the Confederate forces.

The Union march would not be easy. "Many fell out of the ranks and became stragglers," wrote Charles Francis of Illinois. He said that "surplus baggage strewed the roads, and whenever a halt was made the men took the opportunity [of jettisoning what they had come to consider surplus]. . . . Whole knapsacks . . . from shaving appliances and shoe brushes to portable writing desks were thrown away. . . . The heat by day was excessive and pure drinking water was scarce; many suffered on that account."[113] Yet, despite the problems and the criticisms of Buell, many Federals—probably most—were eager to engage the enemy.

"That old poke-easy general of ours [Buell] has allowed the thieving rebels to overrun the best portion of the State and they are now in full possession of our homes," was the opinion of a Kentucky Union soldier. "All we care now is to . . . have a thrash and drive the lousy devils out, or kill or capture the whole army of thieves, with all their long [wagon] train of stolen goods."[114]

☆☆☆

The final stage of the struggle for Kentucky was at hand. From the perspective of Braxton Bragg, the prospects were not encouraging. Summarizing the situation for the benefit of Richmond, the Confederate general had written on September 25, "At Munfordville I was between Buell's forces and General E. K. Smith, by which the latter was secured." Stating that efforts had been made to bring Buell to an engagement, "but he declined," Bragg then explained that, "for want of provisions it was impossible for me to . . . stay where I was, the population being nearly all hostile and the country barren and destitute, having been ravaged by the enemy." With only three days provisions, Bragg said he had "marched on [Bardstown] (59 miles) and reached it after some privation and suffering." Bragg considered it "a source of deep regret" that such a move was necessary, because it "enabled Buell to reach Louisville, where a large force is now concentrated."

Some questions may be raised about Bragg's presentation and interpretation of the message above, but what he said next was factual and revealed the worst news of all: "I regret to say we are sadly disappointed at the want of action by our friends in Kentucky." There had been "no accession to [Bragg's] army," and Kirby Smith had only "secured about a brigade—not half our losses by casualties of different kinds. We have 15,000 stand of arms and no one to use them." Kentucky's failure to rise to the support of the Confederacy was explained, in Bragg's judgment, by "the love of ease and fear of pecuniary loss." Following this verbal slap at the Kentuckians (far from a full explanation, but understandable considering the general's frustrations), Bragg presented, however belatedly, the most sober and realistic appraisal of what would be required for the campaign to succeed that ever was penned by him or any other contemporary that the author has read.

He told Richmond "at least 50,000 [recruits] will be necessary, and a few weeks [perhaps he might better have said 'days'] will decide the question. Should we have to retire, much in the way of supplies and *morale* will be lost, and the redemption of Kentucky will be indefinitely postponed, if not rendered impossible." He closed with a limited expression of hope that Van Dorn and Price might yet render some much-needed assistance, but it is clear that Bragg was very discouraged.[115]

Was Bragg correct in saying that fifty thousand Kentuckians would have been required to "redeem" the Bluegrass State? It seems highly unlikely that his fifty thousand figure was the result of a careful analysis and calculation. Rather, Bragg was exaggerating—although perhaps not a great deal—to make a point. The point, clearly valid, was that he and Kirby Smith needed far more recruits than they were gaining. We can only guess what might have been done for recruiting by a major achievement, such as striking for and taking Louisville immediately after the surrender of the Federals at Munfordville, when that strategic city on the Ohio was lightly held. What a major victory over the Federal army—if attainable, once Bragg and Kirby Smith were united—might do for recruiting likewise was anyone's guess.

Maybe such a triumph would bring out the Kentuckians in huge numbers to take up arms for the Confederacy. But events thus far were not encouraging. Both Rebel columns were deep into the heart of Kentucky. Each had already gained a small victory, Bragg at Munfordville and Kirby Smith more impressively at Richmond, the latter having resulted in a rout of Federal forces. Yet recruitment of Kentuckians had been a meager affair. That a big Rebel triumph could bring about a major change in the number of Kentuckians choosing to support the Confederacy was anything but certain.

Bragg's pessimism is understandable. He was right in saying that tens of thousands of Kentuckians would have been required to "redeem" Kentucky—that is, to establish a permanent Confederate presence in the state, on a scale that could achieve anything of lasting strategic significance. He also was right in saying that failure in this campaign probably meant failure ultimately.

Nor was Bragg the only one disappointed in the Kentucky turnout. Major George Winchester, on September 23, wrote: "I have but little confidence in Kentucky. There are many who express southern principles who do not exemplify it." Mentioning the many barefooted soldiers in the ranks, "with blistered and bleeding feet," Winchester said, "We have been unable to procure the necessary supplies of clothing and shoes." Six days later he wrote. "It is said Kentuckians are coming to the rescue. I have no confidence in those not now in the field."[116]

As if, from General Bragg's perspective, conditions were not already bad enough, his subsequent experience in Kentucky's capital of Frankfort must have been terribly discouraging—like a stark omen of failure. While Buell was moving out from Louisville, advancing to engage the Confederate forces earlier than Bragg had thought possible, Bragg was in Frankfort making plans for the inauguration of Richard Hawes as provisional Confederate governor of the State. It was hoped that this action might encourage enlistments in the Rebel cause, as well as provide some legal justification for the enforcement of the Confederacy's conscription act. On October 4, with an impressive crowd in attendance, the ritual of inauguration was observed, with Hawes promising the audience that his government represented a permanent Confederate presence in the Bluegrass and that the Federal troops would soon be gone from the state. But, even as Hawes spoke, a Yankee division led by Joshua Sill (who died less than three months later at Murfreesboro, Tennessee) was nearing Frankfort; indeed, the sound of Federal shells bursting interrupted his address. The capital was evacuated as quickly as possible, the great ball planned for that evening in celebration of the occasion was canceled, and the new Confederate government of Kentucky spent the war in exile.[117]

Whatever Braxton Bragg thought about the Kentuckians, and whether he was right or wrong, events were rapidly moving toward a climax that would decide which side would prevail in the Bluegrass. A portion of the Rebels and a majority of the Yankees were moving on a collision course toward a clash at a little town in central Kentucky. Its name was Perryville.

Chapter 7

Searching for Water

☆☆☆

The small country town called Perryville was bustling in the warm early morning hours of Wednesday, October 8. Lying along the banks of the Chaplin River, the settlement originally had been known as Harberson's Station, in honor of James Harberson, who had led a group of Pennsylvanians to the site during the American Revolution and acquired hundreds of acres in that Bluegrass region. For protection amid the constant danger of Indians, Harberson and the other inhabitants had constructed a fort on the bank of the river, encompassing a spring to guarantee water if the settlers were besieged. While the fort disappeared long ago, the spring, as well as a cave where people could hide from the Indians, may still be seen.[1]

As for Harberson, it is said that he met a gruesome fate while on a scouting expedition. Apparently he was a victim of Indians; only his head was recovered, about a mile from the fort, where it had been severed from his body. Equally macabre is the account told by a long-time resident of the region, Dr. Jefferson J. Polk: Harberson's wife then "took the head and managed to keep it in a complete state of preservation for many years."[2] It is a fascinating story.

After the War of 1812, two men, Edward Bullock and William Hall, developed plans for a village along the river, calling it Perryville in recognition of Commodore Oliver H. Perry, hero of the naval engagement on Lake Erie, not far from Put-in-Bay. For several decades after the Indians had been driven out of the region, the town, halfway between the Ohio River and the state line of Tennessee, remained undisturbed in the pleasant, rolling hills and rich, productive soil of central Kentucky.[3] Now the long tranquillity was broken. Gray uniformed soldiers could be seen everywhere. Several citizens, fearing a battle, had fled from their homes, seeking safety in nearby towns. Those who remained waited anxiously. Fighting was already going on only a short distance to the west of the village.

Several facts combined to give an unlikely military importance to this quiet hamlet of less than five hundred people in the heart of the Bluegrass country. Perryville was a crossroads where armies easily could concentrate their forces; and the town's streams—Chaplin River, Doctor's Creek, Bull Run, and Wilson's Creek—promised water, a necessity wanted badly by both Blue and Gray in the exceptionally dry fall of 1862. The Chaplin River flowed through the town, meandering from south to north. It was not a major stream; neither wide nor deep, the Chaplin was picturesque but presented no significant impediment to an army's movements. On the contrary, the Chaplin River and its tributary, Doctor's Creek, would be possessions welcomed by either army during the pronounced drought then plaguing Kentucky.

Doctor's Creek snaked through the farms and woods on the west side of Perryville, flowing in a generally northeastern direction until its confluence with the Chaplin River approximately two miles north of town. There the streams joined at a loop of the Chaplin, which had been dubbed Walker's Bend long before the war. Doctor's Creek had a tributary called Bull Run, which emptied into Doctor's Creek about a mile south of the latter's confluence with the Chaplin. Located farthest from the town was Wilson's Creek. It was a tiny stream off to the west and north from Doctor's Creek, which meandered to a confluence with the Chaplin River some distance downstream from where Doctor's emptied into the Chaplin.

As Federal and Confederate armies plodded along the hot, dry roads of central Kentucky, lack of water became a serious problem. Routes of march sometimes were altered in hopes of locating water. The Confederate troops were pleased, to say the least, when they discovered the streams near Perryville. Soon the Federals became aware of them, too, and were equally pleased. True, stretches of the creek beds were dry, but there were pools of brownish water to be found, too. While such liquid did not look particularly inviting, it still had the great virtue of being wet. Thirsty soldiers, carrying empty canteens, were in no position to be discriminating. Indeed, they were ready to fight for such water holes, however uninviting their appearance might be—sometimes fighting even their own comrades in arms. "Every well and spring was drained," remembered a Federal soldier. "Tormented by heat and thirst," men crowded about any water source, "pushing, scrambling, often fighting for a few muddy drops" of the precious liquid.[4]

The Rebels got into Perryville first, of course, as General William J. Hardee, with Simon Buckner's division, tramped in from the west along the Springfield Road on October 6. They were falling back from the Bardstown area, intending to shift the march northeast from Perryville to Harrodsburg and a junction with Bragg's forces to the north. In fact, as ordered by General Polk, J. Patton Anderson's division had moved on to camp at Salt River, on the road between Perryville and Harrodsburg. But Hardee, also complying with Polk's order, had stopped Buckner's division at Perryville in order to get water, planning to resume the trek to Harrodsburg the next day.[5]

It was not to be. That night, Hardee was disturbed and puzzled by the strength of the enemy that was following him. He thought, just as Bragg did, that the bulk of the Yankee force was farther north in the direction of Frankfort. However, the Union troops coming after him on the Springfield Pike, "pressing with heavy force upon his position,"[6] concerned Hardee. Joe Wheeler's cavalry had been skirmishing with the Yankees much of the day, Wheeler developing a general impression of Federal strength, although he knew nothing specifically. John Wharton's Texas cavalry, which might have helped with scouting duties, still was not at hand, having been ordered by Polk to Lebanon for supplies. (Wharton would not reach Hardee at Perryville until the next night.)[7]

Thus it was that Hardee, uncomfortable about continuing north to Harrodsburg with a Federal force of unknown strength shadowing his left flank—Stanley F. Horn wrote that Hardee "sensed that it was more than he could handle"—asked Polk to reinforce him with Anderson's division and Pat Cleburne's brigade, now reunited with Bragg's army.[8] The bishop-general complied, ordering Anderson to move out at 3:00 A.M. on October 7, with Cleburne following an hour later.[9] Informing Bragg of these movements, Polk said, "I have directed General Hardee to ascertain, if possible, the strength of the enemy which may be covered by his advance." Although Polk was several miles removed at Harrodsburg and had received no specific information from any source, his next and concluding sentence—a striking observation quoted by many who have written about Perryville—offered an opinion of the size of the Federal force approaching Hardee. He said: "I cannot think it large."[10]

Never was the bishop-general's opinion more wrong. The Yankee force converging on Perryville was three corps strong, a total of between fifty-five and sixty thousand men. General Buell's plan had been to keep the Rebels guessing about his line of advance, hoping thus to prevent Bragg and Kirby Smith from joining forces. The strategy worked marvelously, aided by Bragg's strongly-held conviction that Buell could not take the field for several weeks anyway.

While Buell moved southeast from Louisville with his main force, the Yankee general also launched a strong feint toward Frankfort. The feint consisted of a division detached from Alexander McCook's corps, led by Joshua W. Sill, a vigilant, competent, Ohio West

Union General Alexander McCook.
Courtesy, Tennessee State Library and Archives.

Pointer, and supported by another division of new recruits commanded by Ebenezer Dumont. Numbering about twenty thousand men, this column was intended both to cover Louisville, if a Rebel move were made toward that city, and, equally important, to confuse the enemy as to the real direction of Buell's line of march, thus keeping Bragg and Kirby Smith divided.

The feint actually worked better than Buell reasonably could have expected. Again, to quote Stanley Horn: "Bragg gullibly accepted it at full face value, and thought Buell's whole army was about to fall on Kirby Smith at Frankfort."[11] Bragg was "badly confused, whether he knew it or not," observed Shelby Foote.[12] So were Bragg's subordinates. Not only were Bragg and Kirby Smith kept separated; but Bragg had been unable even to concentrate his own army, because of the perplexing circumstances. First believing that a battle would be fought near Frankfort, then vacillating in favor of Harrodsburg, Versailles, or Salvisa, Bragg never realized, until the struggle was over, that most of Buell's army was in front of Perryville.[13] As historian Kenneth P. Williams wrote: "It was all a fine illustration of the fact that when one side starts an offensive move and employs a diverting column, the enemy may be much bewildered."[14]

The Union Army approached Perryville on three roads. On the Federal left, moving in by the Mackville Road, was the three-division corps (although Sill's division, as previously noted, had been detached as the main force composing the feint toward Frankfort) of Major General Alexander McDowell McCook. A thirty-one-year-old graduate of the U.S. Military Academy McCook had ranked thirtieth in a class of forty-seven. Known to some of his classmates as "Guts" because of his hefty midsection, McCook had seen frontier service, engaged in the Indian Wars, and taught tactics at West Point.[15] Inclined to be rather boisterous and swaggering, the general irritated many people. "General McCook prides himself on being General McCook," observed a Union soldier at Nashville.[16] One of the famous "fighting McCooks" of Ohio, Alexander was a brother of Dan McCook, who was also serving in Buell's army, and of the late Robert McCook, who, as we have seen, had been killed during the summer near Dechard, Tennessee, a victim of the brutal guerrilla war in northern Alabama and southern Tennessee.

On the Federal right flank, advancing on Perryville via the Lebanon Road, was the corps of Major General Thomas Leonidas Crittenden. This command also was composed of three divisions. General Crittenden was the son of Senator John C. Crittenden, the well-known Kentucky politician who had tried to effect a compromise between North and South in the critical weeks after South Carolina led the way to the secession of the Deep South. Born in 1819 in Russellville, Kentucky, Thomas Crittenden was the younger brother of Confederate General George B. Crittenden. As a young man, he had pursued a legal career but soon interrupted it to fight in the Mexican War, where he served part of the time as an aide to General Zachary Taylor. Crittenden's most notable service to date in the Civil War had been at Shiloh, where he, like McCook, commanded a division in General Buell's army on the second day of that battle.[17] One observer, a person with a favorable attitude toward the general, reported that, in ability, Crittenden was fundamentally a country lawyer.[18] Whatever his ability, or lack thereof, in appearance Crittenden was very noticeable, another observer commenting that the general had a "thin, staring face, and hair hanging to his coat collar—a very wild-appearing major general, but quite a kindly man in conversation."[19]

Occupying the center position in the Yankee advance was the corps of forty-year-old Charles Champion Gilbert, who was acting as a major general, although even his recent promotion to a brigadier generalship had not been approved by the U.S. Congress. (In fact, that approval would never be given.)[20] Gilbert's corps was moving toward Perryville on the Springfield Road, the most direct route. His vanguard kept up a running fight with Joe Wheeler's cavalry, which stubbornly contested the Federal advance.[21] Some of Wheeler's men were captured, and the Union officer in charge paid tribute to their valor, saying that "they certainly are possessed of the devil and have acted bravely the part their masters commanded them to play."[22] Not surprisingly, Gilbert's corps, which had a shorter distance to march, was approaching Perryville ahead of both McCook and Crittenden.

All three Union corps commanders were short on experience in their positions, having been promoted during the recent and rapid army reorganization at Louisville, when Buell was trying to get his forces ready to advance as soon as possible. Gilbert's ability probably was the most questionable. Born at Zanesville, Ohio, Gilbert had graduated from West Point, ranking twenty-first in a class of fifty-nine cadets and had served in the Mexican War, then on the western frontier, and in the Indian Wars. He also had done a stint as an instructor at West Point. In the Civil War, he had fought at Dug Springs, been severely wounded in Missouri at Wilson's Creek, and recovered to fight at Shiloh.[23] Now he led a corps—primarily because he had been "at the right place at the right time"; in this case, at Louisville, in the crisis when Buell needed a professional army officer after the murder of General Nelson. In all the haste and uncertainty of that unsettling event, Buell garnered a mistaken impression that Gilbert was a major general.

As a corps commander, Gilbert proved to be petty, self-centered, and an unbending disciplinarian. The general possessed a colossal ego, one that seemingly required continual nourishment. This the soldiers quickly detected and strongly disliked. There were several confrontations with his officers and men, one such incident leading to the arrest of the Eighty-Sixth Illinois's colonel—over the alleged pilfering of persimmons by a soldier in the colonel's regiment, according to the diary of Allen L. Fahnestock.[24]

James Shaw of the Tenth Indiana told of the following confrontation with Gilbert, at midnight on the road between Springfield and Perryville. Much of the regiment, after a hard day's march, was already asleep when several riders pulled up in a cloud of dust, and one of them roared out: "What regiment is this?" A captain replied that it was the Tenth Indiana, to which the infuriated rider rejoined: "Damn pretty regiment. Why in hell don't you get up and salute me when I pass?" "Who in the hell are you?" asked the captain, and received the answer, "Major General Gilbert!" Gilbert, according to Shaw, then demanded the captain's sword, telling him he was under arrest. At that point, the regiment's colonel, hearing all the commotion, appeared and told General Gilbert that, after marching his regiment hard for a week, he would "hold no dress parade at midnight for any damn fool living" and warned the general that he had better move on.

But Gilbert was not through, next demanding that the regiment's color-bearer surrender the regimental flag. The color-bearer's response was to curse the general, telling him that if he so much as touched the colors, he would kill him. Another soldier rose and told Gilbert to "get out of here, or you are a dead man." Still another fired a weapon, and Gilbert's horse was jabbed with a bayonet by yet another soldier. "The horse," reported Shaw, "reared, plunged and nearly threw Gilbert off." Then away the horse went at a gallop, followed by the general's escort, several of whose horses also were jabbed by bayonets. "There was ever afterwards an enmity against Gilbert in the regiment," wrote Shaw, "and some threatened to shoot him if he got into action."[25]

Later, at the Buell Commission, General James B. Steedman would testify about Gilbert:

> There was a great deal of dissatisfaction in the First Division with General Gilbert prior to the battle of Perryville, and a great deal of feeling among all of the officers of the corps that I ever heard say anything about it, after it was ascertained that he had not the right to exercise that command. There was a feeling that he was somebody's pet, and put where he had no right and for which he was not qualified. He quarreled with nearly all the officers of the First Division about very unimportant and trifling things, and there was a general opinion that he gave his attention entirely to small things instead of attending to the important duties of his position.[26]

Such was the nature of the man commanding the Federal corps that would first make violent contact with the Confederates at Perryville.

The Union soldiers may well have been more irritable than normal—although General Gilbert likely was capable of provoking almost anyone's wrath, regardless of conditions—because of suffering from the acute shortage of water. General Speed S. Fry said the men "were suffering very much" from the lack of water.[27] The summer-long dry weather—which had afflicted much of the Kentucky–Tennessee–North Mississippi–North Alabama region, impeding transport of Buell's supplies by river during his move on Chattanooga—had extended into a hot, dusty fall. Creeks and even some rivers were dry, their shriveled beds accentuated by numerous repulsive cracks.

Uppermost in the minds of many of the soldiers, certainly, were not such matters as better food, a tougher pair of shoes, a warmer coat, a loving woman, or even a comfortable night's rest, but rather a cool stream of water. A deep-seated thirst probably is more engrossing than anything else which one may imagine. If perchance a pond or some small body of water were discovered, which was a rarity, it usually was stagnant, covered with scum, and disagreeable to sight, smell, and taste.

One of the soldiers in the Seventy-Ninth Indiana, John H. Tilford, recorded in his diary on October 7, that "we took up our line of march about 10 o'clock this morning. Marched quite fast all day; our army suffers terribly for water, it is almost impossible to get any." Tilford remarked that some "fellows take water out of mud holes, and drink as if it was the best water they ever tasted," a sight Tilford said he had "never seen before."[28] Perry Hall was another soldier in the Seventy-Ninth Indiana who was keeping a diary. His thoughts on October 7 were much the same as Tilford's, differing only in that he said the march started at nine in the morning: "I never saw men suffer for *water* as we have done for a few days. We marched till *midnight* in search of it. It is horrible to think what we have been compelled to drink!"[29]

Some of the soldiers gave a better idea than others of just what they had "been compelled to drink." Allen L. Fahnestock wrote in his diary that, near Springfield, "we were compelled to fill our canteens out of hog puddles and hold our noses while drinking."[30] Apparently the swine were abundant wherever a pocket of water could be found. The Fiftieth Ohio's Erastus Winters proclaimed: "I drank water on this march that hogs had wallowed in."[31] Hogs were not the only problem, however. Winters also recorded, "It was said that some of the boys got water out of a pond one dark night and used it at supper for to make their coffee and to quench their thirst. . . . What was their disgust next morning to find a dead mule . . . in the pond."[32]

No one summarized the situation better than the Thirty-First Indiana's Jesse B. Connelly, whose diary entry reads in part: "After leaving Bardstown, water became very scarce, and men and horses suffered greatly for want of it. Most that we had until the battle of Perryville was found in stagnant pools in the beds of creeks, in which water had long since quit flowing, and which from evaporation was very brackish and strong. A very little of it was all a man could drink at a time, and soon his thirst was more intense than before."[33]

Perhaps nothing seemed more precious than water, but it was not the only commodity in short supply. Garrett Larew of the Eighty-Sixth Indiana wrote that he "marched all day yesterday [October 6] without a thing to eat at all." Larew also recorded in his diary that "the boys steales chickens and turkeys and meat and everything else they want that they can get their hands on. The colonel tries to keep them from it but they are too sharp for him." Larew added that the colonel had "arrested about a dozen [men] for it and says the next time he takes them for stealing he will shoot them."[34]

As if the circumstances were not bad enough, at least one man worsened his plight with regard to water by a foolish action. George Morgan Kirkpatrick, a soldier in the Forty-Second Indiana, recorded: "We expected to fight, and had heard that the Johnies would take all our grub away from us if they captured us." Consequently, said Kirkpatrick, who apparently lacked confidence in the Federal army's ability to successfully contend with the Rebels, "I ate my two pounds of pickled pork, raw, and chewed up the coffee which I had from fear of its being taken from me. Water was very scarce and the salt meat took effect with a vengeance. While still four miles from the scene of battle, we could hear cannonading in front. What with this, and the dry weather and the salt pork, we were sorely in fear and distress." At last Kirkpatrick reached a creek, but it "was dry except for a few puddles of water with green scum over it." Desperately in need, he "skimmed the water, and put it into a pot and boiled it."[35]

The search for water became one more source of the Union soldiers' animosity toward General Gilbert. Whenever a fresh spring actually existed, sarcastically alleged a member of the Thirty-Sixth Illinois, it was "usually monopolized by General Gilbert, who would send an aide in advance to select a romantic spot, where was pitched the General's marquee and a detachment of body guards was sent to protect the sacred precinct as well as the spring from intrusion."[36]

In fairness to Gilbert, it should be noted that the general's actions in this matter are a debatable point. General Speed S. Fry, for example, when questioned at the Buell Commission about the story of Gilbert's having taken possession of a spring for the exclusive use of himself and his staff, replied, "I know nothing of it personally; I only heard that such was the fact. General Gilbert ordered me the night before the battle to place a guard over a pool of water for the use of the men."[37]

Perhaps Gilbert did have the welfare of his soldiers in mind—and then again, perhaps he merely said that he was securing the water for the use of the men, his real concern being his own needs. Whatever Gilbert's motivations, the search for water was coming to a climax. October 7 had been another "hot and dusty [day] making us look like mullattos," as a Federal private described it, during which the Union army had experienced extreme thirst.[38] Marching armies must have water for the soldiers and the animals. Clearly, the creeks and springs of the parched region through which the Yanks and Rebs plodded were about dry. Ahead lay Perryville, where the Federals could expect to find a good if not adequate supply of water. The Confederates already were there. To get the water, the Yankees would have to fight the Rebels. That, of course, was what they had expected to do when they marched out of Louisville. Now they simply had an additional reason for fighting, a reason that was immediately and intensely motivating: to quench their thirst.

Historian Robert Selph Henry, in *The Story of the Confederacy*, states the matter candidly. Perryville, he writes, "was a fight for water."[39]

☆☆☆

"If he wishes to fight, let him come on." Those were General William J. Hardee's words to Joe Wheeler, as he contemplated the enemy advance on the night of October 6.[40] The enemy did "come on," of course, and Hardee intended, among other things, to deny the Yankees water as long as possible.

With that objective in mind, Hardee deployed his forces. After positioning two of Simon Buckner's three brigades between the Harrodsburg Pike and Chaplin River—S. A. M. Wood's brigade constituting the left flank near Perryville, and Bushrod Johnson's brigade composing the right flank, extending northward along the river's east bank—Hardee then rode west on the Springfield Road with his staff and St. John Richardson Liddell, Buckner's third brigade commander. Hardee was seeking an advanced position in which to station Liddell's unit.

St. John Liddell was a Mississippian, leading five Arkansas regiments whose baptism of fire had come at Shiloh. Hardee had been impressed by Liddell and wanted his veterans out front where they could cover the roads into Perryville from the west. They would also be in position to fight the Federals for the water holes. Hardee and Liddell, fortunately for their peace of mind, had no realistic idea of the strength of the oncoming Yankees, as they selected their ground approximately one mile outside Perryville.[41]

There a range of hills ran generally north-south. Paralleling the range, along its western base, was the small stream known as Bull Run, which flowed to join Doctor's Creek one mile north of the

Confederate General William J. Hardee.
Courtesy, Tennessee State Library and Archives.

Springfield Road. Also about one mile north of the Springfield route lay the Mackville Road, running roughly parallel to the Springfield Pike and, like it, bisecting the north-south hill range.

Hardee's eye for terrain and roads showed him that this was the position for Liddell. He ordered the brigadier general to station his brigade on the hills between the Springfield and Mackville roads. Thus he would be in position to defend both routes by which the Federals might march on Perryville from the west. (The Lebanon Road, on which Crittenden's corps was marching, lay far to the south and actually entered Perryville from the south.)

Liddell agreed with Hardee that the position was a good one and began placing his Arkansas regiments in line on the high ground just east of Bull Run. From left to right, the crest was occupied by the Sixth, Second, Fifth, Seventh, and Eighth Arkansas Infantry.[42] The general reported:

> As my left flank rested on the Springfield Road, all on that side, having no support, was exposed to a flank movement of the enemy; but feeling satisfied that he must be in need of water, and that he would push for that point whence it could be obtained from pools lower down on Doctor's Fork, on my right, I separated my battery, and placed one section on a high hill on my right, commanding the woods opposite and the open valley below.[43]

Considering the importance of water to men who had been on the march for miles, it did seem reasonable that Yankee pressure would likely develop to Liddell's right, in the direction where Doctor's Creek flowed, and, still farther to the right, where Chaplin River snaked its way through the rolling countryside. Liddell retained the other section of his battery in advance on his left flank, where it commanded a field in front of the Rebel line and, to some extent, also the fields on the southern side of the Springfield Road.[44]

But as Liddell contemplated a map, studied the ground in his front, and mulled over the situation facing him, he was not satisfied. Three-quarters of a mile across the valley of Bull Run lay the summit of another clump of hills ranging north-south. Directly in front of Liddell's position was the rise known as "Peters Hill," named for the local farmer Jacob Peters, whose house lay at the western base of the hill, beside the Springfield Road and close to the crossing of Doctor's Creek. On top of Peters Hill stood the house of a family named Turpin, destined to become another landmark of the coming battle. If Liddell held this hill, it would give him a forward post to observe any enemy movements and thus would make his position more secure. Liddell decided to occupy this hill with the Seventh Arkansas, then under command of Lieutenant Colonel Peter Snyder. The soldiers of this regiment were picked to man the advanced position because of the enviable reputation they had earned at Shiloh.[45]

Meanwhile, by the night of October 7, General Buell was less than five miles from Perryville. Not all of his army was so close. McCook's corps to the north, moving through Mackville, had been delayed by a rough road and had made camp seven or eight miles out from Perryville. Crittenden's corps, off to the south on the Lebanon Road, was even farther away, having taken a detour, approved by General Thomas, searching for water. But the advance of Gilbert's centrally located corps, which had been slowed up much of the day by skirmishing with Wheeler's cavalry—"Our advance was vigorously resisted by Wheeler's cavalry," wrote Gilbert—was finally nearing the village, still moving on the Springfield Road. At this point, within six miles of Perryville, the road runs through a rather narrow valley with hills rising perhaps some fifty feet on each side. Upon sighting the Rebels to their front, Robert Mitchell's division, which had been in the lead, was halted and formed in order of battle across the Springfield Road, while the division of Phillip Henry Sheridan was brought up, passed to the front, and formed on the front and right of Mitchell. Albion Schoepf's division was held in reserve.[46]

Not quite all of Schoepf's division remained in reserve, however. Brigadier General Speed S. Fry, born and raised near Perryville, who had practiced law at Danville,[47] knew the country well, and for that reason had been named officer of the day by Buell.[48] General Fry selected a regiment from his own brigade, the Tenth Indiana, led by Lieutenant Colonel William B. Carroll, and ordered that regiment to the front for picket duty. Fry himself went along as the pickets pushed out toward Perryville a mile and a half in advance of the Federal camps.[49]

It was a comfortable, resplendent, moonlit night.[50] If one could have disassociated himself from the trials of the campaign, the area seemed an unlikely setting for a bloody struggle on the morrow. But most of the men in the camps of Gilbert's corps would not have qualified as dispassionate observers.

Conditions were hardly conducive to serene feelings. If one of the soldiers did stumble on a pocket of stagnant water, not even a foul, muddy cup of coffee was to be had—at least not officially—because no fires were allowed. Neither were rations issued. Thirsty, hungry, and tired, the men of Gilbert's corps bedded down for the night, except for the Indiana pickets, who cautiously edged their way forward, perhaps thinking what an excellent target for Confederate sharpshooters the moonlight made of them.

About midnight, Lieutenant Colonel Carroll sent two of the companies, A and E, still farther in advance as skirmishers, to determine, if possible, whether the enemy was still in the immediate area.[51] After all, they just might find water in addition to intelligence concerning the Rebel's location. Groping their way about a mile to the east, crossing Doctor's Creek, these Federal soldiers scrambled over part of Peters Hill and then stumbled upon "a considerable force of the enemy and engaged them," reported Colonel William C. Kise.[52] For several minutes, the Hoosier skirmishers blazed away at the shadowy Confederates in the moonlight. The enemy fired back with such determination that the Federals, convinced they faced superior numbers, retreated.[53]

A report soon went back to corps headquarters, telling of the Rebel position and its apparent strength; and also saying that water could be found in quantity at Doctor's Creek if the Confederates could be driven away. The latter, one supposes, got General Buell's

Union General Phil Sheridan.

Courtesy, Tennessee State Library and Archives.

attention. As soon as Buell knew of the situation, he determined to beat back the Rebels and seize control of the water holes. To do the job, General Phillip Sheridan's division was selected.[54]

☆☆☆

In retrospect, it seems fitting that Sheridan's division had just been passed to the front of Gilbert's corps,[55] for the fiery Ohio native had begun his fast-paced rise to ultimate fame as one of the four or five best Union generals of the war. Gilbert, on the other hand, soon after this campaign, would be relegated to the relative obscurity from which he so recently had emerged.

Sheridan was a brash, thirty-one-year-old graduate of West Point, in the class of 1853. He had worn a brigadier general's star for only a few days, having been promoted after an impressive attack at Booneville, Mississippi, during the campaign for Corinth, when he was greatly outnumbered—possibly as much as four to one.[56] "He is worth his weight in gold," said William S. Rosecrans in recommending promotion, an evaluation that often has been quoted.[57] The son of Irish immigrants, although he himself did not look Irish, Sheridan was an unamiable man who made enemies easily.[58]

Standing about five feet, five inches tall, he was an energetic person, not particularly concerned with dress,[59] and in that respect he was much like two other soldiers who eventually emerged as top Union generals: Grant and Sherman. Sheridan was, as the saying goes, "a man in a hurry." An intriguing description of his appearance was once penned by the much taller Abraham Lincoln, who said that Sheridan was "a brown, chunky little chap, with a long body, short legs, not enough neck to hang him, and such long arms that if his ankles itch he can scratch them without stooping."[60]

Sheridan had a well-deserved reputation for a quick temper, a reputation that went back to a confrontation during his academy days when he had accosted another cadet with a bayonet. Perhaps with manslaughter charges flashing through his mind, Sheridan opted for fisticuffs instead of cold steel but still was set back from graduating for a year.[61] Undoubtedly there existed a coarseness about "Little Phil." "Sheridan was a good hater," observed one of his biographers.[62] As Russell Weigley wrote, "He had a streak of downright cruelty and brutality."[63] Possibly this contributed toward making him a good general. Always Sheridan's generalship evinced, again to quote Weigley, "ruthless aggressiveness" and an "overwhelming thirst for combat and an unwavering determination to drive the enemy into the ground."[64]

Right then, Sheridan's thirst for combat was tied to a thirst for water, and the new brigadier intended to drive the enemy off the ground ahead—the ground around Doctor's Creek—rather than into it. About two o'clock on the morning of October 8, Sheridan ordered the brigade of Colonel Daniel McCook to execute this duty: "I directed Colonel Daniel McCook, with his brigade and [Charles M.] Barnett's battery, to occupy the heights in front of Doctor's Creek, so as to secure that water for our men."[65]

Like Sheridan, McCook was an Ohio native. A veteran of the battle of Wilson's Creek, and chief of staff for the First Division, Army of the Ohio, in the Shiloh campaign, McCook was the colonel of the Fifty-Second Ohio and commander of one of Sheridan's three brigades.[66] At once he awakened his men and began making preparations, consulting with, among others, cavalry Captain Ebenezer Gay, who had some knowledge of the terrain in their front. Then McCook moved forward.[67]

The Confederate picket line was still on the crest of Peters Hill as McCook deployed his veteran regiments in the eerie silence of the early morning. In McCook's words:

> I formed the Eighty-fifth Illinois on the right of the Springfield Pike, the Fifty-second Ohio (my own regiment) on the left of the Springfield Pike, throwing forward well to the front and flanks two companies of each regiment as skirmishers. I formed the One hundred and twenty-fifth Illinois, another regiment composing my brigade, the right wing on the left side of

> the road and the left wing on the right side. My skirmishers had scarcely taken intervals, it being a bright moonlight night (between 3 and 4 o'clock in the morning), when the enemy opened upon me with a heavy musketry fire.[68]

But this time the Federals had mustered sufficient manpower. Up and over the top of the ridge they fought. Throwing the Rebels back, they seized both a stretch of Doctor's Creek and the dominant heights beyond. In the dim twilight before sunrise, McCook sent word back to Sheridan and Buell that he occupied the high ground.[69]

The Confederates were not ready to give up the position just yet, however. St. John Liddell ordered his units to reform for a counter-attack. The Seventh and Fifth Arkansas regiments drew the assignment. While the Rebel infantry quickly responded and deployed for an assault, the cannoneers of C. Swett's Mississippi Battery (Warren Light Artillery) unlimbered their guns and opened fire across the valley of Bull Run, using spherical case and concentrating their barrage on the woods of Peters Hill. Particularly hard hit was the area held by the Eighty-Fifth Illinois. Dan McCook ordered his troops to lie down, but several had already become casualties.[70]

The Yankee cannoneers fought back, quickly and effectively. Captain Charles M. Barnett's six-gun battery answered the Rebel fire. The Federals more than held their own in this artillery duel, even though Barnett was unable to use two of his guns because of the inexperience of the soldiers detailed to man them. The Federal gunners kept shifting their pieces effectively, getting the range on the Confederate artillerists, forcing them several times to move to avoid a concentrated fire. Nevertheless, a lot of Rebel fire smashed into the woods on Peters Hill.[71]

Then Liddell signaled for his infantry to advance. Tense Yankees waited, men of the Fifty-Second Ohio and the One Hundred and Twenty-Fifth Illinois, as well as the Eighty-Fifth Illinois, while the Rebels moved steadily forward, their colorful battle flags waving in the early morning light. "I restrained the impatience of the men," said McCook, until the Confederates "got within 200 yards of me."[72]

At last McCook ordered his men to open fire, the cracking report of the Federal rifled-muskets sounding up and down the line. The Rebels responded with a volley of their own, and a soldier of the Fifty-Second Ohio later remarked how men were so often struck without crying out: "An arm is shattered, a leg carried away, a bullet pierces the breast, and the soldier sinks down silently upon the ground or creeps away if he can."[73]

From the Confederate perspective, St. John Liddell summarized the assault which he had ordered: "The attempt was promptly and cheerfully made," he reported, "but the force of the enemy had been increased so largely and suddenly as to force back both lines, the officers and men contesting the ground with resolute determination, unwilling to yield it to even the great odds against them."[74] But yield they did, in the face of superior Yankee numbers who were holding the dominant terrain. Sheridan was then with McCook, up where he could see what was going on, and fending off messages from Gilbert instructing his aggressive brigadier not to bring on a general engagement before Buell was ready. Sheridan replied that he was not bringing on an engagement, although he thought the Rebels intended to do so.[75] Whatever the Rebels intended, it was clear they would not be able to drive the Yankees off Peters Hill without a major effort. Clearly two infantry regiments and a handful of guns would not suffice to do the work.

Sheridan soon set up his headquarters, commandeering for that purpose the house belonging to a family named Turpin. Meanwhile, his blue-clad soldiers headed for Doctor's Creek to quench their thirst. The aggressive Sheridan, not satisfied with securing his hold on Peters Hill, then determined to force Liddell's Arkansans off their ground across Bull Run and back on Perryville. Thus he ordered Lieutenant Colonel Bernard Laibolt's brigade to attack Liddell's Rebels. But the Arkansans stubbornly held their position against Laibolt's determined advance. Laibolt's response was to reinforce his attack, committing two Illinois regiments in support of the Missouri regiments that had led the Yankee assault. One of these Illinois units became famous as the "Preacher Regiment." The Seventy-Third Illinois was so named because about a dozen of its officers were Methodist preachers.[76]

The Rebels continued to fight vigorously, and the Yankees increased the pressure still again, sending two more regiments into the fray. The swelling Union numbers at last became too great—so it seemed to the Federals—and Liddell's brigade retreated in haste. Sheridan had triumphed again. The wisdom of this attack, however, was highly questionable. When General Gilbert came up and saw Sheridan's situation, he immediately told him to pull back. Not only had Sheridan's advance carried considerably beyond the main line of the corps; but also both of his flanks were unanchored.[77] In spite of all the criticism, much of it justified, that has been leveled against Gilbert, his concern about Sheridan's rash advance was well founded.

Roy Morris suggests that the success of Sheridan's last assault, ironically, gave Buell a "false impression" of Rebel strength that led to "crucial misconceptions." Pointing out that Liddell's Confederates "had been forced to fall back" and take their places among the Rebel forces massing for a major attack, Morris says that the consequent ease of Sheridan's triumph misled Buell "into thinking that the enemy had fallen back in disarray and that he had the luxury of taking his time." Thus he decided to delay his plans for attack until the next day. "By doing exactly what he had been told not to do, Sheridan had unwittingly contributed to a general relaxation of tension among the Union high command," wrote Morris, and that "at the very moment . . . Bragg's Confederates were assembling to launch a devastating frontal assault on Alexander McCook's unwary corps."[78]

☆ ☆ ☆

In fact, it was a question of who would first launch a major assault. Some of the Federal officers would have wagered that it would not be Buell, for they considered him too slow both in deliberation and in action, even if he was making preparations for an attack. In the event that Buell did attack first, they worried about the outcome of any fight under his direction, unconvinced that he could adjust to changing conditions in the confusion of battle.

There was so much concern that, according to testimony later offered at the Buell Commission, several Yankee officers held a secret meeting on the night of October 7. They gathered in the house of a citizen at Rolling Fork, a few miles from Lebanon. Behind closed doors, to prevent the enlisted men from knowing what was occurring, some twenty to thirty officers assembled. They came from both Crittenden's corps and Gilbert's corps. According to the testimony of General James B. Steedman, the result of the meeting was the framing of a dispatch, although it was never sent, to President Lincoln, "asking him to relieve Buell from the command of the army, for the reason that, in the opinion of the signers, he had lost its confidence." Steedman said the petition was signed by all the officers present.[79]

General Buell apparently knew nothing of this clandestine gathering. Perhaps he sensed something of the discontent with his leadership, however, for it was pronounced, among both soldiers and officers. Certainly Buell knew the administration in Washington was unhappy with him, for, as previously recounted, he had barely escaped removal from command, thanks to General Thomas. Thomas also was unaware of the secret meeting at Rolling Fork; at least, there is no evidence that he knew about the gathering.

It was fortunate that Buell had no information about the Rolling Fork meeting. Buell had enough problems on the night of October 7 without the added burden of knowing that his officers were preparing to ask the president to remove him from command. He had been bruised during the afternoon when he was thrown from his horse.[80] But even though he was suffering physically, he fully intended to attack the enemy. Much of the Rebel army, Buell thought, was in his front near Perryville. Thus he must coordinate the concentration of his own forces, which were then closing in on the western outskirts of the little town. The feint toward Frankfort having deceived the Confederates about the location of his main body, a surprise attack might even be possible. Already Buell had instructed Alexander McCook to have General Sill, commanding the diversionary column, to make forced marches in order to join up as quickly as possible.

Meanwhile, the Federal forces close at hand needed to be properly positioned at once. "On discovering that the enemy was concentrating for battle at Perryville," Buell reported, "I sent orders on the night of the 7th to General McCook and General Crittenden to march at 3 o'clock the following morning, so as to take position respectively as early as possible on the right and left of the center corps, the commanders to report in person for orders on their arrival, my intention being to make the attack that day if possible."[81] This is a straightforward, accurate summation. Buell's actual orders to Thomas, written by Chief of Staff Colonel James Fry, with the time of 7 P.M. noted, read: "From all the information received today it is thought the enemy will resist our advance into Perryville. They are said to have a strong force in and near the place. We expect to attack and carry the place tomorrow. March at 3 o'clock precisely tomorrow morning without fail, and if possible get all the canteens filled and have the men cautioned to use water in the most sparing manner."[82]

Attempting to make sure that all would go well at the high command level, Buell also told General Thomas that, when Crittenden's column was in position, "you will please report in person at these headquarters with all the information you may have been able to obtain, and instructions for the further movements will be given." The last sentence of the message said: "Nothing has been heard of you since we parted this morning."[83]

But General Thomas did not report to Buell in person. His failure to do so is puzzling. Buell had informed Thomas clearly that he intended to attack. Thomas also had a specific order to report, and he was second in command of the army. Historian Kenneth P. Williams observes that Thomas "knew Buell's weakness; and he should have realized that his presence might be highly important, might greatly influence instructions that might be given." Furthermore, contended Williams, as second in command, Thomas "should have wanted to be something more than a companion or prompter to a corps commander."[84] Williams's criticism of Thomas for not reporting in person to Buell is well taken.

One might speculate that Thomas's refusal to report to Buell had something to do with a subtle tension between the two men, especially since Thomas had been named to replace Buell, even if he had refused to do so. Perhaps something about the wording, the tone of Fry's message to Thomas from Buell, did not set well with Thomas. The stalwart Virginian could be touchy at times. There is no way of knowing why Thomas acted as he did. Whatever the reason, it was unfortunate for the Union army that the man who probably was the most competent general in the army was not in Buell's immediate presence as the time for battle drew near.

Clearly, General Buell needed all the help he could get. Buell's concept of the situation, especially of the number of Confederates at Perryville, was highly inaccurate. No more than half of Bragg's army was in front of the village, whereas Buell supposed he was confronting the entire Rebel force. "Seldom in the annals of warfare have the commanders of two contending armies been so completely befuddled as to the location and plans of the other," wrote Stanley Horn.[85] For his part, Bragg was convinced that only a small portion of Buell's force was near Perryville and that the main Yankee army was moving to strike the Rebels to the northeast, near Frankfort or Versailles. Thus Bragg had been striving to rendezvous with Kirby Smith's forces in that direction and counter the supposed Federal strength.[86]

☆☆☆

Bragg had intended to leave Harrodsburg on October 8 and join Kirby Smith. However, he rode south to Perryville that morning, concerned both about the Blue force near that village, which had disrupted his timetable for reuniting his army, and about the lack of information from Polk and Hardee concerning the Yankee numbers. It is easy—perhaps too easy—to be hard on Bragg for failing to locate the main force of the Union army. For example, Basil Duke bitterly censured Bragg, noting that he was "completely misled by the mere demonstration upon Frankfort," and stating that the general kept "more than two-thirds of the force under his command idly maneuvering in a quarter where nothing could be accomplished, and permitted less than twenty thousand men to become engaged upon a field where more than forty-five thousand of the enemy could have been hurled against them."[87]

But the employment of a diversionary column, such as Buell sent toward Frankfort, often can be very effective in confusing an enemy. Information from Kirby Smith's front seemed to indicate that a strong force was approaching. Indeed, the "mere demonstration," as Duke called it, was twenty thousand strong. And the truth is, neither Hardee nor Polk had indicated to Bragg that most of the Federal army was near Perryville, although both generals later claimed that they knew the fact. If they did, it is strange indeed that they did not inform Bragg.[88] Quite the contrary, it will be recalled that Polk's 11 P.M. message to Bragg on October 6 had said of the Federal force approaching Perryville, "I cannot think it large."[89] The most that can be made of Hardee's words to Bragg on the night of October 7—and certainly Hardee had sent no clear-cut information before then—is that he implied that a sizable force in his front was a possibility. Of course this was a factor, perhaps the decisive one, in Bragg's ultimate decision to ride to Perryville early on the morning of October 8 and form his own judgment about developments on that front.

As Bragg's biographer, Grady McWhiney, writes, "It seems clear that Hardee and Polk were as poorly informed about the enemy's location as Bragg."[90] When Polk and Hardee afterward maintained that their counsel had been ignored, Colonel William K. Beard, the inspector general of the army, wrote to Bragg: "I had occasion to see you frequently during the days preceding the battle of Perryville and well recollect that you were led to believe from the information given you by the officers commanding both at Perryville and Versailles that the main attack would be in the direction of the latter place."[91] Also, McWhiney wrote that Colonel David Urquhart said that Kirby Smith begged Bragg to send reinforcements to him, "confident that the feint was against Perryville, and that the main attack would surely fall on him. Thus urged, General Bragg, against his own judgment, yielded, and detached two of his best divisions."[92]

It *was* a very muddled picture of the enemy's location that Bragg had before him as he rode to Perryville. While en route, he heard from Polk, a communiqué which cheered him for the moment. Bragg later reported: "Having ordered the attack and that no time should be lost, I was concerned at not hearing the commencement of the engagement early in the morning, but was much relieved for the time by receiving from General Polk a note, dated Perryville, 6 A.M., October 8, informing me that the enemy's pickets commenced firing at daybreak and that he should bring on the engagement vigorously."[93]

But Bragg's relief was short-lived. As the Confederate commander approached the town of Perryville, he heard no sounds indicative of battle. Instead of attacking, Polk had held a council of war with Hardee, Buckner, and Cheatham, laying before them Bragg's order of the previous evening to "give the enemy battle immediately. Rout him, and then move to our support at Versailles."[94]

Polk found the order very disturbing, especially as increasing evidence of growing Federal might was uncovered. Joe Wheeler's information indicated that Yankee infantry were out on the Springfield Road in at least division strength. There was skirmishing on the Lebanon Road southwest of Perryville. Most alarming of all was St. John Liddell's situation a mile west of town, where Federal infantry were applying increasing frontal pressure, while the Blue cavalry operated on Liddell's flank, and artillery fire tore into his lines.[95] Simon Buckner later reported that Liddell "became so hotly engaged with the enemy as to require either that he should be supported by the other brigades of my division, or that he should be withdrawn; on reporting which fact to General Polk, I was directed to withdraw Liddell's brigade . . . and establish my line in rear of Chaplin's Fork."[96]

Polk and Hardee were still unsure of the Federal strength, and they determined to be cautious. Bragg reported: "To my surprise . . . no gun was heard, and on my arrival, about 10 A.M., I was informed that it was determined not to attack, but to assume the 'defensive-offensive.'"[97] Polk's report said they had resolved "to adopt the defensive-offensive, to await the movements of the enemy, and to be guided by events as they were developed."[98] Polk explained, six months later when a trial for disobedience of orders loomed as a possibility, that he had not regarded Bragg's message instructing him to give battle at Perryville as a "mandatory" attack order, "but simply suggestive and advisory."[99]

It reasonably may be contended that Bragg's order to "give the enemy battle immediately" was predicated upon his belief that the enemy's main force was not in front of Perryville, but the order—if words mean anything—certainly was more than "simply suggestive and advisory."

This "Perryville Affair," as Polk styled the matter,[100] soon would become a sore point between Bragg and his generals. Hardee, Buckner, and Cheatham all declined, six months later, to tell Bragg what advice they had given Polk at the council of war. Buckner wrote Bragg a long letter listing reasons why he would not respond, the whole message couched in conciliatory language. Cheatham, whose relationship with Bragg was badly strained after the Stones River battle in December, responded with two sentences. He told Bragg that his "sense of duty" compelled him "to decline to answer" concerning what part he had taken in the council of war at Perryville.[101]

One of Bragg's biographers has presented a compelling case against Polk.[102] While there is no doubt that Bragg was in a difficult position, being unsure where the main body of the enemy lay—and that he deserved criticism for not having established an adequate means of gathering intelligence about the enemy's whereabouts—it is also true that Bragg was not well served by Kirby Smith, nor by his two chief subordinates, Hardee and Polk, particularly Polk.

Actually, when Polk failed to attack on the morning of October

8, it was the second time he had disobeyed Bragg's orders within a week. Earlier Bragg had told the bishop-general, when the latter was at Bardstown, that the Federals were "certainly advancing on Frankfort," and had ordered him, on October 2, to put his "whole available force" in motion the next day and "strike [the Yankees] in flank and rear."[103] Bragg also had ordered Kirby Smith to assault the Federals—General Sill's diversionary column, of course—from the front. But Polk never moved from Bardstown, until eventually he retreated toward Perryville, because he was convinced that Bragg was mistaken about the location of the Union's main force.

Polk claimed that he never disobeyed Bragg's order. His reasoning was that Bragg had told him to move with his whole "available" force, and that, "since the largest part of Buell's army" was in "my immediate front," there were simply "no troops . . . available."[104] Grady McWhiney makes a pertinent observation when he says that Polk's explanation about his "available" force is really "the argument of a bishop, not a general."[105] Perhaps McWhiney is even more on the mark when he observes that "Polk probably had been a bishop too long to be a successful subordinate."[106]

Some historians have excused the bishop-general's disobedience of Bragg's orders, contending that he was justified, considering the circumstances, and pointing out that Bragg was wrong about the location of the Union's main force.[107] Nevertheless, it is entirely possible that Polk's failure to move on October 3, as Bragg had instructed, cost the Confederates a victory. Steven Woodworth, in his recent book, *Jefferson Davis and His Generals*, candidly states: "Polk's disobedience probably cost the army a victory and might have been much more costly had Bragg not learned of it in time to call off Kirby Smith's attack."[108] Grady McWhiney writes:

> Had Polk moved rapidly to Frankfort on October 3 or 4 and cooperated with Smith, the outcome of the Kentucky campaign might have been different. The Confederates, who would have outnumbered [the Yankees under] Sill and Dumont, might have crushed these two Union divisions. . . . In any

> event, the armies of Bragg and Smith would [finally] have been united and better able to meet Buell's main force.[109]

If Polk had moved, as ordered and when ordered, he would not, as his son later claimed,[110] have exposed himself to attack in flank by Buell's army. The Federal force was not concentrated for an attack on October 3, and the Rebel cavalry, "if properly used, could have screened the army's march."[111] What "Polk's partisans" have overlooked, writes McWhiney, "is that Buell's army from October 3 through October 5 occupied positions which just might have allowed Bragg's original plan to work."[112] Each of Buell's corps was on a different road, one heading toward Shepherdsville, one toward Mount Washington, and one toward Taylorsville, with the diversionary column moving toward Frankfort. They were about a day's march apart from each other, and not one had blocked Polk's possible routes north. Certainly the road from Bardstown through Bloomfield and Mount Eden was open. If that route had been blocked, there was yet another, farther to the east, through Chaplin and Lawrenceburg.[113]

Also, if Polk had been thinking more about what he could do to the enemy rather than what the enemy might do to him, it might have occurred to the bishop-general that, if indeed the main force of the Yankees was advancing toward him, a great opportunity was at hand to slip away, concentrate with Kirby Smith's forces, and mass their superior numbers against a much smaller segment of the enemy.

Such a move by Polk also would have taken Buell by surprise, that principle of generalship recognized through the ages as one of the most important—if not *the* most important, as Napoleon thought—that a successful commander may employ, often leading to results far out of proportion to the numbers and resources expended. Obviously no one knows how Buell might have reacted, but with the Rebels thus applying the military principals of maneuver, mass, and surprise, Buell would have been placed under great pressure. The "fortunes of war" just might have taken a decidedly different turn.

Instead, as Woodworth caustically concludes, "Polk, the actual culprit," ironically was "sending off a dispatch to Bragg admonishing his commander for allowing the army to become too scattered, even though it was Polk's obstinacy that had kept the army from being united and had added to the dispersion."[114]

Whatever may be concluded about Bragg's attack orders and Polk's interpretations, there is no question that Polk twice disobeyed orders and that Bragg, when he reached Perryville about ten o'clock on October 8, was surprised and upset to find that Polk had not made the attack ordered for that morning. Instead, the Rebels were in a defensive line behind the Chaplin River, hardly what Bragg had expected. Anxious to smash the Yankees in his immediate front and then move north to what he still thought would be the main Federal force, Bragg decided to attack even if the hour would be much later than anticipated. He soon learned, however, upon examining the Rebel position, that the attack must be delayed still longer, because Polk had the troops badly positioned. When Bragg studied the ground, and the positions held by the Confederate divisions, he may well have thought it fortunate that the Rebels had not launched an attack before he got to Perryville.

The major problem was that the Confederate right (northern) flank, if advanced against the Yankees, was highly vulnerable to a turning movement by the Federals.[115] The position was not good, thought Colonel George Brent: "General Polk's line was weak, his right if outflanked by the enemy would have cut us off from Harrodsburg and General Smith."[116] Also, a Federal turning movement would secure control of the confluence of Doctor's Creek and Chaplin River. The Federals already had control of virtually all of Doctor's Creek, as the Confederate units were positioned to the east of that stream.

An attack under such circumstances was a flirtation with disaster. The Rebel front, Bragg felt, first must be adjusted to cope with the problem on the right flank. "General Bragg at once, therefore," recalled J. Stoddard Johnston, "ordered Cheatham's division to be marched by the right flank as rapidly as possible. The distance to be marched was about two miles."[117] Clearly this would expend a lot more time, but Bragg probably reasoned that he had no choice in the matter. The general would launch his attack north of the Springfield Road, which ran directly west from Perryville. He would concentrate his men to crush the Federal left and center. Cheatham would be on the Rebel's far right, Simon Buckner's division to Cheatham's left, and Patton Anderson's division to the left of Buckner.

Cheatham's move "was soon underway, the hot sun beating on [the men] as they marched northward. . . . The movement attracted sporadic artillery fire, but Cheatham's men were periodically sheltered by the undulating hills along Chaplin's Fork."[118] When the march was completed, sometime around noon, Cheatham's division and a Texas cavalry command, led by John A. Wharton, anchored the Grayclads' northern flank.[119] To further strengthen the attack against the Federal left, where the main Rebel effort was to be made, Bragg shifted two brigades from Anderson and a reserve brigade from Buckner to take position on Cheatham's left, these soldiers to come into the gap between Cheatham and Buckner.[120]

The plan of attack called for Cheatham's division, "in echelon from the right," to move rapidly against the Yankee's left flank, positioned on the ridge to their front. When Cheatham's guns were heard, the divisions of Buckner and Anderson would move to the assault on the center and left. In immediate command on the army's right was Polk, with Hardee commanding on the left. The plan explained, Bragg and his staff selected a site on the east side of Doctor's Creek, in rear of Cheatham's division.[121] At last the Rebels were ready to begin their attack.

☆☆☆

Back on the Springfield Road, three and a half miles from Perryville, General Buell was at the house of a family named Dorsey, where he had established his headquarters. On a hill close to the house, some soldiers of the Seventeenth Ohio observed the general's position. Years later, one of them, Colonel John M. Connell, spoke at a reunion in Lancaster, claiming that at the base of the hill "was Buell's peaceful tent, where we could occasionally see him bareheaded and in his shirt sleeves comfortably at home."[122]

It would be surprising if Buell really were "comfortable" in any meaningful sense of the word. The general was very sore because of the fall from his horse the previous day. He was anticipating a battle—one that he knew (or surely should have known) he had to win if he hoped to keep his command. Yet all known factors seemed to indicate that his plan to attack on October 8 would have to be abandoned. At the least, any attack would have to be delayed until sometime in the afternoon.

The advance of General Alexander McCook's corps would not come up on the Federal left before mid-morning. Time would be consumed getting those men into position for an attack, and as yet there was no word from Crittenden's corps on the right flank. Apparently Buell, by late morning, was thinking of postponing his attack until October 9.[123] Perhaps, shaken by his fall, the general welcomed that prospect.

Actually, however, Buell's situation was not bad at all. The columns of his army were coming together quite well, even if not as rapidly as he had intended. Crittenden was coming up on the Lebanon Road. Except for Joshua Sill's division of McCook's corps, still on the march from Frankfort, and the inexperienced division under Dumont, which was continuing the feint to the north, Buell had all his troops along a front of about six miles.[124] The overall strength was about fifty-five thousand. The latest intelligence on Confederate strength placed only two divisions at Perryville.[125] Quite possibly more Rebels were present, as Buell thought, but, even so, the Federals could expect to have a numerical advantage—in the worst possible case, an equality.

The basic problem was that Buell did not have a grip on his army. There was a disturbing looseness about the whole operation, a looseness which was accepted and even symbolized by Buell himself.[126] His staff officers did not serve him well, coming back from the front to headquarters at the Dorsey House for the noon meal on October 8. Kenneth Williams cuttingly remarks: "Their synchronized stomachs served notice of emptiness at the same hour and they returned to headquarters, not one having sufficient curiosity or sense of responsibility to remain and keep an eye on developments."[127] Also, as noted previously, Buell was not served well by his second-in-command, George Thomas, who, moving with Crittenden's corps, remained virtually out of contact with the army's commander.

Even fate seemed to be against Buell. The landscape, combined with the direction and intensity of the wind, kept the noises of heavy musketry firing, which would have announced a battle, from being heard by Buell at his headquarters. This amazing phenomenon, sometimes called "acoustic shadow," results in loud sounds "being inaudible to persons a short distance from the source while the same sounds may be heard over a hundred miles away in another direction."[128] Unfortunately, "acoustic shadow" left Buell unaware, until about four o'clock in the afternoon,[129] that his army had been attacked and was fighting desperately. Buell's victimization through this odd quirk of nature has aroused a degree of sympathy for his plight, especially when coupled with his injury and seemingly reasonable explanation that he supposed "information of anything of serious import" would have been "promptly conveyed to me."[130]

Yet, nothing obscures the fact that Buell was about to miss a rare opportunity, essentially because he did not possess the controlling and aggressive instincts of a first-rate field commander. His was the command. His was the responsibility. But he did not seize the moment.

☆☆☆

Meanwhile, out on the Mackville Road, as McCook's corps moved toward the outskirts of Perryville, Lovell H. Rousseau's division was in the lead—minus John C. Starkweather's brigade, which had been delayed at Mackville while receiving supplies. General James S. Jackson, after waiting a while for Starkweather to advance, decided to march his division behind Rousseau's, with Starkweather's unit eventually coming on in the rear.[131] In Starkweather's brigade, the colonel of the Seventy-Ninth Pennsylvania Infantry spoke to motivate his men on the dry, dusty march: "Boys, you have longed to meet the enemy on the battlefield, and you have a chance today or do without water, as the enemy holds the spring." The soldiers replied that both "a fight and water" they would have before the day was finished.[132]

When McCook was about three miles out of Perryville, he halted his men west of the Benton (White) Road and set up corps headquarters a short distance in front, near the house of a family named Russell, located on the Mackville Road just east of its intersection with Benton Road. He told Rousseau and Jackson where to position their divisions. Rousseau was to take position along Benton Road, on Gilbert's left flank, from which he was separated by a valley nearly half a mile wide, in which lay the bed of Doctor's Creek. Jackson was to place his command, composed largely of green troops, on Rousseau's left. McCook then rode to report to Buell at army headquarters, which he said he reached about half an hour past noon, while Rousseau and Jackson watched their divisions filing into line.[133]

Forty-four-year-old Lovell Harrison Rousseau, born in Lincoln County, Kentucky, was a lawyer by profession. Having practiced in Indiana before serving in the Mexican War, he returned from that conflict to become Louisville's leading criminal lawyer. In 1860, Rousseau was elected to the Kentucky state senate, where he played a prominent role in opposing secession. Resigning in 1861 to recruit for the Union army, he fought under Buell's command at Shiloh. Intelligent and experienced, he was one of the army's most dependable division commanders.[134]

Leading the Federal division that prolonged Rousseau's line to the left was thirty-nine-year-old James Streshly Jackson. Like Rousseau, Jackson was a native Kentuckian, a lawyer, and a veteran of the Mexican War. A member of Congress in 1861, he gave up his seat to organize the Third Kentucky Union Cavalry. Jackson was a man who evoked contradictory feelings and evaluations. He had provoked a duel with a fellow officer during the Mexican War and had resigned to avoid court-martial.[135] A *New York Times* article of October 11, 1862, described Jackson as "brusque and overbearing, . . . a party to numerous quarrels, which sometimes resulted in duels," and also accused him of killing his antagonist in a street fight in Hopkinsville. If the *Times* was less than sympathetic to Jackson, one wonders about the Kentucky battlefield marker's quite different evaluation: "Impressive in person, graceful in manner, kindly, chivalrous, he was the highest type of Kentucky gentleman."

Whatever the truth about Jackson's character and temper, according to some accounts, a discussion had been held on the night of October 7 among Jackson, William Rufus Terrill, his senior brigade commander, and Colonel George Webster, concerning the chances of being struck in battle by enemy fire. They decided that they should not be worried, thinking that the chances of any particular soldier's being killed were very slight. By the next night, all three would be dead.[136]

Right then, many of the Yankees, both officers and enlisted men, were more interested in water than anything else, especially since unfortunate rumors had begun to circulate through the Federal units that only an insignificant Confederate force was present at Perryville. General Rousseau later reported: "Everything indicated that the enemy had retired and it was so believed."[137] Thirsty Yankees were easily lulled into a false sense of security. General Rousseau, in fact, now focused his attention on the quest for water. "Waiting perhaps an hour," he wrote, "I concluded to resume the march" to the creek, "to get water for my men, who were suffering intensely for the want of it."[138]

Thus Rousseau ordered Colonel William H. Lytle, commanding the lead brigade, to advance and permit his soldiers to fill their canteens. The plan was for one regiment at a time to go down the hill to the creek. As soon as the first regiment returned, another would follow. The Forty-Second Indiana moved down the hill first, passed the house of Squire Henry P. Bottom, stacked arms, and began trying to fill their canteens with the stagnant water, of which, according to Lytle, "there was little or none there."[139]

Union General William R. Terrill.
Courtesy, Hart County Historical Society.

It is unlikely that McCook would have objected to Rousseau's action. In fact, McCook returned to the front from army headquarters with instructions from Buell to make a reconnaissance to Chaplin River to get water. "I went forward in person, examined the ground, and saw the water," McCook later told the Buell Commission.[140]

On the left of Jackson's division—that is, on the extreme left of the whole Union line—the brigade of General William Rufus Terrill was going into position. "Our Brigadier General Terrill," said a soldier in the One Hundred and Fifth Ohio, "is a tall, light haired man with a coarse voice which makes him quite a target for the boys to mock at. He loves good liquors and beef for his table."[141] Terrill was a twenty-eight-year-old Virginian who had graduated from West Point in 1853, the cadet whom Sheridan had threatened with a bayonet.[142] His younger brother James, a graduate of Virginia Military Institute, had joined the Confederate army and was serving under A. P. Hill in Virginia, but William remained loyal to the Union.[143]

Terrill's inexperienced brigade was closest to the Chaplin River. Already Terrill had announced, looking toward the stream, "That's my water."[144] To take it, he had the approval of both Jackson and McCook, just as soon as his full brigade was formed in line. The Yankee quest for water probably would have brought on a battle even if the Confederates had not been poised to attack.

Chapter 8

A Ghastly Scene of Dead and Dying

☆☆☆

Benjamin Franklin Cheatham stood on the bank of Chaplin River at Walker's Bend. He watched his brigades form and looked up at the bluff they must climb. As commander of the division that would lead the Confederate attack, Cheatham's role was highly important.

A native of Nashville, descended on the maternal side from James Robertson, founder of the city, the colorful, forty-two-year-old Cheatham was a veteran of both the Mexican War and the California Gold Rush. He had returned to Tennessee and participated prominently in the state militia in the years preceding the war. He was commissioned a major general shortly before commanding a division at bloody Shiloh. Generally popular with his men, Cheatham already possessed a reputation as a fierce fighter. Standing five feet, eight or nine inches tall, he was powerfully built, with light blue eyes, light brown hair, and a heavy mustache. An English visitor later remarked that Cheatham was "stout, rather rough-looking," while a Yankee soldier wrote that his "looks did not belie his reputation as a rough and ready fighter." According to one of the men under his command, Cheatham looked like a soldier should look, being a "quite commanding figure." His physical strength and cursing were becoming legendary. So too, if the allegations of some are accepted, was his drinking, although it is unlikely that he could have retained a high position of command, as he did throughout the war, had he been a habitual drunkard.[1]

Cheatham's attack had been delayed when it was discovered by John Wharton's cavalry that the Federal flank was being extended farther to the north. (These Yankees were the men of Jackson's division, of course, moving into position on the left of Rousseau's line.) In order to strike the Blueclads in flank, Cheatham's division obviously had to be shifted farther to the north before his assault could be launched. Also, Wharton's cavalry had to drive the Union pickets from the ground just above the bluff, if a surprise attack were to be achieved.[2]

Riding with Wharton were the Eighth Texas Cavalry Regiment and portions of two other regiments, the Fourth Tennessee and the First Kentucky, as they passed behind Cheatham's lines to the far right, crossing the Chaplin and moving into attack formation while still concealed by hills from Federal observation. The sudden charge of the horsemen completely surprised the skirmishers from the Thirty-Third Ohio Infantry Regiment on the bluff above the river. A participant wrote that the cavalry maneuver "was made in a sweeping gallop and as if on parade,"[3] while General Polk reported that "Wharton charged the enemy's extreme left with great fury, passing on over stone walls and ravines and driving back [the pickets] several hundred yards."[4]

The charge was effective. The Yankee pickets fled for security, scrambling back to the main body of their regiment, a part of Leonard Harris's brigade of Rousseau's division, which then opened fire and stopped the Confederates from further pursuit. As Wharton's cavalry hastily retired from Union view, not only was the ground clear for Cheatham's attack, but also the Federals, rather than interpreting the move as possibly heralding a Confederate assault, believed the contrary. Again seeing their enemy give ground, just as Liddell's brigade had done farther south, many Yankees were convinced that there was no impending threat of attack. "Everything indicated that the enemy had

Confederate General B. Franklin Cheatham.
Courtesy, Tennessee Historical Society.

retired and it was so believed," wrote division commander Brigadier General Lovell H. Rousseau in his report after the battle.[5] In fact, many men in the Forty-Second Indiana were engaged in cooking and eating when the Rebel attack broke upon them. Others were still involved in procuring water.[6]

It was approaching two o'clock when Cheatham gave the order for his infantry to advance.[7] The first line of the Grayclads moved forward. Across the river they splashed, the stream being barely deep enough to break their stride. Up the far bank they clambered, continuing to the top of the bluff. Still hidden from Yankee view, they stopped to catch their breath and adjust their lines. Then, as they swung forward in battle formation into the open area, for the first time they were visible to the astonished Federals of Jackson's and Rousseau's divisions, the former still assembling.[8]

George W. Landrum of the Second Ohio, a regiment in Harris's brigade, had his telescope resting on a gun as he watched the hills and woods to the front of the northerners. A few minutes earlier, he had observed ten or twelve Confederates on horseback, "evidently taking a survey of the field," who then disappeared. "For some reason, I know not what," wrote this young man who was to die eleven months later at Chickamauga, "I kept my glass on the point they had left. . . . Suddenly there emerged from the wood the head of a column of men, and as they came out, their bayonets glistened in the sun, and then I knew they were coming for us."[9]

Thus the battle began with a surprise attack. However, contrary to the hopes of General Buell, it was the southerners who achieved the surprise. It was not an absolute surprise, of course, but it was effective. A member of Bragg's staff, the Kentuckian J. Stoddard Johnston, wrote that Cheatham's "noble division of Tennesseans" moved forward, "as if on dress parade, with a spirit not excelled by anything I afterwards witnessed . . . , taking the enemy by surprise."[10]

"Give 'em hell, boys!" shouted General Cheatham as the men charged. According to legend, Bishop-General Polk was nearby and

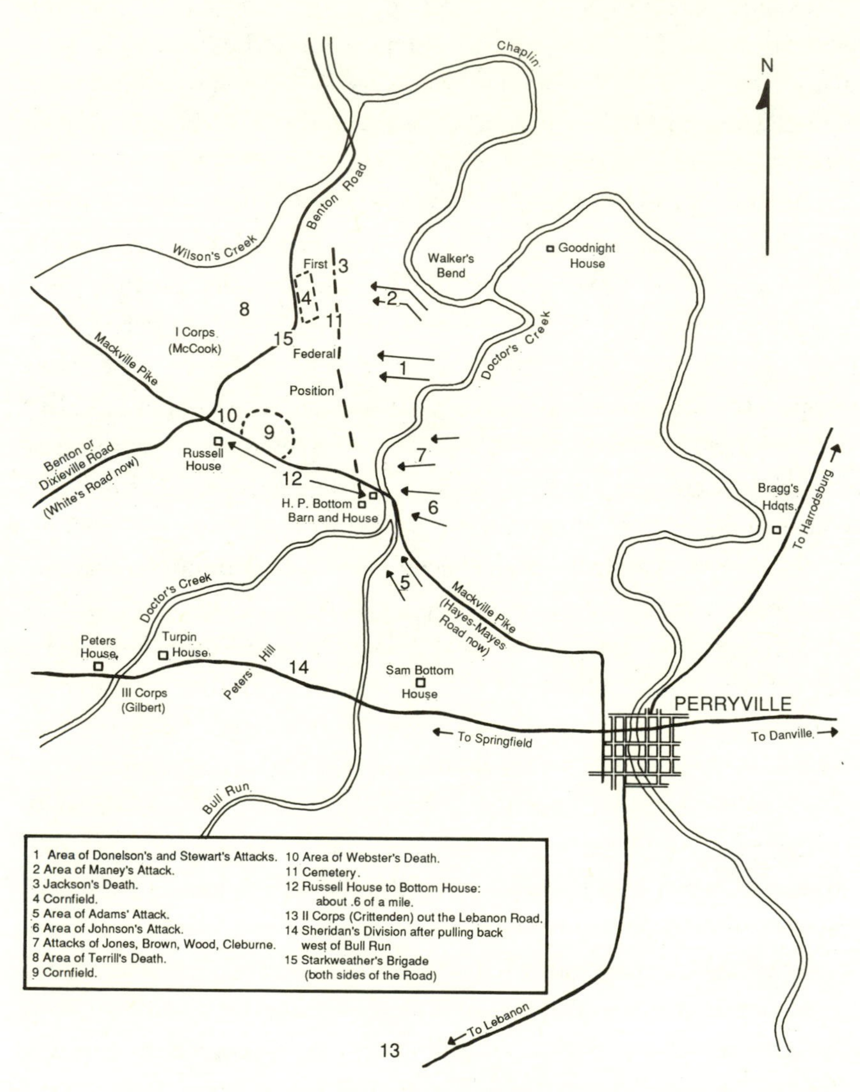

Perryville battle area.
Map prepared by Sharon McDonough.

heard Cheatham. Polk's voice also rang out: "Give it to 'em boys; give 'em what General Cheatham says!"[11]

Daniel S. Donelson's brigade was in the lead, followed by the men of Alexander P. Stewart's command. Brigadier General Donelson, a West Point graduate who had ranked fifth in his class of thirty-seven, was a Tennessee plantation owner who had served in the state legislature. A long-time participant in the state militia, he had chosen the site for strategic Fort Donelson on the Cumberland River, which was named for him. At sixty-two years of age, Donelson was older than most officers, as well as most men in the ranks, and had less than a year to live.[12] His brigade was composed entirely of units from the Volunteer State, consisting of, from right to left, the Sixteenth, Fifteenth, and Thirty-Eighth regiments, with the Eighth and Fifty-First regiments held in reserve.[13]

These Grayclads, yelling and shrieking, swept forward toward the Yankee position, intent on giving their enemy exactly what General Cheatham had said.[14] "'Victory' for our motto was shouted all along our line and fearlessly and gallantly we charged them," remembered a Confederate in the Sixteenth Tennessee.[15] "And now the battle was upon us," related a Federal in the Thirty-Third Ohio who watched the Confederate charge. He said that it was the first time he had heard the Rebel yell and that "they came like veterans, and the onslaught was terrible."[16] The Union line lay a few hundred yards to the front of the Confederates, along the crest of a hill that ran in a northwestern direction, gradually rising in elevation toward the flank.

But what Donelson's men glimpsed ahead of them was not what they had hoped to see. Before they could reach the Federals on the crest of the low-lying ridge in their front, they first had to cross a rather pronounced depression in the terrain, which paralleled the enemy line. Bad as it was, this factor was relatively minor compared to what else they saw. Although the Yankees were surprised to find the Rebels charging toward them, and although General Terrill's green regiments—the Eightieth Illinois, the One Hundred and Twenty-Third Illinois, and the One Hundred and Fifth Ohio—still were tak-

Looking east from site of Parson's Guns toward Rebel attackers.
Photograph by Peggy Nims.

ing position to form the Federal left, the Confederate attack was not enveloping the Yankee line as planned; instead it was striking straight toward their line. Donelson's regiments actually were facing some units of Rousseau's division, the Second and the Thirty-Third Ohio regiments of Harris's brigade, and the Twenty-Fourth Illinois, sent forward from John Starkweather's brigade, as well as Jackson's units to their right front.[17]

Worse yet for the Rebels, as fate would have it, Charles C. Parson's Federal battery, located beyond the line where Terrill's infantry was forming, soon enfiladed Donelson's regiments with artillery fire on their right flank, while Samuel J. Harris's battery opened against their left flank. The Confederate attack indeed had surprised the Federals, but when it did not envelop their flank as intended, the result was that Donelson's brigade found its own flanks raked by a devastating artillery barrage, and its front swept by heavy musketry

View west as Confederates approach Parson's Guns.
Photograph by Peggy Nims.

fire. Nevertheless, reported Donelson, the men moved "forward at a double quick . . . , amid yells and cheers at every step."[18]

From the Yankee line, a Union soldier who said that "the bullets whistled around us and I was truly astonished that I was not hit," affirmed the élan of the Rebel charge: "I could see them fall, and waver, and fall back, only to come on again, yelling and cheering like so many devils. . . . As fast as a man fell, another stepped into his place."[19]

A Rebel was equally impressed with what he saw of the Federal line in his front. "It looked to me like the whole face of the earth was covered with Yankees," said C. H. Clark, a charging Confederate in Colonel John Savage's Sixteenth Tennessee regiment.[20] Even today, if one stands in the depression gazing up the hill toward the Union position, it is possible to understand something of what Clark must have felt. Likely it did look worse to soldiers in the Sixteenth

Tennessee than those in the other regiments of Donelson's brigade. According to Clark, "The whole line of battle was expected to keep in line in the forward movement, but some of the boys, seemingly anxious to close in on the enemy, raised the yell and rushed forward, which caused our regiment to get far in advance of our main line."[21]

Clark was not exaggerating about the Sixteenth Tennessee's advanced and isolated position. Cheatham's biographer states that an officer on Cheatham's staff ordered the Sixteenth to move forward rapidly, which it did, before the Fifteenth and Thirty-Eighth regiments could connect up with the Sixteenth.[22] Perhaps it was a combination of an unfortunate order and the zeal of the Sixteenth that moved the regiment forward so quickly—too quickly.

C. H. Clark said, too, that the men were "falling dead and wounded all about me . . . , school mates and playmates, neighbors and friends, and I thought all would be killed. . . . I had no hope of getting out alive." He recalled a man named George Sparkman who "was severely wounded and took refuge behind a tree, but a grape shot from a cannon killed him." In addition to the soldiers who were falling dead and wounded, Clark remembered some terrorized sheep and rabbits caught between the two enemy lines, "either scrambling to get away or immobilized by fright."[23]

Donelson's brigade was stymied, in the process losing a third of its strength, as its regiments moved in an uncoordinated manner. Donelson tried to shift his direction of advance farther to the right, toward the enemy flank, but this only resulted in confusion. Alexander P. Stewart's brigade was coming to Donelson's aid.[24] A forty-year-old Tennessean, Stewart was known as "Old Straight" from the days when he had taught mathematics, first at West Point and later at Cumberland University in Lebanon, Tennessee.[25] With five Tennessee regiments, he was advancing to reinforce the Rebel assault. But the pressing need was to do something about Parson's Federal battery and the supporting infantrymen who were raking the Confederate right flank with artillery and rifle fire.[26]

General Cheatham had recognized the problem, and he assigned

George Earl Maney's brigade the task of silencing those Yankee guns. Maney was another Tennessean in Cheatham's predominantly Volunteer State division. A graduate of the University of Nashville and a veteran of the Mexican War, Maney was to fight in most of the major battles and campaigns of the Western Theater, surviving the Civil War to become a railroad president, legislator, and minister to several Latin American countries.[27]

Maney moved his brigade well to the right, ascended the bluff, and was able to go into attack formation while concealed from the Yankees both by a wooded area and a slight depression of the ground. From left to right, his brigade was formed with the Ninth Tennessee, the Sixth Tennessee, and the Forty-First Georgia. These three regiments composed the attacking force, making up, as Maney explained, "as much front as could be brought advantageously against the battery."[28] In reserve he placed the First Tennessee and the Twenty-Seventh Tennessee. Two soldiers of the latter regiment, William Rhodes and Frank Buck, demonstrated the fear and anxiety that can plague people when facing a trial such as the impending charge. They went to their company captain, John W. Carroll, and told him they were going to be killed. Carroll later recalled that "their pale features, their calm demeanor, their determined looks impressed me much." Although the captain had no authority to do so, he said, "yet I did offer that they take a pass and drop out, which they refused to do."[29] Then the brief moment for reflection was gone, and action once more absorbed the attention of all.

The men of Maney's brigade plunged forward. Up and over the top of the rise they advanced, surprising the Federals by their unexpected appearance.[30] A Yankee remarked that it was as if they came out of nowhere. They were only about three hundred yards away and moving through a wooded area toward the open ground on the left of the Union position.[31] Even so, three hundred yards can be a long distance, and the Rebel attack would not be easy.

General James Jackson was with Charles Parsons's battery. At once he instructed Parsons to shift his guns leftward and halt the oncoming enemy. Parsons's eight guns blasted canister into Maney's ranks, and the Federal supporting infantry of the One Hundred and Twenty-Third Illinois—at last in position after advancing with the rear rank in front, which produced much confusion, according to Captain William P. Anderson, since the regiment was a new one—also opened fire, sweeping the Rebels with deadly effect.[32]

"One of the most deadly and destructive fires that can possibly be imagined," reported the Sixth Tennessee's Colonel George C. Porter, "was poured into [the brigade's] whole line by the enemy, who occupied a strong and well chosen position on an eminence in an open field about 300 yards to the front."[33] Major John Knight, commanding the Forty-First Georgia, reported that "owing to the situation of the enemy, the Forty-first Regiment was first exposed to the fire, and as soon as it was in view, the enemy opened upon them a most terrific and deadly fire. . . . It was a fearful time."[34]

The Twenty-Seventh Tennessee, due to the confusion that so often manifests itself on a battlefield, had followed the main line through the woods, instead of remaining in reserve as had been intended, and Major A. C. Allen of that regiment later recalled: "During the whole time of passing through the woods the [enemy] battery was playing upon us with terrible effect. . . . Large boughs were torn from the trees, the trees themselves shattered as if by lightning, and the ground plowed in deep furrows."[35]

Maney's Confederates, soon after emerging from the woods, confronted a high rail fence, and their advance quickly came to a stop. Colonel Porter remarked that, at this point, "it seemed impossible for humanity to go farther, such was the havoc and destruction that had taken place in their ranks. A temporary halt was the inevitable result."[36]

Penned down behind the fence and facing a murderous artillery barrage from the slope above, Maney's brigade was in a death trap. If they hoped to escape from the awful mess in which they were entangled, they would have to silence the Yankee battery and drive the Yankee infantry from the hill. This was the reality, cold and brutal. They must kill the Federals before the Federals killed them.

Perhaps no one recognized this truth more keenly than George Maney. "Our only chance of success," he later wrote, "was to move rapidly forward."[37] Maney was on foot, his horse having been shot. Thus, at the crisis of the advance, fearing his brigade would be destroyed if it remained long at the fence, the general ignored the danger and showed the kind of personal leadership that makes the difference between victory and defeat. Moving down the line from right to left, Maney urged the men forward.

Colonel Porter, whose Sixth Tennessee was in the center of the Rebel line, gave this account of the dramatic moment: "Here, at this critical juncture, General Maney passed along the line from the right of the Georgia regiment to the left of the Ninth Tennessee, ordering and encouraging us to still press forward, as it was our last and only chance of safety and success."[38] Porter said Maney's "presence and manner . . . imparted fresh vigor and courage among the troops,"[39] while Major Knight of the Forty-First Georgia reported that, "At this critical moment General Maney passed down the line, encouraging the men by his personal presence and urging them forward."[40]

The Confederates responded, many of them undoubtedly realizing that no acceptable alternative existed. If they were going to die anyway, then they wanted to die fighting. Major Allen said that the Twenty-Seventh Tennessee "as one man leaped the fence and most gallantly charged at a double-quick, firing at every opportunity." Maney himself wrote that his men charged as if "reckless of the danger and death before them."[41]

The Confederates were taking severe casualties, but they were also moving relentlessly up the hill, pausing only to reload their weapons. When they fired, thought one Rebel, "it looked as if it were a solid sheet of flame."[42] The momentum of battle was abruptly changing, turning against the Yankees.

General Braxton Bragg had advanced to a bluff on the river from which he viewed the action.[43] J. Stoddard Johnston was with the general. "I recall, with a feeling of horror, the sight which presented itself. . . . It was a square, stand-up, hand-to-hand fight. The batteries and lines of battle of both sides could be seen distinctly, except

Looking north from federal monument to the line of Parson's Guns and the site of General Jackson's death marker. Photograph by Peggy Nims.

when occasionally obscured by the dense smoke, which alternately hung over the scene or was blown off by the western breeze. Never was a battle scene more perfectly spread out to the eye."[44] Bragg and his staff watched in hope that the Yankee left was about to be driven from the field in rout.

Federal General Jackson was still with Parsons's guns and apparently sensed the change taking place in the struggle since the Rebels cleared the fence. According to Captain Samuel M. Starling, inspector general of the Union Tenth Division, who was standing within three or four yards of the general, "the minnie balls . . . with their peculiar whizzing noise" seemed to be coming in greater and greater numbers from the Confederate ranks, when Jackson remarked, "Well I'll be damned if this is not getting rather particular." Almost as soon as Jackson had uttered the words, enemy fire hit him in the chest. Starling thought the general was killed instantly, stating "I am sure he breathed not once."[45] Captain Percival Oldershaw also was nearby when the division commander fell: "I found him on his back, struggling to speak, but unable to do so. He died in a few moments." Oldershaw said two bullets had entered the general's right breast.[46]

About the same time that Jackson was killed, the One Hundred and Twenty-Third Illinois Infantry fell back in panic. Unfortunately for the Union, General Terrill had ordered the big regiment of some seven hundred men forward when Maney's Rebels began their advance. The Illinois soldiers, organized only one month earlier, had had hardly any drill instruction. They came into the fight in confusion, and, after a brief flurry, were no match for Maney's brigade, which could load and fire faster than they could. Once the Rebels had advanced beyond the fence, they raked the One Hundred and Twenty-Third with a devastating volley. The inexperienced regiment went to pieces, scurrying up the hill, many in a panic, leaving the slope dotted with the bodies of their dead and wounded. In the battle, the regiment suffered about 190 casualties, and most of those came in the minutes when they engaged Maney's brigade.[47]

"Perryville was a quick and brutal initiation of new Illinois regiments to warfare. For some soldiers, just weeks away from home, it had all happened too suddenly." Such was the summation penned by one man from Illinois.[48] Certainly the One Hundred and Twenty-Third Illinois was not the only raw Yankee regiment struggling to cope with the Rebels on the left flank. The One Hundred and Fifth Ohio, which had been formed on August 20, was attempting to take position as the last regiment on the flank when the Rebels attacked. Like the vanquished Illinois unit, it also moved up with the rear rank in front.[49]

Private Josiah Ayre of the Ohio men's Company E vividly recorded in his diary the confusion among the green troops: "By some reason or another we could not form into proper line and after going through several maneuvers in order to do so we became mixed and confused, not knowing what our officers said or anything about it. Finally we were ordered to load and fire the best we could, although I could not see a rebel at the time on account of the shape of the ground."

Private Ayre continued to describe how he and some of the men would move forward to get sight of the enemy, fire and then fall back to reload. "I repeated this two or three times," he said, "when we were ordered to fall back, the enemy not being over 15 rods from us, steadily advancing. By this time every man seemed to be looking out for himself as we were all broken up. For my part, I could not tell whether we had any regiment or not." Ayre said he finished loading his gun and started off. "I did not go far however before a musket or rifle ball struck me in my left leg just below the calf, breaking it and passing clear through. I of course fell and that finished my fighting." Soon the advancing Rebels swept by and Private Ayre said "one of them cut off my cartridge box and took it away from me."[50]

George Maney's fierce attack, pressed home by the now relentless Tennesseans and Georgians, finally overcame the Yankee position on the extreme left. Parsons's battery was devastated by their assault, losing well over half of its officers and men and most of its horses. The story was told that Parsons himself continued alone to fire one of the guns, and, in the words of Stanley Horn, historian of the Army of Tennessee, "When the Confederate infantry closed in on him he did not flee but drew his sword, stood at 'parade rest' and awaited the fire of the advancing force." The outcome, continued Horn, was that Parsons's courage deeply impressed an oncoming Rebel colonel who ordered his troops to withhold fire, allowing Parsons to walk away from the field of conflict.[51]

Another version of the story was that one of Parsons's own men pulled him away when the enemy was almost upon him.[52] (Surviving the war, Parsons became an Episcopal minister in Memphis; he stayed at his post while the yellow fever epidemic of 1878 ravaged the city, contracted the disease, and died.[53]) Only one of Parsons's guns was hauled away by the Federals, the others falling into the hands of the cheering attackers.

The Rebels did not need to depend on captured guns, however. After a different kind of struggle—one that many of those facing the bullets probably would have welcomed—the Grayclads had succeeded in dragging their own artillery to the top of the bluff, from which the Yankee lines were being blasted with telling effect. The Thirty-Third Ohio's Henry Lewis said that a soldier "near him had his head torn from his shoulders by a shot from the Rebel guns." Amazingly, "the same ball bounced off a tree and hit Lewis, breaking his right arm." According to the continuing saga that Lewis related, he was then "struck in the left shoulder by infantry fire."[54]

What happened to Lewis, his decapitated companion, and the Thirty-Third Ohio, whose Lieutenant Colonel Oscar F. Moore was also wounded, left behind, and taken prisoner as the regiment fell back, typified the situation on a much broader scale.[55] While some of the Yankees of McCook's corps had fought like the veterans they were, to be sure, and some of the recruits also had fought well, others, particularly many of the green troops in Jackson's division, had raced for the rear. The Second Ohio's George Landrum believed that the men in the regiments that turned and fled were not so much to blame as their officers. He observed that "several of the new regiments, who have brave men to lead them, behaved nobly, and would have done as well as any if they had only *known how*; *but* a great number of the Colonels and other field officers of the new regiments fled before their men." Landrum thought it was not surprising that "then the men, finding themselves deserted by their officers, turned and ran like curs—in some instances running completely over some of our old and tried regiments, creating the wildest confusion." Also, some officers apparently could not identify the enemy when they directed the fire of their regiments, according to Landrum: "I saw one regiment (a new one), I could not find out where it is from, or its number, deliver its fire into another of our regiments, and then turned and fled."[56]

One wonders how many Yankees—having correctly identified the enemy—then experienced the disconcerting problem of a defective weapon. An Indiana private, reporting that the men were ordered to rise and fire at the oncoming Rebels, remembered that "our bullets . . . strewed the ground with their mutilated carcasses—the legitimate fruit of [their] treason and folly," but that soldier's subsequent efforts to fire his weapon were futile. Throwing down his gun "in disgust," the private searched for another weapon, claiming he tried about six before finding one that could be depended upon to shoot.[57]

George M. Kirkpatrick, a member of the Forty-Second Indiana, who was in battle for the first time, quickly lost faith in his sergeants: "We had two sergeants, Jack Jones and Nath Matheney," wrote Kirkpatrick. Jones had "told us what to do if we heard a cannon shot. He had said, 'Don't dodge, as when you hear it, it is past.' Jack was running in front of me, and every time a . . . ball or shell would go over, he would duck to the ground. . . . Both of those men had seen service in the Mexican War, and we young fellows looked to them for information, or had been doing so; but after that we would not take their word anymore."[58]

Regardless of whether the Federals fought or ran—or tried to duck—the tide of battle had turned against the Union left flank. The Confederates of Cheatham's division—the brigades of Maney, Donelson, and Stewart—at last had mustered sufficient manpower. Up and over the top of the crest the Grays' line swept, collapsing half of McCook's line and driving the Federals back. Retreating to the next hill to the rear, the northerners halted at the Benton Road.

Among the Federal units being forced to retreat in this sector was the One Hundred and Twenty-First Ohio regiment. It had been ordered to the support of Parsons's battery, only to learn upon drawing near that, in the words of Lieutenant Ellis E. Kennon, acting assistant adjutant general of the Thirty-Fourth Brigade, "the battery had been taken and the enemy were approaching in very considerable force. The One Hundred and twenty-first abandoned their position in bad order, but were subsequently partially reformed some distance to the rear and fought in a creditable manner. I deem it due to Colonel [W. P.] Reid to here state that he acted bravely and used his utmost exertions to rally his men."[59]

The "bones" of this report are interestingly fleshed out by the letters of two soldiers in the ranks of the One Hundred and Twenty-First regiment. "It was a bloody day and the greatest exhibition of the Providence of God was that we were not all 'cut to pieces'—to use the common expression," wrote Harvey Lewis four days after the battle. "'Twas owing to our greenery that we were brave enough to go scale the hill in the face of the enemy as we did. Our Colonel supposed we were going to support a battery, and so did we, but on arriving at the brow of the hill a masked battery was opened upon us simultaneously with that of musketry and the balls flew round us thicker than hail." Then Lewis's account differs from Lieutenant Kennon's, saying, "We tried to sally three or four times notwithstanding, when the old regiment that was in front of us broke and ran against us, which caused our boys to do alike . . . and when we did go—'twas sorrowfully and with our faces to the foe . . . ; we were followed for a mile by shot and shell and my only feeling was that of sorrow that we had retreated."[60]

A companion of Lewis in the One Hundred and Twenty-First Ohio was Silas Emerson, a young man anxious to get into a battle, whose account gives another intriguing perspective from the man in the ranks. Writing to "Dear Ann!" (his wife) on the sixth day after the fight, Emerson said he had not been well when the battle took place, but was half a mile behind his regiment resting in a wagon. Yet, "when I heard that our boys would soon go into the fight, I got out and ran all the way to our regiment and went into the fight about 3 o'clock. . . . We had a great battle with the enemy," he wrote; "all marched boldly and even cheerfully forward until the enemy opened on us with cannon and musketry which made sad havock in our ranks. . . . We were not in line of battle when they first fired on us. We formed however as soon and well as we could and returned their fire." But orders soon came to retreat which, said Emerson, "we done in some confusion but quite as well as could be expected even from an older regiment under the same murderous circumstances but we left some brave men on the field." Emerson wrote that he was right beside his company captain, their elbows touching, when the man was struck by a cannon ball; "his blood and flesh flew all over me. I don't know how I escaped. I felt no fear at any time. I had no time to think. After the captain fell the command of the company devolved upon me."[61]

The Rebels, as they compelled the Yankees to retreat, also left a pavement of their dead and wounded. C. H. Clark of the Sixteenth Tennessee in Donelson's brigade, later recalling the fearful circumstances of Donelson's charge, thought that the advance of Maney's brigade—coming "to our rescue on the right"—was the only thing that "saved the remainder of our regiment from being killed or captured."[62] J. J. Womack, also with the Sixteenth Tennessee, wrote that "at the onset we suffered very much both in officers and men."[63] John Gold of the Twenty-Fourth Tennessee in Stewart's brigade, remembered that a large number of his regiment were killed as they tried to crowd through a gap in a rail fence rather than going over the fence.[64]

Major Knight of the Forty-First Georgia thought that "one-half, if not two-thirds, of their entire loss during the battle" occurred as a result of the charge to silence Parsons's battery.[65] Colonel Porter of the Sixth Tennessee, like the Forty-First Georgia a part of Maney's brigade, said that the enemy battery had been taken and their infantry support driven from the field, but only "with terrible slaughter." Porter reported that the regiment had lost "five color-bearers, three of them in this assault."[66] And finally, William M. Pollard of the First Tennessee in Maney's brigade, reported simply in his diary: "We charged and captured several pieces of artillery at a terrible loss." Then he gave some devastating casualty figures: Company B lost twenty out of twenty-six men, Company D lost nineteen out of thirty-eight, including "every commissioned and non-commissioned officer except the fourth corporal, a boy of 19 years of age, who came out in command of the company."[67]

The battle was fearful and bloody, but Cheatham's assault had forced the Federal left to fall back, some of its units in panic.

☆☆☆

Meanwhile, on Cheatham's left, Simon Bolivar Buckner also was driving the Yankees before him—once a certain amount of confusion and bungling had been overcome. Buckner's men were up against the two brigades of Leonard Harris and William Lytle of Rousseau's division. Actually, while Buckner's division bore the brunt of the fight in this sector, it was the small supporting brigade from Anderson's division, led by Brigadier General Thomas M. Jones, that first made contact with the Yankees on Buckner's right flank.

Tom Jones was a native Virginian. An 1853 graduate of West Point, he served as colonel of the Twenty-Seventh Mississippi Infantry before rising to brigade commander.[68] Jones took his three Mississippi regiments, in battle formation, down a rather steep hill just north of the Mackville Road and across the nearby dry bed of Doctor's Creek. There the Federals hit them with a volley of rifled musketry and artillery. The Mississippians returned fire and struggled forward.

The Yankee fire came from the hillside straight ahead, where the Tenth Wisconsin was posted on the left and the Forty-Second Indiana on the right. Peter Simonson's Indiana battery, positioned between the regiments, raked the Mississippians with canister as fast as his artillerists could load and fire. A second volley from the Federal infantry line ripped the Confederate ranks, cutting down men by the score and bringing the advance to a halt. When a third volley blasted the outnumbered and combat inexperienced Mississippians, the brigade collapsed, the survivors rapidly retreating in disorder over their dead and wounded.[69]

Tom Jones's brigade had attempted the impossible: a frontal assault with inferior numbers against a strong defensive position supported by artillery. Even in an action this one-sided, however, there were also Federal casualties. In the Forty-Second Indiana, Company A's Captain Charles G. Olmstead, encouraging and cheering his men, called out to them: "This is as good a place to die as any other"—a cry that has been heard more than once and on more than one battlefield. Scarcely had he uttered the words, according to Captain S. F. Horrall, when he was shot in the forehead and instantly killed. Another member of the Forty-Second, Private George Kirkpatrick, said he was beside Olmstead when he was struck, the captain's brains spattering on Kirkpatrick.[70]

The Mississippians had been compelled to retreat, but a much larger force of Confederates was preparing to advance. On Jones's left, the weight of Simon Buckner's Rebel command was about to go in against Rousseau's Yankees. These Confederates had been maneuvering, with considerably less than parade-ground precision, to launch their attack. Buckner had Bushrod Johnson's big brigade of six regiments advancing to spearhead the assault, while Daniel W. Adams of J. Patton Anderson's division, assigned to cooperate with Buckner, was positioning itself on Johnson's left. Bushrod Johnson, forty-five years old the previous day, was a West Pointer and a veteran of the Seminole and Mexican wars, who had been captured at Fort Donelson but had escaped to fight at Shiloh. There he was seriously wounded but had recovered to fight now at Perryville.[71] His brigade was composed of the Seventeenth Tennessee, Twenty-Third Tennessee, Twenty-Fifth Tennessee, Thirty-Seventh Tennessee, Forty-Fourth Tennessee, and the Fifth Confederate.[72]

Johnson's brigade approached Doctor's Creek at the crossing of the Mackville Road, near the farm of Squire Henry P. Bottom, and attempted to make an oblique wheel to the left before advancing to the attack.[73] The result of the wheeling movement, due to lack of communication, confusion, and blundering, was a comedy of errors that must have resembled a gigantic parade-ground drill gone berserk. The Fifth Confederate regiment, approaching on the extreme left, did not turn at all and so diagonally crossed the brigade's line of march, finally coming up on the right flank in front of two other regiments. At the same time, the march of the Forty-Fourth Tennessee and the Twenty-Fifth Tennessee angled too far to the left—the latter much too far—eventually approaching the right rear of Adams's on-coming brigade and being fired upon by Confederate artillery under Captain Cuthbert H. Slocomb, because it was thought the two units were Yankees moving to attack Adams.[74]

The Forty-Fourth Tennessee, supposing that the battery firing on them was Union, reacted accordingly, as Colonel John S. Fulton of the Forty-Fourth reported: "We charged rapidly up the hill with fixed bayonets to silence and take the battery on our left, and having gained the top of the hill we found it to be the [Confederate] Washington Artillery, and immediately reported to them that they had been firing upon their own men, when the firing ceased."[75]

The confusion of the whole episode is clearly revealed in other reports as well. Colonel Moses White of the Thirty-Seventh Tennessee said, "We discovered that we were separated from the brigade, which was to us a matter of no little surprise, as we had received no command but forward."[76] And Colonel John M. Hughs, Twenty-Fifth Tennessee, reported that "the 44th [regiment] having passed entirely around us and the Fifth Confederate having disappeared, I do not know where, I was left on the extreme left of the brigade, and meeting General Adams, was advised by him to advance by the left flank and take position on the left of his batteries, then firing upon the enemy."[77]

As Adams's brigade marched to join up with Johnson's left flank, its band struck up a tune, playing the men onto the field of conflict with a rousing rendition that was said to have "filled the woods full of music."[78] Cheering as they approached the right flank of the Yankee line, which was stationed on the hill just west of the Bottom House, the soldiers of Adams's brigade were jolted back to reality, as this colorful Rebel pageantry was soon greeted by a hail of fire from the Union line.[79]

The Yankee position, still manned on its left by the Tenth Wisconsin and the Forty-Second Indiana, which had thrown back Jones's attack, was prolonged to its right by the Tenth Ohio, the Third Ohio, and the Fifteenth Kentucky. The latter protected the right flank, while the Thirty-Eighth Indiana and the Eighty-Eighth Indiana waited in reserve.[80]

At last Bushrod Johnson's Tennesseans lurched forward in disjointed fashion, units intermingled, two regiments now moving with Adams's brigade, and engaged Rousseau's Yankees in some of the most intense fighting of the battle. The Confederate advance drove back the Federal skirmishers, then quickly came to a halt. Several stone fences were in the area south of the Mackville Road, and both sides tried to take advantage of these, some Confederate units firing from behind a stone wall along the west bank of Doctor's Creek, while Federals of the Third Ohio and Fifteenth Kentucky crouched behind stone fences on the hillside west of the Bottom House.[81]

The Thirty-Seventh Tennessee's Colonel White testified to the "overwhelming storm of lead" that the Federals poured into his ranks. The Tennesseans, upon White's order, scrambled for better cover, exchanging their post-and-rail fence for the more solid protection of a stone wall, from which they immediately opened fire on their tormentors. As Colonel White reported, "The fire raged with unabated fury for about one hour and a half," when the Thirty-Seventh's ammunition was exhausted and the regiment had to be relieved.[82]

From the Federal perspective, the smoke, noise, and fury of the fight could not have seemed greatly different from the view of the Confederates. John Beatty, colonel of the Third Ohio, particularly remembered the artillery fire. Slocomb's Rebel battery blasted the Yankee troops; Beatty wrote in his memoirs that the enemy's batteries "reopened with redoubled fury, and the air seemed filled with shot and exploding shells. . . . For a time, I do not know how long thereafter, it seemed as if all hell had broken loose; the air was filled with hissing balls; shells were exploding continuously, and the noise of the guns was deafening." Beatty described how a nearby barn was set afire by a shell, the intense heat therefrom nearly panicking some of his troops, as "the flames bursting from roof, windows, doors, and interstices between the logs, threw the right of the regiment into disorder; the confusion, however, was but temporary. The boys closed up to the left, steadied themselves on the colors, and stood bravely to the work." When "the work" was over, Beatty counted nearly two hundred dead and wounded from his five-hundred-man regiment.[83] Thus came to a bloody end the Third Ohio's long-held notion that, because it had somehow missed several previous engagements, it was destined never to fight a battle.[84]

There could be no doubt in the minds of the participants on both sides that this was a battle. General Rousseau later remarked that "Shiloh was nothing" compared to it.[85] While Shiloh obviously had been a much bigger and longer encounter than Perryville, the severity of Perryville probably was comparable to Shiloh's worst moments.

The intensity of the struggle is evident from many accounts of soldiers who experienced it. In the Forty-Second Indiana, George

Kirkpatrick was among a group of Hoosiers who charged down a hill toward a band of Rebels. "About half way down the hill two Johnies were sitting behind a rail cut log," said Kirkpatrick, "with their guns cocked ready, and one of them shot for my head, his bullet passing below my ear, clipping the hair; the other drew blood from Lockwood, my file leader. As soon as they shot they squatted close to the log, and threw up their old gray hats and said 'We will surrender.'" It was not to be. Kirkpatrick concluded: "I don't know just how it was, but others said they saw two guns come down on those two Johnies' heads, and I found my gun broken. . . . The whole thing was all over in thirty seconds or less."[86]

Kirkpatrick and his comrades soon were compelled to fall back, scampering up the hill they had just descended, and Kirkpatrick was grazed by a bullet, "blistering my forehead," he wrote. "In my fright, I thought that my brains were laid bare, because of the stinging pain and the blood pouring down into my eyes, and . . . I was afraid to put my hand up there, for fear to disturb my brain, which I supposed to be exposed by the wound."[87] The Forty-Second's lieutenant colonel was shot in the mouth, yet continued to set a forceful and demanding example for the regiment. "As he rode hither and thither, the blood covering his mouth and face, the officers and men [were inspired to nerve] themselves to the greatest possible exertions," said a member of the regiment.[88]

The pressure on the Federals continued to build. The southern brigade of Daniel W. Adams now had worked itself into position to fire on the flank of the line held by the Third Ohio and the Fifteenth Kentucky, already being tormented by Slocomb's Rebel battery. Adams was something of a seasoned fighter by now. Born in Frankfort, Kentucky, he began a law practice in Louisiana after graduating from Yale. Aggressive and slavishly devoted to the values of the time, he once challenged and killed a newspaper editor in a duel. For his service at Shiloh, where he was blinded in one eye, Adams was promoted to brigadier general.[89] Now his fighting energy, unleashed on the Federal flank, was complemented by Bushrod Johnson's pressure on their front.

It would take a lot of force to break the Bluecoats at this point, posted as they were behind stone fences. "The position was a very strong one," reported Johnson. "There was perhaps none stronger in the enemy's lines."[90] And these Federals were fighting as if they believed that the outcome of the battle depended upon them. Colonel Curran Pope of the Fifteenth Kentucky, seeking to inspire his troops, tramped down his line from soldier to soldier "patting them on the back, cheering and encouraging them to fight to the end." Colonel Pope himself was wounded but stayed with his men. The Fifteenth's color-guard, composed of nine soldiers, was annihilated, as each successive color-bearer was killed or wounded, the colors shot full of holes and the flag staff finally blasted in two.[91]

Color-bearers in the Third Ohio fared no better. "In the opening of the battle," according to Whitelaw Reid's account, "color-sergeant William V. McCoubrie stood a little in advance of the color-guard, bearing the regimental standard proudly aloft." Instantly "a fierce fire" was directed at his exposed position, "and the gallant fellow was killed." Such was the fate of five others, until "a beardless boy of seventeen, named David C. Walker," rushed forward "and caught the colors ere they touched the ground," successfully carrying the flag through the remainder of the action. His reward for this feat was to be named, on the morrow, color-sergeant of the regiment.[92]

Obviously, the Rebel fire directed at the Yankee color-guards was devastating; however, shooting at the enemy's colors certainly was not confined to the Confederates. Captain S. F. Horrall, of the Forty-Second Indiana, recorded that "some practiced marksmen of Company G of the Forty-second were ordered to keep the rebel flag down." Several times the flag, with its bearer, fell, said Horrall, but "was taken up again."[93]

Taking down the enemy's colors would not win a battle, as both sides surely knew, in spite of their enthusiasm for trying. Maximum force at the proper pressure points was what was needed. And at last the Rebels, just as they did farther to the north on Cheatham's flank, were bringing together a concentrated force, front and flank. Although Bushrod Johnson's troops were running out of ammunition,[94] reinforcements were moving up rapidly. On Johnson's right, the brigade of John Calvin Brown, from Anderson's division, had moved into the area from which Tom Jones had been repulsed, applying pressure to the Federal left flank; and coming to Johnson's immediate support, Pat Cleburne's crack division was moving to the front between Brown and Johnson.

Cleburne's report, vivid and precise, is worth quoting: "The enemy lined the ridges west and south of the creek. They were strongly posted behind stone walls and were keeping up a rapid fire on the brigade of General Johnson, which was trying to ascend the ridges in the face of this galling fire. We now received the order to advance quickly to his support."[95] At double-quick time, Cleburne led his men across the creek, a witness saying they moved (quite in contrast to the earlier approach of Johnson's brigade) like "a dress parade under fire on the battlefield."[96] During the advance, Cleburne, who had been seriously wounded in the mouth during the battle at Richmond, was painfully wounded in the ankle, but stayed in the fight, skillfully directing the brigade. His horse "Dixie," one of his favorites, was killed. A captain later said: "Only such a man as Cleburne . . . could inspire men to go up against such odds, and win—and he did."[97]

Cleburne first got his Fifteenth Arkansas regiment into a position, partially protected by a stone wall, to level an enfilading fire on the left flank of those Yankees of the Fifteenth Kentucky and Third Ohio who had made such a tough fight behind their own appropriated stone fences.[98] Shortly before, as previously noted, shellfire had set ablaze a nearby barn filled with hay that was behind the Bottom House. Soon flames shot high into the air.[99] The smoke and heat from the blaze was one factor that, in combination with the Confederate fire on both flanks as well as their front, finally forced the Third Ohio and the Fifteenth Kentucky to pull back up the hill.

Elated as he saw the Yankees retreating, W. E. Yeatman wrote that "as their line broke, we had them, and gave it to them in the back. It was a hot evening, and the grass being dry, caught fire, the flames spreading to a barn just to our right. Rather than burn, out hustled a lot of blue coats to surrender."[100]

As Cleburne's men advanced, Bushrod Johnson's exhausted soldiers, out of ammunition, fell back toward the creek bed to regroup.[101] The Confederates now had too many men and too much fire power. The Federal soldiers could stand no longer, and their entire line retreated up the hill. A Union staff officer described them as "like men who had been beating against a great storm." The fresh troops of Cleburne, supported by Adams and Brown on the left and right, rejuvenated the attack by Buckner's brigade. But once again a distressing and disheartening blunder had to be endured. Cleburne told the story: "As we ascended the hill we were fired into by our own artillery in the rear. Several of our men were killed and wounded, and we had to fall back. I sent an aide to stop this battery. I can only account for this blunder from the fact that most of our men had on blue Federal pants."[102]

With this "friendly fire" silenced, Cleburne once again ordered his line forward. Their battle flags flying, the Rebels moved to the crest of the hill and continued to drive the Yankees who were attempting to rally just beyond the hill. "The moment our flags, carried by the line of skirmishers, appeared above the crest of the hill," Cleburne wrote, "the enemy, supposing our line of battle was in view, emptied their guns at the line of skirmishers. Before they could reload, our true line of battle was upon them; they instantly broke and fled, exposed to a deadly fire."[103]

Colonel Lytle tried to rally these Federals, persuading perhaps a hundred (Cleburne's estimate) to stand with him. "They were routed in a moment," remarked Cleburne, "with heavy loss."[104] Lytle himself was wounded, "as he thought, fatally, and refusing to be taken from the field, was taken prisoner," reported General Rousseau.[105] The Confederates continued to advance through a cornfield, firing into the rear of the retreating Yankees, but, said Cleburne, they "became so scattered in the pursuit I found it necessary to halt the brigade and reform line of battle."[106]

J. Stoddard Johnston recalled the scene: "The sun shines hot and red through the smoke. The long agony of doubt is passed, and the whole line advances. . . . General Bragg, crossing the creek, rides forward rapidly to the right, to order a more vigorous advance. A ghastly scene of dead and dying meets our view at every step; the blue and the grey mingled together in sickening confusion."[107]

A Yankee in the Thirty-Sixth Illinois of Sheridan's division observed the action from Peters Hill, as did many another soldier in Gilbert's corps, and saw the Union line off to his left break under the pressure of the Rebel attack. Afterward he expressed the consternation felt by those watching—unengaged—as their comrades of McCook's corps were mauled, broken, and driven by the Confederate attack: "When our lines went down before the irresistible charge, many a prayer went up to heaven, 'God help our poor boys now.'"[108]

This soldier's prayer calls forth a rather obvious question: why did God need to help when the left flank of Sheridan's division was only a few hundred yards away? It will be remembered that, earlier in the day, General Gilbert had urged Sheridan, when fighting with Liddell's brigade, not to bring on a general engagement. Later, when the trek of Daniel Adams from the Springfield Road took his brigade across Sheridan's front, "Little Phil" observed and allowed those Rebels to pass without a contest. Sometime after noon, while Gilbert was at army headquarters with General Buell and distant noise of artillery was audible, the testy Buell instructed Gilbert to send an order to Sheridan to stop wasting powder.[109] Gilbert remained at army headquarters to eat with Buell, who informed him that dinner was nearly ready. Sheridan, receiving Gilbert's message, quieted his artillery. Also, Sheridan never notified his corps commander, nor the army commander, that a battle was being fought off to his left.

Was Sheridan simply being petty (as he certainly could be; one of his biographers observed "a cruel pettiness" in the little man[110]), piqued at the way he had been treated by his superiors? Or did he assume, even after the order to stop the waste of powder, that Gilbert and Buell surely must know that a battle was under way? Sheridan's report, brief and oversimplified when addressing this part of the action, merely says, "I directed the fire of my artillery across the valley on this advance of the enemy, forcing them to retire, thus very much relieving General McCook. This ended the operations of the day, it being dark and the enemy having retired from the field."[111]

Actually, it would be surprising indeed if General McCook had agreed that Sheridan's actions had "very much relieved" him during the fighting on the afternoon of October 8. Some writers have given Sheridan great credit—certainly more than he deserved—for his role at Perryville. Two biographers, perhaps overly conscious of "Little Phil's" subsequent contributions to the war, credited him with having "saved the Union army" on October 8.[112] (At the Battle of Stones River in Middle Tennessee, less than three months later, a solid case might be developed for just such a thesis, but not at Perryville.)

Sheridan was in a position at Perryville to have made a major contribution. From the advanced and high ground near the Chaplin River, to which he had aggressively charged, Sheridan later, in his memoirs, claimed he had "discovered the Confederates forming a line of battle on the opposite bank, with the apparent purpose of an attack in force."[113] This discovery prompted Sheridan to pull his troops back to the entrenchments already thrown up on the crest of Peters Hill. From that vantage point, which offered a good view to his left (north), Sheridan saw McCook's corps advancing toward the Chaplin River, unaware of and unable to see the Rebels massing in force on the opposite side of the stream. He said he tried, "by the use of signal flags," to warn McCook's troops of the danger in their front, but "my efforts failed."[114]

Soon Sheridan and his soldiers were watching in fascination and dismay as the Confederate attack surprised McCook's men and drove them back across the rolling hills.[115] When McCook sent a message calling for Sheridan's help on his right flank, Sheridan said he advanced a battery [Hescock's], "supported by six regiments," to a "very good position . . . on my extreme left, whence an enfilading fire could be opened on that portion of the enemy attacking the right of [McCook's] Corps, and also on his batteries across Chaplin River."[116]

But Sheridan did not keep up this fire for long. The Rebels were soon placing two batteries on Sheridan's flank and massing troops behind them, as if about to assault. General Gilbert, who by then had come up in the rear, saw what the southerners were doing and feared that Sheridan would be overrun. He told Sheridan to pull back his guns and their infantry support. Complying with his corps commander's order, Sheridan instructed them to fall back to his entrenched position. "I had no sooner got back to my original line than the Confederates attacked me furiously," wrote Sheridan. But, continued the general, "our telling fire made them recoil."[117]

The Confederates never even got to Sheridan's line, in fact. According to Captain George S. Roper's account, Sheridan, carried away by adrenaline, at that moment said that he had "whipped them like hell!"[118] However, as Roy Morris, Jr., the recent and most thorough biographer of Sheridan's Civil War career, points out, "not only had Sheridan enjoyed the advantage of holding the high ground" as the Rebels attacked him, "but he also outnumbered the Confederates . . . four to one."[119] We might also note, as Captain Roper did, that Sheridan "was supported by two brigades of General Robert Mitchell's command on his right."[120]

After repulsing the four Confederate regiments that had attempted to carry his entrenched position, Sheridan once again swung his artillery to his left, seeking to aid McCook. The nervous General Gilbert, who seemed perhaps more concerned about Sheridan's behavior than anything else at Perryville, was alarmed again. "What does that mean? What are they doing over there? Can you see?" Captain Roper was the man whom Gilbert was bombarding with the questions. Then Gilbert ordered Roper to ride to Sheridan and find out what was going on.

When Roper returned with Sheridan's reply that he "was changing front to assist General McCook" with his artillery, Gilbert seemed greatly relieved and satisfied, thought Roper. "Now we've got them; now we've got them; now is the time to push everything."[121] (At least that is what Roper said that Gilbert said.) The fact, of course, is that Gilbert did not "push" anything. What he did was send a message to Buell, informing him of Sheridan's actions and urging Buell to "push everything."[122]

Gilbert's corps, then, was virtually unengaged throughout the battle. He might have played a decisive role, but apparently either did not understand how to use a portion of his large force to support McCook, or would not take responsibility of doing it. After all, while given the rank of major general, actually he was only a captain, *and* an officer without any battlefield experience at any rank.[123]

Sheridan himself was new to division command, of course, and with a force of approximately 6,500, he had some three times as many troops as he had ever led before.[124] While "Little Phil" probably realized that Gilbert was not equal to his responsibility as a corps commander, it probably would be expecting too much of the young Sheridan to suggest that he should have played a saving role such as that later assumed by Gordon Granger, who, without orders, came to the aid of General Thomas at Chickamauga. Sheridan did direct the fire of his artillery, once more, against the Confederates attacking McCook, which, according to Sheridan's claim previously noted, "very much relieved" McCook.[125] But what McCook really needed, and earlier, was Sheridan's infantry—or somebody's infantry—from Gilbert's corps.

Twenty-eight-year-old Dan McCook, the younger brother of Alexander McCook, was commanding one of Sheridan's brigades. Later he gave enlightening testimony to the Buell Commission—enlightening even when one allows for a probable bias in favor of aiding the corps of his brother. After the Rebel attack on Sheridan had been driven off, Dan McCook said, "the excitement which attends such little affairs as this subsided. I turned around and saw the barn on General Rousseau's right in flames, and saw the rebels [advancing]. . . . They were so near I could see the daylight through their ranks with my glass." The younger McCook said the Confederates, as he watched, enveloped and drove back Colonel William Lytle's right flank. "At that time our division, with two batteries, was lying idle. I begged General Sheridan to at least allow us to open on them with artillery, for . . . I felt satisfied that the Rebels were concentrating their whole force against our [left] wing." When again Sheridan did open artillery fire on the Rebels attacking Rousseau, Dan McCook thought it helped to check them, but he also said that by marching his command "250 yards over an open-plain corn field I could have taken the rebels in rear and flank and had them between Lytle's battery and my own."[126] Obviously, Dan McCook felt that Sheridan's division, or at least some of it, should have been deployed against the Confederates attacking Rousseau.

Another Federal in Gilbert's corps, Captain T. J. Wright of the Eighth Kentucky, was of like mind. "Thus the battle raged," he said, "with only a part of our forces engaged, and *our whole corps* ready, willing and waiting, within supporting distance, . . . eager . . . to be led on to support our brave, battling comrades. But no orders came."[127]

The failure to use the Federal forces available to assist McCook's corps would be long remembered. Almost two decades later, Colonel John M. Connell, speaking to veterans of the Seventeenth Ohio at a reunion in Lancaster, asked, "What soldier under Buell will forget the horrible affair at Perryville, where 30,000 men stood idly by to see and hear the needless slaughter in McCook's unaided, neglected and even abandoned command, without firing a shot or moving a step in its relief?"[128] Connell exaggerated, but the broad picture he painted was accurate, and certainly McCook's corps, fighting essentially alone, made an inordinate contribution to what Stoddard Johnston described as a "ghastly scene of dead and dying."

Chapter 9

I'll Fight 'Em as Long as I Live

☆☆☆

While fierce, bloody fighting raged along the Mackville Road near the Bottom House and westward, the outcome of the battle was being determined on the northern flank of McCook's corps. There, along the Benton Road, McCook's second line struggled to hold its ground against the Rebels of Cheatham's division, who had broken and driven Terrill's brigade from the front line, killing division commander Jackson. If McCook's line at the Benton Road could be shattered, it would probably wreck his entire corps, bringing about the complete destruction of the Union left. Gilbert's corps in the center, with its inexperienced leadership, then would be vulnerable. The result might be a Federal retreat from the field. The relatively small number of Confederates would not matter. Two corps of the Union army were virtually unengaged, and the Federal forces did not know how few were the southerners they faced. Anything might be possible—perhaps not probable, but possible—if McCook's corps could be crushed.

Certainly Captain William P. Anderson, the U.S. Army's assistant adjutant general, Thirty-Third brigade, thought the Rebels were on the verge of victory: "Had the enemy pursued his advantage at this crisis the most disastrous results must have followed. . . . Nothing but a very small, disorganized fragment of the division [Jackson's Tenth] remained to dispute [the enemy's] possession of . . . our ammunition train, ambulances, and such supplies as had accompanied us. . . . General Terrill rallied the few troops he had left."[1]

"If our left was turned," stated General Rousseau, "our position was lost and a total rout of the army corps would follow."[2]

Fortunately for the U.S. Army, the ridge along which the Benton Road ran for several hundred feet was held by the brigade of John Converse Starkweather, a thirty-two-year-old lawyer, born in Cooperstown, New York, who had entered the war as colonel of the First Wisconsin Infantry.[3] If anybody may be said to have "saved the Union army" at Perryville, it is Starkweather's command. The good thing about Starkweather's brigade, which belonged to Rousseau's division, was that it consisted of four veteran regiments and only one green regiment. Moreover, it occupied high ground that was very defensible.

The factor of chance in war is always intriguing, and here it was quite significant. Starkweather probably would not have been in this strategic location if, as previously noted, General Jackson had not tired of waiting for him to march that morning and decided to proceed with his division, thus separating Starkweather from the rest of Rousseau's division and forcing him to bring up the rear. As a result, Starkweather was stationed where his men likely determined the battle's outcome.

As the beaten troops of William Terrill's brigade retreated, many of them in panic, they ran pell-mell through the lines of Starkweather's advanced regiment, the Twenty-First Wisconsin, that was deployed in a cornfield east of the Benton Road. The men of the Twenty-First, most of them, held their position as they watched Terrill's fleeing troops pass through in their headlong dash to the rear.[4] A captain in Terrill's command, Robert B. Taylor, later wrote that "our Brigade in less than an hour ceased to be a Brigade." While Taylor's appraisal was an exaggeration, his words attest to the widespread confusion and panic. General Terrill himself thought the situation was dire.

Union General John C. Starkweather.
Courtesy, Hart County Historical Society.

"The Rebels are advancing in terrible force," he shouted to an officer of the Twenty-First Wisconsin.[5]

Soon the Wisconsin men saw the cause of the chaos. The triumphant Confederates—George Maney's command—topped the ridge in their front and began streaming down its western slope, coming for them. The two sides at once were blazing away at each other. Also, Federal artillery from Starkweather's main line along the Benton Road opened on these Confederates. At the point where the Benton Road turns west, away from the ridge, David Stone's Battery A, Kentucky Light Artillery, was posted, with Asahel Bush's Fourth Battery, Indiana Light Artillery, on his left. These batteries opened a devastating fire on the Rebels, although some of their shots fell into the lines of the Twenty-First Wisconsin, wounding and killing some of the Federal soldiers, according to Michael H. Fitch's account of the fight. After several volleys were exchanged in the hollow between the ridges, the Rebels seemed on the verge of another triumph, as the Wisconsin troops gave ground, struggling up the slope to Starkweather's main line.[6]

But the final decision of battle was not to be with the Grayclad forces. The troops of Wisconsin, joining with their own brigade as well as with men who had rallied from Terrill's brigade, stood with soldiers from Pennsylvania, Illinois, Ohio, and Indiana, composing a formidable line on ground favorable for repelling an attack, supported by Bush's and Stone's artillery, which proved equal to the Confederate challenge.[7]

The Rebels could see that the Yankee position was a strong one. But A. P. Stewart's brigade was moving to Maney's support on the Confederate left. Maney's and Stewart's two-brigade line, composed mainly of Tennesseans, except for the Forty-First Georgia regiment, might yet break the Federals and gain a costly victory. Maney gave the signal, and his troops moved forward once more, in concert with Stewart's command, determined to drive the Union troops from the ridge.[8]

As the Rebels approached, the Union line laid down a murderous barrage of artillery and infantry fire. Sam Watkins of the First Tennessee, which was Maney's right flank regiment, was one of the southerners moving toward Bush's Indiana Battery, less than a thousand feet away. His graphic account conveys something of the horror of the charge made by those Tennesseans: "The guns were discharged so rapidly that it seemed the earth itself was in a volcanic uproar. The iron storm passed through our ranks, mangling and tearing men to pieces. The very air seemed full of stifling smoke and fire, which seemed the very pit of hell, peopled by contending demons."[9]

The "contending demons" were Yanks and Rebs, of course, and the way they fought left a lifelong imprint on the mind of many a person who experienced the carnage of that fall afternoon in central Kentucky. A veteran of Shiloh wrote, "Such fighting I never witnessed and in fact never had been witnessed on the battlefields of America." He said that "there was no cringing, no dodging. The men stood right straight up on the open field, loaded and fired, charged and fell back as deliberately as if on drill."[10]

This last comment about the order being like a drill is probably a bit of overstatement, as evidenced by several after-action reports that confirm a considerable amount of confusion. However, the quotation does convey something of the fearlessness with which many men on both sides fought. "It was a life to life and death to death grapple," added Sam Watkins. "The sun was poised above us, a great red ball sinking slowly in the west, yet the scene of battle and carnage continued." Watkins later would write that he "was in every battle, skirmish and march that was made by the First Tennessee Regiment during the war" and that he was never in "a harder contest and more evenly fought battle than that of Perryville."[11]

A member of the Sixteenth Tennessee of Maney's brigade, C. H. Clark recalled in his memoirs of the war that such a trial had a disorienting impact. There was, he thought, "a tendency to temporarily derange the minds of some, at least it was the case with me. If you ask me if I was scared, I answer, I don't know, but I do know I was scared before we got in the thickest of the fight."[12]

Perhaps there was no time, "in the thickest of the fight," to be scared. Advancing with Company A, Fifth Tennessee Infantry, in

Stewart's brigade, was Benjamin A. Hagnewood (or Haguewood), who found himself the recipient of a hurtling ramrod. Sometimes in the confusion and excitement of battle, a soldier, hurriedly loading his weapon, would forget to remove the rammer from the barrel before firing, thus sending an awful missile speeding toward the enemy (as well as depriving himself of the ability to fire his weapon again). Hagnewood, who lost consciousness instantly when the ramrod struck him, recalled that he only knew what had happened to him when he later regained consciousness and "discovered the butt end of a steel rammer sticking out of my left breast." Hagnewood said he extracted the rammer with his own hand and then was taken to "what was called a hospital," where he expected medical assistance, but "from that good hour to this," claimed Hagnewood, "never has as much as a wet cloth been applied to that wound." Many a soldier in Stewart's brigade was killed or wounded, but probably few, if any, were felled in such a unique manner.[13]

Along the Union lines, a reporter who watched Stewart's brigade advance toward Starkweather's position was impressed by "the desperate valor of the Rebels. Led by mounted officers, their broad columns came to the attack in quick movement and with death defying steadiness, uttering wild yells, till staggered by the sweeping cross fire of our artillery and volleys from Starkweather's regiments."[14] An Ohio soldier, Erastus Winters, who fought in the Benton Road line, said that "the ground was covered with [the] blood" of the dead and wounded in his regiment.[15]

The Confederates moved steadily up the slope, although suffering from the close-range fire of the Yankee line. Despite taking heavy losses, Maney's men struggled to the top of the ridge and grappled hand-to-hand with the Federals, particularly those around the cannon, who were equally determined to hold their ground against the southern onslaught. H. R. Feild, colonel commanding the First Tennessee, gives a good account of the tremendous, though ultimately futile, effort of his regiment as it fought to silence Bush's Battery: "After deploying the regiment to the extreme right it was ordered to charge, which it did in splendid style, with close, compact ranks, killing all the horses and men of the battery and driving its support away."[16]

Then, according to Feild's report, Maney's whole brigade, disorganized and confused, relinquished the crest and fell back down the slope. Whether the retreat was due to the pressure of Yankee fire or confusion, as Feild said, the First Tennessee prepared to attack again. "I rallied the regiment at the foot of the hill, no other regiment forming but mine, some 30 or 40 men of the other regiments falling into the ranks," reported Feild.[17] "In the meantime the enemy came back to the guns . . . , and also marched two regiments on our left on a wooded hill." Feild stated his regiment once more charged up the ridge, this time alone, "under a heavy fire of musketry, driving the enemy back and taking his guns again. The regiments on our left then opened fire upon us, killing and wounding a dozen officers and men at each discharge."[18]

The Thirty-Second Kentucky's Captain Robert Taylor, a member of Terrill's brigade, testified that "many of the [Union] Artillerists had been killed" and that "the ground around was slippery with blood." Taylor added that many a "powder begrimed Artillery man was laying stretched out upon the ground around us, torn and mutilated, their countenance plainly indicating the awful manner of their death."[19]

The grit required to fight as the Federals and Confederates did at Perryville is well illustrated by Sam Watkins's account of Rebel W. J. Whittorne, "a strippling boy" of fifteen, who fell, "shot through the neck and collarbone," but then got up, grabbed his gun, and began loading and firing once more, exclaiming, "Damn 'em, I'll fight 'em as long as I live!" The boy probably did think that he soon would be dead. Actually, he lived long after the war.[20] A considerable number of Whittorne's comrades, of course, did not survive to witness another dawn.

The Rebels could gain no more. Stewart's advance was halted by a barrage of fire from the Yankees. After several determined but futile assaults, Stewart's men were compelled to retire. Maney's troops on Stewart's right then faced a destructive fire raking their left flank. The combined frontal and flanking fire was too much. Maney's soldiers, too, retired down the slope. Seeing the hopeless situation, Colonel Feild said he ordered his First Tennessee to retreat, "which it did in much better order than could have been expected, leaving half their number dead and wounded on the top of the hill."[21]

In fact, Maney's entire brigade suffered casualties numbering nearly half of its strength. Starkweather, fighting defensively from a good position, nevertheless took casualties numbering about one-third of his command. Among the Union losses was General Terrill, whose brigade had been swept back by the first Rebel assault. He collapsed, mortally wounded, while fighting with the remnants of his command near Stone's Battery, apparently the victim of an exploding artillery shell.[22]

"I was within five feet of Terrill when he was killed," wrote James A. Connelly of the One Hundred and Twenty-Third Illinois. "I . . . raised him to a sitting position and saw that nearly his entire breast was torn away by the shell. He recognized me and his first words were: 'Major, do you think it's fatal?'" Connelly felt sure the wound was mortal, but trying to encourage Terrill, told the general that he hoped not. Probably Terrill sensed the reality, because Connelly reported that he exclaimed, "My poor wife, my poor wife!" Connelly said that Terrill died about two o'clock the next morning.[23]

Possibly some of the Federal soldiers felt that Terrill had gotten just what he deserved—at least according to an interesting letter written by Stanley Lockwood of the One Hundred and Fifth Ohio. Alleging that Terrill had struck a soldier over the head with a saber because the man left the ranks on an extremely hot day, Lockwood stated that, soon afterward, many a soldier had loaded his weapon for self-protection against the general. Terrill, wrote Lockwood, "is a drunken old tyrant and deserves to be shot by his own men and if he don't come to that fate it will be because the oath of hundreds of men in the 105th Regiment is good for nothing." It is well that Connelly noted that the cause of Terrill's death was an exploding shell; otherwise, in view of the Lockwood letter, one might wonder if the general had not been killed by his own men.[24]

The battle was ending on the extreme Yankee left flank. Starkweather had held. The Rebels finally were stopped, and neither side seemed inclined to renew the fight in that vicinity. Cheatham's exhausted Confederates fell back beyond the ridge from which they had driven the original Union line. Starkweather's Federals pulled back, along the Benton Road to the west. The Confederates had not killed all the horses of Bush's Battery, as Feild reported, but with thirty-five horses lost, two of Bush's four guns had to be dragged away by the men of the First Wisconsin. General Rousseau, who had been with Starkweather earlier in the afternoon, was not present to see the climax of the engagement along the Benton Road, having been told that his presence was required on the right, where his two other brigades were sorely pressed.[25]

General Rousseau had galloped toward the right of his division to learn that the bloodied brigades of Lytle and Harris had been driven back to the vicinity of the Russell House, where, Lytle having been wounded and captured, Harris struggled to form a new defensive position with the battered remains. The Fifteenth Kentucky, which had fought so stubbornly before falling back from its stone fence barricade and which would finish the battle with sixty-six men dead and one hundred and thirty wounded, was in front of the Russell House as Rousseau galloped up. "On approaching the Fifteenth Kentucky (though broken and shattered) it rose to its feet and cheered," Rousseau reported. Ordering the men to lie down, Rousseau also reported that a heavy force of the enemy was advancing upon his right flank, "the same that had turned Lytle's right flank." Pointedly, Rousseau remarked in his report that the Rebels were "moving steadily up, in full view of . . . General Gilbert's army corps . . . , the left flank of which was not more than 400 yards" away. A few months later, Rousseau testified that "almost any part of [Gilbert's force] might have been sent to reenforce us. . . . He was certainly near enough to render us assistance had he been inclined to do it."[26] Rousseau got no help from these Federals, however. The failure of Gilbert's corps to come to the assistance of McCook's corps, when the latter was driven back and was on the brink of destruction, very nearly enabled the Rebels to roll up the Union left flank. Obviously Rousseau was disturbed by Gilbert's failure to help him.

Whatever he may have been thinking about Gilbert, General Rousseau had no alternative but to do the best he could with the troops under his command. Immediately in rear of the Fifteenth Kentucky was the Michigan Battery of Cyrus O. Loomis, posted on higher ground. Here, for sure, Rousseau could expect some assistance. Hurriedly riding to the side of Loomis, Rousseau directed him to open fire on the Rebels at once. But Loomis refused, replying that General McCook had instructed him to reserve what ammunition he had "for close work." In a somewhat amusing account, Rousseau reported that he pointed to the enemy advancing and said that they were "close enough, and would be even closer in a moment." Apparently Loomis agreed, for he at once opened fire with what Rousseau described as "fearful effect" on the Confederate ranks.[27]

But Rebel artillery, which was particularly well handled during this attack, was continuing to take its toll among the Yankees. Rousseau said that enemy shells were so thick that he thought "as many as four or five burst at a time."[28]

Rousseau was doing everything he knew to rally the regiments from Lytle's and Harris's brigades. He rode along the line near the Russell House, under fire, with his hat held high on the point of his sword, setting an example of the courage required to face their attackers, as he reportedly shouted: "My brave boys, I know you will never desert me in the day and hour of danger." To Rousseau's immediate left, George Webster's brigade had formed a line of battle a little farther up the hill, where the men awaited the southern charge.[29]

George Landrum of the Second Ohio, who had been one of the very first Yankees to spot the Rebels advancing, as he had surveyed the front with his telescope, was impressed with Rousseau: "At this time I saw General Rousseau, with his hat on his sword high up above his head, waving it and cheering the men on, perfectly fearless, his countenance all aglow." Landrum thought that "the enemy appeared to know him and made him an especial mark, but he escaped without a scratch."[30] In another letter a couple of weeks later, Landrum noted that "General Rousseau has been promoted. All the credit of the fight that any general can claim is due to him; but," he observed, "there was no great amount of generalship displayed on that field."[31]

At the moment, in the heat of battle, Landrum was doing all he could to help General Rousseau hold the line. His account reveals the intensity of the fight, the pressure the Federals faced, and the presentiment of imminent defeat: "The enemy made their advance about 2 o'clock, and they steadily advanced, forcing our men back, the fight raging with the most terrible ferocity on both sides." Recalling the noise as like "one great roar of musketry," the artillery "pouring in shot and shell," Landrum said, "The air was thick with balls. Men were flying in all directions from the field and I thought all was lost." Landrum wrote that he was able to talk some of the men into returning and fighting again, "but some of them I *drove* back to their places with my sword. I had become perfectly reckless. I never felt my blood rush so wildly, and the sight of our men lying lifeless maddened me to desperation."[32]

Indeed, it was a desperate situation, for now the Confederates prepared for what they hoped would be the final attack in this sector, an assault that would shatter the makeshift Union right flank of McCook's corps. General Hardee, observing the Federal troops forming near the Russell House, directed S. A. M. Wood's brigade across Doctor's Creek to strengthen the attack, Wood's men taking position on Cleburne's right flank. While Wood advanced to their support, Cleburne and Adams assaulted the Yankees at the Russell House.

A soldier of the Thirty-Third Ohio, Angus Waddle, who informed Colonel Harris that his regiment needed ammunition, said that the colonel, anxiously glancing up at the sun, replied that he wished the sun "would soon disappear and thus put an end to the fight, which was so unequally waged."[33] But the sun was not yet setting, and a Federal in Webster's brigade, Colonel Joseph W. Frizell of the Ninety-Fourth Ohio, reported that Cleburne's troops "opened upon me" with a "most murderous and incessant fire."[34] The Union fire proved equally destructive, however, as Frizell's men "stood their ground," he estimated, "for about three quarters of an hour," and the Confederate advance could not continue.[35] The fight in this sector had evolved into a mishmash of units charging and countercharging, neither side able to gain an advantage.

Soon Daniel Adams decided that the Yankee position was too strong and ordered his brigade to fall back, communicating his intention to Cleburne.[36] Cleburne continued to fight, sending out a few sharpshooters to watch his left flank. But, said Cleburne, "a large regiment posted in the valley to my right gave way, and most of them, in spite of my entreaties, fled to the rear, leaving my small brigade of not over 800 men in the center of the battle, unsupported on either flank."[37] Then Cleburne's command was pinned down by an artillery duel being waged across his lines. W. E. Yeatman, Second Tennessee Infantry, thought it was a "novel experience" to witness "a grand artillery duel fought over our heads, while we were comparatively safe."[38] Cleburne said that the artillery fight, "together with the fact that [we] were almost out of ammunition, prevented us from advancing farther. We held the position we had taken until night closed in."[39] The main Confederate effort thus shifted to Cleburne's right.

There Wood's brigade had come up, striking George Webster's Yankees with force, compelling part of his brigade to give way and mortally wounding Webster. Thus died all three Union officers—Jackson, Terrill, and Webster—who, according to legend, had decided the previous night that the chances of being killed were so slim as not to concern them.[40]

Finally, as Webster's men were being forced back, McCook's corps got some help, albeit limited, from the infantry of Gilbert's corps. McCook later reported that, at 2:30, he dispatched his aide-de-camp, First Lieutenant L. M. Hosea to General Sheridan, commanding Gilbert's left division, requesting Sheridan to see that his

(McCook's) right flank was not turned by the enemy. Also, McCook had dispatched another officer, Captain Horace N. Fisher, to find assistance from the nearest commander of troops. Fisher had quite a ride. First he located and asked aid of General Albion Schoepf's division, but Schoepf, while saying that he would like to help, referred Fisher to General Gilbert (then arriving on the field from General Buell's headquarters). Gilbert in turn referred Fisher to Buell, still back at the Dorsey House. Fisher at last reported to Buell at about 3:30. Meanwhile, the anxious McCook had sent yet another aide, Captain W. T. Hoblitzell, to General Schoepf or whoever he might find who could send reinforcements.[41]

At last Gilbert responded. When the general had examined his front, deciding there was no immediate threat to his command, he sent one brigade (fifteen hundred men, according to McCook) to help McCook. Commanding that brigade was Colonel Michael Gooding, who reported: "Precisely at 3:30 o'clock P.M. I received orders directly from Major General Gilbert . . . to proceed immediately to the support of General McCook, on my left."[42]

Gooding's men, proceeding at double-quick pace, reached the intersection of the Mackville and Benton roads, where Gooding said he "found the forces badly cut up and retreating . . . hotly pressed by the enemy." Three regiments strong, Gooding's brigade included the Fifty-Ninth Illinois, the Seventy-Fifth Illinois, and the Twenty-Second Indiana. Forward into the melee Gooding ordered his troops, advancing across the intersection, with Oscar F. Pinney's battery located "on an eminence in our rear, . . . bordered by a dense wood." Rousseau then withdrew his battered brigades, fought out in the struggle with Cleburne, and Gooding faced the Rebel onslaught of Wood's brigade.[43]

S. A. M. Wood struck Gooding's regiment so hard that Gooding, as his report shows, thought that Wood commanded a division. Gooding was outnumbered, to be sure, and had to fight fiercely to hold his ground. "The battle now raged furiously," he reported; "one after one my men were cut down, but still, with unyielding hearts, they severely pressed the enemy, and in many instances forced them to give way. Here we fought alone and unsupported for two hours and twenty minutes." In addition to the pressure from Wood's men, Confederate artillery, positioned near the Bottom House, was pounding Gooding's ranks. But these Yankees were fighting as if they intended to hold their ground, whatever the cost.[44]

"Fiercer and fiercer grew the contest and more dreadful became the onslaught," continued Gooding's report. "Almost hand-to-hand they fought. . . . At one time the Twenty-second Indiana charged on [the enemy] with fixed bayonets and succeeded in completely routing and throwing them from their position on our right, but at the same time they brought in a reserve force on our left."[45]

The Rebels had decided to put in one more brigade, General Liddell's Arkansans, even if its ranks were depleted from the earlier clash with Sheridan. "With deafening cheers" Liddell's brigade moved against Gooding's flank, reported General Polk.[46]

It was about five o'clock, nightfall was near, and the danger of firing into one's own men was now greater than earlier in the day. General Polk rode to Liddell's position and thought he saw another line of Rebels firing into the flank of the Confederate brigade. Polk rode at once to the colonel of the offending regiment. "I asked him in angry tones what he meant by shooting his own friends," said Polk, and demanded that he cease firing at once. The colonel responded that he was sure, in fact "damned certain," that he was shooting at the enemy. Polk was equally sure that he was not. "Cease firing, sir; what is your name, sir?" Polk demanded to know. The bishop was shocked to hear the man reply that he was the colonel of an Indiana regiment; in turn, the Yankee colonel shot back, "And, pray sir, who are you?"

Fortunately for Polk, he thought fast, his instincts were good, his gray clothing helped hide his identity in the deepening twilight—and he was lucky. Later Polk described the incident: "Well, I saw there was no hope but to brazen it out; my dark blouse and the increasing obscurity befriended me, so I approached quite close to him and shook my fist in his face, saying, "I'll soon show you who I am, sir; Cease firing, sir, at once!" Polk then turned and rode away, "shouting in an authoritative manner to the Yankees to cease firing." Continuing the account, Polk said that "at the same time I experienced a disagreeable sensation, like screwing up my back, and calculating how many bullets would be between my shoulders every moment. I was afraid to increase my pace until I got to a small copse, when I put the spurs in and galloped back to my men."[47] Certainly luck rode with Polk at Perryville. (He was not to be so fortunate on a mountaintop in Georgia in the late spring of 1864, when a Federal cannon shot ended his life.)

Once back on the Confederate side, Polk ordered Liddell's brigade to direct their fire at the Indiana regiment. Later he described the well-directed blasts that tore through those Federals as "a succession of the most deadly volleys I have witnessed. The enemy's command in their immediate front was well nigh annihilated." Again, Polk wrote that "three thousand muskets blazed as one gun. And I assure you, Sir, that the slaughter of that Indiana regiment was the greatest I had ever seen in the war." It evidently was a devastating fire that the Rebels laid down, even if Polk did exaggerate the number of Grayclads who were engaged. "When the smoke had cleared away," said General Liddell, "nothing was visible of the enemy but their wounded, dying and dead." Among the Union dead was Lieutenant Colonel Squire I. Keith, "at the head of his regiment and in the act of flourishing his sword and urging his men onward to victory" when he fell, according to Michael Gooding's report.[48]

Gooding's line collapsed when struck by the withering fire from Liddell's brigade. These Federals had fought gallantly against Wood's men, but the added pressure from Liddell's unit was more than they could withstand. In falling back, Gooding reported that "my horse was shot from under me, and before I could escape through the darkness I was taken prisoner and conveyed from the field."[49] Gooding's brigade halted its retreat northwest of the intersection of the Mackville and Benton roads, while Liddell's men stopped their advance at the intersection. It was about dark, as noted by both Gooding and Polk, and—like the combatants farther to the north—neither side seemed inclined to continue the action. In fact, Polk said that he "ordered the troops to cease firing and to bivouac for the night."[50] While many a soldier expected that the struggle would resume on the morrow, actually the Battle of Perryville had ended.

J. Stoddard Johnston described the last moments of the engagement in moving terms: "The sun was declining in a cloudless sky, rank, red and fiery in the West, while almost simultaneously, the full moon, its counterpart in bloody mean, rose opposite." Still the Rebel artillery kept firing from an elevation on his left, Johnston said, sending forth "continuous flames, deepening in their lurid glare as it became darker, until only the sheet of fire, without the smoke, could be seen. . . . Gradually the fire slackened, the moon rose higher and lit up the ghastly faces of the dead, until at 8 o'clock, all was the stillness of death. The battle was over."[51]

☆☆☆

McCook's corps had waged a hard fight on the Federal left flank. Gilbert's center corps had seen only limited action, and Crittenden's right flank corps had been engaged hardly at all. Crittenden's corps, well over twenty thousand strong, had been deceived by Joe Wheeler's cavalry into believing that a large Confederate force was in their front. Actually, Wheeler had about twelve hundred troopers and a couple of artillery pieces operating on the Lebanon Road. Upon this occasion, Wheeler exaggerated only mildly when he praised his command a few days later: "And upon the memorable field of Perryville alone and unsupported, you engaged and held in check during the entire action at least two infantry divisions of the opposing army."[52] While "Fighting Joe" deserves credit for a colossal bluff, Crittenden should have conducted a reconnaissance in force, to learn if the enemy really was in his front in strength.

General Buell, as it turned out, never knew that a battle was being waged until at least 3:30 P.M. (Horace Fisher of McCook's staff said he reached Buell's headquarters seeking help for the left

Confederate General Joseph Wheeler.
Courtesy, Tennessee State Library and Archives.

flank at 3:30) and possibly, according to some accounts, not until four o'clock. Buell, obviously, had no direct influence on the course of the fight. That night Buell ate supper at the Dorsey House with Gilbert and Sheridan. Apparently he was slow to realize the scope of the battle.[53] General Rousseau arrived about nine o'clock and reported what had happened on the Union northern flank. He left headquarters feeling that Buell had not yet understood that anything more than heavy skirmishing had taken place during the day. Later Rousseau testified: "I told the general about the fight . . . , but [he] was pretty cool about it. I told him that I thought he did not appreciate the fight we had had, and that it was the hardest fight I had ever seen. He said he did appreciate it; that late in the afternoon he had heard of the battle; and my impression was that it was between 3 and 4 o'clock that he got the information."[54]

Sheridan's impression was the same as Rousseau's. He said "the conversation indicated that what had occurred was not fully realized, and I returned to my troops impressed with the belief that General Buell and his staff-officers were unconscious of the magnitude of the battle that had just been fought."[55] Sheridan's recent biographer is less charitable in his analysis of Buell. "The fact was that Buell," wrote Roy Morris, "could not bring himself to admit that he had allowed one-third of his army to absorb a frightful beating while Gilbert's corps had been content to defend itself against sporadic attacks by a single brigade of enemy troops, and Crittenden's corps had scarcely been used at all."[56]

Many a soldier, Yank or Reb, could have assured the Union commander that indeed a battle had been waged. Nearly every building in and around the town was converted to a hospital for one side or the other. Union casualties were over 4,200, and the Confederates' about 3,400. When one reflects that total Rebel forces engaged numbered only 15,000 to 16,000, that most of the Yankee fighting was done by the single corps of McCook, and that the battle did not begin before about 2 P.M. and was over by nightfall, then the casualty figures, relative to the numbers engaged and the time involved, were heavy indeed.[57] General Bragg, perhaps with the memory of the two-day clash of Shiloh in his mind, would write that the Battle of Perryville was "for the time engaged . . . the severest and most desperately contested . . . within my knowledge."[58]

The intensity of the struggle impressed many participants. General Bragg's estimate of the battle's severity was echoed by a Confederate of the Fifty-First Tennessee, Major J. T. Williamson, who later wrote of Perryville: "This was the hottest fight for the time it lasted that I was in during the war. We slept right on the ground where we had made the last charge. The dead Yankees were lying thick on the ground." Williamson, continuing his account, said that "a very pathetic scene took place that night. A Federal soldier boy was wounded and lying near where we were bivouacked. He begged piteously for his mother and to be taken away as [he feared] the fight would be renewed the next day."[59]

Typically in the Civil War, companies—even many regiments—had been recruited from a single community, which explains why a soldier's letter often gave, for the information of those back home, a brief accounting of the men wounded and killed. Andrew J. McGarrah wrote thus to his wife in Indiana of the fighting at Perryville, detailing the wounds of those in his company: "william hunter was wounded in the foot ralph skelton . . . in the leg william sanders . . . in the thie capten Barett had the buttens shot of his hat and was nocked down but was not hurt major shanklen was shot in the neck kernal denby was shot in the mouth but none of our connection was hert."[60] Seemingly McGarrah's and his wife's "connection" were fortunate, because his Forty-Second Indiana Regiment, according to the historian of the unit, suffered casualties equaling one-third of its strength, in no more than two hours of fighting.[61]

Confederate C. H. Clark, who had been severely wounded in his right side above the hip, related that "the moaning and sighing of the wounded and dying that night was heartrending and enough to make any man oppose war." Clark said he was carried to the courthouse at Harrodsburg, where nine of the wounded in the hospital with him that night died. Years later, Clark remembered that "the dead were laying thick on both sides. That was sixty years ago, but the terrible slaughter there yet haunts me in my dreams."[62]

At least Clark, who was a member of the Sixteenth Tennessee, was with his fellow Confederates. George W. Parks, also of the Sixteenth, was suffering from a broken leg and had been captured by the Federals. Parks said that "after some days" he was "put in a stable" where he was made miserable by the swarms of flies and "was most eat up by magets." Parks also said that his "clothes was shot off. Hunger and starvation is undescribable."[63]

One of the most vivid accounts of the day's death and misery was recorded in a diary kept by Confederate Major George Winchester, as he described the night: "I returned about 9 o'clock to the principal hospital to witness a scene revolting to humanity—the house, yard and every available space upon an acre of ground were covered with the wounded. The night was as quiet, and the moon shone as calmly and as placidly down as if nature looked with approving smile upon the terrible drama which had just been enacted." Winchester testified to the hopelessness of many wounds: "It seemed the climax of impotence to see the surgeon peering wisely into a hole through the small of a man's back that you could put an elephant's head in."[64]

Many a soldier was still thirsty, the day's fighting having compounded the misery engendered by hard marching in the abnormally dry weather. Certainly the wounded soldiers suffered because of the scarcity of water. One Federal particularly remembered that, all through "the long dreary night," he could "hear the poor, wounded boys calling for water."[65] Years afterward, soldiers still remembered keenly the quest for water and the battlefield horror associated with it. Confederate John W. Henderson, a young man in Buckner's division, wrote to Buckner in 1889, recalling the misery of the night after the Battle of Perryville: "I was very thirsty but . . . afraid to ask to hunt water . . . and while thinking what would I do for water I heard you say you wished you had a drink. I told you I would go and get some if you would give me your canteen." Carrying the general's canteen, Henderson made his way "to one of the pools we had passed and filled yours and my own. I returned it to you with the fear you would ask me where I got it for there were a great many dead and wounded lying around the pool . . . whose wounds had been washed in the same." If Buckner was troubled by the polluted water, Henderson did not mention the fact, saying only, "I thought it was splendid I was so thirsty."[66]

Union Corporal George W. Morris, a member of the Eighty-First Indiana, said, "The enemy's wounded lay in every fence corner. Our boys behaved themselves, and treated them kindly, bringing water whenever they desired it. They were mostly Tennessee troops. Some of them deserved no compassion for they spoke impudently and disdainfully. Nevertheless, on account of their wounds, no notice was taken of it." Morris further testified that "we felt sad over the sights we had seen, but all the boys felt that our flag must be upheld, and that the country should not be divided."[67]

Not until the next morning did some soldiers realize more fully the large number who were dead and wounded, even though many of the wounded had been hauled away by then. The Ninety-Eighth Ohio's William Spencer, who was sick and lying in a surgeon's wagon, soon to die of typhoid and pneumonia, garnered a full picture of the horrors, both late on the day of battle and on the morrow. He said attendants "were continually passing by leading and carrying and hauling the wounded who were crying and screaming with pain. But the most horrible sight I witnessed was in passing over the battlefield, where were to be seen men lying one on another and for rods one might have walked on the dead bodies."[68]

At sunrise on October 9, Samuel Starling and another Federal officer were seeking the body of General Jackson, which they had not been able to remove at the time of his death because of the rapidity of the Confederate advance. Starling wrote: "We found quite a number of Rebel and Union soldiers, ministering to the wounded and looking at the [battle] ground." Starling thought that it seemed "all animosity had ceased and they were mixing like friends." He and his companion found Jackson's body "just where we left him," but boots, hat, and buttons were gone.[69]

A soldier in the Fifteenth Wisconsin wrote of the battlefield, "The sight that met my gaze next morning when going through the field was horrendous, the shattered legs and arms and the thickly strewed bodys of the fallen soldiers made the sight terrible."[70] Another Federal, from the Fifty-Second Ohio, simply wrote that the area was an "awful sight," while the One Hundred and Fifth Ohio's Bliss Morse spoke of dead men shot through the head, "some with arms, heads, legs . . . torn off. Some lay with their tongues swelled out of their mouths, and others laid with hands stuck out as if surprised, with an expression of amazement on their faces. They were very much distorted." Morse thought the Rebels were darker than the Federals and wrote that "some were liquored and showed the effects of gunpowder." Relative to the alleged darker appearance of dead Confederates, another Federal said that "because of the black swollen condition of many of the bodies of the slain southerners," a report circulated and "was believed to be true by many . . . that our enemies had been fed on gun-powder and whiskey . . . to so fire them that they should become animated to fight with desperation, and that the gun-powder caused the discoloration."[71]

A week after the engagement, a Federal officer thought the ground "the most horrid sight that ever man beheld." In a letter to his wife, he wrote "there are hundreds of men being eaten up by the buzzards and hogs." Equally repelled was a private in the ranks of the Eighty-Eighth Illinois, who recorded that he saw four or five bodies of Confederate officers, around which a rail fence had been erected to protect the remains from being attacked by "the swine that prowled in the woods. The disgusting sight of these animals feeding upon human gore was more than sufficient to give them immunity from sacrifice by the hungry of our army. No one could be found sufficiently hardy to talk of eating the flesh of hogs captured near the battlefield." Clearly the hogs were indeed feasting upon the dead humanity. The Ninety-Sixth Illinois's Joseph Whitney observed "a great many rebel dead lying over the ground," and he said that those who "had been buried were rooted up by hogs that were tearing the bodies up and eating them."[72]

Such sights and experiences as a battlefield presents affect different persons in different ways. For some, the result is drastic changes in their perspective on war. The Second Ohio's George Landrum, who said he went into the battle "determined to see the *fun*" (emphasis in the original), apparently revised his feelings considerably as the carnage unfolded all about him. Writing to his sister-in-law, he continued: "I have seen men shot in the head, breast and legs, and still stand up and fire till they dropped down either dead or exhausted. . . . I will not attempt to describe [all] the horrible scenes I there witnessed. . . . You have no doubt read descriptions of this fight, but no one can describe the scenes of that field." Then, as if to give an example of the greatest horror, Landrum said, "I saw a Rebel officer who had fallen on a fence that was burning, half charred."[73]

Samuel Starling, writing to his daughters, remarked that he was "sickened with this cursed strife. . . . The poor, dust covered, ghastly looking fellows dead in every posture, some with heads half shot off and some with their knapsacks under their heads and hats over their faces, evidently adjusted by themselves before death. Altogether there is a horrible, sickening feeling produced beyond anything I ever before felt."[74]

Surely the fear of being killed or wounded was the greatest fear of many soldiers. Sometimes, however, even when soldiers were fortunate enough to escape these horrors, they still suffered deeply from the loss of friends, or the destruction of simple possessions worth little or nothing in monetary terms but laden with great emotional value. Such was the case with the Forty-Second Indiana's William Stuckey, who did his duty at the Battle of Perryville, although, as we have seen, his enthusiasm for soldiering had long since passed. Writing to his wife Helen, addressed as "My Dear Love," Stuckey said he was in "the hottest of the battle all the time," and, obviously referring to a friend known to both of them, reported, "Oliver was killed by my side as we retreated up a hill he was struck with a ball in the back he fell and ask me to help him but there was no place to stop and help wounded men[75] the secesh was in all over the ground

Cemetery where H. P. Bottom buried Confederate dead.
Photograph by Peggy Nims.

in few minutes . . . our dead they stript of there shoes and blankets and other close I had your Portrait in my shot pouch a bullet struck it severing it from one end to the other I never seen your likeness again . . . I feel lost without it."[76]

As for burying the dead, Union bodies would be interred along the Springfield Road in temporary graves and later removed to various national cemeteries in Kentucky. Squire Henry P. Bottom gathered up about four hundred Confederate bodies, identifying some, and buried them in pits near the position where Cheatham's division had begun to fight. The burial pits are now enclosed by cemetery walls, close to the battlefield's visitor center. Other Confederate dead were buried in unmarked graves near the Goodnight House beside the Chaplin River. There was ample evidence that at Perryville both sides generally had managed to give the other, in Polk's words, "what General Cheatham said."

Among the Union casualties, in a sense, was General Buell, even though his only physical suffering resulted from the fall from his horse. Basically, Buell failed to keep a firm hand on his army and failed to show the proper instincts of a first-rate field commander, when he knew his forces were in close proximity to the enemy. Coupled with Lincoln's prior conviction that the general was not aggressive, Buell's performance at Perryville soon was to bring his career as an army commander to a close.

Chapter 10

I Never Hated Them till Now

☆☆☆

The Battle of Perryville "was really a very hard one considering the numbers engaged, and one of the worst features in the matter is that it was one of those engagements which do nothing toward settling the contest." So observed Dr. William W. Blair, a surgeon with the Fifty-Eighth Indiana Infantry, in a letter to his wife Margaret which was written four days after the battle.[1] Many a soldier, Union and Confederate, would have endorsed the Indiana doctor's evaluation. Both sides had indeed fought fiercely. The casualties, relative to the numbers engaged, certainly were heavy, and neither side felt that it had been whipped.

A host of Federal soldiers also would have agreed with Dr. Blair's opinion of General Buell, whom the surgeon characterized as overly cautious; as, in fact, basically unwilling to engage the enemy. "Buell is certainly acting very strangely, if not traitorously," stated Blair.[2] Jesse B. Connelly, Thirty-First Indiana, later related that "since it is known now that but one corps of Buell's army was engaged in the battle, the other two in reach but not ordered to advance, there begins to be talk among the men that Buell is not just right." Connelly continued, stating, "It is reported and believed among the men that Buell purposely held back the two corps so that Bragg might escape with his army and the large amount of plunder he had gathered. It is also reported that Buell and Bragg had a conference in Perryville the night after the battle, and many men believe it."[3] There were variations of this story, as "many rumors were afloat," according to the Fiftieth Ohio's Erastus Winters. Among the rumors, reported Winters, was the one asserting, wrongly, "that General Bragg and General Buell were brothers-in-law, and that they had eaten supper together the night before the battle."[4]

More briefly and crudely phrased, but no less damning of Buell, was the response of the Eighty-Eighth Indiana's Frank McKinzie to Louis Nettelhorst's question about General Buell: "You wanted to know how i like Buel he is an old traitor." Equally laconic and also lacking in punctuation was the diary entry of Thomas M. Small, Tenth Indiana Infantry: "Old Buell is a coward or a Rebel Shoot him."[5] Yet another claimed that "thousands of privates in the army" considered Buell to be "a traitor to the cause of the Union."[6]

Dr. Blair declared that there would have been no battle at Perryville if General McCook had not "run on the Rebs before he or they were aware of it!!!" After further castigating General Buell's lack of aggressiveness, the doctor summarized: "I think I have as little inclination to see our army butchered up in a general battle as any one can have, but this way of putting down the rebellion will not be successful."[7]

Perryville never became a general engagement for all of the Federal forces, of course, but McCook's corps on the left flank, which bore the brunt of the action, was, to use Dr. Blair's words, "butchered up" rather badly. The situation was especially difficult for the wounded of both sides, because Perryville was a little town, in an isolated area, and did not begin to have the medical supplies, physicians, nurses, food, and clothing necessary to care for several thousand casualties. Nor was the Federal army, which was soon to be left in possession of the battlefield, equipped to care for them properly.

The condition of the wounded in this battle was "peculiarly distressing," thought J. S. Newberry, secretary for the Western Department of the U.S. Sanitary Commission. Reporting to the general secretary of the commission, Newberry said that "no adequate provision had been made" for the care of the wounded. Continuing, Newberry noted: "The stock of medicines and hospital stores in the hands of the surgeons was insignificant. They had almost no ambulances, tents, no hospital furniture, and no proper food." Observing that the hamlet of Perryville afforded very little means of ministering to the wounded, Newberry added that "the surrounding country had been overrun and devastated by two great armies, and the inhabitants impoverished in all possible ways. As a consequence, nearly everything necessary to the proper care of sick or wounded men had to be imported from a considerable distance."[8]

Among those ministering to the wounded was Dr. A. W. Reed, who had hired a buggy in Louisville and, accompanied by an assistant named Thomasson, set out for Perryville as rapidly as possible after learning of the battle. "We found the first hospital for the wounded at Maxville," recorded Dr. Reed. It was a tavern, with sixteen rooms, containing 150 wounded and 30 sick, mostly from a Wisconsin regiment. Twenty-five men were on cots, said Reed, some on straw, and the others on the floor with blankets. "The cooking was all done at a fire-place, with two camp-kettles and a few stew-pans. The ladies of the town, however, were taking articles home, and cooking them there; thus giving great assistance" to the surgeon in charge, who was Dr. P. P. White of the One Hundred and First Indiana.

"From this place to Perryville, some ten miles, nearly every house was an hospital," said Reed. "At one log cabin we found 20 of the Tenth Ohio, including the major and two captains. At another house were several of the Ninety-Third Ohio; and the occupants were very poor, but doing all in their power for those in their charge." The mother of the family, reported Reed, "promised to continue to do so, but said, with tears in her eyes, she feared that she and her children must starve when the winter came."

Reaching Perryville after dark, Dr. Reed discovered that the number of wounded was much larger than expected. Every house was a hospital, all crowded and with very little to eat. "Instead of 700, as first reported, at least 2,500 Union and rebel soldiers were at that time lying in great suffering and destitution. . . . In addition to these, many had already been removed, and we had met numbers of those whose wounds were less severe walking and begging their way to Louisville." Reed echoed a theme common among those describing the aftermath of the battle: "There had been almost no preparation for the care of the wounded at Perryville, and as a consequence the suffering from want of *help* of all kinds, as well as proper accommodations, food, medicines and hospital stores, was excessive." Reed thought the fault lay with the military authorities who withheld "information, and denied [the surgeons] the resources which alone would have enabled them to meet the emergencies of the case."[9]

A local surgeon, Jefferson J. Polk, recalled the large number of wounded who "were left upon our hands. My house was made a hospital for eight or ten of these. I was likewise appointed surgeon to a hospital containing forty wounded soldiers. Here I labored day and night until my health gave way, and I was compelled to desist from my work."[10]

Many a soldier, in letters, memoirs, and other documents, testified to the awful suffering that followed the struggle at Perryville. Perry Hall, a chaplain with the Seventy-Ninth Indiana, wrote to his wife that "a mile or so from Perryville we passed a hospital where there were some 200 wounded. Many of their wounds never got dressed, and our men, who were on picket duty near them all night, describe their cries and moans as piteous in the extreme." Hall also said that he "was only partly over the rebel side of the [battle] field and I saw 37 of their dead. . . . You may allow they were in no very pleasant condition to look upon. *Hogs* were running around near *some* of them."[11]

Perhaps such a gruesome sight among the Rebel dead would have been just fine with the Twenty-Ninth Indiana's John A. Berger, who told his parents: "We got on the battlefield 2 days after the Battle and there were some 300 or 400 hundred dead Sesh on the field unburied and I guess they lay there yet (they had ought to)."[12]

Also commenting on the host of dead bodies littering the general area was George W. Landrum, of the Second Ohio, in a long letter to "Dear Amanda," dated four days after the battle. Twice marveling that he himself had not been harmed, even though in the midst of fierce fighting, the Ohio native said that he had ridden over the field the day after the battle. Confederates, he wrote, were "lying two and three deep in some places." But the scenes of Federal dead were equally horrible and, he thought, more disturbing—"men with their heads shot off, and mangled in every possible manner. The Rebels stripped our wounded. By the side of every one of our dead men you would see an old pair of shoes and a greasy, filthy pile of clothes."

Then, as if all the stress and pent-up emotion occasioned by the awful experience suddenly burst forth, Landrum wrote: "I never hated them till now. I have now a thirst for vengeance; the sight of our men lying scattered over that field has added ten fold to my hatred for them."[13]

It is one thing to think of dead men in the aggregate, but something else again to consider them as individuals, whether Yank or Reb. When one knows something of the real person, a degree of sympathy sometimes develops. Ira Nye, Company F, One Hundred and Fifth Ohio, was an example of "those strange instances of presentiment fulfilled." From the time of his enlistment, Nye had predicted that he would be killed in the first battle in which he was involved. "This impression he repeated about the time the regiment left Louisville," wrote the regiment's historian, "and when nearing the field of action bade his friends in Company E farewell, saying to one of them that his time had come." The young man's conviction was soon proven correct, as he was shot through the chest at Perryville.[14]

Another member of the One Hundred and Fifth Ohio, whose fate arrests one's interest, is Elbridge T. Early of Company K. Sick in a hospital in Lexington, Kentucky, when the Confederates took the city, and suffering from fever, Early nevertheless "crawled from his cot and made his escape." He evaded the enemy as he avoided the roads and traveled by night through woods and fields, until, after struggling over one hundred miles, he at last rejoined his regiment at Louisville. Although worn and considerably underweight from his ordeal, Early moved out with his regiment and endured the hard march that culminated in the battle at Perryville. Determined to fulfill his obligation, Early "fought in the front line, and though wounded in the hip, kept fighting still, until stricken down by a ball, piercing his temple."[15]

The Battle of Perryville occurred four months to the day, minus one, after the Forty-First Mississippi's Captain T. J. Koger, complaining of "our ditch-digging Generals . . . who . . . retreat," had told his wife that he preferred "a little more daring, go-ahead fighting . . . , even tho it cost . . . more lives." The Kentucky campaigning cost the lives of hundreds of Confederates, and Perryville cost Captain Koger his life. Right up to the moment that Koger's unit formed line of battle to make its attack, the captain, not surprisingly, was writing another of the many letters to his wife. Early on in the battle—probably within the first thirty minutes of the Rebel attack—Koger took a bullet near the heart and was killed. The man who conveyed the sad news to the family also observed that only twenty-five hundred recruits had joined the Confederate army, and offered the opinion "that Kentucky would come with the South if voting could accomplish it—but generally they won't fight for it."[16]

Some soldiers, of course, were fortunate in that, in one way or another, they were exempted by chance from the heat of battle. Sickness proved to be a blessing for the Ninety-Eighth Ohio's William Spencer, who was confined to the surgeon's wagon. He said "the shells were whistling all around me" and some "passed over me not more than 6 inches but I consider that nothing compared to what some had to go through." Spencer wrote that men "were continually passing by leading and carrying and hauling the wounded who were crying and screaming with pain."[17]

The majority of Buell's force, as previously noted, never was engaged in the fight at Perryville. In a few instances, this seemingly was due to poor management on the part of some officer or officers. The Seventy-Ninth Indiana's John H. Tilford recorded in his diary that "the whole division was put on quick time, sometimes on double-quick." Tilford said the unit was "taken into a large open field, and drawn up in line of battle," only to then be "marched through a corn field into a wood, then back into the field again." By that time, said Tilford, the firing was quite heavy, and "quite a battle [was] going on." But Tilford was not to be involved in the struggle and concluded his diary entry for October 8 by saying that he "slept very well" that night.[18]

The Thirty-Second Kentucky's Robert Taylor wrote that "night gathered her mantle over a field strewn with Union dead, who had called vainly for help, and died unaided at their posts." Taylor's own "slight" wound was dressed around midnight in a makeshift hospital, after which, the captain wrote in his diary, "I sat down upon the steps of the hospital and gazed up into the face of the moon in thankfulness and gratefulness to its maker for bringing me through the . . . clash of arms that day in safety."[19]

Among the soldiers who had been engaged in the awful, bloody melee, some were desirous of more formally expressing their gratitude to a Divine Power for having spared their lives. Captain Edward V. Bowers of the One Hundred and Fifth Ohio, a Christian minister, gathered a few of the more religiously inclined of the regiment when the battle was over, and in a depression of the hill where his Company K rested, held a prayer service. "It was very quietly done," recorded an observer, "but when the notes of a hymn reached the ears of the [regiment's] Colonel, . . . he sent at once to 'stop the racket that old fool Bowers [is] making to draw the enemy's fire on us!'" Perhaps the colonel's angry command could be heard farther than the words of "the softly chanted hymn." That, at least, was the opinion of the man who recorded the incident.[20]

Despite the widespread suffering and misery following the battle, there was no guarantee, even if the engagement was ended, that anyone was safe from the possibility of guerrilla action or marauding by some type of irregular troops. A soldier of the Eighty-Seventh Indiana, Johnson W. Culp, related in his diary that he and two other men were "detailed to take care of 17 sick men that was laying under an apple tree." Since these sick men had no shelter, Culp said that "we tore down a rye stack and built a rail pen and covered it with rye and got all 17 fellows in it but there was no room for us and as we had been on short rations for a while we went to a farm house to get something to eat." Culp said that he and the others received "a tolerably fair supper of corn bread and mutton" from a reluctant farmer who "had a son in the Rebel army that was severely wounded in the Battle of Perryville right at home and they had him there." Leaving the farmhouse, the Federals slept in the loft of a sheep stable on some hay. It "rained all night," according to Culp, and when he and the two others returned to check on their charges the next morning, the Indiana native reported that, during the night, "the guerrillas gobbled our 17 sick men."[21] And thus it went, each individual with his own story of events following the battle.

Josiah Ayre of the One Hundred and Fifth Ohio was among the wounded who spent the night on the battlefield unattended. Shot below the calf of the left leg and unable to walk, Ayre said that he "crawled up behind a tree where I remained till taken from the field which was not until the next day. . . . My wound was dressed sometime in the afternoon and has felt pretty easy since." Ayre recorded that "it has been wet and cold for the last thirty six hours." Despite this weather and his wound, the young soldier conveyed an optimistic note as he also wrote, three days after the battle: "Take it all together, I think myself lucky." Actually, Private Ayre was anything but lucky, dying of complications from his wound on October 14. He was twenty-one years old.[22]

☆☆☆

On the night of October 8, while thousands of wounded soldiers attempted to cope with their traumatic fate, and while the healthy men played out their various roles in the battle's aftermath, General Bragg, who had thought he was confronting only a small portion of

Buell's force, at last learned the truth about the enemy's numbers. The information came from intelligence garnered while overrunning McCook's position. Bragg discovered that actually some forty to fifty thousand Federals were in his front. If the Yankees realized how few were the Rebels they faced, they well might launch a major attack as soon as possible on the morning of October 9. Thus, during the night, Bragg began pulling his troops out of Perryville, falling back some ten or twelve miles to the northeast, to Harrodsburg. There all of Bragg's army finally could be united with the forces of Kirby Smith, making the southerners at least equal to the Federals in strength.[23]

Buell followed the next day, and the Blue and Gray lines soon lay across from each other once more. The possibility of another engagement seemed likely. On October 10, Kirby Smith arrived at Harrodsburg and apparently urged Bragg to fight. "For God's sake, General, let us fight Buell here," were the words Kirby Smith addressed to Bragg, according to Kirby Smith's recollection, written after the war. "I believe," he continued, quoting himself, "that without a command even, our men would run over Buell's army composed, as it more than half is, of new levies." Supposedly Bragg responded, "I will do it, sir," upon hearing which the soldiers of Kirby Smith were said to have burst forth with loud shouts of approval.[24]

But Bragg did not attack. Occupying a good defensive position, Bragg hoped that Buell would do the attacking, but the Union commander would not oblige him, leaving students of the Kentucky campaign with yet another question to ponder: Should Bragg not have fought the decisive battle for Kentucky at Harrodsburg? Regardless of whether Kirby Smith was encouraging Bragg to attack or not, the Confederate situation is intriguing. Not only Bragg's and Kirby Smith's forces were at hand; but Humphrey Marshall's three thousand soldiers[25] also were within supporting distance. Bragg probably would have had superior numbers if he had engaged Buell again. Clearly, he would have had more battle-seasoned troops, many of them "fired up" over their victories at Richmond and Perryville. And McCook's Federal corps had been so hard hit that it was in no shape for further

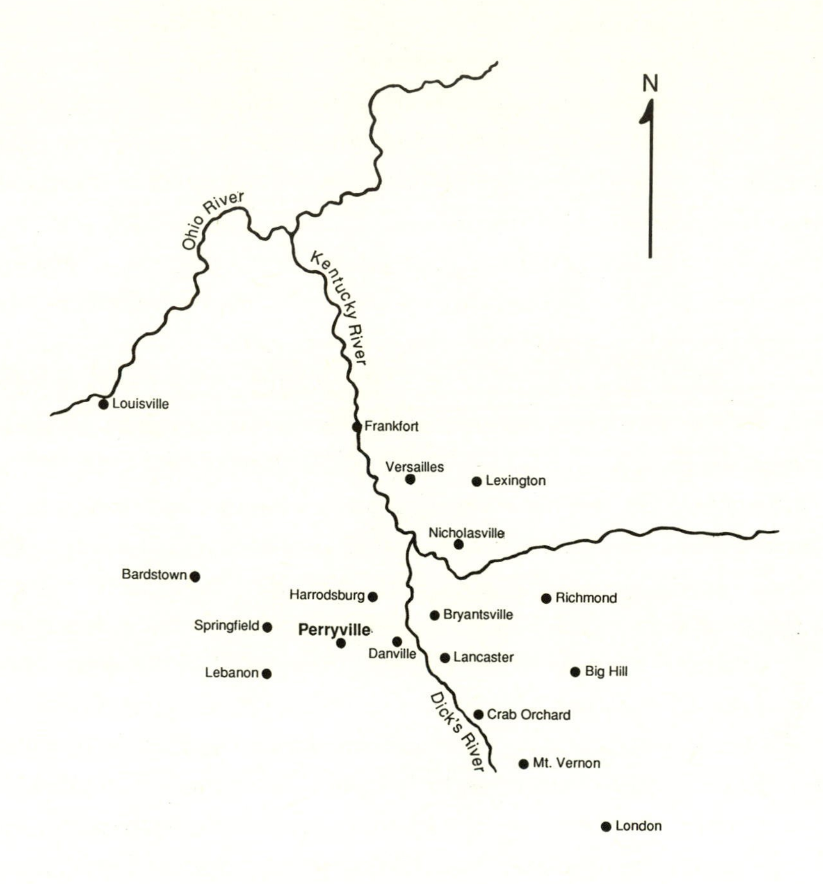

Central Kentucky.
Map prepared by Sharon McDonough.

battle. It is interesting to speculate what Thomas Jonathan Jackson or Robert E. Lee might have done if he had been in command of the Confederate forces at Harrodsburg.

This is not to say that a decision to attack again was an obvious choice. No doubt Bragg was concerned about the possibility that Buell might move southeast to Danville and cut his line of retreat, the road back to Cumberland Gap. No doubt he was worried as well about the Union brigade of Ebenezer Dumont, reportedly approaching from the north. If Bragg had withdrawn due east from Perryville to Danville, instead of Harrodsburg, he would have secured his most direct line of retreat; he also would have been moving farther away from Kirby Smith and presenting the enemy with an opportunity to knife between the Rebel commands and turn upon one or the other with superior numbers. By falling back to Harrodsburg, Bragg assured that all the Confederates could be united—which was his best move—although simultaneously he made his line of retreat more vulnerable. When Buell began feeling for the Rebel flanks, it seemed to Bragg that the time had come to retire once more. Indeed, there were indications that Buell might be pushing hard to gain Danville. Thus Bragg fell back across Dick's River (Dix today) and established a position on high ground, with his headquarters at Bryantsville, again ready to accept battle if Buell should attack. Once more the Union general declined, planning instead to swing right, moving to turn the Rebel left flank. It was then that Bragg made the decision to leave Kentucky without waging another battle.[26]

The Confederate commander was discouraged about the problems associated with feeding his army. His own supply of flour and meal was sufficient for only a few more days. The Federals had sent raiding parties over the countryside, destroying mills and granaries, making it extremely difficult to obtain more. Reports were coming in—and they were accurate—that a large Federal force was advancing from Cincinnati to unite with Buell. Probably weighing most heavily upon Bragg's mind was the disappointing fact that Kentucky recruits for his army had been far less numerous than expected.[27]

Already the general had concluded that the Kentuckians would not rise to support the Confederacy. Recent days had only confirmed that judgment. Bragg still had wagonloads of weapons that he had carried along to arm recruits who never had enlisted. Kirby Smith, for all his earlier enthusiasm, had done little better. At best, his recruiting had been only marginally successful. Without large numbers of Kentucky recruits, Bragg correctly concluded, the campaign could not achieve anything of lasting significance.

On October 12, in a report written at Bryantsville, Bragg said: "The campaign here was predicated on a belief and the most positive assurances that the people of this country would rise in mass to assert their independence. No people ever had so favorable an opportunity, but I am distressed to add there is little or no disposition to avail of it. Willing, perhaps, to accept their independence," Bragg concluded, "they are neither disposed nor willing to risk their lives or their property in its achievement."[28]

"Why should I stay with my handful of brave Southern men," he asked in a revealing letter to his wife, "to fight for cowards who skulked about in the dark to say to us, 'We are with you. Only whip these fellows out of our country and let us see you can protect us, and we will join you'?" Then Bragg added: "In the midst of this comes the news of Van Dorn's defeat in Mississippi."[29]

Long-awaited news from northern Mississippi finally had come to Bragg, and it, too, was unpleasant. Sterling Price and Earl Van Dorn had united, attempting to wrest Corinth from the hands of William S. Rosecrans's entrenched Federals on October 3. Each side had had a strength of about twenty-two thousand men. With a valiant effort, the Rebels attacked from the west, penetrating to the second Yankee line, about a mile from the center of the little railroad town. The battle went on into the next day. Several southern frontal assaults were thrown back, as the Union, fighting defensively from a protected position, enjoyed a winning advantage. At last the Confederates had retreated, ending the struggle after suffering approximately the same number of casualties that Bragg's forces had taken at Perryville. Once again, as after Shiloh, Corinth was inundated with dead and wounded men. Once again, as at Shiloh, a Confederate attack had failed to achieve anything of importance. Van Dorn and Price would not even be advancing into West Tennessee, much less joining Bragg in Kentucky. (In fact they were retiring to Holly Springs.) And west of the Mississippi River, the Rebel forces, although winning the Battle of Newtonia on September 30, nevertheless had retired from Missouri into northwestern Arkansas during the first week of October.

Bragg knew, of course, that in the East, Lee had been driven back into Virginia, and, it seemed to Bragg, there were armed Unionists all over Kentucky. Jefferson Davis was expressing a deep concern for the safety of Bragg's army. The Confederacy, Davis was warning, could not afford the loss of Bragg's force, for then a Federal army could move, unopposed, into Chattanooga and control its vital railroads. Even if Bragg were to fight again and win—and victory was far from a certainty—what now, Bragg must have wondered, would be the significance of the triumph? Without the massive support of Kentucky, militarily and politically, there could be no sequel of any consequence. Bragg's force alone could not occupy and control Kentucky. Thus Bragg decided, with the concurrence of Hardee, Polk, and Kirby Smith, to fall back into Tennessee.[30]

Abandoning much of the spoils they had gathered and leaving behind hundreds of men—altogether probably some three thousand—who were too sick or badly wounded to be moved, the Confederates, slowly and painfully trudged southward, away from the Bluegrass region that earlier had been thought so promising, struggling over the mountain roads, tramping toward Knoxville. All the Confederates, that is, except for Humphrey Marshall's smaller force, which would retire into Virginia. At Lancaster, Bragg and Kirby Smith, who despite vows of cooperation had spent virtually the whole campaign apart from one another, once more went their separate ways, Bragg's Army of the Mississippi moving on the road to Crab Orchard, while the Army of Kentucky marched farther to the east, heading toward Big Hill. Placed in charge of the Rebel rear guard was Joe Wheeler.[31]

Kirby Smith, increasingly pessimistic as he contemplated the problems of getting back over Big Hill, informed Bragg that he feared the loss of all his wagon train.[32] This well might have occurred, had not General Cleburne, traveling with the trains, taken control when one of Kirby Smith's officers was about to destroy them, and, with Herculean efforts on the part of the soldiers, managed to get them over the great barrier. Not a wagon was lost.[33] Another general who rendered splendid service to the Confederate cause was Wheeler, whose cavalry command again and again warded off and halted the Yankee pursuers.[34] General Buell continued following until the Confederates reached London. There he abandoned the pursuit, began shifting forces westward, and prepared to move into Nashville once more. Suddenly—after the longest Confederate campaign, in terms of miles covered, that the war had seen or would see—it was evident that conditions were much the same as before it all began, except for the casualties and, perhaps most important, the devastating blow to Confederate morale, an inevitable consequence when the high hopes of mid-summer and early fall could not be realized.

Having started out with abundant optimism, it was a disillusioned and disheartened force that retreated into Tennessee.[35] If wounded men had to be left behind, at least there were many Confederate sympathizers in the Bluegrass to comfort them. The Ninety-Sixth Illinois's Joseph Whitney, who upon crossing the Kentucky River said there were not but half a dozen Union men "in this country," tramped into Harrodsburg a few days after the Rebels left and affirmed that he was "in the enemy's country," that hundreds of wounded "sessesh" were in the hospital, and that the women of Harrodsburg were "very saucy to us," saying "they would like to have us in a place where they could kill every one of us." Whitney also added that "one of the men in our regiment was poisoned last night . . . by . . . whiskey . . . from one of the sessesh."[36]

Some of the worn and dispirited men in the ranks of the retreating Rebels were vehement in their criticism of Bragg. W. E. Yeatman, Second Tennessee Infantry, who had lost several of his schoolmates and friends in the battle at Perryville, called the order to fall back into Tennessee "cowardly." He claimed that he nearly starved to death on the march to Knoxville. Another Rebel, John Gold of the Twenty-Fourth Tennessee, likewise said that he thought he would starve on the trek back from Perryville. A man in the Seventeenth Tennessee said that he was among "the barefoots," who were "started for Cumberland Gap without a mouthful of rations over 100 miles . . . and being nearly naked and starved I took sick." At last, by train from Knoxville, he arrived at a "hospital at Chattanooga with pneumonia." If there was a positive aspect to all this, perhaps it was that his condition kept him out of the Stones River battle at Murfreesboro in late December. Major J. T. Williamson, commenting on the lack of food, wrote that "we had to put guards over the teams to keep the men from taking all the corn from the mules and horses. I have seen the men pick up the shelled corn on the ground when the stock had been fed, wash it and parch it. I did it several times myself."

Still another soldier reported that "the retreat from Perryville was one of fearful suffering." More than two hundred men in his brigade were barefooted, he reported. "We were ordered to draw ten days rations and march to Knoxville by way of Cumberland Gap," but, he continued, "we failed to draw the ten days rations, as we did not overtake any provision-wagons and those we guarded were loaded with ordinance. For ten days we had nothing to eat save what we could find on the march . . . through a mountainous and sparsely settled country . . . ravaged by both armies before our retreat."[37]

"We have seen some very hard times in Kentucky," said a soldier of the Fifty-Second Georgia in a letter to his mother. "I am glad," he continued, "that Pa did not try to go with us for he could not have stood the exposure and fatigue which we had to suffer."[38] Another Tennessean remembered: "We thought Kentucky was ours, alas, how soon the scene shifted. The retreat from Kentucky was one of the greatest trials and hardships of any march made during the war."[39] The First Arkansas's William Bevens observed that the men who did get back from Kentucky "were tough as whitleather, ready for anything."[40] But, of course, to toughen the troops was hardly the purpose of the campaign.

In early November, Confederate James Travis was writing from Ringgold, Georgia, where he was hospitalized, to his sister Artalisa Merrell of Jasper County, Mississippi, reflecting on the campaign, and perhaps expressing the thoughts of many: "We have been on a long march through tenese and nearly through Kentucky and back. . . . I never thought men could stand what they can untill we took this march. I think the rout we took must of been seven hundred miles."

Travis then commented about Perryville: "I reckon you have heard of the perryvill fite. . . . We was in the hard part of the battle . . . I don't see how any one can go in battle and come out safe, balls whistled all round my head . . . I thought every minet it would be my time next, men falling all around on every side, some with their heads shot off, some their bodeys shot in two." In this respect, reflecting on how he escaped being hit when firing was so heavy, Travis seemed to echo Union soldier George Landrum, of the Second Ohio, who also marveled, as previously noted, that he had not been wounded or killed. Doubtless many soldiers on both sides felt the same.

Travis continued, complaining of cowardly officers and the war in general: "I tell it is and awful . . . sight. narry one of our officers was in the fight all sick it loucks like we have cowardly officers in this company. the boys is all satisfied of fiting and wish they was back at Mobile or at home. . . . If I ever did wish for anything in earnest it is peace for I am giting tired of such foolishness."[41]

No brilliant flash of perception is required to realize that many a soldier must have felt as Travis did. John J. Hogg, writing a series of letters to his wife in Georgia after the campaign, said: "Susan, I thank God I am on the south side of the Cumberland River again. . . . I am still in a state of sanity but God only knows how long. . . . Susan, I can not describe to you the sufferings of a poor soldier. Oh wretched war! Oh cruel and destructive war! When will it all end. . . . The Confederate States of America I think will soon know its doom."

Frequently calling upon Susan to send him brandy—once calling for two gallons but cautioning her to be sure it will get through to him—Hogg also talked about his unsuccessful attempts to hire a substitute, and urged his wife to hire one for him, something she "must" do "if you want me at home again." This miserable soldier had become aware of the "Twenty Slave Law," by which a man could escape military service if he was in "charge of twenty negroes," and sought his wife's help in an attempt to qualify by arranging something with his grandmother's slaves. If this would not work, he suggested yet another possibility for combining his own slaves with someone else's in order to qualify for the necessary twenty.[42]

Certainly not all the men were ready to get out of the army, not by any means. But many were disappointed and unhappy after the Kentucky campaign, sensing that a major setback had just occurred. "We move toward Cumberland Gap," wrote a Confederate officer a few days after the battle at Perryville. "Kentucky . . . is hopelessly lost, her people now, prompted by an avaricious love of prosperity . . . have bartered away, in a position of neutrality, the birthright descended from revolutionary ancestors." The Confederate continued: "The long and weary marches, the sleepless nights, and thirst and hunger . . . will be long remembered. My recollections of Kentucky are not pleasant."[43] Another officer wrote, "We started . . . from Kentucky with heavy hearts, as we had expected to remain there and get a great many recruits and a large amount of army supplies, which our army needed so much."[44]

Such feelings often apparently were manifested in anger, and the target of the anger was General Bragg. Some of the men, according to historian Allan Nevins, "would gladly have burned [General Bragg] at the stake."[45] Some of the generals, too, were angry and disgusted with Bragg. Perhaps the most vocal of all—ironically, considering the major problems that he had caused Bragg—was Kirby Smith. He wrote to the War Department, bitterly complaining about Bragg's conduct of the campaign. He requested a transfer, preferably to Mobile, but to anywhere, he said, if staying in his present capacity would necessitate further cooperation with Bragg.[46] To his wife, Kirby Smith said, "No one could have anticipated [the exodus from Kentucky]—Bragg's movements since taking command in Kentucky have been most singular and unfortunate."[47]

When Bragg arrived in Knoxville, a summons to Richmond awaited him. Flooded by complaints of dissension in the ranks of the army, as well as insistent demands that Bragg be removed from command, Jefferson Davis had decided that he must confer with his general in person. "The President desires," wired the adjutant general, "that you will lose no time in coming here."[48] The Kentucky campaign was over, but the recriminations and blame would long continue. Although the president decided to sustain General Bragg in command, in the perceptions of many officers and soldiers, whether deservedly or not, Bragg's ability to lead had suffered grave damage. Be that as it may, shortly after Bragg rejoined his army, he ordered it forward to concentrate in Middle Tennessee around the town of Murfreesboro, thirty miles southeast of Nashville. Just west of Murfreesboro, a small, usually sluggish stream meandered its way northward to join the Cumberland. It was known locally as Stones River.

Chapter 11

Season of Folly, Season of Decision

☆☆☆

"Among them all, I fear, there is not a Napoleon," remarked a Rebel engineer, earlier in the year, as he contemplated the talents of the western Confederate generals.[1] By late October 1862 his judgment would have seemed even more valid—and applicable to Yankees as well as Rebels. A lot of blundering had been going on, and going on for a long time, with both sides contributing significantly. Understanding such folly is in the best historical tradition.

Even though the Federals finally won at Shiloh, their performance was hardly impressive. Possibly the Confederates blundered even more—enough, perhaps, to cost them the victory. Both Yankees and Rebels stumbled about remarkably, and, in the campaigning that followed Shiloh, a pattern of folly was clearly identifiable.[2]

While some historians have faulted General Halleck for not advancing from Corinth to Vicksburg, his decision to go for Chattanooga instead was not without merit. But when Halleck sent Buell against Chattanooga, he needed to hold the enemy's main force at Tupelo. This he could have done by advancing troops south on the railroad, to pin Bragg in position.

The movement would have been relatively simple, with nothing like the numbers required, or the problems posed, by a Vicksburg campaign. A much deeper commitment of forces would have been necessary for a move on Vicksburg, and a railroad supply line did not exist for the latter part of such a movement, unless the Federals first went into Jackson. (Later in the year, of course, General Grant was to learn about these difficulties, when he launched his first effort toward that fortress on the Mississippi.)

But Halleck did not create a diversion to distract Bragg, nor advance troops to occupy the Confederates at Tupelo. Having decided upon Chattanooga as the objective, Halleck's one clear mistake was leaving Bragg free to maneuver, which the southerner did very effectively, transferring his army to Chattanooga and making Buell's position in northern Alabama untenable.[3]

Buell's subsequent retreat from Alabama, once the Confederates were moving into Tennessee and threatening to eliminate his railroad line from Louisville (with which they already had played havoc and which still was blocked at the tunnels north of Gallatin), is quite understandable. Once committed to falling back, however, Buell seemed not to know where to stop. The Buell Commission concluded that he could have assumed a satisfactory position in Middle Tennessee, east of Nashville, to confront the Rebel advance. There his supply line was shorter than in Alabama, formidable defensive terrain options were his for the taking, and offensive action seemed possible.

Instead, he retreated to Nashville and opened the way for the Confederates to move into Kentucky. A Confederate soldier's observation, entered in his little pocket diary on September 14, is a succinct indictment of Buell's leadership: "And now we have crossed Tennessee and have advanced 50 odd miles into Kentucky without ever firing a gun at Yankees. Who would ever have dreamed such a thing. I certainly expected we would encounter Buell and have one desperate battle before leaving Tennessee, but that gentleman seems to have taken to himself wings and left the country in double quick time."[4] Buell made it easy for the Rebels, so easy that a trap well might have been expected. Buell had laid no trap, however. In fact, for a while he actually was cut off from Louisville and in a precarious situation, as Bragg held the railroad and the pike at the Green River. Buell only got into Louisville without a scratch because Bragg chose to allow him to pass.[5]

Buell's performance at Perryville, while well begun with a diversionary column that fooled the Rebel commander about the location and objective of the main Union force, finally, in addition to the generally loose administration of his command, was so lacking in energy and aggressiveness, in understanding and perception, that he came close to making one of the war's inadequate commanders, Braxton Bragg, look relatively competent.[6] Probably Lincoln, who before Perryville had wanted to relieve Buell, afterward wished that he had done so despite the arguments of General George Thomas.

Having fought the Battle of Perryville badly, Buell followed up that engagement with less than aggressive pursuit of Bragg's retreating army, a pursuit that the general abandoned just when the president and Secretary of War Stanton thought that he might, at last, move into East Tennessee. Instead, Buell changed direction and headed back for Nashville. Preoccupied with the supply problems of an East Tennessee campaign, Buell apparently preferred Nashville for his operations and seemingly failed to discern—despite his near removal from command before Perryville—the precariousness of his standing with Lincoln. This time Lincoln would not be put off. Buell was removed, and forty-three-year-old William Starke Rosecrans—"Old Rosy," as the men called him—who had turned back Van Dorn and Price at Corinth, was the president's choice to take over the Union forces at Nashville.[7]

Rosecrans's coming to command was greeted by the soldiers with almost universal approval. "We were glad to be delivered of Buell," wrote William Hartpence of the Fifty-First Indiana Infantry.

Hartpence told of a song concerning Rosecrans that was popular among the men, claiming that thousands of them would loudly bellow out:

Old Rosy is the man, Old Rosy is the man;
We'll show our deeds where'er he leads;
Old Rosy is the man![8]

Don Carlos Buell soon may have been forgotten in the Federal army, but Braxton Bragg would long remain with the Confederate forces. Actually, he would lead the ill-fated Army of Tennessee, as it was known for the remainder of the war, longer than any other general. Bragg had begun his first campaign impressively, skillfully conducting the transfer of his army to Chattanooga, an excellent movement that placed him in position to unite with Kirby Smith's forces, advance westward, and recover Middle Tennessee, while at the same time compelling Buell to withdraw from northern Alabama. This was the plan as Bragg conceived it.

Unfortunately for the Confederates, Kirby Smith undermined that plan, as he struck northward into Kentucky. Bragg probably could have stopped him early on, but, for whatever reasons, instead acquiesced, and the Florida native quickly moved deep into the Kentucky Bluegrass. With both command and forces divided, and guided by an objective that was vaguely defined at best—to encourage the "rise" of Kentucky for the Confederacy—the Rebel campaigning probably was doomed from the start.[9]

The "what ifs" admittedly are intriguing. What if Bragg had fought Buell south of the Green River? What if he had struck for Louisville when it was not adequately defended? What if Polk had obeyed Bragg's orders, before Perryville, to march from Bardstown and join him for an attack on the Federal column approaching Frankfort? What if, after Perryville, Bragg and Kirby Smith, having joined forces, had decided to fight at Harrodsburg?

All such speculations must take into account the fact that the Kentuckians were not enlisting in the Rebel forces in sufficient numbers to have any real impact. Together with the previously noted violations of the principles of generalship, that fact insured that the Confederate movement would not succeed. Ominously for the future, Bragg came away from Kentucky having lost the confidence of many men and officers, whether deservedly or not.

Of course, the general did have some defenders. Among the staunchest was Surgeon Carlisle. Talk of General Bragg's being superseded "is all nonsense," he wrote to his wife. "He stands higher with the President and army today than he ever has and his whole campaign in Kentucky was [conducted] with wisdom and meets with the warmest approval at Richmond in spite of the barking puppies who [criticize it]." The Kentucky campaign, Carlisle continued, "was one which has never been equaled [under] the same circumstances."[10] The surgeon, from beginning to end of the Kentucky venture, had nothing but praise for Bragg. His, definitely, was a minority opinion.

Major George Winchester was more representative. After neglecting his diary for a number of days, the major took up his pen once more in mid-November, to state his estimate of the general: "Bragg is a humbug," he wrote. "He has no brain and is unfit for his position. His Kentucky campaign should cost him his head, and his further continuance in command of the army should cost Davis his."[11]

Many a Federal was correspondingly elated. "We have driven Bragg out of Kentucky," exulted Horace N. Fisher. "The 8th of October will be a memorable day in the history of the war."[12]

☆☆☆

Without the border slave states, the Confederacy never had much chance of winning its independence. Kentucky, especially because of the rivers and the railroads, was the most vital of those states. In 1862, the summer and fall campaigning made it clear that not only Kentucky, but Maryland as well, would stand with the Union. (Already the issue seemed to have been decided in Missouri, the guerrilla war that continued to ravage that state notwithstanding.)

In retrospect, the Kentucky situation is clarified by the knowledge that the majority of Kentuckians who fought in the war did so on the side of the Union—nearly fifty thousand whites and twenty-four thousand blacks, while perhaps thirty-five thousand served in the Rebel forces. The Federals likewise dominated enlistments in Missouri and Maryland.[13] In the trite but popular jargon of present-day America, the "bottom line" is that the Confederacy simply did not possess the resources, in either men or material, to occupy and control the strategic border slave states, especially when, as now seems evident, the majority of people in those states did not favor the Confederacy. But this knowledge, it must be remembered, is retrospective.

Bragg and Kirby Smith—and Lee as well—were hopeful that their 1862 border state campaigns would bring impressive numbers of recruits to the southern armies. It was hoped that political leaders could be inspired to take action on behalf of the Confederacy and to lead secession movements. In the case of Kentucky, it was vital that a strong and permanent Confederate presence be established in that state if the course of the war were going to be reversed in the Western Theater. At the time, no one could know that these events would not happen, that these states were not going to either supply the number of soldiers hoped for, or rise and join the Rebels.

Following Lee's defeat in September at Antietam (Sharpsburg, the South called it) and his retreat to Virginia, it was clear that Maryland would not cast her lot with the Confederacy. Equally important, Lincoln's Emancipation Proclamation, issued soon afterward, changed forever the complexion of the war, making it very unlikely that England would recognize the Confederacy.[14] And although it has not been widely understood, when the Rebel forces retreated from Kentucky in mid-October, the strategic picture of the rest of the war became starkly visible. Kentucky could not be controlled by the Confederacy, and thus the war, in the Mississippi Valley, in all likelihood never could be turned around. No less a leader than Robert E. Lee had remarked on the implications of defeat in the Western Theater: "If the Mississippi Valley is lost, the Atlantic

States would be ruined."[15] Obviously the Mississippi Valley was well on its way to being lost—the Mississippi River, except for the stretch from Vicksburg to Port Hudson, being already dominated by Union naval forces—before Lee ever initiated his late summer campaign that ended in Maryland, despairingly for the Rebels, at bloody Antietam; and also before Bragg and Kirby Smith began their move into Kentucky.

Here it seems appropriate to comment on a question which many students of the war have long contemplated: whether the Eastern or the Western Theater of conflict was the more important. While the author would affirm that the Western Theater—because of its vastness, its resources, and its numerous avenues (particularly rivers and railroads) for Union strategic gain—was the more significant, the point which should not be obscured in the discussion is that the Western Theater (whether more or less important) is, undeniably, where the Federals first dealt extensive damage to the Confederacy. The terrible losses inflicted there were of such nature and on such a scale that the Confederacy, ever after, was fighting from a drastically impaired position, a situation from which she could not recover. The Western Theater was, as our British friends might express it, where the rot set in.

The sum of all events in 1862, concluding with the failure of the Kentucky campaigning, was that the Confederacy, strategically, was in a very precarious situation. One is tempted to say that the Confederacy had lost the war—unless the Federals lost the will to prosecute it. To be sure, the United States still had to win the war—that is, to carry the war to the South until the southern will to resist was broken. And that would not be easy.

Sometimes one had to wonder if the United States would persevere long enough to win. Certainly Lincoln, at times, was very discouraged, one of his lowest points, in fact, occurring in the late fall 1862, when, overall, the war had gone well through that year. Thirty-two seats in the U.S. House of Representatives had been lost to the Democrats in the off-year elections; soldiers opposing the Emancipation Proclamation threatened and sometimes did desert, rather than fight for the freedom of blacks; while the number of antiwar Democrats seemed to be increasing in the lower northern states adjacent to the border slave states. These were just some of the problems weighing upon the president's mind. He also was shaken to the core by the effort of Republican senators to compel a reshaping of his cabinet—ostensibly to remove Secretary of State Seward, but actually, Lincoln seemed to think, as a possible step toward getting rid of him. This political crisis was occurring at the same period when he and the nation were confronted with the heavy casualties of the badly mismanaged engagement—basically a series of frontal assaults—at Fredericksburg. This fiasco proved the incapacity of yet another Federal commander in the East and prompted the president to say, "If there is a worse place than hell, I am in it."

Jefferson Davis could have spoken the same words—and with more justification. An ultimately ruinous inflation was already fastening its unrelenting grip upon the Confederacy's economy. "King Cotton" diplomacy, that will-o'-the-wisp of southern hope upon which so much had been predicated, already had proven to be a cruel hoax. Fighting a war without an industrial base was yielding its predictable long-term fruit, in the scarcity of all manner of equipment, from clothing and shoes to iron rails and armored vessels. The states' rights philosophy, which had contributed mightily to secession and the establishment of the Confederacy, now, ironically, was playing a major role in bringing down the very structure it had helped to create. The philosophy continually hampered any effective centralized direction of the war effort; and the Confederacy's inadequate manpower base had forced it to resort to conscripting men for the army—an action viewed by many southerners as a blight infesting the new nation—as early as spring 1862, a full year before the Union was to take a similar step.

Much of the problem, with which both sides found it hard to cope, centered around the fact that the war was not at all what they had expected it to be. Already it had gone on far longer than most had originally expected, and the end was not yet in sight. The casualties were horrendous, the dead eventually totaling approximately 622,000 people—more than were killed in all the rest of America's wars put together until well into the Vietnam conflict. By the end of 1862, the awful scale of the war had become clearly evident and was deeply disturbing to both sides.

With a much smaller manpower pool than the Union, the Confederacy's percentage of loss was far greater than the North's. In 1860, the North had a population of twenty-two million, which continued to be increased by immigration as the war progressed. In contrast, the eleven Confederate states had only some nine million, of which about three million were slaves, and these states received very little immigration during the war. The Union military was able to absorb what sometimes was a two-to-one casualty rate in favor of the South, better than the Confederacy could accept its losses, which, relative to its total population, were actually heavier than the North's.

The southern Confederacy, in a word, was being devastated. Whatever problems the North and Abraham Lincoln were experiencing by late fall 1862, if viewed in an objective light, paled in comparison with those of the South and Jefferson Davis. The Rebel hope of foreign assistance was virtually destroyed after the failed Confederate campaigns and the Emancipation Proclamation, coupled with the disasters in the Western Theater, which neither Shiloh nor the Kentucky campaigning had reversed. In this situation, the Confederacy, after 1862, needed something of a miracle if it were going to succeed—as long as, and its importance justifies repetition, the Union determination to put down the rebellion remained firm.

Probably the Confederacy's best chance was to prolong the struggle, in the hope that the North would grow weary of the cost before the task could be finished. But the Confederacy did not conduct the war with that aim in mind; thus, even though Lee's army would yet win some great victories—in fact, perhaps the greatest of all his triumphs, the Battle of Chancellorsville, was to come in May 1863—the Union military continually grew stronger.

In part—and probably it was a very large part—the perception of ever-increasing Federal strength, combined with the Western Theater's 1862 collapse, motivated Lee to wage offensive warfare aggressively in summer 1863, again carrying the fight north, into Pennsylvania, resulting in the monumental clash at Gettysburg. Lee has been criticized by some historians for allegedly focusing too narrowly upon the Eastern Theater at the expense of the strategic needs of the Confederacy overall, as well as for a penchant for offensive action. But as one notable historian has pointed out, significantly, if Lee had won at Gettysburg, "nothing would ever have been heard of the defects in Lee's strategic vision."[16] Apparently, after 1862, Lee believed that only a bold, fateful stroke could possibly save the Confederacy; that time was short in which to attempt such a move; that a choice between East and West was dictated by lack of resources to strike in both theaters; and that chances of significant accomplishment in the West—both because of the dire situation there and because of generals such as Bragg and John Pemberton, whose leadership was suspect—were much slimmer than in the East. Moreover, if a victory could be achieved in the East, the impact on public opinion likely would be greater. Given what he and Jefferson Davis knew at the time, the decision which led to Gettysburg was not without merit. Sometimes lost from view in all the critical analysis is the fact that, whatever move the Rebels made at this stage of the war, the chances of any far-reaching achievement were slim.

It is with the benefit of hindsight that conserving Confederate manpower in an attempt to prolong the war appears, perhaps, the wiser move. Today's students of the conflict know what a burden war weariness became for the United States in 1864. As the presidential election approached, it appeared likely that Lincoln would be defeated, a scenario that raised the specter of success for the Confederacy. Is it not asking the impossible of Lee and other Confederate leaders to have had, in early 1863, such insight relative to possible events more than a year away—particularly when the Rebel losses of 1862 were so obvious, recent, pervasive, and devastating?

Furthermore, war weariness is the proverbial two-edged sword that cuts both going and coming. After the disasters and failures of 1862, war weariness may have seemed more likely to impact the Confederacy heavily, rather than the Union. Clearly, the Rebel setbacks of that year made it seem that time was running out for the South. There is no question that 1862 was the year when the war turned against the Rebels—suddenly, dramatically, strategically. The fall of Fort Henry and Fort Donelson, the loss of New Orleans, the occupation of Nashville, the capture of Memphis, the Federal triumph at Shiloh, the Union takeover of the Memphis and Charleston Railroad, the strategic southern defeat at Antietam, and the Emancipation Proclamation are among the numerous pieces of evidence that the war had gone against the Rebels.

Perhaps nothing demonstrated this fact more clearly, or dramatized the southern reverses of 1862 more compellingly, than the abysmal failure of the campaign to claim the Bluegrass State for the Confederacy. Despite missed opportunities, the campaign turned into a great strategic triumph, from the Union perspective, when the Rebels not only failed to gain Kentucky, but also were unable to inflict any serious damage to the western Federal forces. Never again would the western Confederacy have the strength in numbers, supplies, or transportation even to make the attempt to take Kentucky. And never again, except for small forces such as John Hunt Morgan's cavalry (which to the Federals never was more than an irritation), would a Confederate army set foot upon the dark and bloody ground of the Bluegrass.

Notes

☆☆☆

Abbreviations

ALDAH	State of Alabama, Dept. of Archives and History, Montgomery
CWD	Mark Mayo Boatner III, *Civil War Dictionary* (New York, 1959)
FCHS	Filson Club Historical Society, Louisville, Ky.
GDAH	State of Georgia, Dept. of Archives and History, Atlanta
HCHS	Hart County Historical Society, Munfordville, Ky.
HL	Huntington Library, San Marino, Calif.
IHS	Indiana Historical Society, Indianapolis
MDAH	State of Mississippi, Dept. of Archives and History, Jackson
OHS	Ohio Historical Society, Columbus
OR	*War of the Rebellion: A Compilation of the Official Records of the Union and Confederate Armies.* 129 vols. Washington, D.C., 1880–1901. All references are to serial 1.
SHC	Southern Historical Collection, Univ. of North Carolina, Chapel Hill
SCUTK	Special Collections, Library of the Univ. of Tennessee, Knoxville
TSLA	Tennessee State Library and Archives, Nashville
UKSC	Special Collections, Univ. of Kentucky, Lexington
WKU	Lewis-Starling Manuscript Collection, Manuscript Section, Kentucky Building, Western Kentucky Univ., Bowling Green
WRHS	Western Reserve Historical Society, Cleveland, Ohio
YLUF	P. K. Yonge Library of Florida History, Special Collections, Univ. of Florida, Gainesville

1. A Long Way from Shiloh to Perryville

1. OR, vol. 17, pt. 2, 599, 601, 606, 614.
2. T. Harry Williams, *P. G. T. Beauregard: Napoleon in Gray* (Baton Rouge, La., 1954), 51.
3. James Lee McDonough, *Shiloh—In Hell Before Night* (Knoxville, Tenn., 1977), 60, 62.
4. *Memphis Daily Avalanche*, 7 Mar. 1862.
5. T. Harry Williams, *Beauregard*, 1.
6. McDonough, *Shiloh*, 64–67.
7. CWD, 78, 54. Ezra J. Warner, *Generals in Gray: Lives of the Confederate Commanders* (Baton Rouge, La., 1959), 30–31, 22–23.
8. Eugene H. Berwanger, ed., *My Diary North and South*, by William Howard Russell (New York, 1988), 149.
9. Glenn Tucker, *Chickamauga: Bloody Battle in the West* (Dayton, Ohio, 1972), 78.
10. Ibid.
11. Steven E. Woodworth, *Jefferson Davis and His Generals: The Failure of Confederate Command in the West* (Lawrence, Kans., 1990), 92.
12. Tucker, *Chickamauga*, 79.
13. Woodworth discusses the Bragg-Davis problem in *Davis and His Generals*, 92–93.
14. Grady McWhiney, "Braxton Bragg at Shiloh," *Tennessee Historical Quarterly* 21 (Mar. 1962): 20. James Lee McDonough, *Stones River: Bloody Winter in Tennessee* (Knoxville, Tenn., 1980), 23.
15. Don C. Seitz, *Braxton Bragg: General of the Confederacy* (Columbia, S.C., 1924), 9.
16. Edward H. Moren to Mary Frances Moren, 20 Feb. 1862, Edward Moren Papers, ALDAH. Samuel R. Watkins, *"Co. Aytch," Maury Gray's, First Tennessee Regiment* (Jackson, Tenn., 1952), 67. Tucker, *Chickamauga*, 76.
17. Tucker, *Chickamauga*, 75,76.
18. Woodworth, *Davis and His Generals*, 94.
19. Daniel E. Sutherland, ed., *Reminiscences of a Private: William E. Bevens of the First Arkansas Infantry, C.S.A.* (Fayetteville, Ark., 1992), 89.
20. Charles P. Roland, ed., *Destruction and Reconstruction*, by Richard Taylor (Waltham, Mass., 1968), 94.
21. Grady McWhiney, *Braxton Bragg and Confederate Defeat* (New York, 1969), 20, 390.
22. McDonough, *Shiloh*, 168–70.
23. Stanley F. Horn, *The Army of Tennessee: A Military History* (New York, 1941), 155.
24. OR, vol. 17, pt. 2, 599.
25. Horn, *Army of Tennessee*, 155.
26. See the accounts of Horn, *Army of Tennessee*, 155; T. Harry Williams, *Beauregard*, 158–59; and McWhiney, *Braxton Bragg*, 260–61, all of which are very similar. Horn is listed first because he wrote first. The original source of this information appears to be Alfred Roman, *The Military Operations of General Beauregard in the War Between the States, 186l–1865*, 2 vols. (New York, 1884). Horn does not cite anyone, while T. Harry Williams cites Roman, and McWhiney cites T. Harry Williams.
27. T. Harry Williams, *Beauregard*, 160.

28. Ibid., 161, 165.
29. William I. Hair, *The Kingfish and His Realm: The Life and Times of Huey P. Long* (Baton Rouge, La., 1991), 21, 22.
30. CWD, 63, 935, 41.
31. Thomas L. Livermore, *Numbers and Losses in the Civil War in America, 1861–1865* (New York, 1901), 79–80, 77, 78. Livermore calculated a total of 23,741 casualties for Shiloh, compared with 4,689 for Bull Run and 2,419 for Wilson's Creek.
32. Robert Selph Henry, *The Story of the Confederacy* (New York, 1931; rpt. 1957), 81.
33. Quoted in Benjamin Franklin Cooling, *Forts Henry and Donelson: The Key to the Confederate Heartland* (Knoxville, Tenn., 1987), xiii.
34. Ibid., 245.
35. Henry, *Story of the Confederacy*, 79.
36. James M. McPherson, *Ordeal by Fire: The Civil War and Reconstruction* (New York, 1982), 222.
37. Horn, *Army of Tennessee*, 83.
38. McDonough, *Shiloh*, 6.
39. McPherson, *Ordeal by Fire*, 222.
40. George W. Johnson to wife, 15 Feb. 1862, George W. Johnson Papers, Manuscript Dept., FCHS. (Johnson also asked his wife to "give their third son, Junius, to the Confederacy." She was not interested in complying with his request.)
41. McDonough, *Shiloh*, 6.
42. Cooling, *Forts Henry and Donelson*, xiii.
43. Quoted in Herman Hattaway and Archer Jones, *How the North Won: A Military History of the Civil War* (Chicago, 1983), 156. Also see note, p. 202.
44. Walter Durham, *Nashville, The Occupied City: The First Seventeen Months—February 16, 1862, to June 30, 1863* (Nashville, Tenn., 1985), 31. Also see Stanley F. Horn, *The Decisive Battle of Nashville* (Baton Rouge, La., 1956), 24.
45. Horn, *Army of Tennessee*, 75. See also Hattaway and Jones, *How the North Won*, 76: "With the exception of New Orleans, Nashville was the largest and most important city south of the Ohio River. Occupying a strategic position on the Cumberland River, Nashville had extensive rail connections further enhanced by its giant arsenal, two powder mills and supply depot."
46. Robert C. Black, *The Railroads of the Confederacy* (Chapel Hill, N.C., 1952). Particularly see the railroad map therein.
47. Horn, *Army of Tennessee*, 75. See also Horn's account in "Nashville During the Civil War," *Tennessee Historical Quarterly* 4 (Mar. 1945): 3–22.
48. J. P. Lesley, *Iron Manufacturer's Guide to the Furnaces, Forges and Rolling Mills of the United States* (New York, 1859), 130–36. J. B. Killebrew, *Middle Tennessee as an Iron Center* (Nashville, Tenn., 1879), 9–15. Allan Nevins, *The War for the Union*, 4 vols. (New York, 1960), 2: 74. Cooling, *Forts Henry and Donelson*, 45. Thomas L. Connelly, *Army of the Heartland: The Army of Tennessee, 1861–1862* (Baton Rouge, La., 1967), 8–10.

49. Henry, *Story of the Confederacy*, 111, 112. The number of guns is from Shelby Foote, *The Civil War: A Narrative*, 3 vols. (New York, 1958–75), 1: 307–8.
50. Mrs. Braxton Bragg to Bragg, March 26 and April 2, 1862, William P. Palmer Collection, Braxton Bragg Papers, WRHS.
51. OR, vol. 7, 889.
52. OR, vol. 6, 398, 828. Nevins, *War for the Union*, 2: 74.
53. McDonough, *Shiloh*, 221–22.
54. Horn, *Army of Tennessee*, 145.
55. Ibid., 145, 144.
56. Frank E. Vandiver, *Blood Brothers: A Short History of the Civil War* (College Station, Tex., 1992), 121.
57. McPherson, *Ordeal by Fire*, 230.
58. Ibid. See also McPherson's account in *Battle Cry of Freedom: The Civil War Era* (New York, 1988), 419, 420.
59. Charles Dufour, *The Night the War Was Lost* (New York, 1960).
60. McPherson, *Ordeal by Fire*, 231.
61. McDonough, *Shiloh*, 6.
62. For a full discussion of this battle, see William L. Shea and Earl J. Hess, *Pea Ridge: Civil War Campaign in the West* (Chapel Hill, N.C., 1993).
63. Charles Roland, *An American Iliad: The Story of the Civil War* (Lexington, Ky., 1991), 64. For more information about the war in the West, see Alvin M. Josephy, Jr., *The Civil War in the American West* (New York, 1991).
64. McPherson, *Ordeal by Fire*, 161.
65. McDonough, *Shiloh*, 168–83. McWhiney, *Braxton Bragg*, 231. OR, vol. 10, pt. 1, 483, 493, 498, 574, 575. Clarence C. Buell and Robert U. Johnson, eds., *Battles and Leaders of the Civil War*, 4 vols. (New York, 1887–88), 1: 605.
66. Horn, *Army of Tennessee*, 157.
67. The first letter cited was written on a Friday in June, from a camp near Tupelo, but the date was not given; the second (earlier) letter was dated 13 May 1862; both in Koger Collection, MDAH.
68. *New Orleans Daily Picayune,* 18 April 1862, quoted in McWhiney, *Braxton Bragg*, 253.
69. Terry Carlisle to "My Darling Wife," 25 June 1862, Terry Carlisle, M.D., Civil War Letters, AC 47-001, GDAH.
70. McWhiney, *Braxton Bragg*, 253.
71. James Lee McDonough and James Pickett Jones, *War So Terrible: Sherman and Atlanta* (New York, 1987), 46.
72. Quoted in McWhiney, *Braxton Bragg*, 255.

2. Working on the Railroad

1. McDonough, *Shiloh*, 37, 220, 221. Warner, *Generals in Blue*, 195–97. Nevins, *War for the Union*, 2: 112.

2. McDonough, *Shiloh*, 9.
3. McDonough, *Shiloh*, 37–41, 220. Stephen E. Ambrose, *Halleck: Lincoln's Chief of Staff*, (Baton Rouge, La., 1962), 27–54.
4. Bruce Catton, *Grant Moves South* (Boston, 1960), 278–80. Ulysses S. Grant, *Personal Memoirs of U. S. Grant*, 2 vols. (New York, 1885), 1: 381–83. Nevins, *War for the Union,* 2: 112.
5. Hattaway and Jones, *How the North Won*, 205.
6. Nevins, *War for the Union*, 2: 112.
7. OR, vol. 16, pt. 2, 14, 62.
8. Kenneth P. Williams, *Lincoln Finds a General: A Military Study of the Civil War*, 5 vols. (New York, 1952), 4: 26. McPherson, *Ordeal by Fire*, 233–34.
9. OR, vol. 16, pt. 2, 62.
10. OR, vol. 10, pt. 1, 671.
11. Catton, *Grant Moves South*, 280.
12. McPherson, *Battle Cry of Freedom*, 512. For further defense of Halleck, see Ambrose, *Halleck*, 56–57.
13. Gilbert E. Govan and James W. Livingood, *The Chattanooga Country, 1540–1962: From Tomahawk to TVA* (New York, 1952), 21.
14. James Lee McDonough, *Chattanooga: A Death Grip on the Confederacy* (Knoxville, Tenn., 1984), 73. See also "Chattanooga," *Encyclopedia Britannica*, 1966 ed., vol. 5.
15. Roy P. Basler, ed., *The Collected Works of Abraham Lincoln*, 8 vols. (New Brunswick, N.J., 1953), 5: 91.
16. Ibid.
17. Ibid., 4: 544–45, 458; 5: 60, 90, 91, 98, 99, 276, 295, 300, 308; 6: 377, 378, 439, 470, 471, 484, 498, 510; 7: 35, 53, 321.
18. Thomas L. Connelly, *Civil War Tennessee: Battles and Leaders* (Knoxville, Tenn., 1979), 8, 11. Also see Connelly, *Army of the Heartland*, 6, 8. OR, vol. 52, pt. 2, 324.
19. OR, vol. 16, pt. 2, 8.
20. Ambrose, *Halleck*, 56–57. Catton, *Grant Moves South*, 279. Foote, *The Civil War*, 1: 542, 558–59. McPherson, *Ordeal by Fire*, 233. Kenneth P. Williams, *Lincoln Finds a General*, 4: 27.
21. OR, vol. 16, pt. 2, 9.
22. OR, vol. 16, pt. 1, 473, 479.
23. OR, vol. 16, pt. 1, 30, 31.
24. Warner, *Generals in Blue*, 51. CWD, 96, 97.
25. Foote, *The Civil War*, 1: 563.
26. McDonough, *Shiloh*, 178–81. Warner, *Generals in Blue*, 52.
27. Foote, *The Civil War*, 1: 560.
28. OR, vol. 16, pt. 1, 297.
29. The author personally has examined the tunnel, bridge, and trestle. The length of the bridge is taken from OR, vol. 16, pt. 1, 248.

30. OR, vol. 16, pt. 1, 608.
31. The author has examined the tunnel near Cowan, as well as the area south of it. The length of the tunnel is taken from information available at the Railroad Museum in Cowan.
32. OR, vol. 16, pt. 1, 391, 392.
33. James A. Ramage, *Rebel Raider: The Life of General John Hunt Morgan* (Lexington, Ky., 1986), 137. Edison H. Thomas, *John Hunt Morgan and His Raiders* (Lexington, Ky., 1975), 48.
34. OR, vol. 16, pt. 1, 248, 325–27, 603, 608; pt. 2, 38–39.
35. OR, vol. 16, pt. 1, 248.
36. OR, vol. 16, pt. 1, 326.
37. OR, vol. 16, pt. 1, 604.
38. OR, vol. 16, pt. 1, 297.
39. OR, vol. 16, pt. 1, 297–98.
40. OR, vol. 16, pt. 1, 33–35.
41. OR, vol. 16, pt. 2, 104.
42. OR, vol. 16, pt. 2, 122.
43. OR, vol. 16, pt. 2, 122–23.
44. OR, vol. 16, pt. 2, 128.
45. OR, vol. 16, pt. 1, 333.
46. Robert Selph Henry, *"First With the Most" Forrest* (Indianapolis, Ind., 1944), 86.
47. John Allan Wyeth, *That Devil Forrest: Life of General Nathan Bedford Forrest* (1899; rpt. New York, 1959), 28–68.
48. Henry, *Forrest*, 13–71.
49. Andrew Nelson Lytle, *Bedford Forrest and His Critter Company* (New York, 1931), 91.
50. OR, vol. 16, pt. 2, 722–23. Lytle, *Bedford Forrest*, 89. Henry, *Forrest*, 85.
51. OR, vol. 16, pt. 1, 810.
52. Ibid. Henry, *Forrest*, 86, 87. Lytle, *Bedford Forrest*, 92. Wyeth, *That Devil Forrest*, 72.
53. OR, vol. 16, pt. 1, 810.
54. Lytle, *Bedford Forrest*, 91.
55. Lytle, *Bedford Forrest*, 92.
56. OR, vol. 16, pt. 1, 794.
57. OR, vol. 16, pt. 1, 797.
58. OR, vol. 16, pt. 1, 794, 795, 797.
59. Henry, *Forrest*, 86.
60. Henry, *Forrest*, 87.
61. Wyeth, *That Devil Forrest*, 72, 73. Henry, *Forrest*, 87.
62. Henry, *Forrest*, 88.
63. Bromfield L. Ridley, *Battles and Sketches of the Army of Tennessee* (Mexico, Mo., 1906), 111.

64. Henry, *Forrest*, 87, 88. Lytle, *Bedford Forrest*, 95–97.
65. On Forrest's background, see Wyeth, *That Devil Forrest*, 1–20; Lytle, *Bedford Forrest*, 3–28; Henry, *Forrest*, 13–31. Forrest's exact height is not known. Some students of the general say he was 6'2" tall.
66. Henry, *Forrest*, 88.
67. Henry, *Forrest*, 89.
68. Henry, *Forrest*, 89.
69. Wyeth, *That Devil Forrest*, 76. OR, vol. 16, pt. 1, 805.
70. Henry, *Forrest*, 89.
71. OR, vol. 16, pt. 1, 811. Wyeth, *That Devil Forrest*, 78. Lytle, *Bedford Forrest*, 99. Henry, *Forrest*, 90.
72. OR, vol. 16, pt. 1, 811, 35, 604, 607.
73. Foote, *The Civil War*, 1: 562.
74. OR, vol. 16, pt. 1, 609; pt. 2, 230–31.
75. OR, vol. 16, pt. 2, 279.
76. OR, vol. 16, pt. 1, 248.
77. OR, vol. 16, pt. 2, 302.
78. OR, vol. 16, pt. 2, 236.
79. Ibid.
80. OR, vol. 16, pt. 2, 266. Buell replied to Halleck: "It is difficult to satisfy impatience, and when it proceeds from anxiety, as I know it does in this case, I am not disposed to complain of it. My advance has not been rapid, but it could not be more rapid under the circumstances. . . . Our lines of communication . . . have been twice seriously broken [by enemy cavalry] just as they were finished. . . . We have therefore found it necessary to fortify every bridge over more than 300 miles of road. This could only be done with safety by distributing a large force along the road until the works were complete. They will be done this week and I am already concentrating the troops again."
81. OR, vol. 16, pt. 2, 302.
82. Ramage, *Rebel Raider*, 1–7.
83. Ibid., ix. Those especially interested in Morgan should also consult Cecil F. Holland, *Morgan and His Raiders* (New York, 1943); Basil W. Duke, *The Story of Morgan's Cavalry* (New York, 1867); and Thomas, *Morgan*.
84. Ramage, *Rebel Raider*, 111.
85. Horn, *Army of Tennessee*, 452.
86. Ramage, *Rebel Raider*, 112. Durham, *Nashville*, 107. Thomas, *Morgan*, 48–49.
87. OR, vol. 16, pt. 1, 298. Ramage, *Rebel Raider*, 112. Durham, *Nashville*, 108.
88. OR, vol. 16, pt. 1, 300.
89. OR, vol. 16, pt. 1, 251.
90. Ibid.
91. OR, vol. 16, pt. 1, 300.

92. Thomas, *Morgan*, 49.
93. Ramage, *Rebel Raider*, 115. Walter T. Durham, *Rebellion Revisited: A History of Sumner County, Tennessee, from 1861 to 1870* (Gallatin, Tenn., 1982), 93–94.
94. Ramage, *Rebel Raider*, 116.
95. Ibid.

3. God and Kentucky

1. Basler, *Works of Lincoln*, 4: 532. James A. Rawley, *Turning Points of the Civil War* (Lincoln, Neb., 1966), 11.
2. Basler, *Works of Lincoln*, 4: 532.
3. McPherson, *Battle Cry*, 284.
4. Rawley, *Turning Points*, 14.
5. Woodworth, *Davis and His Generals*, 41, 39.
6. Ibid., 40–41.
7. McPherson, *Ordeal by Fire*, 153–54. Woodworth, *Davis and His Generals*, 38–41. Roland, *American Iliad*, 56. Also see Horn, *Army of Tennessee*, 44–46.
8. McPherson, *Ordeal by Fire*, 154.
9. A helpful article on this topic is Gary Donaldson, "'Into Africa': Kirby Smith's and Braxton Bragg's Invasion of Kentucky," *Filson Club Historical Quarterly* 61 (Oct. 1987): 444–65.
10. Joseph H. Parks, *General Leonidas Polk, C.S.A.: The Fighting Bishop* (Baton Rouge, La., 1962), 10, 12.
11. Warner, *Generals in Gray*, 279–80. CWD, 769.
12. Joseph H. Parks, *General Edmund Kirby Smith, C.S.A.* (Baton Rouge, La., 1962), 6–121. CWD, 769–70. Warner, *Generals in Gray*, 279–80.
13. Foote, *The Civil War*, 1: 83.
14. CWD, 770.
15. Parks, *Kirby Smith*, 134–43.
16. OR, vol. 10, pt. 2, 597.
17. OR, vol. 10, pt. 2, 476, 597; vol. 16, pt. 2, 685.
18. OR, vol. 10, pt. 2, 554, 584, 596, 597; pt. 1, 921.
19. OR, vol. 10, pt. 2, 554.
20. OR, vol. 10, pt. 2, 480, 481, 483.
21. OR, vol. 16, pt. 2, 679, 701, 702, 707–9, 711, 720.
22. OR, vol. 16, pt. 2, 727.
23. Ibid.
24. OR, vol. 16, pt. 2, 729.
25. Ibid.
26. OR, vol. 16, pt. 2, 730.
27. OR, vol. 17, pt. 2, 626.
28. T. J. Koger to "My Darling Wife," 9, 12, and 22 June 1862, Koger Collection, MDAH.

29. Quoted in Larry J. Daniel, *Soldiering in the Army of Tennessee: A Portrait of Life in a Confederate Army* (Chapel Hill, N.C., 1991), 84.
30. T. J. Koger to wife, 10 June 1862, Koger Collection, MDAH.
31. McWhiney, *Braxton Bragg*, 267, 268. Also see Woodworth, *Davis and His Generals*, 130–34; Horn, *Army of Tennessee*, 156–60; Connelly, *Army of the Heartland*, 197–201; Foote, *The Civil War*, 1: 569–74.
32. OR, vol. 52, pt. 2, 330.
33. Ibid.
34. OR, vol. 52, pt. 2, 331.
35. OR, vol. 7, pt. 2, 655–56.
36. McWhiney, *Braxton Bragg*, 271.
37. Terry Carlisle to wife, 13 July 1862, Terry Carlisle, M.D., Civil War Letters, GDAH.
38. Thomas Benton Ellis Diary, June 1861–April 1865, YLUF.
39. Augustus Oswald McDonnell Diary, 10 Aug. 1862, YLUF.
40. M. Jinkins to Col. E. S. Jinkins, "Dear Father," 15 Aug. 1862, SCUTK.
41. Woodworth, *Davis and His Generals*, 135–36.
42. OR, vol. 16, pt. 2, 745–46.
43. OR, vol. 16, pt. 2, 734–35.
44. OR, vol. 16, pt. 2, 746.
45. Donaldson, "Into Africa," 450–51.
46. Parks, *Kirby Smith*, 201.
47. Manuscript notes made by Edmund Kirby Smith, in Edmund Kirby Smith Papers, SHC.
48. OR, vol. 16, pt. 2, 741.
49. Ibid.
50. Ibid.
51. OR, vol. 16, pt. 2, 746.
52. OR, vol. 16, pt. 2, 751.
53. OR, vol. 16, pt. 2, 724.
54. OR, vol. 16, pt. 2, 733–34.
55. E. Merton Coulter, *The Civil War and Readjustment in Kentucky* (Chapel Hill, N.C., 1926), 151–65.
56. OR, vol. 16, pt. 2, 733–34.
57. J. Stoddard Johnston Diary, FCHS. OR, vol. 16, pt. 2, 751.
58. Humphrey Marshall to Alexander H. Stephens, 22 Feb. 1862, Humphrey Marshall Papers, FCHS. For facts about Marshall, see John E. Kleber, ed., *The Kentucky Encyclopedia* (Lexington, Ky., 1992), 610.
59. OR, vol. 16, pt. 2, 748.
60. OR, vol. 16, pt. 2, 749.
61. OR, vol. 16, pt. 2, 995.
62. OR, vol. 16, pt. 2, 751.
63. OR, vol. 16, pt. 2, 752–53.

64. Ibid.
65. Edmund Kirby Smith Papers, SHC.
66. J. Stoddard Johnston Diary, FCHS.
67. OR, vol. 52, pt. 2, 340.
68. OR, vol. 17, pt. 2, 675–76.
69. OR, vol. 17, pt. 2, 687.
70. OR, vol. 17, pt. 2, 690.
71. OR, vol. 17, pt. 2, 691, 692, 696.
72. OR, vol. 17, pt. 2, 696, 697.
73. OR, vol. 16, pt. 2, 698.
74. OR, vol. 16, pt. 2, 544–45.

4. Retreat to Nashville

1. OR, vol. 16, pt. 2, 398, 409, 445, 451, 452.
2. Basler, *Works of Lincoln*, 5: 295.
3. Theodore R. McBeath to "Dear Nannie," 2 July 1862, in Theodore Robert McBeath Papers, UKSC.
4. George Morgan Kirkpatrick, *The Experiences of a Private Soldier of the Civil War* (N.p., "the Hoosier Bookshop," 1973), 9.
5. George W. Landrum to "Dear Amanda," 28 April 1862, and Landrum to "Dear Sister," 15 April 1862, both in George W. Landrum Papers, OHS.
6. John Beatty, *The Citizen Soldier: Or, Memoirs of a Volunteer* (Cincinnati, Ohio, 1879), 132, 133.
7. Bergum H. Brown to "Dear Mother," 2 Aug. 1862, in Bergum H. Brown Letters, IHS.
8. Beatty, *Citizen Soldier*, 144.
9. George W. Landrum to "Dear Sister," 23 April 1862, Landrum Papers, OHS.
10. Jack F. Pase to "Dear Parents," 16 and 22 May 1862, John A. Berger and Jack F. Pase Letters, IHS.
11. William R. Stuckey to "My Dear Love," 13 and 14 Nov. 1861, 18 and 29 Dec. 1861, 3 Jan. 1862, 3 Feb. 1862, and 15 Aug. 1862, William R. Stuckey Letters, IHS.
12. Jesse B. Connelly Diary, IHS.
13. Kirkpatrick, *Experiences of a Private*, 9.
14. James S. Thomas Letters, IHS.
15. Beatty, *Citizen Soldier*, 132, 140.
16. James F. Mohr to "Dear Brother," 16 May 1862, 25 July 1862, James F. Mohr Letters, FCHS.
17. W. E. Patterson Diary, SCUTK.
18. Bergum H. Brown to "Dear Mother," 2 Aug. 1862, Bergum H. Brown Letters, IHS.
19. Beatty, *Citizen Soldier*, 143.

20. Ibid., 138–39.
21. Loraine B. Pabst, "The Sack and Occupation of Athens, Alabama," *Bulletin of the North Alabama Historical Association* 4 (1959): 18–20. Hugh C. Bailey, "Reaction in the Tennessee Valley to Federal Invasion," *Bulletin of the North Alabama Historical Association* 5 (1960): 7. Mary Ellen McElligott, ed., "'A Monotony Full of Sadness': The Diary of Nadine Turchin, May 1863–April 1864," *Journal of the Illinois State Historical Society* 70 (Feb. 1977): 27. OR, vol. 16, pt. 1, 634, 637, 478, 479. Warner, *Generals in Blue*, 511.
22. Theodore R. McBeath to "Dear Nannie," 2 Aug. 1862, Theodore Robert McBeath Papers, UKSC.
23. OR, vol. 16, pt. 1, 838, 839.
24. *Nashville Daily Union*, 8 Aug. 1862, TSLA.
25. OR, vol. 16, pt. 1, 839.
26. Quoted in *Nashville Daily Union*, 13 Aug. 1862, TSLA.
27. Bergum H. Brown to "Dear Mother," 2 Aug. 1862, Bergum H. Brown Letters, IHS.
28. *Nashville Daily Union*, 2 Aug. 1862, TSLA.
29. OR, vol. 16, pt. 1, 636.
30. John W. Large Letter, 7 July 1862, IHS.
31. OR, vol. 16, pt. 1, 328.
32. OR, vol. 16, pt. 1, 637. McElligott, "Diary of Nadine Turchin," 28. Warner, *Generals in Blue*, 511.
33. OR, vol. 16, pt. 1, 639, 640.
34. OR, vol. 16, pt. 1, 639, 640, 641.
35. OR, vol. 16, pt. 1, 640.
36. Quoted in the *Nashville Daily Union*, 1 Aug. 1862, TSLA.
37. *Nashville Daily Union*, 3 Aug. 1862, TSLA.
38. *Nashville Daily Union*, 21 Aug. 1862, TSLA.
39. OR, vol. 16, pt. 1, 641.
40. OR, vol. 16, pt. 2, 361.
41. Kenneth P. Williams, *Lincoln Finds a General*, 4: 46. Durham, *Nashville*, 111. Durham, *Rebellion Revisited*, 95–99. Ramage, *Rebel Raider*, 117.
42. Durham, *Rebellion Revisited*, 95–99. OR, vol. 16, pt. 2, 387, 388.
43. OR, vol. 16, pt. 2, 389.
44. OR, vol. 16, pt. 2, 278–79.
45. OR, vol. 16, pt. 2, 390, 395, 396, 398, 408, 418, 432, 438, 442, 445.
46. OR, vol. 16, pt. 1, 604.
47. Kenneth P. Williams, *Lincoln Finds a General*, 4: 46.
48. Durham, *Nashville*, 113.
49. OR, vol. 16, pt. 1, 604.
50. OR, vol. 16, pt. 1, 602.

51. OR, vol. 16, pt. 1, 604, 608.
52. OR, vol. 16, pt. 1, 707.
53. OR, vol. 16, pt. 1, 472, 475.
54. OR, vol. 16, pt. 1, 603.
55. OR, vol. 16, pt. 1, 604–5.
56. OR, vol. 16, pt. 1, 33.
57. OR, vol. 16, pt. 1, 707.
58. Kenneth P. Williams, *Lincoln Finds a General*, 4: 25–51.
59. OR, vol. 16, pt. 1, 109.
60. OR, vol. 16, pt. 2, 357.
61. OR, vol. 16, pt. 1, 376.
62. OR, vol. 16, pt. 2, 392.
63. OR, vol. 16, pt. 2, 399.
64. Quoted in *Nashville Daily Union*, 10 June 1862, in TSLA.
65. OR, vol. 16, pt. 1, 38–43, 87–88, 154, 189–92.
66. OR, vol. 16, pt. 2, 392.
67. OR, vol. 16, pt. 1, 155.
68. OR, vol. 16, pt. 1, 110.
69. *Nashville Daily Union*, 28 Aug. 1862, TSLA.
70. OR, vol. 16, pt. 2, 421.
71. Ibid.
72. OR, vol. 16, pt. 2, 445–46.
73. OR, vol. 16, pt. 1, 182–83, 189–91, 202–3.
74. OR, vol. 16, pt. 1, 9.
75. OR, vol. 16, pt. 2, 451.
76. *Nashville Daily Union*, 29 Aug. 1862, TSLA.
77. James King to Jenny, 10 Sept. 1862, James King Papers, Manuscripts Division, TSLA.
78. OR, vol. 16, pt. 1, 182.
79. OR, vol. 16, pt. 1, 202.
80. OR, vol. 16, pt. 1, 17.
81. OR, vol. 16, pt. 2, 451.
82. OR, vol. 16, pt. 1, 9.
83. This was also the conclusion of the Buell Commission. See ibid.
84. OR, vol. 16, pt. 2, 766.
85. Edmund Kirby Smith to wife, 19, 20, and 21 Aug. 1862, Edmund Kirby Smith Papers, SHC.
86. Paul F. Hammond, "General Kirby Smith's Campaign in Kentucky in 1862," *Southern Historical Society Papers* 9 (1881): 247.
87. Alfred Fielder Diary, TSLA.
88. William Lowrey Diary, ALDAH.

89. Hugh Black to "Dear Wife," 15 Aug. 1862, and Hugh Black Diary, both in Capt. Hugh Black Letters, Special Collections, Florida State Univ., Tallahassee.
90. Hammond, "Kirby Smith's Campaign," 248–49.
91. William Lowrey Diary, ALDAH.
92. Frank Ryan, "The Kentucky Campaign and Battle of Richmond," *Confederate Veteran* 26 (1918): 158.
93. Edmund Kirby Smith to wife, 24 and 26 Aug. 1862, Edmund Kirby Smith Papers, SHC.
94. Edmund Kirby Smith to "My Dear Major," undated, Edmund Kirby Smith Papers, SHC.
95. Edmund Kirby Smith to wife, 24 Aug. 1862, Edmund Kirby Smith Papers, SHC.

5. A General Stampede to the Rear

1. OR, vol. 16, pt. 1, 907, 908.
2. Hammond, "Kirby Smith's Campaign," 249–50. This source is particularly valuable, since Hammond was with Kirby Smith on this campaign and wrote his account reasonably soon after the event, in spring 1863. "It had been feared," he wrote, that the Federals would post themselves upon "the high bluffs of the Kentucky river and . . . the few places at which the passage could be effected were susceptible of every defence against greatly superior numbers." Donaldson, "Into Africa," 444–65, is also valuable when studying the Richmond engagement.
3. OR, vol. 16, pt. 1, 931.
4. Hammond, "Kirby Smith's Campaign," 249.
5. OR, vol. 16, pt. 1, 908, 909, 911; pt. 2, 467.
6. Warner, *Generals in Blue*, 343–44.
7. OR, vol. 16, pt. 2, 467; pt. 1, 909.
8. OR, vol. 16, pt. 1, 909.
9. OR, vol. 16, pt. 1, 908.
10. OR, vol. 16, pt. 1, 911. Kenneth P. Williams, *Lincoln Finds a General*, 4: 53.
11. OR, vol. 16, pt. 1, 913.
12. 6 April 1878, copy in possession of Prof. Dean W. Lambert, Berea College, Berea, Ky.
13. OR, vol. 16, pt. 1, 914–15.
14. OR, vol. 16, pt. 1, 918–19.
15. OR, vol. 16, pt. 1, 915.
16. Hammond, "Kirby Smith's Campaign," 249.
17. OR, vol. 16, pt. 1, 911.
18. *Louisville (Ky.) Courier-Journal*, 6 April 1878.
19. CWD, 698.
20. Today there is a small community at the northern base of the ridge, on the road to Richmond, that is called Big Hill. Also there is a promontory north of this com-

munity, known as Joe's Lick Knob, that sometimes is mistakenly referred to as Big Hill. This information was acquired while the author was researching the terrain, thanks particularly to Prof. Dean W. Lambert, Berea College, Berea, Ky.

21. CWD, 698.
22. Hammond, "Kirby Smith's Campaign," 249.
23. Kirby Smith Papers, SHC.
24. Hammond, "Kirby Smith's Campaign," 249.
25. Edmund Kirby Smith to wife, 29 Aug. 1862, Kirby Smith Papers, SHC.
26. Ryan, "The Kentucky Campaign," 158–59.
27. McDonough, *Shiloh*, 99. James Lee McDonough and T. L. Connelly, *Five Tragic Hours: The Battle of Franklin* (Knoxville, Tenn., 1983), 138. Warner, *Generals in Gray*, 53–54.
28. McDonough, *Shiloh*, 99. McDonough and Connelly, *Five Tragic Hours*, 138. Warner, *Generals in Gray*, 53–54. For more information on Cleburne, see Captain Irving A. Buck, *Cleburne and His Command*, by Capt. Irving A. Buck (rpt. Wilmington, N.C., 1987), and Howell Purdue and Elizabeth Purdue, *Pat Cleburne, Confederate General: A Definitive Biography* (Hillsboro, Tex., 1973). On the battle flags, see Howard Michael Madaus and Robert D. Needham, *The Battle Flags of the Confederate Army of Tennessee* (Milwaukee, Wisc., 1976).
29. Warner, *Generals in Blue*, 310. CWD, 508.
30. Sam Reid to "Dear Mary," 27 Aug. 1862, Samuel Reid Family Papers, IHS.
31. Henry H. Aye Autobiography, IHS.
32. Ryan, "The Kentucky Campaign," 160.
33. OR, vol. 16, pt. 1, 911.
34. OR, vol. 16, pt. 1, 911, 944.
35. Rogersville sometimes is referred to as White's Farm. It no longer exists but was in the area now called Terrill.
36. OR, vol. 16, pt. 1, 911.
37. OR, vol. 16, pt. 1, 944.
38. Ibid.
39. Ibid.
40. OR, vol. 16, pt. 1, 949.
41. OR, vol. 16, pt. 1, 944.
42. OR, vol. 16, pt. 1, 944, 949.
43. Hammond, "Kirby Smith's Campaign," 249. OR, vol. 16, pt. 1, 934, 944–45.
44. Hammond, "Kirby Smith's Campaign," 250.
45. OR, vol. 16, pt. 1, 912.
46. CWD, 698.
47. Kentucky Historical Marker.
48. OR, vol. 16, pt. 1, 912, 916, 920, 934, 940, 945, 949.

49. OR, vol. 16, pt. 1, 945.
50. OR, vol. 16, pt. 1, 950.
51. Ibid.
52. OR, vol. 16, pt. 1, 945.
53. OR, vol. 16, pt. 1, 920.
54. Robert M. Frierson, "General E. Kirby Smith's Campaign in Kentucky," *Confederate Veteran* 1 (1893): 295.
55. OR, vol. 16, pt. 1, 912.
56. OR, vol. 16, pt. 1, 945–46.
57. OR, vol. 16, pt. 1, 946.
58. Ibid.
59. Frierson, "General E. Kirby Smith's Campaign in Kentucky," 295.
60. Buck, *Cleburne and His Command*, 107.
61. OR, vol. 16, pt. 1, 934, 940, 942. Hammond, "Kirby Smith's Campaign," 250.
62. Author's conclusion after an on-site examination.
63. OR, vol. 16, pt. 1, 940.
64. The student of the Richmond battle can not help being disappointed that more reports of the battle were not written and preserved. Two reports that never found their way into the OR were preserved in Frank Moore, ed., *The Rebellion Record: A Diary of American Events*, 11 vols. (New York, 1861–68), vol. 5. These were by the Ninety-Fifth Ohio's Lt. Col. J. B. Armstrong and the Sixty-Ninth Indiana's Col. Herman J. Korff.
65. OR, vol. 16, pt. 1, 912.
66. Oliver Haskell Diary, IHS.
67. Henry H. Aye Autobiography, IHS.
68. OR, vol. 16, pt. 1, 912.
69. OR, vol. 16, pt. 1, 929.
70. Moore, *Rebellion Record*, 5: 412–13.
71. OR, vol. 16, pt. 1, 913.
72. OR, vol. 16, pt. 1, 920.
73. Ibid.
74. OR, vol. 16, pt. 1, 913.
75. OR vol. 16, pt. 1, 942, 940.
76. Ibid.
77. Ibid.
78. Ibid.
79. OR, vol. 16, pt. 1, 921, 913.
80. Hammond, "Kirby Smith's Campaign," 251. Parks, *Kirby Smith*, 214.
81. OR, vol. 16, pt. 1, 909, 913, 921. Robert E. McDowell, *City of Conflict: Louisville in the Civil War, 1861–1865* (Civil War Round Table, Louisville, Ky., 1962), 791.
82. Haskell Diary, IHS.

83. McDonough, *Shiloh*, 178.
84. Moore, *Rebellion Record*, 5: 413. Donaldson, "Into Africa," 457. McDowell, *City of Conflict*, 79.
85. Thomas D. Clark, *A History of Kentucky* (Lexington, Ky., 1954), 321.
86. Ryan, "The Kentucky Campaign," 160. Hammond, "Kirby Smith's Campaign," 253. OR, vol. 16, pt. 1, 921. Parks, *Kirby Smith*, 215.
87. Parks, *Kirby Smith*, 215.
88. Hammond, "Kirby Smith's Campaign," 253.
89. Frierson, "General E. Kirby Smith's Campaign," 295.
90. Ibid.
91. McDowell, *City of Conflict*, 79. Dean W. Lambert, "Battle of Richmond, Kentucky," tour guide for the Richmond Tourism Commission, Richmond, Ky. Foote, *The Civil War*, 1: 652. OR, vol. 16, pt. 1, 909.
92. OR, vol. 16, pt. 1, 921.
93. OR, vol. 16, pt. 1, 938. Hammond, "Kirby Smith's Campaign," 253.
94. Byron Smith, "Battle of Richmond, Kentucky," *Confederate Veteran* 30 (1922): 298.
95. Hammond, "Kirby Smith's Campaign," 253.
96. Captain Haynie, "Captain Haynie Captured a Regiment," *Confederate Veteran* 7 (1899): 203. The captain's name is given as Haynie, of Cave Spring, Ga. No first name is recorded.
97. OR, vol. 16, pt. 1, 914. Parks, *Kirby Smith*, 215.
98. OR, vol. 16, pt. 1, 938–39.
99. Foote, *The Civil War*, 1: 650.
100. Livermore, *Numbers and Losses*, 89. CWD, 698. OR, vol. 16, pt. 1, 909.
101. Ryan, "The Kentucky Campaign," 160.
102. Vaughan to Tipton, 2 June 1892, in French Tipton Papers, John Wilson Townsend Room, Eastern Kentucky Univ., Richmond.
103. Parks, *Kirby Smith*, 217. Ryan, "The Kentucky Campaign," 160. Kentucky Historical Marker at Mt. Zion Church.
104. Captain Hugh Black Diary, Special Collections, Florida State Univ., Tallahassee.
105. Lucia Burnam, "What I Remember," John Wilson Townsend Room, Eastern Kentucky Univ., Richmond.
106. Ibid. Some Confederates, she said, "gloried in the name of Rebel and sometimes they said they were *not* Rebels at all."
107. Henry Aye Autobiography, IHS.
108. Ryan, "The Kentucky Campaign," 160.
109. Glover Moore, *William Jemison Mims, Soldier and Squire* (Birmingham, Ala., 1966), 35. See also William H. Townsend, *Lincoln and the Bluegrass: Slavery and Civil War in Kentucky* (Lexington, Ky., 1955; rpt. 1989), 295.
110. Captain Hugh Black Diary, Special Collections, Florida State Univ., Tallahassee.
111. Ryan, "The Kentucky Campaign," 160. Parks, *Kirby Smith*, 219.

112. T. Otis Baker to "Dear Father and Mother," 26 Sept. 1862, Otis T. Baker Papers, MDAH.
113. OR, vol. 16, pt. 1, 933.
114. OR, vol. 16, pt. 2, 797.
115. Kirby Smith Papers, SHC. Donaldson, "Into Africa," 457.
116. James A. Ramage, "Panic on the Ohio," *Blue and Gray Magazine* 3 (May 1986): 12.
117. McDonough, *Shiloh*, 47, 156–61. *Chicago Times*, 26 Mar. 1862.
118. Ramage, "Panic on the Ohio," 12, 13. Horn, *Army of Tennessee*, 164–65.
119. Ramage, "Panic on the Ohio," 13.
120. Kleber, *Kentucky Encyclopedia*, 194.
121. Ramage, "Panic On The Ohio," 13–15.
122. Horn, *Army of Tennessee*, 164–65. McDowell, *City of Conflict*, 81.
123. Major Alfred Pirtle, "Biographical Sketches," in *The Union Regiments of Kentucky, Published Under the Auspices of the Union Soldiers and Sailors Monument Association,* ed. Alfred Pirtle (Louisville, Ky., 1897), 61. Coulter, *Civil War and Readjustment in Kentucky*, 151.
124. OR, vol. 16, pt. 2, 465, 466, 469.
125. OR, vol. 16, pt. 2, 475–76.
126. Ibid.
127. OR, vol. 16, pt. 2, 478–79.
128. OR, vol. 16, pt. 2, 476.
129. Livermore, *Numbers and Losses*, 88–89. CWD, 105.
130. Horn, *Army of Tennessee*, 165.
131. OR, vol. 16, pt. 2, 766, 768–69.
132. Kenneth P. Williams, *Lincoln Finds a General*, 4: 54. Horn, *Army of Tennessee*, 164.
133. Parks, *Kirby Smith*, 220.
134. OR, vol. 16, pt. 2, 495, 496, 497, 500.
135. OR, vol. 16, pt. 2, 822.
136. Watkins, *"Co. Aytch,"* 79.
137. Diary of Augustus McDonnell, 14 Sept. 1862, YLUF.
138. A. T. (or F.) Boyd to "Dear Sister," 26 Oct. 1862, Boyd/Sitton Family Civil War Letters, 1861–65, AC 70-004, GDAH.
139. John J. Hogg Diary, and Hogg to "Dear Susan," 16 Sept. 1862, both in John J. Hogg Papers, Georgia Historical Society, Savannah.
140. Various Koger letters, Koger Collection, MDAH. Terry Carlisle to wife, 23 Aug. 1862, Terry Carlisle, M.D., Civil War Letters, GDAH.

6. An Unauthorized and Injudicious Attack

1. OR, vol. 16, pt. 1, 963.
2. Information about Munfordville was acquired at the Hart County Historical Society, Munfordville, Ky. (HCHS). The information about Andrew Jackson comes from Judge Roy A. Cann's unpublished notebook, HCHS.

3. Quoted in Hal Engerud, "The Battle of Munfordville," booklet, 1984, HCHS, 3.
4. Engerud, "Battle of Munfordville," booklet, 8.
5. OR, vol. 16, pt. 1, 963–64.
6. Hal Engerud, "The History of the Siege of Munfordville," Louisville Civil War Round Table, 23 June 1962, p. 4., copy in HCHS.
7. OR, vol. 16, pt. 1, 963–64.
8. OR, vol. 16, pt. 1, 964. Engerud, "Siege," 4.
9. OR, vol. 16, pt. 1, 974.
10. OR, vol. 16, pt. 1, 960.
11. Col. Hal Engerud, USA, Retired, "The Battle of Munfordville," address at Civil War Centennial Commemorating the Battle of Munfordville, Courthouse Square, Munfordville, Ky., 15 Sept. 1962, copy in HCHS.
12. OR, vol. 16, pt. 1, 974.
13. E. T. Sykes, "An Incident of the Battle of Munfordville, Kentucky, September, 1862," *Publications of the Mississippi Historical Society* 2 (1918): 537.
14. Ibid., 536–37.
15. OR, vol. 16, pt. 1, 974.
16. Ibid.
17. OR, vol. 16, pt. 1, 975.
18. OR, vol. 16, pt. 1, 972.
19. Ibid.
20. Engerud, "Battle of Munfordville," Booklet, 6.
21. OR, vol. 16, pt. 1, 959, 974–75.
22. OR, vol. 16, pt. 1, 960–61.
23. OR, vol. 16, pt. 1, 975.
24. Ibid. Engerud, "Battle of Munfordville," Booklet, 10.
25. Sykes, "Incident of Battle of Munfordville," 538.
26. OR, vol. 16, pt. 1, 960, 972, 973. Edison H. Thomas, "The Battle at the Bridge," *L and N Employees Magazine* (May 1955): 9.
27. Engerud, "Battle of Munfordville," Booklet, 10–11. OR, vol. 16, pt. 1, 972, 973.
28. Wiley Sword, *Shiloh: Bloody April* (New York, 1974), 320. OR, vol. 16, pt. 1, 976.
29. OR, vol. 16, pt. 1, 976.
30. OR, vol. 16, pt. 1, 977.
31. OR, vol. 16, pt. 1, 976.
32. OR, vol. 16, pt. 1, 987.
33. OR, vol. 16, pt. 1, 977.
34. Sykes, "Incident of Battle of Munfordville," 538. OR, vol. 16, pt. 1, 987.
35. OR, vol. 16, pt. 1, 977. Engerud, "Battle of Munfordville," Booklet, 11.
36. OR, vol. 16, pt. 1, 981.
37. OR, vol. 16, pt. 1, 961, 981.
38. Sykes, "Incident of Battle of Munfordville," 539.

39. Ibid., 539–40.
40. Mary E. Brent Roberts, "Memories of Life on a Farm in Hart County, Kentucky, in the Early Sixties," *Filson Club Historical Quarterly* 14 (July 1940): 152–53.
41. Engerud, "Siege," 6.
42. OR, vol. 16, pt. 1, 972.
43. OR, vol. 16, pt. 1, 980.
44. J. Stoddard Johnston, "Bragg's Campaign in Kentucky: From Chattanooga to Munsfordville" (*sic*), in J. Stoddard Johnston Papers, FCHS.
45. Marmaduke B. Morton, "Last Surviving Lieutenant-General: Visit to the Home of General S. B. Buckner," *Confederate Veteran* 17 (1909): 85. "Simon Bolivar Buckner," *Hart County Historical Society Quarterly* 13 (July 1981): 12.
46. Buckner's letter to Bragg with Bragg's inscription, Simon Bolivar Buckner Manuscripts, HL.
47. Buckner's presence actually produced few recruits, as most Confederate sympathizers hesitated to take a stand until after Rebel triumphs took place in the Bluegrass.
48. Hal Engerud, "Munfordville: The Home of Two Civil War Generals," originally published in *Hart County News*, Bicentennial ed.; reissued in pamphlet form, 8 Feb. 1974, copy in HCHS.
49. Morton, "Last Surviving Lieutenant-General," 61. CWD, 95, 96. On Buckner and "Glen Lily," see "Glen Lily," *Hart County Historical Society Quarterly* 19 (Oct. 1987): 3–4. Also see Arndt M. Stickles, *Simon Bolivar Buckner, Borderland Knight* (Chapel Hill, N.C., 1940), for a more thorough treatment of the general.
50. Morton, "Last Surviving Lieutenant-General," 85. "Simon Bolivar Buckner," 12.
51. OR, vol. 16, pt. 1, 968–69.
52. Engerud, "Siege," 9. OR, vol. 16, pt. 1, 209. Johnston, "Bragg's Campaign."
53. OR, vol. 16, pt. 1, 970.
54. OR, vol. 16, pt. 1, 970–71. Also see p. 209 for Wilder's account.
55. "Simon Bolivar Buckner," 12.
56. Ibid.
57. OR, vol. 16, pt. 1, 210. Morton, "Last Surviving Lieutenant-General," 85.
58. OR, vol. 16, pt. 1, 210, 211. Morton, "Last Surviving Lieutenant-General," 85.
59. Engerud, "Siege," 10.
60. Morton, "Last Surviving Lieutenant-General," 85.
61. Ibid.
62. Johnston, "Bragg's Campaign." John T. Wilder, "The Siege of Munfordville," in Samuel C. Williams, *General John T. Wilder, Commander of the Lightning Brigade* (Bloomington, Ind., 1936), 62–63. Connelly, *Army of the Heartland*, 230.
63. Sykes, "Incident of Battle of Munfordville," 542.
64. Connelly, *Army of the Heartland*, 230.
65. Engerud, "Siege," 10.
66. T. J. Koger to wife, 20 Sept. 1862, Koger Collection, MDAH.

67. George Stewart, Sr., 2nd Kentucky Volunteer Cavalry, U.S., "Reminiscence of War Experiences," 30 Nov. 1915, HCHS.
68. Hal Engerud, "Anthony L. Woodson's Travail," written for the *Hart County News,* Bicentennial ed.; reissued in pamphlet form, 8 Feb. 1974, copy in HCHS.
69. Connelly, *Army of the Heartland*, 230.
70. OR, vol. 16, pt. 2, 841–42.
71. Connelly, *Army of the Heartland*, 228.
72. Ibid.
73. OR, vol. 16, pt. 2, 842.
74. Horn, *Army of Tennessee*, 170.
75. Horn, *Army of Tennessee*, 170, 171, 172.
76. Horn, *Army of Tennessee*, 453. Buell and Johnson, *Battles and Leaders*, 3: 20, 22. Also see McWhiney, *Braxton Bragg*, 286–92.
77. Henry, *Story of the Confederacy*, 195.
78. Roland, *American Iliad*, 84.
79. Horn, *Army of Tennessee*, 172, 453.
80. OR, vol. 16, pt. 2, 815.
81. OR, vol. 16, pt. 1, 968.
82. Lowell H. Harrison, *The Civil War in Kentucky* (Lexington, Ky., 1975), 46.
83. OR, vol. 16, pt. 1, 968.
84. McWhiney, *Braxton Bragg*, 288.
85. OR, vol. 16, pt. 2, 830; pt. 1, 47. Buell and Johnson, *Battles and Leaders*, 3: 21. See preceding chs. 3 and 5.
86. Woodworth, *Davis and His Generals*, 152.
87. Horn, *Army of Tennessee*, 172.
88. Kleber, *Kentucky Encyclopedia*, 194.
89. Bruce Catton, *This Hallowed Ground* (New York, 1956), 205.
90. Livermore, *Numbers and Losses*, 92–93. Bruce Catton, *The American Heritage Short History of the Civil War* (New York, 1960), 95–97. Catton, *This Hallowed Ground*, 199–207.
91. Henry, *Story of the Confederacy*, 197.
92. George Winchester Diary, Confederate Collection, TSLA.
93. T. J. Koger to wife, 24 and 27 Sept. 1862, Koger Collection, MDAH.
94. James H. Jones to "Father and Mother," 28 Sept. 1862, James H. Jones Letters, IHS.
95. W. E. Patterson Diary, 1861–64, SCUTK.
96. Hambleton Tapp and James C. Klotter, eds., *The Union, The Civil War and John W. Tuttle: A Captain's Account* (Frankfort, Ky., 1980), 125.
97. William Spencer to "Dear Sister," Covington, Ky., n.d., and Spencer to "Dear Father," Louisville, 22 Sept. 1862, OHS.
98. Hal Engerud, "Louisville's Civil War Civil Defense," *Louisville Courier-Journal Magazine*, 30 Sept. 1956, 41.

99. Horn, *Army of Tennessee*, 176.
100. McDowell, *City of Conflict*, 83–84.
101. Engerud, "Louisville's Defense," 41.
102. James Mitchell Reminiscences, OHS.
103. OR, vol. 16, pt. 2, 540.
104. Charles Lewis Francis, *Narrative of a Private Soldier in the Volunteer Army of the United States* (New York, 1879), 51. Connelly Diary, IHS.
105. Henry, *Story of the Confederacy*, 197.
106. Kleber, *Kentucky Encyclopedia*, 193. McDowell, *City of Conflict*, 92–93.
107. Henry, *Story of the Confederacy*, 197. McDowell, *City of Conflict*, 99–101.
108. Thomas C. James to "Dear John," Louisville, Ky., 29 Sept. 1862, Jefferson C. Davis file, IHS.
109. James A. C. Dobson, *A Historical Sketch of Company K, of the Seventy-ninth Indiana Volunteers* (Plainfield, Ind., 1894), 3.
110. Kleber, *Kentucky Encyclopedia*, 193.
111. McPherson, *Battle Cry of Freedom*, 518.
112. Horn, *Army of Tennessee*, 176.
113. Francis, *Narrative of a Private*, 53.
114. T. J. Wright, *History of the Eighth Kentucky Regiment Volunteer Infantry* (St. Joseph, Mo., 1880), 61.
115. OR, vol. 16, pt. 2, 876.
116. Maj. George Winchester Diary, Confederate Collection, TSLA. See also J. Winston Coleman, Jr., *Lexington During the Civil War* (Lexington, Ky., 1938), 35.
117. Harrison, *Civil War in Kentucky*, 48–49.

7. Searching for Water

1. Kleber, *Kentucky Encyclopedia*, 110. Richard C. Brown, *A History of Danville and Boyle County, Kentucky, 1774–1992* (Danville, Ky., 1992), 167. Jefferson J. Polk, *Autobiography, Occasional Writings and Biographies of Worthy Men and Women of Boyle County, Kentucky* (Louisville, Ky., 1867), 68, 69. Kenneth A Hafendorfer, *Perryville: Battle for Kentucky* (Utica, Ky., 1981), 115.
2. Polk, *Autobiography*, 69.
3. Kleber, *Kentucky Encyclopedia*, 110. Brown, *History of Danville*, 167. Hafendorfer, *Perryville*, 115.
4. A. W. Tourgee, *The Story of a Thousand: Regimental History of the One Hundred and Fifth Ohio* (Buffalo, N.Y., 1895), 93.
5. OR, vol. 16, pt. 1, 1109, 1119. Nathaniel Cheairs Hughes, Jr., *General William J. Hardee: Old Reliable* (Baton Rouge, La., 1965), 125.
6. OR, vol. 16, pt. 1, 1109.
7. Connelly, *Army of the Heartland*, 253.
8. Horn, *Army of Tennessee*, 180. Connelly, *Army of the Heartland*, 256.
9. OR, vol. 16, pt. 1, 1095.

10. Ibid. Polk's observation is quoted by Kenneth P. Williams, Shelby Foote, Kenneth Hafendorfer, Grady McWhiney, and T. L. Connelly, and probably by others as well.
11. Horn, *Army of Tennessee*, 178. CWD, 643.
12. Foote, *The Civil War*, 1: 727.
13. OR, vol. 16, pt. 1, 897, 903, 904, 1095, 1096.
14. Kenneth P. Williams, *Lincoln Finds a General*, 4: 129.
15. Warner, *Generals in Blue*, 294. CWD, 526.
16. David Lathrop, *The History of the Fifty-ninth Regiment Illinois Volunteers* (Indianapolis, Ind., 1865), 192.
17. McDonough, *Stones River*, 67.
18. Foote, *The Civil War*, 1: 728.
19. CWD, 208. Warner, *Generals in Blue*, 100.
20. Warner, *Generals in Blue*, 173–74. CWD, 342.
21. Horn, *Army of Tennessee*, 180.
22. L. G. Bennett and William M. Haigh, *History of the Thirty-sixth Regiment Illinois Volunteers, During the War of the Rebellion* (Aurora, Ill., 1876), 241.
23. CWD, 342. Warner, *Generals in Blue*, 173–74.
24. Allen L. Fahnestock Diary, cited in Hafendorfer, *Perryville*, 80.
25. James B. Shaw, *History of the Tenth Indiana Volunteer Infantry* (Lafayette, Ind., 1912), 171–72, cited in Hafendorfer, *Perryville*, 96.
26. OR, vol. 16, pt. 1, 136.
27. OR, vol. 16, pt. 1, 221.
28. John H. Tilford Diary, FCHS.
29. Perry Hall Diary, IHS.
30. Allen L. Fahnestock Diary, quoted in Hafendorfer, *Perryville*, 109. Johnson W. Culp, who was serving in the Eighty-Seventh Indiana, though sworn in as a musician, said he "carried a gun in preference to a drum." Culp commented on the water and mules, writing in his diary that, while he found a creek, "many mules and horses" filled it, and "as some went out others came in." Johnson W. Culp Diary, 7 Oct. 1862, FCHS.
31. Erastus Winters, *In the Fiftieth Ohio Serving Uncle Sam* (Cincinnati, Ohio, 1895), 15.
32. Ibid.
33. Jesse B. Connelly Diary, IHS. One of Connelly's comrades said that there was no water except "some holes which contained very bad water." Lancelot Ewbank Diary, IHS.
34. Garrett Larew Diary, IHS.
35. Kirkpatrick, *Experiences of a Private*, 13, 14. Virtually every person, Federal or Confederate, who left any account of this campaign recalls the dire water problem. Other examples are the W. E. Patterson Diary, SCUTK; and Harvey Lewis to "Dear Folks," 2 Oct. 1862, Harvey Lewis Papers, OHS.
36. Bennett and Haigh, *Thirty-sixth Illinois*, 240–41.

37. OR, vol. 16, pt. 1, 220.
38. Josiah Ayre, "The Civil War Diary of Private Josiah Ayre, Company E, 105th Ohio Volunteer Infantry," transcribed by James Glauser, with additional notes by Mrs. Charles A. McCarthy, Whitehall, Mich., 1975, p. 18, copy in the Perryville Battlefield Museum files.
39. Henry, *Story of the Confederacy*, 199.
40. OR, vol. 16, pt. 2, 917.
41. Hughes, *General Hardee*, 126. Hafendorfer, *Perryville*, 105, 106. Warner, *Generals in Gray*, 187–88.
42. OR, vol. 16, pt. 1, 1158. Hughes, *General Hardee*, 126. Hafendorfer, *Perryville*, 107.
43. OR, vol. 16, pt. 1, 1158.
44. Ibid.
45. Ibid. "The General's Tour Guide—The Battle of Perryville," *Blue and Gray Magazine* 1 (Oct.-Nov. 1983): 27. Hafendorfer, *Perryville*, 109.
46. Horn, *Army of Tennessee*, 181, 182. Kenneth P. Williams, *Lincoln Finds a General*, 4: 123. Foote, *The Civil War*, 1: 729, 730. Buell and Johnson, *Battles and Leaders*, 3: 52. OR, vol. 16, pt. 1, 1072, 1076. Crittenden's column did find water, "an abundant supply of water with which to quench our thirst," according to John J. Hight and Gilbert R. Stormont, *History of the Fifty-eighth Regiment of Indiana Volunteer Infantry* (Princeton, N.J., 1895), 100–101.
47. Pirtle, "Biographical Sketches," 62–63.
48. OR, vol. 16, pt. 1, 219.
49. Ibid.
50. "It was a beautiful, quiet, moonlight night," according to Bennett and Haigh, *Thirty-sixth Illinois*, 248. "The moon was shining brightly," according to Edna J. Shank Hunter, *One Flag, One Country and Thirteen Greenbacks a Month: Letters from a Civil War Private and His Colonel (125th Illinois)* (San Diego, Calif., 1980), 40. A number of contemporaries mention the moonlight.
51. OR, vol. 16, pt. 1, 1074.
52. Ibid.
53. Ibid.
54. Buell and Johnson, *Battles and Leaders*, 3: 47. OR, vol. 16, pt. 1, 238.
55. OR, vol. 16, pt. 1, 1072.
56. CWD, 747. Warner, *Generals in Blue*, 437–38.
57. CWD, 73. Foote, *The Civil War*, 1: 732.
58. Russell Weigley, "Philip H. Sheridan," *Civil War Times* 7 (July 1968): 5, 8.
59. Roy Morris, Jr., *Sheridan: The Life and Wars of General Phil Sheridan* (New York, 1992), 1. Weigley, "Phil Sheridan," 5, 8.
60. Robert M. Utley, *Cavalier in Buckskin: George Armstrong Custer and the Western Military Frontier* (Norman, Okla., 1988), 27.

61. John P. Dyer, *The Gallant Hood* (Indianapolis, Ind., 1950), 32. Weigley, "Phil Sheridan," 5. Foote, *The Civil War*, 1: 732, 735.
62. Paul A. Hutton, *Phil Sheridan and His Army* (Lincoln, Neb., 1985), 19.
63. Weigley, "Phil Sheridan," 6.
64. Ibid., 7–8.
65. OR, vol. 16, pt. 1, 238, 1081.
66. Warner, *Generals in Blue*, 295. CWD, 527.
67. OR, vol. 16, pt. 1, 238.
68. Ibid. This is from the testimony of the Buell Commission. See also McCook's report: OR, vol. 16, pt. 1, 1083.
69. OR, vol. 16, pt. 1, 238–39.
70. OR, vol. 16, pt. 1, 1158, 1083.
71. OR, vol. 16, pt. 1, 239, 1083, 1158.
72. OR, vol. 16, pt. 1, 239.
73. Quoted in Hafendorfer, *Perryville*, 144.
74. OR, vol. 16, pt. 1, 1158.
75. Morris, *Sheridan*, 90. Kenneth P. Williams, *Lincoln Finds a General*, 4: 128. Buell and Johnson, *Battles and Leaders*, 3: 53. Philip H. Sheridan, *Personal Memoirs of P. H. Sheridan*, 2 vols. (New York, 1888), 1: 195.
76. "The General's Tour Guide," 28, 33. OR, vol. 16, pt. 1, 1081. Morris, *Sheridan*, 90–91.
77. "The General's Tour Guide," 33.
78. Morris, *Sheridan*, 92.
79. OR, vol. 16, pt. 1, 135–36, 138, 221.
80. Kenneth P. Williams, *Lincoln Finds a General*, 4: 133. Foote, *The Civil War*, 1: 730. Francis McKinney, *Education in Violence: The Life of George H. Thomas* (Detroit, Mich., 1961), 160.
81. OR, vol. 16, pt. 1, 1025.
82. OR, vol. 16, pt. 2, 580.
83. OR, vol. 16, pt. 2, 581.
84. Kenneth P. Williams, *Lincoln Finds a General*, 4: 129.
85. Horn, *Army of Tennessee*, 181.
86. McWhiney, *Braxton Bragg*, 300–301. Seitz, *Braxton Bragg*, 190. William M. Polk, *Leonidas Polk: Bishop and General*, 2 vols. (New York, 1894), 2: 142–43.
87. Buell and Johnson, *Battles and Leaders*, 3: 27.
88. Connelly, *Army of the Heartland*, 260–61. McWhiney, *Braxton Bragg*, 309–10.
89. OR, vol. 16, pt. 1, 1095.
90. McWhiney, *Braxton Bragg*, 310.
91. Ibid.
92. Ibid.
93. OR, vol. 16, pt. 1, 1092.

94. Bragg to Polk, 7 Oct. 1862, Simon B. Buckner Manuscripts, HL. OR, vol. 16, pt. 1, 1096.
95. Connelly, *Army of the Heartland*, 259–60.
96. Simon Bolivar Buckner, "Report of the Battle of Perryville," 6 Nov. 1862, Simon B. Buckner Manuscripts, HL.
97. OR, vol. 16, pt. 1, 1092.
98. OR, vol. 16, pt. 1, 1110.
99. OR, vol. 16, pt. 1, 1102.
100. Ibid.
101. OR, vol. 16, pt. 1, 1101, 1105–7.
102. McWhiney, *Braxton Bragg*, 298–312.
103. OR, vol. 16, pt. 2, 897.
104. OR, vol. 16, pt. 1, 1101.
105. McWhiney, *Braxton Bragg*, 306.
106. Ibid., 307.
107. Horn, *Army of Tennessee*, 178–79. "Polk, fortunately for the safety of the army, took the liberty of disobeying orders," says Horn. Connelly, in *Army of the Heartland*, 248, says, "Polk's decision was a necessary one. . . . He certainly could not move north as requested." See also Kenneth P. Williams, *Lincoln Finds a General*, 4: 126.
108. Woodworth, *Davis and His Generals*, 157.
109. McWhiney, *Braxton Bragg*, 305.
110. Polk, *Leonidas Polk*, 2: 140.
111. McWhiney, *Braxton Bragg*, 303–4.
112. Ibid.
113. Ibid.
114. Woodworth, *Davis and His Generals*, 157.
115. Horn, *Army of Tennessee*, 182.
116. Quoted in McWhiney, *Braxton Bragg*, 314.
117. "Bragg's Campaign," J. Stoddard Johnston Papers, FCHS. Buckner, "Report of the Battle of Perryville," 6 Nov. 1862, Simon B. Buckner Manuscripts, HL. Horn, *Army of Tennessee*, 183.
118. Christopher Losson, *Tennessee's Forgotten Warriors: Frank Cheatham and His Confederate Division* (Knoxville, Tenn., 1989), 65.
119. Ibid.
120. Connelly, *Army of the Heartland*, 263.
121. Ibid. Losson, *Frank Cheatham*, 65. Buckner, "Report of the Battle of Perryville," Simon B. Buckner Manuscripts, HL. OR, vol. 16, pt. 1, 1087, 1120, 1121.
122. C. T. DeVelling, *History of the Seventeenth Ohio Regiment* (Zanesville, Ohio, 1889), 99.
123. OR, vol. 16, pt. 1, 50, 1022. Kenneth P. Williams, *Lincoln Finds a General*, 4: 129. Hafendorfer, *Perryville*, 169. "The General's Tour Guide," 33.

124. OR, vol. 16, pt. 1, 1025, 1026.
125. Foote, *The Civil War*, 1: 733. OR, vol. 16, pt. 1, 660.
126. See Kenneth P. Williams, *Lincoln Finds a General*, 4: 133–35.
127. Ibid., 4: 128.
128. CWD, 2.
129. OR, vol. 16, pt. 1, 1023, 1025.
130. OR, vol. 16, pt. 1, 51.
131. OR, vol. 16, pt. 1, 1045, 344, 293–94.
132. Hafendorfer, *Perryville*, 154.
133. OR, vol. 16, pt. 1, 50, 1039, 1044. Horn, *Army of Tennessee*, 182. Hafendorfer, *Perryville*, 162–63.
134. CWD, 710. Warner, *Generals in Blue*, 412–13. Hafendorfer, *Perryville*, 310.
135. Warner, *Generals in Blue*, 247–48. CWD, 431.
136. Buell and Johnson, *Battles and Leaders*, 3: 57.
137. OR, vol. 16, pt. 1, 1044. See also the testimony of William H. Lytle, p. 69.
138. OR, vol. 16, pt. 1, 1044–45.
139. OR, vol. 16, pt. 1, 69. William McDowell, "Reminiscences of the Battle of Perryville," FCHS.
140. OR, vol. 16, pt. 1, 90.
141. Loren J. Morse, ed., *Civil War Diaries and Letters of Bliss Morse, Company D, 105th Ohio Volunteer Infantry* (Wagoner, Okla., 1985), 29.
142. CWD, 830. Warner, *Generals in Blue*, 437, 496–97. Foote, *The Civil War*, 1: 732, 735.
143. CWD, 830. Warner, *Generals in Blue*, 496.
144. OR, vol. 16, pt. 1, 90.

8. A Ghastly Scene of Dead and Dying

1. McDonough and Connelly, *Five Tragic Hours*, 40. Clement Evans, ed., *Confederate Military History*, 12 vols. (Atlanta, Ga., 1889), 8: 302–4. Joe Spence Diary, 1861–62, Confederate Collection, TSLA. Christopher Losson, "Major General Benjamin Franklin Cheatham and the Battle of Stone's River," *Tennessee Historical Quarterly* 41 (Fall 1982): 278–92. Warner, *Generals in Gray*, 47–48.
2. Losson, *Cheatham*, 65. OR, vol. 16, pt. 1, 1110. Hafendorfer, *Perryville*, 195–96. Connelly, *Army of the Heartland*, 263.
3. L. B. Giles, *Terry's Texas Rangers*, 46, cited in Hafendorfer, *Perryville*, 210, 396.
4. OR, vol. 16, pt. 1, 1110.
5. OR, vol. 16, pt. 1, 1044.
6. Spillard F. Horrall, *History of the Forty-second Indiana Volunteer Infantry Regiment* (Indianapolis, Ind., 1892), 150.
7. J. Stoddard Johnston, "Battle of Perryville," Oct. 1862, FCHS, says it was a few minutes after 2 P.M. See also Losson, *Frank Cheatham*, 66.

8. Losson, *Frank Cheatham*, 66. Foote, *The Civil War*, 1: 735. OR, vol. 16, pt. 1, 1110–11. Hafendorfer, *Perryville*, 213, 217.
9. George W. Landrum to "Dear Amanda," 12 Oct. 1862, Landrum Papers, OHS.
10. Johnston, "Battle of Perryville."
11. Hafendorfer, *Perryville*, 217. This story also has been told of other battles. Certainly the events could have happened more than once.
12. Warner, *Generals in Gray*, 74–75. CWD, 243.
13. OR, vol. 16, pt. 1, 1108. J. J. Womack, *The Civil War Diary of Captain J. J. Womack, Company E., Sixteenth Regiment, Tennessee Volunteers (Confederate)* (McMinnville, Tenn., 1961), 62. Buell and Johnson, *Battles and Leaders*, vol. 3, 30. Losson, *Frank Cheatham*, 66.
14. Losson, *Frank Cheatham*, 66.
15. Womack, *Civil War Diary of Womack*, 62.
16. Angus L. Waddle, *Three Years with the Army of the Ohio and the Cumberland* (Chillicothe, Ohio, 1889), 30.
17. OR, vol. 16, pt. 1, 1060, 1062. Losson, *Frank Cheatham*, 66–67. Hafendorfer, *Perryville*, 218–21. "The General's Tour Guide," 34. Connelly, *Army of the Heartland*, 263. B. Franklin Cheatham, "Report of the Engagement Near Perryville, Kentucky," 19 Nov. 1862, William P. Palmer Collection of the Braxton Bragg Papers, WRHS. Daniel S. Donelson, "Report of the Part Taken in the Battle of Perryville by the 1st Brigade, 1st Division, Right Wing, Army of the Mississippi," 26 Oct. 1862, William P. Palmer Collection of the Braxton Bragg Papers, WRHS.
18. OR, vol. 16, pt. 1, 1060, 1063; Donelson, "Report of the Part Taken"; Cheatham, "Report of the Engagement"; Losson, *Frank Cheatham*, 67.
19. George W. Landrum to "Dear Amanda," 12 Oct. 1862, Landrum Papers, OHS.
20. C. H. Clark Memoirs, Civil War Collection, TSLA.
21. Ibid.
22. Losson, *Frank Cheatham*, 66.
23. C. H. Clark Memoirs, Civil War Collection, TSLA.
24. Losson, *Frank Cheatham*, 66–67. Hafendorfer, *Perryville*, 221.
25. CWD, 798.
26. Losson, *Frank Cheatham*, 67.
27. Warner, *Generals in Gray*, 210. CWD, 507. Evans, *Confederate Military History,* 8: 322–23.
28. Losson, *Frank Cheatham*, 67. "The General's Tour Guide," 35. George Earl Maney Papers, William P. Palmer Collection of the Braxton Bragg Papers, WRHS.
29. John W. Carroll, *Autobiography and Reminiscences of John W. Carroll* (Henderson, Tenn., n.d.), 24.
30. Losson, *Frank Cheatham*, 67.
31. Ibid.
32. OR, vol. 16, pt. 1, 1062–63.
33. OR, vol. 16, pt. 1, 1115.

34. OR, vol. 16, pt. 1, 1113.
35. OR, vol. 16, pt. 1, 1118.
36. OR, vol. 16, pt. 1, 1115.
37. George Earl Maney Papers, in William P. Palmer Collection of the Braxton Bragg Papers, WRHS.
38. OR, vol. 16, pt. 1, 1115.
39. Ibid.
40. OR, vol. 16, pt. 1, 1113.
41. OR, vol. 16, pt. 1, 1118. "The General's Tour Guide," 35.
42. Hafendorfer, *Perryville*, 245.
43. Johnston, "Battle of Perryville."
44. Ibid.
45. Samuel M. Starling to daughters, 16 Nov. 1862, WKU.
46. OR, vol. 16, pt. 1, 1060.
47. Hafendorfer, *Perryville*, 231–35. OR, vol. 16, pt. 1, 1034, 1060.
48. Hunter, *One Flag, One Country*, 42.
49. OR, vol. 16, pt. 1, 1063.
50. Ayre, "Civil War Diary," 20.
51. Horn, *Army of Tennessee*, n50, 454–55.
52. Johnson and Buell, *Battles and Leaders*, 3: 61.
53. Horn, *Army of Tennessee*, n50, 455.
54. "The General's Tour Guide," 35.
55. OR, vol. 16, pt. 1, 1049.
56. George W. Landrum to "Dear Amanda," 12 Oct. 1862, Landrum Papers, OHS.
57. Abstract of diary of Private Gleazen, Eightieth Indiana, in files of Perryville Battlefield Museum, Perryville, Ky.
58. Kirkpatrick, *Experiences of a Private*, 14.
59. OR, vol. 16, pt. 1, 1067.
60. Harvey Lewis to "Dear Folks," 12 Oct. 1862, Harvey Lewis Papers, OHS.
61. Silas Emerson to Nancy, 14 Oct. 1862, Silas Emerson Papers, OHS.
62. C. H. Clark Memoirs, Confederate Collection, TSLA.
63. Womack, *Diary of Womack*, 63.
64. John Gold Reminiscences, TSLA.
65. OR, vol. 16, pt. 1, 1115.
66. Ibid.
67. William M. Pollard Diary, TSLA.
68. CWD, 444.
69. Hafendorfer, *Perryville*, 236, 239, 250. OR, vol. 16, pt. 1, 1054–56, 1126–27.
70. Horrall, *History of the Forty-second Indiana*, 152. Kirkpatrick, *Experiences of a Private*, 15.
71. CWD, 437. Warner, *Generals in Gray*, 157–58.

72. OR, vol. 16, pt. 1, 1124, 1125.
73. OR, vol. 16, pt. 1, 1126, 1133.
74. OR, vol. 16, pt. 1, 1128–33. Hafendorfer, *Perryville*, 251.
75. OR, vol. 16, pt. 1, 1133.
76. OR, vol. 16, pt. 1, 1132.
77. OR, vol. 16, pt. 1, 1131.
78. "The General's Tour Guide," 35, 36.
79. Ibid.
80. OR, vol. 16, pt. 1, 70–71.
81. OR, vol. 16, pt. 1, 1128–1132.
82. OR, vol. 16, pt. 1, 1132.
83. Beatty, *Citizen Soldier*, 178–79.
84. Ibid.
85. George W. Landrum to "Dear Amanda," 12 Oct. 1862, Landrum Papers, OHS.
86. Kirkpatrick, *Experiences of a Private*, 15.
87. Ibid.
88. Horrall, *History of the Forty-second Indiana*, 153.
89. CWD, 3. Hafendorfer, *Perryville*, 179.
90. OR, vol. 16, pt. 1, 1125.
91. Hafendorfer, *Perryville*, 264.
92. Whitelaw Reid, *Ohio in the War: Her Statesmen, Generals and Soldiers*, 2 vols. (Cincinnati, Ohio, 1868), 2: 30. See also Beatty, *Citizen Soldier*, 183.
93. Horrall, *History of the Forty-second Indiana*, 152.
94. OR, vol. 52, pt. 1, 52.
95. OR, vol. 52, pt. 1, 51.
96. Purdue and Purdue, *Cleburne*, 89.
97. W. E. Yeatman, excerpt from address to Confederate veterans, Knoxville, Tenn., quoted in the Knoxville *Sentinel*, n.d., in Scrapbook, United Daughters of the Confederacy, Helena, Ark., cited in Purdue and Purdue, *Cleburne*, 89, 298.
98. OR, vol. 52, pt. 1, 52.
99. Johnston, "Battle of Perryville."
100. W. E. Yeatman Memoirs, TSLA.
101. OR, vol. 52, pt. 1, 52.
102. Ibid.
103. Ibid.
104. Ibid.
105. OR, vol. 16, pt. 1, 1047.
106. OR, vol. 52, pt. 1, 52.
107. Johnston, "Battle of Perryville."
108. "The General's Tour Guide," 36.
109. Ibid., 35.

110. Hutton, *Sheridan*, 19.
111. OR, vol. 16, pt. 1, 1082.
112. Hutton, *Sheridan*, 12, says Sheridan's troops "repelled five rebel assaults at Perryville, Kentucky, to hold his line and save the Union army. The Northern press, starved for authentic heroes, hailed Sheridan as the 'paladin of Perryville.'" Although the book has source notes, no sources are given for this assertion. Richard O'Connor, *Sheridan the Inevitable* (Indianapolis, Ind., 1953), 82, sums up: "Five assaults swept up against Sheridan and his entrenched infantry, but he held the position and saved the army." The only sources cited for O'Connor's account of Sheridan's part in the fight are Sheridan's memoirs and his after-action report. Although not a Sheridan biographer, Fletcher Pratt, in *A Short History of the Civil War* (New York, 1935), 96, 97, also describes the battle in a manner that leaves the reader supposing that Sheridan saved the Federal army. Sheridan was, said Pratt, "a very paladin" of a leader, whose men "stood like a rock amid sheets of rifle fire" and "hurled back" most of the Rebel army—at least he names Cheatham, Hardee, Buckner, and Anderson as having "flooded round Sheridan's hill," from which the general allegedly defeated the oft-cited five assaults.
113. Sheridan, *Memoirs*, 1: 195.
114. Ibid.
115. Ibid., 1: 196.
116. OR, vol. 16, pt. 1, 1040. Sheridan, *Memoirs*, 1: 196.
117. Sheridan, *Memoirs*, 1: 197.
118. OR, vol. 16, pt. 1, 283.
119. Morris, *Sheridan*, 95.
120. OR, vol. 16, pt. 1, 283.
121. Ibid.
122. Ibid.
123. Morris, *Sheridan*, 85.
124. Ibid., 86.
125. OR, vol. 16, pt. 1, 1082.
126. OR, vol. 16, pt. 1, 240.
127. Wright, *History of the Eighth Kentucky*, 63.
128. DeVelling, *History of the Seventeenth Ohio*, 99.

9. I'll Fight 'Em as Long as I Live

1. OR, vol. 16, pt. 1, 1063.
2. OR, vol. 16, pt. 1, 1047.
3. Warner, *Generals in Blue*, 472. CWD, 793.
4. OR, vol. 16, pt. 1, 1155. Michael H. Fitch, *Echoes of the Civil War As I Hear Them* (New York, 1905), 59–60.
5. Hambleton Tapp, ed., "The Battle of Perryville, October 8, 1862, as Described in

the Diary of Captain Robert B. Taylor," *Register of the Kentucky Historical Society* 60 (1962): 276. Fitch, *Echoes of the War*, 59.

6. OR, vol. 16, pt. 1, 1155. Fitch, *Echoes of the War*, 60.
7. OR, vol. 16, pt. 1, 1041.
8. OR, vol. 16, pt. 1, 1155–56. Hafendorfer, *Perryville*, 267–71.
9. Watkins, *"Co. Aytch,"* 82.
10. E. John Ellis to his mother, 21 Oct. 1862, quoted in McWhiney, *Braxton Bragg*, 316–17.
11. Watkins, *"Co. Aytch,"* 81, 80.
12. C. H. Clark Memoirs, Confederate Collection, TSLA.
13. Gustavus W. Dyer and John Trotwood Moore, comp., *The Tennessee Civil War Veterans Questionnaires*, ed. Colleen Morse Elliott and Louise Armstrong Moxley, 5 vols. (Easley, S.C., 1985), 3: 983.
14. J. Cutler Andrews, *The North Reports the Civil War* (Pittsburgh, Penn., 1955), 299.
15. Winters, *In the Fiftieth Ohio*, 20.
16. OR, vol. 16, pt. 1, 1114.
17. Ibid.
18. Ibid.
19. Captain Robert Taylor Diary, 12 Oct. 1862, Kentucky Historical Society, Frankfort.
20. Watkins, *"Co. Aytch,"* 83.
21. OR, vol. 16, pt. 1, 1114.
22. OR, vol. 16, pt. 1, 1041. "The General's Tour Guide," 36. Hafendorfer, *Perryville*, 292.
23. Hafendorfer, *Perryville*, 284.
24. Stanley Lockwood, probably to his mother, n.d. (but pre-Perryville), Lockwood Family Papers, WRHS.
25. OR, vol. 16, pt. 1, 1046, 1156.
26. OR, vol. 16, pt. 1, 1033, 1047, 346.
27. OR, vol. 16, pt. 1, 1047.
28. OR, vol. 16, pt. 1, 345.
29. Hafendorfer, *Perryville*, 311. George W. Landrum to "Dear Amanda," 12 Oct. 1862, Landrum Papers, OHS.
30. Landrum to "Dear Amanda," 12. Oct. 1862. See also Waddle, *Three Years*, 30, who testified of Rousseau's courage and leadership.
31. Landrum to "Dear Amanda," Oct. 28, 1862, OHS.
32. Landrum to "Dear Amanda," Oct. 12, 1862, OHS.
33. Waddle, *Three Years*, 30.
34. OR, vol. 16, pt. 1, 1053.
35. Ibid.
36. OR, vol. 16, pt. 1, 1123.

37. OR, vol. 52, pt. 1, 52.
38. W. E. Yeatman Memoirs, Confederate Collection, TSLA.
39. OR, vol. 52, pt. 1, 52.
40. Buell and Johnson, *Battles and Leaders*, 3: 57. "Their opinion," according to Col. Charles Denby, Forty-Second Indiana, "was that men would never be frightened if they considered the doctrine of probabilities and how slight the chance was of any particular person being killed. Theory failed, as it has often done before; all three were killed in the next day's fight."
41. OR, vol. 16, pt. 1, 1040.
42. OR, vol. 16, pt. 1, 1079.
43. OR, vol. 16, pt. 1, 1079, 1080.
44. Ibid.
45. Ibid.
46. OR, vol. 16, pt. 1, 1111.
47. Horn, *Army of Tennessee*, 185. Polk, *Polk*, 2: 155–56.
48. OR, vol. 16, pt. 1, 1111, 1159, 1080. "The General's Tour Guide," 38. Polk, *Polk*, 2: 156.
49. OR, vol. 16, pt. 1, 1080.
50. OR, vol. 16, pt. 1, 1111.
51. Johnston, "Battle of Perryville."
52. Kenneth P. Williams, *Lincoln Finds a General*, 4: 132–33.
53. Buell and Johnson, *Battles and Leaders*, 3: 48, 58. OR, vol. 16, pt. 1, 345. Sheridan, *Memoirs*, 1: 199.
54. OR, vol. 16, pt. 1, 345.
55. Sheridan, *Memoirs*, 199.
56. Morris, *Sheridan*, 196.
57. Livermore, *Numbers and Losses*, 95.
58. Horn, *Army of Tennessee*, 186. Buell and Johnson, *Battles and Leaders*, 3: 30. OR, vol. 16, pt. 1, 1112, 1036. Tourgee, *Story of a Thousand*, 127, quotes Bragg.
59. J. T. Williamson, "Notes About the War," Jill Garrett Collection, TSLA.
60. Andrew J. McGarrah to wife, 15 Oct. 1862, McGarrah Papers, IHS.
61. Horrall, *History of the Forty-second Indiana*, 153.
62. C. H. Clark Memoirs, Confederate Collection, TSLA.
63. Dyer and Moore, *Tennessee Veterans Questionnaires*, 4: 1688.
64. Maj. George Winchester Diary, Civil War Collection, TSLA.
65. Winters, *In the Fiftieth Ohio*, 21.
66. John W. Henderson to Buckner, 2 Mar. 1889, Simon B. Buckner Manuscripts, HL.
67. George W. Morris, *History of the Eighty-first Regiment of Indiana Volunteer Infantry in the Great War of the Rebellion, 1861–1865* (Louisville, Ky., 1901), 17.
68. William Spencer to "Dear Sister," 11 Oct. 1862, Joseph and William Spencer Letters, OHS.

69. Starling to "Dearest Daughters," 16 Nov. 1862, WKU.
70. Civil War Collection (Federal), TSLA.
71. Ibid. Morse, *Civil War Diaries and Letters of Bliss Morse*, 32. Francis, *Narrative of a Private*, 59.
72. Capt. Alexander M. Ayers to his wife, 16 Oct. 1862, quoted in McWhiney, *Braxton Bragg*, 319. Francis, *Narrative of a Private*, 59. Robert J. Snetsinger, ed., *Kiss Clara for Me: The Story of Joseph Whitney and His Family, Early Days in the Midwest, and Soldiering in the American Civil War* (State College, Penn., 1969), 47.
73. George W. Landrum to "Dear Amanda," 12 Oct. 1862, OHS.
74. Starling to "Dearest Daughters," 12 Oct. 1862, WKU.
75. Some unit commanders had assigned soldiers to shoot instantly those who did stop to help the wounded.
76. William Roberts Stuckey to wife, 19 Oct. 1862, William Roberts Stuckey Letters, IHS.

10. I Never Hated Them till Now

1. Blair Papers, IHS.
2. Ibid.
3. Connelly Diary, IHS.
4. Winters, *In the Fiftieth Ohio*, 22. No doubt many a soldier discounted the rumors. Charles Francis, *Narrative of a Private*, 58, wrote: "It was said that there existed a close relationship between the commanding generals of both armies; but that was only camp talk."
5. McKinzie to Nettelhorst, 25 Nov. 1862, Nettelhorst Papers, IHS. Thomas M. Small Diary, IHS.
6. Clyde C. Walton, ed., *Behind the Guns: The History of Battery I, Second Regiment, Illinois Light Artillery* (Urbana, Ill., 1965), 32.
7. Blair to "Dear Margaret," 12 Oct. 1862, Blair Papers, IHS.
8. Newberry to F. L. Olmsted, Louisville, 24 Oct. 1862, Sanitary Commission Reports, no. 55, p.1, copy in TSLA.
9. Reed to J. S. Newberry, Louisville, 23 Oct. 1862, Sanitary Commission Reports, no. 55, pp. 7, 8, copy in TSLA.
10. Polk, *Autobiography*, 45.
11. Perry Hall to wife, 13 Oct. 1862, Perry Hall Papers, IHS.
12. John A. Berger to "Dear Parents," 18 Oct. 1862, John A. Berger and Jack F. Pase Letters, IHS.
13. George W. Landrum to "Dear Amanda," 12 Oct. 1862, OHS.
14. Tourgee, *Story of a Thousand*, 151–52.
15. Ibid., 150–51.
16. T. J. Koger to "My Darling Wife," 9 June 1862; Julia to James Elder (Julia's husband, the brother of Mrs. T. J. Koger), 25 Oct. 1862; both, Koger Collection, MDAH.

17. William Spencer to "Dear Sister," 11 Oct. 1862, Joseph and William Spencer Letters, OHS.
18. John H. Tilford Diary, FCHS.
19. Captain Robert Taylor Diaries, Manuscripts Division, Kentucky Historical Society, Frankfort.
20. Tourgee, *Story of a Thousand*, 150.
21. Culp Diary, 8–9 Oct. 1862, FCHS.
22. Ayre, "Civil War Diary," 21.
23. OR, vol. 16, pt. 1, 1088, 1093. Horn, *Army of Tennessee*, 186. Edwin C. Bearss, "General Bragg Abandons Kentucky," *Register of the Kentucky Historical Society* 59 (July 1961): 217. Parks, *Kirby Smith*, 235. Harrison, *Civil War in Kentucky*, 54. Connelly, *Army of the Heartland*, 266.
24. Parks, *Kirby Smith*, 237, 238. Horn, *Army of Tennessee*, 186, 187.
25. It is hard to determine how many troops Marshall had. Joe Wheeler, whose numbers generally tend to be low, assigned him 2,160, in Buell and Johnson, *Battles and Leaders*, 3: 12. Connelly, *Army of the Heartland*, 207, credits him with 4,500. Horn, *Army of Tennessee*, 165, and Harrison, *Civil War in Kentucky*, 40, both give him 3,000. The author found no satisfactory way to determine the correct figure.
26. OR, vol. 16, pt. 1, 1093. Bearss, "Bragg Abandons Kentucky," 217, 218. Connelly, *Army of the Heartland*, 268. Horn, *Army of Tennessee*, 188.
27. OR, vol. 16, pt. 1, 1093.
28. OR, vol. 16, pt. 1, 1088.
29. Bragg to wife, 9 Nov. 1862, Bragg Letters, UKSC.
30. See Bragg's report, OR, vol. 16, pt. 1, 1088, 1093–94. See also the accounts of various historians: Horn, *Army of Tennessee*, 172–76, 186–89. Roland, *American Iliad*, 86–87. Woodworth, *Davis and His Generals*, 159–61. Losson, *Frank Cheatham*, 74–75. Henry, *Story of the Confederacy*, 200–201. McWhiney, *Braxton Bragg*, 329–33. Connelly, *Army of the Heartland*, 279–80. Interpretations of characters and events may vary, but Bragg clearly was greatly disappointed in the lack of Kentucky recruits; probably this was the most important reason for his decision to retreat.
31. Bearss, "Bragg Abandons Kentucky," 221.
32. OR, vol. 16, pt. 1, 943, 949.
33. Buck, *Cleburne and His Command*, 116–17.
34. Ibid. Also see Bearss, "Bragg Abandons Kentucky," 219–44.
35. Snetsinger, *Kiss Clara For Me*, 45, 46.
36. W. [H.?] Thomas, Soldier Record, TSLA. J. T. Williamson, "Notes About the War," Jill Garrett Collection, TSLA.
37. W. E. Yeatman Memoirs, Confederate Collection, TSLA. John Gold Reminiscences, TSLA. W. [H.?] Thomas, Soldier Record, TSLA. J. T. Williamson, "Notes About the War," Jill Garrett Collection, TSLA.
38. Boyd to "Dear Mother," 26 Oct. 1862, Boyd/Sitton Letters, GDAH.

39. Thomas Julian Firth, Memoirs, TSLA.
40. Sutherland, *Reminiscences of a Private*, 101.
41. James Travis Letter, 1 Nov. 1862, MDAH.
42. Hogg to wife, 19, 22, 25, and 26 Oct. 1862, Georgia Historical Society, Savannah.
43. Maj. George Winchester Diary, Confederate Collection, TSLA.
44. J. T. Williamson, "Notes About the War," Jill Garrett Collection, TSLA.
45. Nevins, *War for the Union*, 2: 289.
46. Foote, *The Civil War*, 1: 742. Parks, *Kirby Smith*, 241–47. McDonough, *Stones River*, 31.
47. Parks, *Kirby Smith*, 243.
48. Foote, *The Civil War*, 1: 743.

11. Season of Folly, Season of Decision

1. Jeremy F. Gilmer to wife, 29 Mar. 1862, Gilmer Papers, SHC.
2. See McDonough, *Shiloh*, for details of the engagement.
3. For full summation, see chs. 2 and 4.
4. Augustus O. McDonnell Diary, 14 Sept. 1862, YLUF.
5. See chs. 3, 4, 6.
6. See chs. 7–9.
7. McDonough, *Stones River*, 38.
8. William R. Hartpence, *History of the Fifty-first Indiana Veteran Infantry* (Cincinnati, Ohio, 1894), 93–95.
9. See chs. 3 and 6.
10. Terry Carlisle to wife, 11 Nov. 1862, Terry Carlisle, M.D., Civil War Letters, GDAH.
11. Maj. George Winchester Diary, Confederate Collection, TSLA.
12. Horace Cecil Fisher, *A Staff Officer's Story: The Personal Experiences of Colonel Horace Newton Fisher in the Civil War* (Boston, 1960), 46.
13. McPherson, *Ordeal by Fire*, 154, 158, 152. E. Merton Coulter calculated that 20 Bluegrass and western Kentucky counties, with a total of 100,000 slaves, sent only 6,000 soldiers to fight for the Union, while 40 other counties, having only 27,000 slaves, supplied some 18,000 soldiers for the Federals. Coulter, *Civil War and Readjustment in Kentucky*, 285–86.
14. See Roland, *American Iliad*, 165–67.
15. Ibid., 134.
16. McPherson, *Ordeal by Fire*, 325.

Bibliography

☆☆☆

Primary Materials

Records

War of the Rebellion: A Compilation of the Official Records of the Union and Confederate Armies. 129 vols. Washington, D.C., 1880–1901.

Collected Works, Diaries, Memoirs, Papers, Reminiscences

Basler, Roy P., ed. *The Collected Works of Abraham Lincoln.* 8 vols. New Brunswick, N.J., 1953.

Beatty, John. *The Citizen Soldier: Or, Memoirs of a Volunteer.* Cincinnati, Ohio, 1879.

Berwanger, Eugene H., ed. *My Diary North and South,* by William Howard Russell. New York, 1988.

Buck, Captain Irving A. *Cleburne and His Command,* ed. Thomas R. Hay. Reprint. Wilmington, N.C., 1987.

Buell, Clarence C., and Robert U. Johnson, eds. *Battles and Leaders of the Civil War.* 4 vols. New York, 1887–88.

Carroll, John W. *Autobiography and Reminiscences of John W. Carroll.* Henderson, Tenn., n.d.

Confederate Veteran. 40 vols. Nashville, 1893–1932.

Duke, Basil W. *The Story of Morgan's Cavalry.* New York, 1867.

Dyer, Gustavus W., and John Trotwood Moore, compilers. *The Tennessee Civil War Veterans Questionnaires.* Edited by Colleen Morse Elliott and Louise Armstrong Moxley. 5 vols. Easley, S.C., 1985.

Fisher, Horace Cecil. *A Staff Officer's Story: The Personal Experiences of Colonel Horace Newton Fisher in the Civil War.* Boston, 1960.

Fitch, Michael H. *Echoes of the Civil War As I Hear Them.* New York, 1905.

Francis, Charles Lewis. *Narrative of a Private Soldier in the Volunteer Army of the United States.* New York, 1879.

Grant, Ulysses S. *Personal Memoirs of U. S. Grant*. 2 vols. New York, 1885.

Hammond, Paul F. "General Kirby Smith's Campaign in Kentucky in 1862." *Southern Historical Society Papers* 9 (1881): 225–33, 246–54, 289–97, 455–62.

Hunter, Edna J. Shank. *One Flag, One Country and Thirteen Greenbacks a Month: Letters from a Civil War Private and His Colonel (125th Illinois)*. San Diego, Calif., 1980.

Kirkpatrick, George Morgan. *The Experiences of a Private Soldier of the Civil War*. N.p. ["the Hoosier Bookshop"], 1973.

Moore, Frank, ed. *The Rebellion Record: A Diary of American Events*. 11 vols. New York, 1861–68.

Morse, Loren J., ed. *Civil War Diaries and Letters of Bliss Morse, Company D, 105th Ohio Volunteer Infantry*. Wagoner, Okla., 1985.

Polk, Jefferson J. *Autobiography, Occasional Writings and Biographies of Worthy Men and Women of Boyle County, Kentucky*. Louisville, Ky., 1867.

Ridley, Bromfield L. *Battles and Sketches of the Army of Tennessee*. Mexico, Mo., 1906.

Roland, Charles P., ed. *Destruction and Reconstruction*, by Richard Taylor. Waltham, Massachusetts, 1968.

Sheridan, Philip H. *Personal Memoirs of P. H. Sheridan*. 2 vols. New York, 1888.

Snetsinger, Robert J., ed. *Kiss Clara For Me: The Story of Joseph Whitney and His Family, Early Days in the Mid-West, and Soldiering in the American Civil War*. State College, Pa., 1969.

Sutherland, Daniel E., ed. *Reminiscences of a Private: William E. Bevens of the First Arkansas Infantry, C.S.A.* Fayetteville, Ark., 1992.

Tapp, Hambleton, and James C. Klotter, eds. *The Union, the Civil War and John W. Tuttle: A Captain's Account*. Frankfort, Ky., 1980.

United States Sanitary Commission Reports. No. 55. Copy in the Tennessee State Library and Archives, Nashville.

Waddle, Angus L. *Three Years with the Army of the Ohio and the Cumberland*. Chillicothe, Ohio, 1889.

Womack, J. J. *The Civil War Diary of Captain J. J. Womack, Company E., Sixteenth Regiment, Tennessee Volunteers (Confederate)*. McMinnville, Tenn., 1961.

Unit Histories

Bennett, L. G., and William M. Haigh. *History of the Thirty-sixth Regiment Illinois Volunteers, During the War of the Rebellion*. Aurora, Ill., 1876.

DeVelling, C. T. *History of the Seventeenth Ohio Regiment*. Zanesville, Ohio, 1889.

Dobson, James A. C. *A Historical Sketch of Company K, of the Seventy-ninth Indiana Volunteers*. Plainfield, Ind., 1894.

Hartpence, William R. *History of the Fifty-first Indiana Veteran Infantry*. Cincinnati, Ohio, 1894.

Hight, John J., and Gilbert R. Stormont. *History of the Fifty-eighth Regiment of Indiana Volunteer Infantry*. Princeton, N.J., 1895.

Horrall, Spillard F. *History of the Forty-second Indiana Volunteer Infantry Regiment*. Indianapolis, Ind., 1892.

Lathrop, David. *The History of the Fifty-ninth Regiment Illinois Volunteers*. Indianapolis, Ind., 1865.

Lindsley, John B., ed. *The Military Annals of Confederate Tennessee*. Nashville, Tenn., 1886.

Morris, George W. *History of the Eighty-first Regiment of Indiana Volunteer Infantry in the Great War of the Rebellion, 1861–1865*. Louisville, Ky., 1901.

Shaw, James B. *History of the Tenth Indiana Volunteer Infantry*. Lafayette, Ind., 1912.

Tourgee, Albion Winegar. *The Story of a Thousand: Regimental History of the One Hundred and Fifth Ohio*. Buffalo, N.Y., 1895.

The Union Regiments of Kentucky: Published under the Auspices of the Union Soldiers and Sailors Monument Association. Louisville, Ky., 1897.

Walton, Clyde C., ed. *Behind the Guns: The History of Battery I, Second Regiment, Illinois Light Artillery*. Urbana, Ill., 1965.

Watkins, Samuel R. *"Co. Aytch," Maury Gray's, First Tennessee Regiment*. Jackson, Tenn., 1952.

Winters, Erastus. *In the Fiftieth Ohio Serving Uncle Sam*. Cincinnati, Ohio, 1895.

Wright, T. J. *History of Eighth Kentucky Regiment Volunteer Infantry*. Saint Joseph, Mo., 1880.

Manuscripts

Alabama Dept. of Archives and History, Montgomery

William Lowrey Diary

Edward H. Moren Papers

John Wilson Townsend Room, Eastern Kentucky Univ., Richmond

Lucia Burnam, "What I Remember"

French Tipton Papers

Filson Club Historical Society, Louisville, Ky.

Johnson W. Culp Diary

George W. Johnson Papers

J. Stoddard Johnston Papers

William McDowell, "Reminiscences of the Battle of Perryville"

Humphrey Marshall Papers

James Mohr Letters

Terah W. Sampson Letters

John H. Tilford Diary

Special Collections, Florida State Univ., Tallahassee

Hugh Black Letters

Georgia Dept. of Archives and History, Atlanta

Boyd/Sitton Family, Civil War Letters

Terry Carlisle, M.D., Civil War Letters

Georgia Historical Society, Savannah
    John J. Hogg Diary and Papers
Hart County Historical Society, Munfordville, Ky.
    Roy A. Cann Notebook
    George Stewart, Sr., "Reminiscences of War Experience"
Huntington Library, San Marino, Calif.
    Simon B. Buckner Manuscripts
Indiana Historical Society, Indianapolis
    Henry H. Aye Autobiography
    John A. Berger Letters
    William W. Blair Papers
    Bergum H. Brown Letters
    Jesse B. Connelly Diary
    Jefferson C. Davis File
    Lancelot Ewbank Diary
    Perry Hall Diary, in the Perry Hall Papers
    Oliver Haskell Diary
    James H. Jones Letters
    Garrett Larew Diary
    John W. Large Letters
    Andrew J. McGarrah Papers
    Louis Nettelhorst Papers
    Jack F. Pase Letters
    Samuel Reid Papers
    Thomas M. Small Diary
    William R. Stuckey Letters
    James S. Thomas Letters
Kentucky Historical Society, Frankfort
    Robert B. Taylor Diaries
Mississippi Dept. of Archives and History, Jackson
    T. Otis Baker Papers
    T. J. Koger Papers
    James Travis Letters
Ohio Historical Society, Columbus
    Silas Emerson Papers
    George W. Landrum Papers
    Harvey Lewis Papers
    James Mitchell Reminiscences
    Bliss Morse Diary
    William Spencer Papers

Perryville Battlefield Museum Files
Josiah Ayre Diary
Private Gleazen Diary
Tennessee State Library and Archives, Nashville
Civil War Collection (Federal)
C. H. Clark Memoirs
Alfred Fielder Diary
Thomas Julian Firth Memoirs
John Gold Reminiscences
James King Papers
William M. Pollard Diary
Joe Spence Diary
W. [H.?] Thomas, Soldier Record
J. T. Williamson, "Notes About the War," in Jill Garrett Collection
George Winchester Diary
W. E. Yeatman Memoirs
Special Collections, Univ. of Florida, Gainesville
Thomas Benton Ellis Diary
Augustus Oswald McDonnell Diary
Special Collections, Univ. of Kentucky, Lexington
Theodore Robert McBeath Papers
Univ. of North Carolina, Chapel Hill
Jeremy F. Gilmer Papers
Edmund Kirby Smith Papers
Special Collections, Univ. of Tennessee, Knoxville
M. Jinkins and E. S. Jinkins Papers
W. E. Patterson Diary
Kentucky Building, Western Kentucky Univ., Bowling Green
Lewis-Starling Manuscript Collection
Western Reserve Historical Society, Cleveland, Ohio
Braxton Bragg Papers, in William P. Palmer Collection
Lockwood Family Papers

Newspapers

Hart County News, Munfordville, Ky.
Louisville (Ky.) *Courier-Journal*
Memphis Daily Avalanche
Nashville Daily Union

Secondary Materials

Books

Ambrose, Stephen E. *Halleck: Lincoln's Chief of Staff*. Baton Rouge, La., 1962.

Andrews, J. Cutler. *The North Reports the Civil War*. Pittsburgh, Pa., 1955.

Black, Robert C. *The Railroads of the Confederacy*. Chapel Hill, N.C., 1952.

Boatner, Mark Mayo, III. *The Civil War Dictionary*. New York, 1959.

Brown, Richard C. *A History of Danville and Boyle County, Kentucky, 1774–1992*. Danville, Ky., 1982.

Catton, Bruce. *Grant Moves South*. Boston, 1960.

______. *The American Heritage Short History of the Civil War*. New York, 1960.

______. *This Hallowed Ground*. New York, 1956.

Clark, Thomas D. *A History of Kentucky*. Lexington, Ky., 1954.

Coleman, J. Winston, Jr. *Lexington During the Civil War*. Lexington, Ky., 1938.

Connelly, Thomas L. *Army of the Heartland: The Army of Tennessee, 1861–1862*. Baton Rouge, La., 1967.

______. *Civil War Tennessee: Battles and Leaders*. Knoxville, Tenn., 1979.

Cooling, Benjamin Franklin. *Forts Henry and Donelson: The Key to the Confederate Heartland*. Knoxville, Tenn., 1987.

Coulter, E. Merton. *The Civil War and Readjustment in Kentucky*. Chapel Hill, N.C., 1926.

Daniel, Larry J. *Soldiering in the Army of Tennessee: A Portrait of Life in a Confederate Army*. Chapel Hill, N.C., 1991.

Dufour, Charles. *The Night the War Was Lost*. New York, 1960.

Durham, Walter. *Nashville, The Occupied City: The First Seventeen Months, February 16, 1862, to June 30, 1863*. Nashville, Tenn., 1985.

______. *Rebellion Revisited: A History of Sumner County, Tennessee, from 1861 to 1870*. Gallatin, Tenn., 1982.

Dyer, John P. *The Gallant Hood*. Indianapolis, Ind., 1950.

Evans, Clement, ed. *Confederate Military History*. 12 vols. Atlanta, 1899.

Foote, Shelby. *The Civil War: A Narrative*. 3 vols. New York, 1958–75.

Govan, Gilbert E., and James W. Livingood. *The Chattanooga Country, 1540–1962: From Tomahawk to TVA*. New York, 1952.

Hafendorfer, Kenneth A. *Perryville: Battle for Kentucky*. Utica, Ky., 1981.

Hair, William I. *The Kingfish and His Realm: The Life and Times of Huey P. Long*. Baton Rouge, La., 1991.

Harrison, Lowell H. *The Civil War in Kentucky*. Lexington, Ky., 1975.

Hattaway, Herman, and Archer Jones. *How the North Won: A Military History of the Civil War*. Chicago, 1983.

Henry, Robert Selph. *The Story of the Confederacy*. New York, 1931. Rpt. 1957.

______. *"First With the Most" Forrest*. Indianapolis, Ind., 1944.

Holland, Cecil F. *Morgan and His Raiders*. New York, 1943.

Horn, Stanley F. *The Army of Tennessee: A Military History*. New York, 1941.

_____. *The Decisive Battle of Nashville*. Baton Rouge, La., 1956.

Hughes, Nathaniel Cheairs, Jr. *General William J. Hardee: Old Reliable*. Baton Rouge, La., 1965.

Hutton, Paul A. *Phil Sheridan and His Army*. Lincoln, Nebr., 1985.

Josephy, Alvin M., Jr. *The Civil War in the American West*. New York, 1991.

Killebrew, J. B. *Middle Tennessee as an Iron Center*. Nashville, Tenn., 1879.

Kleber, John E., ed. *The Kentucky Encyclopedia*. Lexington, Ky., 1992.

Lesley, J. P. *Iron Manufacturer's Guide to the Furnaces, Forges and Rolling Mills of the United States*. New York, 1859.

Livermore, Thomas L. *Numbers and Losses in the Civil War in America, 1861–1865*. New York, 1901.

Losson, Christopher. *Tennessee's Forgotten Warriors: Frank Cheatham and His Confederate Division*. Knoxville, Tenn., 1989.

Lytle, Andrew Nelson. *Bedford Forrest and His Critter Company*. New York, 1931.

McDonough, James Lee. *Chattanooga: A Death Grip on the Confederacy*. Knoxville, Tenn., 1984.

_____. *Shiloh—In Hell Before Night*. Knoxville, Tenn., 1977.

_____. *Stones River: Bloody Winter in Tennessee*. Knoxville, Tenn., 1980.

_____, and Thomas L. Connelly. *Five Tragic Hours: The Battle of Franklin*. Knoxville, Tenn., 1983.

_____, and James Pickett Jones. *War So Terrible: Sherman and Atlanta*. New York, 1987.

McDowell, Robert E. *City of Conflict: Louisville in the Civil War, 1861–1865*. Louisville, Ky., 1962.

McKinney, Francis. *Education in Violence: The Life of George H. Thomas*. Detroit, Mich., 1961.

McPherson, James M. *Battle Cry of Freedom: The Civil War Era*. New York, 1988.

_____. *Ordeal by Fire: The Civil War and Reconstruction*. New York, 1982.

McWhiney, Grady. *Braxton Bragg and Confederate Defeat*. New York, 1969.

Madaus, Michael, and Robert D. Needham. *The Battle Flags of the Confederate Army of Tennessee*. Milwaukee, Wis., 1976.

Moore, Glover. *William Jemison Mims, Soldier and Squire*. Birmingham, Ala., 1966.

Morris, Roy, Jr. *Sheridan: The Life and Wars of General Phil Sheridan*. New York, 1992.

Nevins, Allan. *The War for the Union*. 4 vols. New York, 1960.

O'Connor, Richard. *Sheridan the Inevitable*. Indianapolis, Ind., 1953.

Parks, Joseph H. *General Leonidas Polk, C.S.A.: The Fighting Bishop*. Baton Rouge, La., 1962.

_____. *General Edmund Kirby Smith, C.S.A.* Baton Rouge, La., 1962.

Pirtle, Alfred, ed. *The Union Regiments of Kentucky, Published Under the Auspices of the Union Soldiers and Sailors Monument Association*. Louisville, Ky., 1897.

Polk, William M. *Leonidas Polk: Bishop and General*. 2 vols. New York, 1894.

Pratt, Fletcher. *A Short History of the Civil War*. New York, 1935.

Purdue, Howell, and Elizabeth Purdue. *Pat Cleburne, Confederate General: A Definitive Biography*. Hillsboro, Tex., 1973.

Ramage, James A. *Rebel Raider: The Life of General John Hunt Morgan.* Lexington, Ky., 1986.

Rawley, James A. *Turning Points of the Civil War*. Lincoln, Nebr., 1966.

Reid, Whitelaw. *Ohio in the War: Her Statesmen, Generals and Soldiers.* 2 vols. Cincinnati, Ohio, 1868.

Roland, Charles P. *An American Iliad: The Story of the Civil War.* Lexington, Ky., 1991.

Roman, Alfred. *The Military Operations of General Beauregard in the War Between the States, 1861–1865*. 2 vols. New York, 1884.

Seitz, Don C. *Braxton Bragg: General of the Confederacy*. Columbia, S.C., 1924.

Shea, William L., and Earl J. Hess. *Pea Ridge: Civil War Campaign in the West.* Chapel Hill, N.C., 1993.

Stickles, Arndt M. *Simon Bolivar Buckner: Borderland Knight*. Chapel Hill, N.C., 1940.

Sword, Wiley. *Shiloh: Bloody April.* New York, 1974.

Thomas, Edison H. *John Hunt Morgan and His Raiders*. Lexington, Ky., 1975.

Townsend, William H. *Lincoln and the Bluegrass: Slavery and Civil War in Kentucky.* Lexington, Ky., 1955; reprinted 1989.

Tucker, Glenn. *Chickamauga: Bloody Battle in the West*. Dayton, Ohio, 1972.

Utley, Robert M. *Cavalier in Buckskin: George Armstrong Custer and the Western Military Frontier*. Norman, Okla., 1988.

Vandiver, Frank E. *Blood Brothers: A Short History of the Civil War*. College Station, Tex., 1992.

Warner, Ezra, Jr. *Generals in Blue: Lives of the Union Commanders*. Baton Rouge, La., 1964.

_____. *Generals in Gray: Lives of the Confederate Commanders*. Baton Rouge, La., 1959.

Williams, Kenneth P. *Lincoln Finds a General: A Military Study of the Civil War*. 5 vols. New York, 1949–59.

Williams, Samuel C. *General John T. Wilder, Commander of the Lightning Brigade*. Bloomington, Ind., 1936.

Williams, T. Harry. *P. G. T. Beauregard: Napoleon in Gray*. Baton Rouge, La., 1954.

Woodworth, Steven E. *Jefferson Davis and His Generals: The Failure of Confederate Command in the West*. Lawrence, Kans., 1990.

Wyeth, John Allan. *That Devil Forrest: Life of General Nathan Bedford Forrest*. 1899; rpt. New York, 1959.

Articles, Booklets, Guides, Etc.

Bailey, Hugh C. "Reaction in the Tennessee Valley to Federal Invasion." *Bulletin of the North Alabama Historical Association* 5 (1960): 3–9.

Bearss, Edwin C. "General Bragg Abandons Kentucky." *Register of the Kentucky Historical Society* 59 (July 1961): 217–44.

"Simon Bolivar Buckner." *Hart County Historical Society Quarterly* 13 (July 1981): 3–13.

"Chattanooga." *Encyclopedia Britannica*. Volume 5. Chicago, 1966.

Donaldson, Gary. "'Into Africa': Kirby Smith's and Braxton Bragg's Invasion of Kentucky." *Filson Club Quarterly* 61 (Oct. 1987): 444–65.

Engerud, Hal. "Anthony L. Woodson's Travail." Written for the *Hart County News*, Munfordville, Ky. Bicentennial ed. Reissued in pamphlet form, 8 Feb. 1974. Copy in files of Hart County Historical Society.

______. "Louisville's Civil War Defense." *Courier-Journal Magazine*, Louisville, Ky. 30 Sept. 1956.

______. "Munfordville: The Home of Two Civil War Generals." Written for the *Hart County News*. Bicentennial ed. Reissued in pamphlet form, 8 Feb. 1974. Copy in files of Hart County Historical Society.

______. "The Battle of Munfordville." Address at the Civil War Centennial Commemorating the Battle of Munfordville. 15 Sept. 1962. In files of Hart County Historical Society.

______. "The Battle of Munfordville." Booklet. Hart County Historical Society, Munfordville, Ky., 1984.

______. "The History of the Siege of Munfordville." Louisville Civil War Round Table. 23 June 1962. Copy in files of Hart County Historical Society.

"General's Tour Guide—The Battle of Perryville." *Blue and Gray Magazine* 1 (Oct.-Nov. 1983): 21–44.

"Glen Lily." *Hart County Historical Society Quarterly* 19 (Oct. 1987): 3–4.

Horn, Stanley F. "Nashville During the Civil War." *Tennessee Historical Quarterly* 4 (Mar. 1945): 3–22.

Lambert, Dean W. "Battle of Richmond, Kentucky." Tour guide for the Tourism Commission, Richmond, Ky. N.d.

Losson, Christopher. "Major General Benjamin Franklin Cheatham and the Battle of Stone's River." *Tennessee Historical Quarterly* 41 (Fall 1982): 278–92.

McElligott, Mary Ellen, ed. "'A Monotony Full of Sadness': The Diary of Nadine Turchin, May 1863-April 1864." *Journal of the Illinois State Historical Society* 70 (Feb. 1977)27–89.

McWhiney, Grady. "Braxton Bragg at Shiloh." *Tennessee Historical Quarterly* 21 (March 1962): 19–30.

Pabst, Loraine B. "The Sack and Occupation of Athens, Alabama." *Bulletin of the North Alabama Historical Association* 4 (1959): 18–22.

Ramage, James. "Panic on the Ohio." *Blue and Gray Magazine* 3 (May 1986): 12–15.

Roberts, Mary E. Brent. "Memories of Life on a Farm in Hart County, Kentucky, in the Early Sixties." *Filson Club Historical Quarterly* 14 (July 1940): 129–53.

"Self-Guide Walking Tour of Perryville Battlefield." Prepared by the staff of the Kentucky Military History Museum, Frankfort, Ky. Guide obtained at the Perryville Battlefield Museum, Perryville, Ky.

Sykes, E. T. "An Incident of the Battle of Munfordville, Kentucky, September, 1862." *Publications of the Mississippi Historical Society* 2 (1918): 536–48.

Tapp, Hambleton, ed. "The Battle of Perryville, October 8, 1862, as Described in the Diary of Captain Robert B. Taylor." *Register of the Kentucky Historical Society* 60 (1962): 255–92.

Thomas, Edison H. "The Battle at the Bridge." *L & N Employees' Magazine* (May 1955): 8–10, 32.

Weigley, Russell. "Philip H. Sheridan." *Civil War Times* 7 (July 1968)5–9, 46–48.

Index

☆☆☆